SIXTH EDITION

FROM CRITICAL THINKING to ARGUMENT

A Portable Guide

Sylvan Barnet
Professor of English, Late of Tufts University

Hugo Bedau
Professor of Philosophy, Late of Tufts University

John O'Hara
*Professor of Critical Thinking, Reading, and Writing,
Stockton University*

bedford/st.martin's
Macmillan Learning

Boston | New York

For Bedford/St. Martin's

Vice President, Editorial, Macmillan Learning Humanities: Leasa Burton
Senior Program Manager: John E. Sullivan III
Executive Marketing Manager: Joy Fisher Williams
Director of Content Development, Humanities: Jane Knetzger
Senior Developmental Editor: Leah Rang
Assistant Editor: Cari Goldfine
Editorial Assistant: Alex Markle
Senior Content Project Manager: Peter Jacoby
Senior Workflow Project Supervisor: Joe Ford
Senior Workflow Project Manager: Paul Rohloff
Production Supervisor: Robin Besofsky
Media Product Manager: Rand Thomas
Media Editor: Julia Domenicucci
Editorial Services: Lumina Datamatics, Inc.
Composition: Lumina Datamatics, Inc.
Text Permissions Manager: Kalina Ingham
Senior Text Permissions Researcher: Elaine Kosta, Lumina Datamatics, Inc.
Photo Permissions Editor: Angela Boehler
Photo Researcher: Brittani Morgan Grimes, Lumina Datamatics, Inc.
Director of Design, Content Management: Diana Blume
Text Design: Lumina Datamatics, Inc.
Cover Design: William Boardman
Printing and Binding: LSC Communications

Manufactured in the United States of America.

2   3   4   5   6   24   23   22   21

For information, write: Bedford/St. Martin's, 75 Arlington Street, Boston, MA 02116

ISBN 978-1-319-19443-7

Acknowledgments

Text acknowledgments and copyrights appear at the back of the book on page 427, which constitutes an extension of the copyright page. Art acknowledgments and copyrights appear on the same page as the art selections they cover.

Preface

He who knows only his own side of the cause knows little.
— JOHN STUART MILL

From Critical Thinking to Argument: A Portable Guide is a book about reading other people's arguments and writing your own arguments—with a strong emphasis on critical thinking, reading, and writing about current issues.

The quotation above by John Stuart Mill reflects the view of argument that underlies this book: In writing an essay, an author engages in a serious effort to discover his or her own ideas and, having found them, to contribute to a multisided conversation. The writer is not setting out to trounce an opponent. That is partly why we avoid expressions such as "marshaling evidence," "attacking an opponent," and "defending a thesis." Edmund Burke once wrote, "Our antagonist is our helper," and we agree that views and perspectives contrary to our own can help us sharpen our own thinking and writing. True, on television and social media we see pundits on the right and left who have made up their minds and who are indifferent or hostile to others' analysis and opinions. But in an academic community, and indeed in our daily lives, we learn by listening to others and by questioning our own ideas.

Two other foundational assumptions of this book are that arguments occur in a variety of forms, including but not limited to words on a page, and that arguments are shaped by the contexts in which they are made. In this edition, we reaffirm these beliefs with an expanded focus on visual rhetoric and information literacy, with heightened sensitivity to the interplay between argument and persuasion. We also recognize that academic and cultural discourses may make different arguments — asking different kinds of questions, making different kinds of claims, and using different kinds of evidence to support their views.

Just as arguments are instruments of inquiry and learning as well as expression, *From Critical Thinking to Argument* aims to help students learn to think, read, and write in more effective ways. As *critical thinkers and readers*, students in courses that use this book should develop their abilities to

- ask good questions about the reasoning processes that shape arguments;
- understand why information is selected and how it is presented persuasively by producers of arguments;
- account for variation and discrepancy in diverse perspectives on issues;
- understand how various contexts inform the production and reception of ideas;
- analyze and evaluate the strength of the evidence, reasoning, and assumptions undergirding arguments; and
- reflect upon, interrogate, and judge the (stated and unstated) consequences of arguments.

As *critical writers*, students develop their abilities to

- summarize an argument accurately, identifying the thesis, support, and conclusion;
- analyze an argument by reasoning logically and convincingly about it;
- produce a clear and purposeful argument of their own appropriate to a situation or discourse;

- communicate effectively for a specific audience (using appropriate language, tone, style, depth, and detail);
- explore sources of information and incorporate them selectively and skillfully, with proper documentation; and
- synthesize all information, ideas, terms, and concepts in an orderly and coherent way.

We think about and draft a response to something we have read, and in the very act of drafting, we may find—if we think critically about the words we are putting down on paper—that we are changing (perhaps slightly, perhaps radically) our own position. In short, one reason we write is so that we can improve our ideas. And even if we do not drastically change our views, we and our readers at least come to a better understanding of why we hold the views we do.

FEATURES

Part One, From Critical Thinking to Argument and Research (Chapters 1–7), offers a short course in methods of thinking about and writing arguments. By "thinking," we mean *critical* thinking—serious analytic thought, including analysis of one's own perspectives, assumptions, and predispositions as one encounters (and produces) arguments; by "writing," we mean *critical* writing—the use of effective, respectable techniques for reasoned, convincing analysis, not merely gut feelings and persuasive gimmicks. We offer lots of advice about how to set forth an argument, but we do not offer instruction in dissembling, deceiving, or practicing one-upmanship; rather, we discuss responsible ways of arguing persuasively. We know that before one can write a persuasive argument, one must learn about an issue and clarify one's own ideas—a process that includes thinking critically about others' positions (even when they are agreeable) and being critical about one's own positions before setting them forth responsibly. Therefore, we devote Chapter 1 to critical thinking; Chapters 2, 3, and 4 to critical reading (including reading images in Chapter 4); Chapters 5 and 6 to critical writing; and Chapter 7 to research, including information on finding, evaluating, and documenting sources and discussing ways to choose topics for research, take notes, avoid plagiarism, and integrate quotations. Two annotated student papers—one in MLA style and one in APA style—provide models for reading and reference.

Part One, then, offers a preliminary (but we hope substantial) discussion of such topics as

- identifying assumptions;
- getting ideas by means of invention strategies;
- finding, evaluating, and citing printed and electronic sources;
- interpreting visual sources;
- evaluating kinds of evidence; and
- organizing material as well as an introduction to some ways of thinking.

In Part Two, Further Views on Argument (Chapters 8–10), we acknowledge and detail some of the different approaches to argument and emphasize their potential usefulness to a particular writing situation—or as a means of framing an argument course or unit.

- Chapter 8, A Philosopher's View: The Toulmin Model, is a summary of the philosopher Stephen Toulmin's method for analyzing arguments, covering claims, grounds, warrants, backing, modal qualifiers, and rebuttals.

- Chapter 9, A Logician's View: Deduction, Induction, and Fallacies, offers a more rigorous analysis of these topics than is usually found in composition courses and reexamines from a logician's point of view material introduced in Chapter 3.

- Chapter 10, A Psychologist's View: Rogerian Argument, with an essay by psychotherapist Carl R. Rogers, complements the discussion of audience, organization, and tone in Chapter 6.

We trust that this book is brief enough and affordable enough to be assigned as an accompaniment to a separate anthology of readings or as a supplement to a selection of individual longer works that do not include necessary instruction in critical thinking and argument.

WHAT'S NEW IN THE SIXTH EDITION

This sixth edition brings significant changes. The authors of the early editions established a firm foundation for the book: Hugo Bedau, professor of philosophy, brought analytical rigor to the instruction in argumentation, and Sylvan Barnet, professor of English, contributed expertise in writing instruction. They have since turned the project over to John O'Hara, professor of critical thinking, to contribute a third dimension, augmenting and enriching the material on critical thinking throughout, especially in the early chapters. Other changes have been made to ensure practical instruction and current topics.

A sharper focus on fostering critical thinking and information literacy. Early chapters on critical reading and writing are updated to include an explanation of confirmation bias, a survey-analyze-evaluate process for working through an issue, an understanding of obstacles to critical thinking, and strategies for approaching an issue (or an assignment). Chapter 7, Using Sources, has been extensively updated to help students interrogate their sources for reliability, relevance, and accuracy. Given that today's digital natives seek and find information online, new sections on finding reliable sources provide instruction and visual examples of sponsored content, fake news sites, and scholarly databases so that students can evaluate and use research effectively.

More visual guidance for understanding argument. In response to reviewer feedback, we have revised and updated some of the instruction to design new Visual Guides and create additional entry points to critical thinking. Graphics and flowcharts aid students in designing their own paths through common argument tasks such as writing a critical summary and organizing an analysis. In addition to the student essays that are marked to show the writers' strategies, this edition features annotated essays that make argument moves visible. Several selections by professional writers provide support for understanding argument during the reading process and highlight writers' rhetorical moves and persuasive strategies.

Sentence Guides for Academic Writers. A new appendix helps students develop the essential skill of working with and responding to others' ideas. This practical module helps students develop an academic writing voice by giving them sentence guides, or templates, to follow in a variety of composing situations.

ACKNOWLEDGMENTS

The authors would like to thank those who have strengthened this book by their comments and advice on the sixth edition: Steve Callaway, Glide High School; Deborah Cordonnier, Rider University; Amanda Drake, University of Central Missouri; Rodney Gabel, University of Toledo; Richard Groper, California State University, Los Angeles; Jefferson Hancock, Cabrillo College; Nozomi Irei, Southern Utah University; Husne Jahan, De Anza College; Adam Kaiserman, College of the Canyons; Yogita R. Maharaj, University of California, Merced; Amanda N. Nicholson, Atlanta Metropolitan State College; Shane Ochoa, East Los Angeles College; Pamela Shen, Chabot College; Nancy Johnson Squair, Douglas College; and Josh Weathersby, University of Alabama.

We are also deeply indebted to the people at Bedford/ St. Martin's, especially to our thoughtful and supportive editor, Leah Rang, whose input, review, and feedback helped shape both the written chapters and the reading selections in this edition. Maura Shea, John Sullivan, and Adam Whitehurst, our editors for preceding editions, have also left a lasting impression on the book; without their work on the first several editions, there probably would not be a sixth. Others at Bedford/St. Martin's to whom we are deeply indebted include Edwin Hill, Leasa Burton, Joy Fisher Williams, Peter Jacoby, Cari Goldfine, and Theresa Carcaldi, all of whom have offered countless valuable (and invaluable) suggestions. Special thanks go to Alex Markle who was there for every step of this edition to provide insight and commentary, particularly so in the selection and layout of visual elements new to this edition. We would also like to thank Hilary Newman, Kalina Ingham, Arthur Johnson, Elaine Kosta, Angela Boehler, and Brittani Morgan Grimes, who adeptly managed art research and text permissions. Intelligent, informed, firm yet courteous, persuasive, and persistent — all these folks know how to think and argue.

BEDFORD/ST. MARTIN'S PUTS YOU FIRST

From day one, our goal has been simple: to provide inspiring resources that are grounded in best practices for teaching reading and writing. For more than thirty-five years, Bedford/St. Martin's has partnered with the field, listening to teachers, scholars, and students about the support writers need. We are committed to helping every writing instructor make the most of our resources.

How can we help *you?*

- Our editors can align our resources to your outcomes through correlation and transition guides for your syllabus. Just ask us.
- Our sales representatives specialize in helping you find the right materials to support your course goals.
- Our *Bits* blog on the Bedford/St. Martin's English Community (**community.macmillan.com**) publishes fresh teaching ideas weekly. You'll also find easily downloadable professional resources and links to author webinars on our community site.

Contact your Bedford/St. Martin's sales representative or visit **macmillanlearning.com** to learn more.

Print and Digital Options for *From Critical Thinking to Argument*

Choose the format that works best for your course and ask about our packaging options that offer savings for students.

Print

- *Paperback.* To order the paperback edition, use ISBN 978-1-319-19443-7.

Digital

- *Innovative digital learning space.* Bedford/St. Martin's suite of digital tools makes it easy to get everyone on the same page by putting student writers at the center. For details, visit **macmillanlearning.com/college/us/englishdigital**.

- *Popular ebook formats.* For details about our ebook partners, visit **macmillanlearning.com/ebooks**.
- *Inclusive Access.* Enable all students to receive their course materials through your LMS on the first day of class. Macmillan Learning's Inclusive Access program is the easiest, most affordable way to ensure that all students have access to quality educational resources. Find out more at **macmillanlearning.com/inclusiveaccess**.

Your Course, Your Way

No two writing programs or classrooms are exactly alike. Our Curriculum Solutions team works with you to design custom options that provide the resources your students need. (Options below require enrollment minimums.)

- *ForeWords for English.* Customize any print resource to fit the focus of your course or program by choosing from a range of prepared topics.
- *Macmillan Author Program (MAP).* Add excerpts or package acclaimed works from Macmillan's trade imprints to connect students with prominent authors and public conversations. A list of popular examples or academic themes is available upon request.
- *Bedford Select.* Build your own print handbook or anthology from a database of more than nine hundred selections and add your own materials to create your ideal text. Package with any Bedford/St. Martin's text for additional savings. Visit **macmillanlearning.com/bedfordselect**.

HOW *FROM CRITICAL THINKING TO ARGUMENT* SUPPORTS WPA OUTCOMES FOR FIRST-YEAR COMPOSITION

The following chart provides information on how *From Critical Thinking to Argument* helps students build proficiency and achieve the learning outcomes set by the Council of Writing Program Administrators that writing programs across the country use to assess their students' work.

Rhetorical Knowledge	
Learn and use key rhetorical concepts through analyzing and composing a variety of texts	**Part One, From Critical Thinking to Argument and Research**, moves students from analyzing and evaluating an issue to analyzing specific written and visual arguments, then from writing analysis to composing their own arguments. • **Chapter 3, Critical Reading: Getting Deeper into Arguments**, gives students a vocabulary for key concepts of Aristotelian rhetoric — *ethos, logos, pathos* — and distinguishes between rational strategies (e.g., induction, deduction) and nonrational appeals (e.g., satire, irony, emotional appeals). • **Chapter 4, Visual Rhetoric: Thinking about Images as Arguments**, shows students how these strategies can be applied to visual arguments such as photographs, political cartoons, advertisements, and graphs. • **Chapter 5, Writing an Analysis of an Argument**, guides students through examining thesis, purpose, methods, persona, and the intended audience. An argument and a student's analysis, annotated to highlight the student's rhetorical strategies (pp. 193–96), explicate the process of assessing and evaluating an argument. • **Chapter 6, Developing an Argument of Your Own**, asks students to imagine and compose for their own audience (Imagining an Audience, pp. 213–15)
Gain experience reading and composing in several genres to understand how genre conventions shape and are shaped by readers' and writers' practices and purposes	**Part Two, Further Views on Argument**, covers three different approaches to argument, providing students with multiple perspectives on how to both examine and craft arguments in different genres: Chapter 8, A Philosopher's View: The Toulmin Model; Chapter 9, A Logician's View: Deduction, Induction, and Fallacies; and Chapter 10, A Psychologist's View: Rogerian Argument. The **Topics for Critical Thinking and Writing** that follow readings in the text point to stylistic choices, heightening students' awareness of how writing works. In **Chapter 7, Using Sources**, helpful tables detail the genre conventions of scholarly, popular, and trade sources (pp. 265–66), as well as types of fake news (p. 276).

Develop facility in responding to a variety of situations and contexts calling for purposeful shifts in voice, tone, level of formality, design, medium, or structure	**Thinking Critically** activities help scaffold composing in different genres. See, for example, Thinking Critically: Identifying Ethos (p. 89) and Thinking Critically: Examining Language to Analyze an Author's Argument (p. 191).
Understand and use a variety of technologies to address a range of audiences	The authors of *From Critical Thinking to Argument* assume students will be composing in different media; therefore, instruction throughout emphasizes the affordances and constraints of composing in analog and digital when taking notes, evaluating and citing sources, and more.
Match the capacities of different environments (e.g., print and electronic) to varying rhetorical situations	In addition to coverage noted above that helps students understand the rhetorical situation, Chapter 4 includes arguments for using images in writing.

Critical Thinking, Reading, and Composing	
Use composing and reading for inquiry, learning, critical thinking, and communicating in various rhetorical contexts	**Chapter 1, Critical Thinking**, emphasizes how the process of critical thinking is a generative process through acts of inquiry, reading, and writing. See Generating Ideas: Writing as a Way of Thinking (pp. 15–22). **Chapter 6, Developing an Argument of Your Own**, includes further guidance on inquiry and invention as part of the composing process. See Getting Ideas: Argument as an Instrument of Inquiry (pp. 200–201), Revision as Invention (pp. 205–6), and Asking Questions with Stasis Theory (pp. 206–9).
Read a diverse range of texts, attending especially to relationships between assertion and evidence, to patterns of organization, to the interplay between verbal and nonverbal elements, and to how these features function for different audiences and situations	The nineteen readings in *From Critical Thinking to Argument* are selected from diverse authors, disciplines, and sources. Several sections highlight the importance of strong organization to deliver sound logic, reasoning, and support for claims. See, for example: • Types of Reasoning (pp. 91–98) • Evidence: Experimentation, Examples, Authoritative Testimony, and Numerical Data (pp. 107–21) • Drafting and Revising an Argument (pp. 219–35) **Part Two, Further Views on Argument**, covers how three different argument approaches — Toulmin, formal logic, and Rogerian — organize and use claims and support according to their different purposes.

| Locate and evaluate (for credibility, sufficiency, accuracy, timeliness, bias, and so on) primary and secondary research materials, including journal articles and essays, books, scholarly and professionally established and maintained databases or archives, and informal electronic networks and internet sources | **Chapter 7, Using Sources**, is a comprehensive resource for finding and evaluating primary and secondary sources.

• Finding Sources (pp. 253–62) advises students on finding sources online, in databases, and in libraries.
• Evaluating Sources (pp. 262–80) helps students analyze the credibility, accuracy, and timeliness of sources.
• Performing Your Own Primary Research (pp. 280–85) guides students through interviewing peers and local authorities as well as conducting surveys and observations.

In this edition, this chapter has been heavily updated to correlate with the Framework for Information Literacy for Higher Education from the Association of College and Research Libraries. Notable new entries that serve students' current research challenges include

• Entering a Discourse (pp. 245–48)
• Why Finding Reliable Internet Sources Is So Challenging (pp. 271–72)
• A Word on "Fake News" (pp. 272–76) |
| Use strategies — such as interpretation, synthesis, response, critique, and design/redesign — to compose texts that integrate the writer's ideas with those from appropriate sources | **Synthesizing Sources** (pp. 285–86) emphasizes the importance of synthesis as a way of thinking.

Chapter 7, Using Sources, covers best practices for paraphrasing and summarizing and avoiding plagiarism. Two sample student papers — one following MLA guidelines (pp. 319–27) and one following APA (pp. 328–33) — model outcomes for the research and writing process. |

Processes	
Develop a writing project through multiple drafts	**Chapter 6, Developing an Argument of Your Own**, guides students through the writing process: generating ideas, developing and supporting a convincing thesis, imagining an audience, using transitions, maintaining a consistent tone and persona, and peer review. A sample student essay (pp. 237–43) shows one student's process from rough notes to a final draft.
Develop flexible strategies for reading, drafting, reviewing, collaborating, revising, rewriting, rereading, and editing	**Chapter 2, Critical Reading: Getting Started**, covers active reading strategies (pp. 40–57) such as previewing, underlining, highlighting, annotating, and rereading. A sample essay and a Thinking Critically: Previewing activity give students practice.

Use composing processes and tools as a means to discover and reconsider ideas	**Chapter 1, Critical Thinking**, and **Chapter 6, Developing an Argument of Your Own**, offer ample means of using composing to discover ideas and interrogate assumptions. Notable sections include • Survey, Analyze, and Evaluate the Issue (pp. 7–9) • Prompting Yourself: Classical Topics and Invention (pp. 20–22) • Three Brainstorming Strategies: Freewriting, Listing, and Diagramming (pp. 201–5)
Experience the collaborative and social aspects of writing processes	A new section on understanding and entering discourse (pp. 235–37) emphasizes the social aspect of writing. **Exercises** throughout the text offer opportunities for practicing and applying critical thinking and argument concepts in small groups.
Learn to give and to act on productive feedback to works in progress	**Chapter 6, Developing an Argument of Your Own**, covers the importance of peer review (pp. 235–37) and includes a Checklist for Peer Review that walks students through questions to ask when reviewing peers' work and providing feedback.
Adapt composing processes for a variety of technologies and modalities	**Reading, Writing, and Research Tip boxes** highlight strategies for adapting writing to specific contexts.
Reflect on the development of composing practices and how those practices influence their work	**Checklists** in every chapter invite students to reflect on their reading and writing processes, and **Thinking Critically** boxes throughout the text prompt students to apply the concepts they've learned via interactive exercises.

Knowledge of Conventions	
Develop knowledge of linguistic structures, including grammar, punctuation, and spelling, through practice in composing and revising	**Chapters 5–7** on critical writing show students how to recognize the characteristics of writing and teach how those qualities contribute to effective (or ineffective) writing (see first outcome for more information). **Chapter 6, Developing an Argument of Your Own**, discusses how to establish an appropriate tone and persona; eliminate *we*, *one*, and *I* in argumentative writing; and avoid sexist language. Thinking Critically: Eliminating *We*, *One*, and *I*, p. 234) gives students a chance to put these concepts into practice, and a Checklist for Establishing Tone and Persona (p. 234) allows students to self-review and revise.

Understand why genre conventions for structure, paragraphing, tone, and mechanics vary	**Chapter 5, Writing an Analysis of an Argument**, helps students examine how an author's methods differ in relation to their purpose and audience. **Part Two, Further Views on Argument**, delves into expectations for different kinds of arguments.
Gain experience negotiating variations in genre conventions	Instruction supports writing in common argument genres, such as a critical summary, rhetorical analysis, and analysis of an argument.
Learn common formats and design features for different kinds of texts	**Previewing** (pp. 41–45) introduces students to design and genre features such as headings, subheadings, and abstracts to aid in basic comprehension and source evaluation. **Chapter 4, Visual Rhetoric: Thinking about Images as Arguments**, includes dozens of examples of visual arguments in different genres and highlights their design features. **MLA and APA style formatting conventions** are covered in detail in Chapter 7, Using Sources. Sample student papers in each style provide models.
Explore the concepts of intellectual property (e.g., fair use and copyright) that motivate documentation conventions	**Chapter 2, Critical Reading: Getting Started**, teaches best practices for recognizing and avoiding plagiarism and offers guidance on ethical paraphrase and summary. See, for example, Patchwriting and Plagiarism (pp. 61–63). **Chapter 7, Using Sources**, includes robust coverage of MLA and APA documentation styles, which discuss formatting conventions and include annotated sample student papers. • **Compiling an Annotated Bibliography** (pp. 289–90) shows students how to properly document and summarize their sources. • **Quoting from Sources** (pp. 290–95) shows students how to responsibly quote and integrate sources into their writing. • **Checklists** for evaluating print sources, websites, and fake news, avoiding plagiarism, and general strategies for source-based papers reinforce these concepts.
Practice applying citation conventions systematically in their own work	**Coverage on MLA and APA style** offers guidance on citation conventions, including dozens of models for in-text citations and reference lists.

Contents

PART ONE

FROM CRITICAL THINKING to ARGUMENT and RESEARCH

Critical Thinking

What is the hardest task in the world? To think.

—RALPH WALDO EMERSON

In all affairs it's a healthy thing now and then to hang a question mark on the things you have long taken for granted.

—BERTRAND RUSSELL

Although Emerson said the hardest task in the world is simply "to think," he was using the word *think* in the sense of *critical thinking*. By itself, *thinking* can mean almost any sort of cognitive activity, from idle daydreaming ("I'd like to go camping") to simple reasoning ("but if I go this week, I won't be able to study for my chemistry exam"). Thinking by itself may include forms of deliberation and decision-making that occur so automatically they hardly register in our consciousness ("What if I do go camping? I won't be likely to pass the exam. Then what? I better stay home and study").

When we add the adjective *critical* to the noun *thinking*, we begin to examine this thinking process consciously. When we do so, we see that even our simplest decisions involve a fairly elaborate series of calculations. Just in choosing to study and not to go camping, for instance, we weighed the relative importance of each activity (both are important in different ways); considered our goals, obligations, and commitments (to ourselves, our parents, peers, and professors); posed questions and predicted outcomes (using experience and observation as evidence); and resolved to take the most prudent course of action (i.e., made a decision).

Many people associate being critical with fault-finding and nit-picking. The word *critic* might conjure an image of a sneering art or food critic eager to gripe about everything that's wrong with a particular work of art or menu item. People's low estimation of the stereotypical critic comes to light humorously in Samuel Beckett's play *Waiting for Godot*, when the two vagabond heroes, Vladimir and Estragon, engage in a name-calling contest to see who can hurl the worst insult at the other. Estragon wins hands-down when he fires the ultimate invective:

V: Moron!

E: Vermin!

V: Abortion!

E: Morpion!

V: Sewer-rat!

E: Curate!

V: Cretin!

E: (*with finality*) Crritic!

V: Oh! (*He wilts, vanquished, and turns away*)

However, being a good *critical* thinker isn't the same as being a "critic" in the derogatory sense. Quite the reverse: Because critical thinkers approach difficult questions and seek intelligent answers, they must be open-minded and self-aware, and they must analyze *their own* thinking as rigorously as they analyze others'. They must be alert to *their own* limitations and biases, the quality of evidence *they themselves* offer, the logic *they* use, and the conclusions *they* draw. In college, we may not aspire to become critics, but we all should aspire to become better critical thinkers.

Becoming more aware of our thought processes is a first step in practicing critical thinking. The word *critical* comes from the Greek word *krinein*, meaning "to separate, to choose"; above all, it implies *conscious* inquiry. It suggests that by breaking apart, or examining, our reasoning we can understand better the basis of our judgments and decisions—ultimately, so that we can make better ones.

THINKING THROUGH AN ISSUE

When thinking about an issue, no matter how simple or controversial, we want to do it in a way that's fair to all parties and not just a snap judgment. Critical thinking means questioning not only the beliefs and assumptions of others, but also *one's own* beliefs and assumptions. When developing an argument, you ought to be identifying important problems, exploring relevant issues, and evaluating available evidence fairly—not merely collecting information to support a preestablished conclusion.

Analyzing and Evaluating from Multiple Perspectives

Let's think critically about an issue related to religious freedom, equality, and the law—one that we hope brings some humor to the activity but also inspires careful thinking and debate. In 2005, in response to pressure from some religious groups, the Kansas Board of Education gave preliminary approval for teaching alternatives to evolution in public school science classes. New policies would require science teachers to present "intelligent design"—the idea that the universe was created by an intentional, conscious force such as God—as an equally plausible explanation for natural selection and human development.

In a quixotic challenge to the legislation, twenty-four-year-old physics graduate Bobby Henderson wrote an open letter to the Kansas school board that quickly became popular on the internet and then was published in the *New York Times*. Henderson appealed for recognition of another theory that he said was equally valid: that an all-powerful deity called the Flying Spaghetti Monster created the world. While clearly writing satirically on behalf of science, Henderson nevertheless kept a straight face and argued that if creationism were to be taught as a theory in science classes, then "Pastafarianism" must also be taught as another legitimate possibility. "I think we can all look forward to the time," he wrote, "when these three theories are given equal time in our science classes. . . . One third time for Intelligent Design; one third time for Flying Spaghetti Monsterism (Pastafarianism); and one third time for logical conjecture based on overwhelming observable evidence."

Since that time, the Church of the Flying Spaghetti Monster has become a creative venue where secularists and atheists construct elaborate mythologies, religious texts, and rituals, most of which involve cartoonish pirates and various noodle-and-sauce images. ("R'amen," they say at the end of their prayers.) However, although tongue in cheek, many followers have also used the organization seriously as a means to champion the First Amendment's establishment clause, which prohibits government institutions from *establishing*, or preferring, any one religion over another. Pastafarians have challenged policies and laws in various states that appear to discriminate among religions or to provide exceptions or exemptions based on religion. In Tennessee, Virginia, and Wisconsin, church members have successfully petitioned for permission to display statues or signs of the Flying Spaghetti Monster in places where other religious icons are permitted, such as on state government properties. One petition in Oklahoma argued that because the state allows a marble and granite Ten Commandments monument on the state courthouse lawn, then a statue of the Flying Spaghetti Monster must also be permitted; this effort ultimately forced the state to remove the Ten Commandments monument in 2015. Since then, individuals in California, Georgia, Florida, Texas, and Utah have asserted their right to wear religious head coverings in their driver's license photos—a religious exemption afforded to Muslims in those states—and have had their pictures taken with colanders on their heads.

Let's stop for a moment. Take stock of your initial reactions to the Church of the Flying Spaghetti Monster. Some responses might be quite uncritical, quite unthinking: "That's outrageous!" or "What a funny idea!" Others might be the type of snap judgment

Gary Nelson/Crossville Chronicle

Under the establishment clause of the First Amendment, members of the Church of the Flying Spaghetti Monster were permitted to install a monument on the lawn of a Crossville, Tennessee, courthouse in 2008.

we discussed earlier: "These people are making fun of real religions!" or "They're just causing trouble." Think about it: If your hometown approved placing a Christmas tree on the town square during the holiday season and the Church of the Flying Spaghetti Monster argued that it, too, should be allowed to set up its holiday symbol—perhaps a statue—as a matter of religious equality, should it be afforded equal space? Why, or why not?

Be careful to exercise critical thinking here. Can one simply say, "No, that belief is ridiculous," in response to a religious claim? What if members of a different religious group were asking for equal space? Should a menorah (a Jewish holiday symbol) be allowed? A mural celebrating Kwanzaa? A Native American symbol? Can some religious expressions be included in public spaces and not others? If so, why? If not, why not?

In thinking critically about a topic, we must try to see it from all sides before reaching a conclusion. Critical thinking requires us to understand our own position and also see the other side. One mainstay of critical thinking is a *willingness to identify and consider objections to our own beliefs*. We conduct an argument with ourselves, advancing and then questioning different opinions. If someone were proposing a Spaghetti Monster holiday display, we should ask

- **Who** is *for* and *against* the proposition?
- **Why** are they *for* or *against* it?
- **What** can be said *for* and *against* the proposition?

When thinking critically, it's important to ask key questions about various positions. It is also important to weigh competing interests and predict the outcomes of any decision or action we take. Remember that to be fair, we must adopt a skeptical attitude not only toward views opposed to our own but also toward our own views and our own common sense—that is, toward ideas that seem to us obviously right. If we assume that we have a monopoly on the truth and dismiss those who disagree with us as misguided fools or if we assume that opponents are acting out of self-interest (or a desire to harass the community) and we don't analyze their views, we're being critical, but we aren't engaging in critical thinking.

Survey, Analyze, and Evaluate the Issue

Seeing an issue such as the Church of the Flying Spaghetti Monster from multiple perspectives will require you to gather information—to find out what people are saying and thinking.

You'll likely want to gather perspectives and opinions from religious leaders, community members, and legal experts and analyze them alongside one another (after all, you wouldn't want the town to be sued for discrimination). You'll want to examine points on which people agree and disagree. Try to familiarize yourself with current debates — perhaps about religious equality, free speech, or the separation of church and state — and consider the responsibility of public institutions to accommodate different viewpoints and various constituencies. Ask yourself: What are the bigger issues at stake? Finally, you'll want to evaluate the evidence used by all sides to support their claims. Remember that the Church of the Flying Spaghetti Monster didn't gain so much traction by being easy to dismiss. You'll certainly have to think beyond a knee-jerk value judgment like, "No, a Spaghetti Monster statue would be ugly."

To summarize our process, consider doing the following to enhance your ability to consider multiple perspectives:

1. **Survey different viewpoints**, considering as many as possible and paying attention to who stands to gain and lose in any debate.
2. **Analyze the conflicts**, identifying and separating out the problems or points of debate and trying to see the bigger issues at stake.
3. **Evaluate the ideas**, judging the merit of various claims and arguments and measuring the weight of the evidence.

If you survey, analyze, and evaluate comprehensively, you'll have better and more informed ideas; you'll generate a wide variety of ideas, each triggered by your own responses and the ideas your research brings to light. In short — and this point is key — *argument is an instrument of learning, decision-making, and persuasion*. You will be able to find your position by thinking through the issue and developing your argument. As you do so, you should be as thorough as possible and sensitive to the ideas and rights of many different people. After all, you may have to present your argument to the town council or community. If you simply decided that a Spaghetti Monster statue was insulting to other religions and ignored the law in your argument, you could be setting up your town for a lawsuit.

Use the Visual Guide: Evaluating a Proposal that follows to pursue some lines of questioning for evaluating a proposed regulation, policy, or procedure. Apply this line of thinking to the Flying Spaghetti Monster issue.

Visual Guide: Evaluating a Proposal

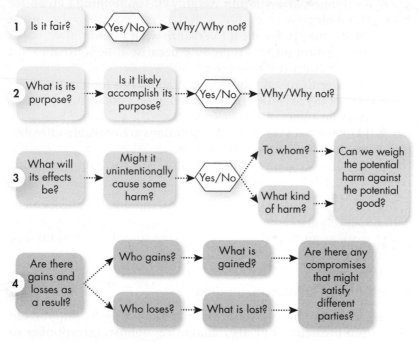

What do you think? If you were on your hometown's city council and a petition came through from the Church of the Flying Spaghetti Monster to permit a Spaghetti Monster display alongside the traditional Christmas tree and menorah on the town square, how would you answer the questions presented in the Visual Guide? How would you vote? Why? How would you explain your vote to opponents of the Spaghetti Monster display?

Obstacles to Critical Thinking

Because critical thinking requires engaging seriously with potentially difficult topics, topics about which you may already have strong opinions, and topics that elicit powerful emotional responses, it's important to recognize the ways in which your thinking may be compromised or clouded. The following attitudes might impede or otherwise negatively affect critical thinking in real life:

1. The topic is too controversial. I do not want to take a position on it.
2. The topic hits "too close to home" (i.e., "I have had direct experience with this").

3. The topic disgusts/angers/bores me.
4. Everyone I know thinks roughly the same thing I do about this topic.
5. Others may judge me if I verbalize what I think.
6. My opinion on this topic is X because it benefits me, my family, or my kind the most.
7. My parents raised me to think X about this topic.
8. One of my favorite celebrities believes X about this topic, so I should agree.
9. I know what I think, but my solutions are probably unrealistic. You can't change the system.
10. The answer is just common sense. Anyone who thinks differently lacks common sense.

Think about how each attitude might be detrimental to engagement with the question of approving a Flying Spaghetti Monster statue or might work as an impediment to drawing sound conclusions and making decisions on any issue.

Anticipating Counterarguments

As we have shown, we generate ideas not only by supporting our initial thoughts, but also imagining opposing responses to them—sometimes called *counterpoints* or *counterpositions*, which help us clarify our thoughts. When we draw conclusions, we may also find **counterarguments** to our own position (other positions and points collected logically together toward a different conclusion). Sometimes, we avoid counterarguments—or avoid taking them seriously—because we do not want to face them or we simply cannot see things from another perspective. But we should try to take counterarguments seriously because they ultimately strengthen our thinking. When we write, they demonstrate that we have taken the time to consider other perspectives. We mention counterarguments here because they're an important component in argument, as you've already seen in our illustrations; we also discuss them in the Rebuttals section in Chapter 8.

CRITICAL THINKING AT WORK: FROM A CLUSTER TO A SHORT ESSAY

Clustering is a type of brainstorming and a way of generating ideas, so it is a good tool for the process of thinking through an issue. Here's an example showing a student developing ideas about an issue related to the Church of the Flying Spaghetti Monster. The student, Alexa Cabrera, was assigned to write approximately 500 words about a specific legal challenge made by a member of the Church of the Flying Spaghetti Monster. She selected the case of Stephen Cavanaugh, a prisoner who had made a complaint against the Nebraska State Penitentiary after being denied the right to practice Pastafarianism while incarcerated there. Because the Department of Corrections had denied him those privileges, Cavanaugh filed suit citing civil rights violations and asked for his rights to be accommodated.

Alexa began thinking through her argument with a cluster, offering an initial idea and then building on it. Notice the role of counterpoints in the beginning of her cluster. Notice, too, that her cluster is not as elaborate as our earlier one. Her cluster was a *first* step, not a road map of the final essay. Finally, notice that Alexa's cluster contains ideas that did *not* make it into the final essay and that her essay—the product of several revised drafts—introduces points she had *not* thought of while clustering. In other words, the thinking process does not end when you begin the writing stage. Instead, writing an argument is a *continuous* process of thinking and learning as well as a method of persuasion.

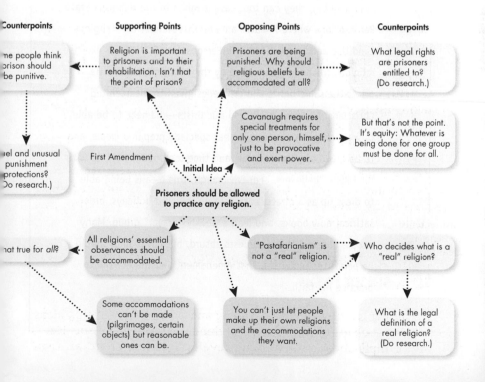

Cabrera 1

Alexa Cabrera

Professor Regina Dacus

English 112

8 October 2016

Title: Plays with words related to pasta and prison. The subtitle states the thesis.

Stirred and Strained: Pastafarians Should Be Allowed to Practice in Prison

Stephen Cavanaugh is a member of the Church of the Flying Spaghetti Monster (FSM), a mostly web-based religious group notable for its members' demands that they be treated under the First Amendment like any other religion. The group strives to show that if Christians can place Nativity scenes on public grounds or if Muslims can wear head coverings in state driver's license photographs, then by god (or by pasta, as the case may be), they can too. Cavanaugh is in the Nebraska State Penitentiary, where inmates are permitted under the Religious Land Use and Institutionalized Persons Act (RLUIPA) to exercise religious freedoms guaranteed by the First Amendment. He wants the same rights and privileges given to incarcerated Christians, Muslims, Jews, and Buddhists — namely, to be able to wear religious clothing, to eat specially prepared meals, and to be given resources, space, and time to conduct worship with his fellow "believers." For Cavanaugh, this means being able to dress up as a pirate, eat pasta on selected holidays, order satirical holy books, and lead a weekly "prayer" group. Many people consider these requests absurd, but Cavanaugh should be permitted under the First Amendment and the RLUIPA to practice his faith.

Paragraph 1: Sets the stage. Nifty turn of phrase engages readers and sets the tone as playful but serious.

Last sentence presents a clear thesis.

Cabrera 2

Some arguments against Cavanaugh are easier to dismiss than others. One of these simply casts aside the spiritual needs and concerns of prisoners: They are being punished, after all, so why should they receive any religious accommodations? This position is both immoral and unconstitutional. Religion is an important sustaining force for prisoners who might otherwise struggle to find meaning and purpose in life, and it is protected by the First Amendment *because* it helps prisoners find purpose and become rehabilitated — the fundamental goal of correctional facilities (even for those serving life without parole). Another argument sees religion as important as long as it conforms to Judeo-Christian belief structures, which has for a long time been the only spiritual path available in American prisons. But today, in our diverse society, the RLUIPA *requires* prisons to provide religious accommodations for all faiths equally unless an undue administrative, financial, or security burden can be proven. Obviously, many religious observances cannot be accommodated. Prisons cannot permit inmates to carry crosses and staves, construct temples and sweat lodges, or make required religious pilgrimages. However, as long as *some* reasonable religious accommodations can be and are made for some groups — such as Catholics being offered fish on Fridays or Jewish and Muslim prisoners receiving kosher and halal meals — then all religious groups must be similarly accommodated.

The more challenging question about the Church of the Flying Spaghetti Monster is whether it is a religion at all, whether it deserves equal treatment among more established religions. When Cavanaugh was first denied his request, the prison claimed

Paragraph 2:
Counter-arguments raised throughout.

Writer cites law's requirements.

Last sentence sustains the thesis and anticipates that readers may agree on this point but still not consider the FSM a religion.

Paragraph 3:
Raises a possible counterposition and gives it due respect.

Cabrera 3

that FSM was not a religion but a "parody" of religion. The Nebraska State Penitentiary suggested it could not grant privileges to anyone who presents his whimsical desires as part of a religious philosophy. In dealing with a humorous and politically motivated "religion" without a strong tradition and whose founder may write a new gospel at any time, should the prison have to keep up with the possibility of constantly changing prisoner demands? Can anyone just make up a religion and then expect to be accommodated?

Responds to opposing position; writer is still discussing reasonable and fair treatment of inmates, not "anything goes."

For better or worse, the answer is yes — as long as the accommodations represent valid forms of observance, are reasonable, and do not pose a substantial burden to the institution. Many religions have councils that at times alter the tenets of their faith. The state does not have the authority to determine what is or is not a "real" religion or religious practice. It does have an obligation under the RLUIPA to accommodate not just some but all forms of faith for incarcerated persons. As long as individuals sincerely hold certain beliefs, and as long as the accommodations requested meet the standards of reasonability and equity, state prisons, like all other government agencies and institutions, cannot discriminate.

Writer reminds readers that the state cannot determine a "real" or "unreal" religion, just as it cannot judge the depth, rigor, or literalness of an inmate's belief.

Some might argue that Cavanaugh's faith is not sincere — that he does not *really* believe that the Earth was literally created by a ball of pasta with meatball-shaped eyes. But this is not the point. The government cannot apply a religious test to measure the degree of one's sincerity or faith. Like others in the Flying Spaghetti Monster movement — secularists, atheists, and professed believers — Cavanaugh should not be treated as an exploiter of religious freedom. In fact, in a pluralistic society with laws to ensure religious freedom and equality, his challenge helps protect all faiths.

Rebuts the counterargument.

Writer makes a shrewd rhetorical move, appealing to the democratic value of fairness.

TOPICS FOR CRITICAL THINKING AND WRITING

1. A paper begins with its title, not with its first paragraph. A good title makes readers curious and may let them know where the essay will take them. Does this title have that effect on you? Why, or why not? What other title would you suggest?

2. Are you convinced from this essay that it would be unfair to deny Cavanaugh and other Pastafarian inmates their demands? Why, or why not?

3. How would you define a "real" religion? Can it be any belief deeply and sincerely felt, or does it require something more? Explain your answer.

GENERATING IDEAS: WRITING AS A WAY OF THINKING

"To learn to write," Robert Frost said, "is to learn to have ideas." But how does one "learn to have ideas"?

Sometimes, we discover ideas while talking with others. A friend shares an opinion about some issue, and we—who have never really thought much about the matter—find ourselves saying that we see their point but have a different opinion. We are, in a sense, offering a counterpoint, saying, "Well, yes, I see your point, but I'm not of that opinion. I see it differently—not as *X*, but as *Y*." For example, imagine someone is arguing against the US border wall proposal put forth by US President Donald Trump. Another person could say:

> *Yes*, I see your point that a wall will be expensive, *but* the fact is we do already have substantial border fences, and we spend a lot of money on enforcement. The wall proposal only strengthens what we already do and may even amount to long-term savings.

A third person might respond, "*Yes*, I see your point about money, *but* the wall will be destructive to the environment, which out-weighs the financial savings." A fourth might add, "*Yes, and* a wall is also a symbol of division." Often, we get ideas when we add to others' observations. Maybe we find ourselves agreeing with someone and would like to extend the observation to include another position, too. We are essentially saying, "Yes, *X*, sure, and also *Y*, too."

Here's another example of how that might play out:

Yes, a "soda tax" on high-sugar beverages would discourage unhealthy behaviors and generate much-needed revenue for the city, *and* come to think of it, it may encourage drink companies to lower the sugar content of their products.

Mere chance — a response a friend's comment — seems to have produced an idea. However, learning to have ideas is not usually a matter of chance. Or if chance *is* involved, well, as Louis Pasteur put it, "Chance favors the prepared mind." Lurking in the mind are bits of information, opinions that may arise in an unexpected circumstance — when talking, when listening to a lecture or a classroom discussion, or especially when reading.

Consider Archimedes, the ancient Greek mathematician who discovered a method to determine the volume of an irregularly shaped object. Here's how the story goes: A king gave a goldsmith a specific weight of gold and asked him to make a crown in the shape of laurel leaves. When the job was finished, the king weighed the crown and found that it matched the weight of the gold he had provided. Nevertheless, he suspected that the goldsmith might have substituted some silver for some of the gold. How could the king find out (without melting or otherwise damaging the crown) if the crown was pure gold?

For Archimedes, meditating on this problem produced no ideas at first, but when he entered a bathtub he noticed that the water level rose as he immersed his body. He suddenly realized that he could determine the purity of the crown by measuring the amount of water it displaced. Since silver is less dense than gold, it takes a greater volume of silver to equal a given weight of gold. In his excitement at his idea to measure equal weights and relative volumes by immersing the crown in water, Archimedes is said to have leaped out of the tub and run naked through the street, shouting *"Eureka!"* (Greek for "I have found [it]!").

Sculpture in Manchester, England, depicting Archimedes's bathtub "Eureka" moment.

Why do we tell this story? Partly because we like it, but chiefly because the word *eureka* captures that moment of unexpectedly finding an idea. Finding an idea can sometimes feel like reaching under the couch to retrieve a dog toy and finding a ten-dollar bill instead: "Hey, look what I found! *Eureka!*" But we rarely luck into ideas in this way. Actually, the word *eureka* comes from the same Greek word that has given us the word **heuristic** (pronounced hyoo-RIS-tik), which refers to a *method* or *process* of discovering ideas.

When you're asked to think about something you've read in this book, if your first response is that you have no ideas, please do not just take a bath like Archimedes did. A better method is to immerse yourself not in water but in the issues at hand. You can do this by listening to what's being said in the world around you—both in and out of the classroom, as well as in the world of magazines, newspapers, books, and other media—and thinking about your responses to what you hear.

One of the most basic methods to discover ideas is the one we mention above—"Yes, *but* I see it differently" or "Yes, *and also.*" This process can help you respond to a work and begin to develop ideas.

Confronting Unfamiliar Issues

Generating ideas can be a challenge when you, as a student, are asked to read about and respond to new or unfamiliar issues. Sometimes, students wonder why they have to engage in particular topics and generate ideas about them. "I want to be a speech pathologist," one might say, "so why do I need to read essays and formulate ideas about capital punishment?"

One answer is that a college curriculum should spur students to think about pressing issues facing our society, so learning about capital punishment is important to all students. But this isn't the only answer. One could never study "all" the important social problems we face (and many of them change very rapidly). Instead, colleges seek to equip students with tools, methods, and habits of mind that enable them to confront arguments about *any* potential issue or problem. The primary goal of a college education (and of this book) is to help students develop an *intellectual apparatus*—a tool kit that can be applied to any subject matter, any issue.

The techniques presented in this book offer a practical framework for approaching issues, thinking about them carefully, asking good questions, identifying problems, and offering reasonable solutions—not necessarily because we want you to form opinions about the specific issues we have selected (although we hope you do), but because we want you to practice critical thinking, reading, and writing in ways that transfer to other aspects of your education as well as to your personal, professional, and civic life.

The Nigerian novelist Chinua Achebe said, "The writer must march up front." Rather than thinking that you must "agree or disagree" with the authors whose positions you'll read about in this book, imagine that you'll be practicing how to discover your own unique point of view by finding pathways into debates, negotiating different positions, and generating new ideas. So when you confront a new or unfamiliar issue in this book (or elsewhere), consider the strategies discussed in this chapter as practical methods—*heuristics*—for generating new ideas from the information at hand. That is what critical thinking (and writing) is all about.

Using Clustering to Discover Ideas

As you can see from the student cluster on the Pastafarian issue, we're big fans of clustering as a practical method for generating ideas and thinking through your argument. If you think with pencil and paper in hand and let your mind make associations by clustering, you'll find (perhaps to your surprise) that you have plenty of interesting ideas and that some can lead to satisfying conclusions. Doubtless you'll also have some ideas that represent gut reactions or poorly thought-out conclusions, but that's okay. When clustering, allow your thoughts to take shape without restriction; you can look over your ideas again and organize them later.

To start clustering, take a sheet of paper and jot down what you think is the most basic issue or the fundamental conflict. This will help shape the questions you ask and frame your initial idea. Write down your initial idea—your opinion on the issue or debate at hand—and then develop supporting ideas, explore counterpositions (and rebuttals), and jot down where you need to do some research, eventually leading you to a tighter argument. Review the cluster on page 11 to help you work through an issue.

WRITING TIP If you decide to generate ideas for your essay by clustering, don't worry that some ideas may be off the cuff or even nonsense. Just get ideas down on paper. You can evaluate them later.

Approaching an Issue (or an Assignment)

Anyone who has played baseball can tell you that one of the most challenging things to do is hit the ball. So, coaches often instruct their players to develop an *approach* to hitting. The hitter's approach begins in the dugout. First, you watch the pitcher. You make observations. What kind of pitches are being thrown? Are they largely inside pitches or outside pitches, high or low, fast or slow? Answering these questions can help determine what you do as you get ready to bat. You must also ask: What is the game situation? Are you attempting to hit long into the outfield or just get the ball in play, perhaps to advance your runners already on the bases? Once you step into the batter's box, where should you set your feet—farther away from the plate or close to it? In short, you are asking questions: *What am I facing? What is my goal?* and, quite literally, *Where do I stand?*

Not everyone plays baseball, but this metaphor is intended to get you thinking about how to prepare for an argument by asking some key questions:

- What should you look for in an issue or problem?
- What kinds of challenges will opponents likely throw at you?
- How will you position yourself?
- What do you want to achieve?

A critical thinker's approach, like a baseball batter's, is the preparation for the argument. It involves assessing issues, identifying key problems, and discovering your ideas.

In real life, and in this book, you may be given an assignment to think critically or make an argument. A professor (or a textbook author) assigning a prompt is much like a coach instructing you on your approach, and examining the assignment prompt carefully is like reading the pitcher. Ask: What is being thrown at you? How should you strategize to meet the challenges?

Perhaps the assignment prompts you to consider a certain aspect of an issue, compare two arguments, or take a side in a debate. Here is an example of an assignment that calls for a specific approach:

> At the time a county clerk in Kentucky named Kim Davis was refusing to sign marriage licenses for same-sex couples, some of her supporters compared her to civil rights activists like Rosa Parks, who intentionally broke segregation laws in order to challenge them. Are Kim Davis's actions justifiable in the same way Rosa Parks's were? Are the two figures equivalent crusaders for justice?

A prompt like this doesn't tell you *what* to think, but *what to ask* and *how to argue*. It tells you to *compare, analyze,* and *evaluate*. In your comparison of Davis and Parks, you must judge whether or not their actions were morally or politically equivalent and then argue yes or no. You are being prompted to consider the motivations, purposes, and justifications for each figure's actions.

Many assignments call for these elements of comparison, analysis, and evaluation. They ask the questions and tell you how to argue. But by figuring out what to ask and how to argue yourself, you can develop arguments without prompts provided by your professors. When facing issues in your life, work, or society, you will sometimes have to prompt *yourself* to figure out what to think (and what to argue).

Prompting Yourself: Classical Topics and Invention

One way of generating new ideas by prompting yourself is to consider what the ancient rhetoricians called **topics**—from the Greek *topoi*, meaning "places." (We see this word as a root in our word *topography*, a description of place.) Today, we often use the word *topic* to describe something very specific, as when a professor or committee leader says, "Today our topic for discussion is the proposed bike lane on our campus drive." But for the ancients, such as Aristotle in Greece and Cicero in Rome, the *topoi* (or topics) were more conceptual and were seen as the basic elements of arguments, debates, and conversations. Among the classical topics were *definition, comparison, relationship,* and *testimony*. When formulated as questions, they prompted thoughtful people to invent (from the Latin *invenire*, "to come upon, to find") ideas.

If you're at a loss for ideas when confronted with an issue—and an assignment to write about it—you might discover ideas by turning to the relevant classical topics, framing them as questions, and jotting down your responses. We'll use our campus bike lane as an example issue.

Definition: **What are the elements in the debate?**

What is a road? What is a bike lane? What is a college campus? How might these definitions help you think through the issues? If, for example, you define a *road* as a way people travel (especially students), a *bike lane* as a pathway for a certain means of safe transportation, and a *campus* as a place where students must be able to live and learn safely, then you may be able to discover a reasonable starting point for an argument: *Because many students use bikes and they need to get to class safely, a bike lane on campus is a reasonable accommodation.* Simply defining the basic elements within an issue may guide your thinking on a question.

Comparison: What are the elements like or unlike?

Comparing students to nonstudents, cars to bikes, or campuses to other public spaces may also help you discover your position. You may find that students have a special need for bikes that nonstudents do not have. Or you may find that bikes, compared to cars, are cheaper and more environmentally friendly. Maybe campus roads are not the same as some other public roads; they may be more like roads in parks, cutting through spaces of leisure, quietude, and study. Making comparisons like these can help you evaluate the various reasons bicycle lanes may be called for on campus. You may also compare other cases: Have other colleges built bike lanes? If so, to what effect?

Relationship: What are the causes and effects in play?

Think of relationships as *"if . . . then"* propositions. If we decided to build bike lanes, then we would likely increase safety and access on campus and help the environment. However, if we build bike lanes, then we would also spend a great deal of money, which may affect other budget priorities, some of which may also increase other kinds of access and safety. The point: Teasing out the relationships of actions to their consequences can help produce ideas. (You may also explore the consequences of non-actions: If we did not build bike lanes, then we would not be keeping up with institutions that are building them, making our school less attractive to new students.)

Testimony: What are the major opinions and forms of evidence?

All ideas need to be justified in consideration of opinions and evidence. What do drivers think? What do students think? What do experts and respected leaders say? What laws or rules are applicable? What evidence has been (or can be) gathered to testify to the need for bike lanes (or the lack of such a need)? Have there been accidents? Are students or drivers complaining about the risks? Gathering testimony—assessing data, trends, currents, opinions, and attitudes—can help inspire ideas.

The classical *topoi* are not solutions to any problems at hand, but a means of discovering solutions. They provide a set of categories that can work as guidelines to formulating an opinion or argument. In other words, they offer a way to organize the *process* of invention, of thinking through an issue to determine what you think and what position you want to take.

AN ESSAY FOR GENERATING IDEAS

Consider the following brief essay about the Food and Drug Administration's approval, in 2015, of a genetically engineered salmon. Although GMO (genetically modified organism) foods and medicines are common in the United States, this salmon will soon be the first genetically modified animal approved for food consumption in the United States. After you read the essay, refer to Thinking Critically: Generating Ideas with Topics (p. 24), which asks you to begin jotting down ideas on a sheet of paper along the lines of the classical topics. As an example of how to respond to the questions, we've included columns related to the Stephen Cavanaugh case. As you attempt to formulate ideas related to the essay about genetically engineered salmon, answer the questions related to the classical topics. There's no need to limit yourself to one answer per item as we did.

Nina Fedoroff

Nina Fedoroff (b. 1942) is a molecular biologist and winner, in 2007, of the National Medal of Science. She served as science and technology advisor to the US secretary of state from 2007 to 2010 and is an emeritus Evan Pugh professor at Penn State University. The following essay originally appeared in the New York Times *in December 2015.*

The Genetically Engineered Salmon Is a Boon for Consumers and Sustainability

This is great news for consumers and the environment. Wild salmon populations have long been in deep trouble because of overfishing, and open-water cage farming of salmon pollutes coastal waters, propagates fish diseases, and sacrifices a lot of wild-caught fish to be consumed as salmon feed.

The fish is virtually identical to wild salmon, but it is a more sustainable food source, growing faster to maturity.

But just imagine, you'll soon be able to eat salmon guilt-free. AquaBounty has spent more than 20 years developing and testing this faster-growing salmon that will require less feed to bring it to a marketable size. It can be farmed economically in closed, on-land facilities that recirculate water and don't dump waste into the sea. Since the fish live in clean, managed water, they don't get diseases that are spread among caged fish in the sea. And the growing facilities could be closer to markets, cutting shipping costs.

All of these elements take pressure off wild salmon and make salmon farming more sustainable.

Much of the concern about AquaBounty's salmon centers 5 around several bits of added DNA, taken from another fish, that let the salmon grow continuously, not just seasonally. That does not make them "unnatural" or dangerous, it just makes them grow to market size on less feed.

We've been tinkering with our plants and animals to serve our food needs for somewhere between 10 and 20 thousand years. We created corn, for example. The seed-bearing structure of the original "wild" version, called teosinte, looked very different from the modern-day ear, packed with hundreds of soft, starch-and-protein-filled kernels. And it's people who developed the tomatoes we eat today. Mother Nature's are tiny: A pioneering breeder described them in an 1893 grower's guide as "small, hollow, tough, watery" fruits.

But there's money (and fame) in being anti-G.M.O. The organic food marketers want to sell their food, which is overpriced because organic farming is inefficient—not because the food's better—so they tell scare stories about the dangers of G.M.O.s.

There is also no reason to fear that these genetically engineered salmon will escape and destroy wild populations. Only sterile females will be grown for food. And since the fish will be grown in contained facilities on land, escapees can't survive either.

AquaBounty's salmon is salmon, plain and simple. I, for one, can't wait to taste it.

THINKING CRITICALLY GENERATING IDEAS WITH TOPICS

Use the classical topics (pp. 20–22) to think through an issue. Provide the relevant information for a topic of your choice or for the topic of genetically engineered salmon explored in Fedoroff's essay. We have provided the issue of Steven Cavanaugh and the Church of the Flying Spaghetti Monster as an example.

Topics	Questions	Example Topic: *Pastafarianism*	Your Topic
Definition *Categories* *Descriptions* *Definitions* *Explanations*	What is it?	Define terms: *creationism* *religious freedom* *civil rights*	
Comparison *Similarities* *Differences* *Analogies* *Applications*	What is it like or unlike?	Civil disobedience Other struggles for religious rights	
Relationships *Antecedents* *Precedents* *Consequences* *Outcomes*	What are some causes and effects? (*If . . . , then*)	If Pastafarianism is permitted to continue, then . . . If prisoners cannot worship freely, then . . .	
Testimony *Statistics* *Maxims* *Laws* *Authorities/ Quotations*	What forms of evidence and opinion exist?	What have courts said in the past? What do supporters and/or detractors say? What laws exist to protect members of religions?	

Thinking Critically about the Issue

What follows is an inner dialogue that you might engage in as you think critically about the question of genetically engineered salmon.

The purpose of genetically engineered salmon is to protect against the ecological effects of overfishing — that seems to be a good thing.

Another purpose is to protect consumers by ensuring that the price of salmon, one of the most commonly eaten fish, will not become so high that few people could afford it.

But other issues are apparent. Should we turn to altering the genes of animals to protect the environment or consumer prices? Are there other solutions, like eating less salmon or regulating overfishing?

Who gains and who loses, and what do they stand to gain or lose, by Federal Drug Administration (FDA) approval of genetically modified salmon?

The author says no one should worry about "several bits of DNA added," but come to think of it, is this modification unethical or dangerous in any way? Is it okay to create a new type of animal by altering genes?

The author attacks anti-GMO activists, saying they're just after money (and fame — why fame?). Isn't money (and fame?) also the goal of AquaBounty and other GMO food producers?

Part of the job is **analytic**, recognizing the elements or complexities of the whole, and part is **evaluative**, judging the adequacy of all the ideas, one by one. Both tasks require critical thinking in the form of analyzing and evaluating, and those processes themselves require a self-conscious and disciplined *approach*.

So far, we have jotted down a few thoughts and then immediately given some second thoughts contrary to the first. Be aware that your own counterpositions might not come to mind right away. They might not occur until you reread your notes or try to explain the issue to a friend, until you do some preliminary reading on the subject, or even until you begin drafting an essay aimed at supporting or undermining the FDA rules. Most likely, some good ideas won't occur until a second or third or fourth draft — or even until after you have published or turned in your work.

Here are some further thoughts on the issue of genetically modified salmon to show how different perspectives and questions lead to different approaches.

According to one article, the FDA is not requiring companies to label the salmon as genetically engineered. Should this information at least be made available to consumers? Maybe their religious, ethical, or personal preferences would be not to eat modified fish species.

If the fish were properly labeled and people knew of any risks associated with eating it, consumers could avoid it if they wished.

- *Possible perspectives:* Social (consumer interest)
- *Questions:* How should consumers expect to be protected by the government in an era of new scientific developments such as GMOs and in relation to their right to know what goes into their food? How should the government respond to new scientific advances such as GMOs?
- *Approach:* Might I argue that the new regulations are okay, but strict labeling should be required?

It's actually pretty amazing that scientists have helped solve the problem of the dwindling salmon population from overfishing by making a genetic modification that allows fish to grow large and fast and sustainably. Like any new thing, people who are uncomfortable with technological change will resist the new processes but will soon become accustomed to them once their fears are allayed. I'll bet at one time, people were hesitant to accept the light bulb as an advancement. Like all new advances, once it is accepted, it will be a boost to consumers, the environment, and business.

- *Possible perspectives:* Scientific (technological change)
- *Questions:* What other technologies were resisted in the past and are now commonplace, and what lessons can we learn from them? Which technologies are now keystones for our economy? How has science contributed to solving food crises and environmental crises?
- *Approach:* Might I argue that people should be more open to technological innovation as a way to solve environmental, social, and economic issues related to the food supply?

Doubtless there is much that we haven't asked or thought about, but we hope you'll agree that the issue deserves careful thought. Some of these questions require you to do **research** on the topic. Some raise issues of fact, and relevant evidence probably is available. To reach a conclusion in which you have confidence, you'll likely have to do some research to find out what the facts — the objective data — are. Merely explaining your position without giving the evidence will not be convincing.

> ✓ A CHECKLIST FOR CRITICAL THINKING
>
> ☐ Does my thinking show open-mindedness and intellectual curiosity?
> ☐ Am I approaching my subject from a particular perspective?
> ☐ Can I examine the assumptions that come with my approach?
> ☐ Am I willing to entertain different ideas, both those that I encounter while reading and those that come to mind while writing?
> ☐ Am I willing to exert myself — for instance, to do research — to acquire information, identify different viewpoints, and evaluate evidence?

Even without doing any research, however, you might want to look over the pros and cons, perhaps adding some new thoughts or modifying or even rejecting (for reasons that you can specify) some of those already given. If you do think further about this issue (and we hope that you will), notice an interesting point about *your own* thinking: It probably isn't *linear* (moving in a straight line from *A* to *B* to *C*) but *recursive*, moving from *A* to *C* and back to *B* or starting over at *C* and then back to *A* and *B*. By zigging and zagging almost despite yourself, you'll reach a conclusion that may finally seem correct. In retrospect, it might seem obvious; *now* you can chart a nice line from *A* to *B* to *C*—but that probably wasn't at all evident at the start.

A SHORT ESSAY CALLING FOR CRITICAL THINKING

When reading an essay, we expect the writer to have thought carefully about the topic. We don't want to read every false start, every fuzzy thought, and every ill-organized paragraph that the writer knocked off. Yes, writers make false starts, put down fuzzy thoughts, and write ill-organized paragraphs, but then they revise and revise yet again, ultimately producing a readable essay that seems effortlessly written. Still—and this is our main point—writers of argumentative essays need to show readers that they have made some effort; they need to show *how* they got to their views. It isn't enough for the writer to say, "I believe X"; rather, he or she must in effect say, "I believe X because I see things from this perspective. Others believe Y or Z, and although from their perspective, their answers might sound reasonable, my inquiry shows another way to think or act about the issue. There may be value in Y or Z (or maybe not), and on the surface they may be plausible (or maybe they are not plausible), but their beliefs do not take into account what I am arguing, that X is a better alternative because. . . ." Obviously you don't need to follow that exact pattern (although you could); the point is that writers often need to make their critical thinking explicit to convince their readers of the argument they make.

Notice in the following short essay — on employers using biometric devices to monitor employees' performance — that the author, Lynn Stuart Parramore, positions herself against new workplace technologies in a compelling way. As you read, think critically about how she presents her position and how she encourages readers to sympathize with her views. Ask questions about what she includes and excludes, whether she presents other perspectives amply or fairly, and what additional positions might be valid on these recent developments in the rapidly growing field of biometrics in business.

Lynn Stuart Parramore

Lynn Stuart Parramore is a senior research analyst at the Institute for New Economic Thinking and a senior editor of AlterNet, *as well as a frequent contributor to* Reuters, HuffPost, *and other outlets. Reprinted here is an essay published by* Al Jazeera America *on September 18, 2015.*

Fitbits for Bosses

> Provocative title leaves readers with a sense of Parramore's argument.

Imagine you've just arrived at your job with the Anywhere Bank call center. You switch on your computer and adjust the height of your chair. Then, you slide on the headset, positioning the mic in front of your lips. All that's left to do is to activate your behavior-monitoring device — the gadget hanging from your neck that tracks your tone of voice, your heart rate, and your physical movements throughout the day, sending real-time reports to your supervisor.

> The writer throws in an ominous proposition, the "behavior-monitoring device," that could become routine.

A scene from a dystopian movie? Nope. It's already happening in America. Welcome to the brave new world of workplace biosurveillance.

It's obvious that wearable tracking technology has gone mainstream: Just look at the explosion of smart watches and activity monitors that allow people to count steps and check their calorie intake. But this technology has simultaneously been creeping into workplaces: The military uses sensors that scan for injuries, monitor heart rate, and check hydration. More and more, professional athletes are strapping on devices that track every conceivable dimension of performance. Smart ice skates that measure a skater's jump. Clothes that measure an athlete's breathing and collect muscle data. At this year's tryouts in Indianapolis, some NFL hopefuls wore the "Adidas miCoach," a device that sends data on speed and acceleration straight to trainers' iPads. Over the objection of many athletes, coaches and team owners are keen to track off-the-field activity, too, such as sleep patterns and diet. With million-dollar players at stake, big money seems poised to trump privacy.

Now employers from industries that don't even require much physical labor are getting in on the game.

Finance is adopting sophisticated analytics to 5 ensure business performance from high-dollar employees. Cambridge neuroscientist and former Goldman Sachs trader John Coates works with companies to figure out how monitoring biological signals can lead to trading success; his research focuses on measuring hormones that increase confidence and other desirable states as well as those that produce negative, stressful states. In a report for Bloomberg, Coates explained that he is working with "three or four hedge funds" to apply an "early-warning system" that would alert supervisors when traders are getting into the hormonal danger zone. He calls this process "human optimization."

People who do the most basic, underpaid work in our society are increasingly subject to physical monitoring, too—and it extends far beyond the ubiquitous

---

Marginal annotations:

Science-fiction language and references to a dystopian "brave new world" assist sense of foreboding.

Presents as "obvious" the fact that biosurveillance technology has gone mainstream, "creeping" into the workplace. "So what?" Parramore is about to tell us.

Single sentence turns the focus from two specialized fields to everyday jobs.

Extends the dystopian theme and sci-fi language: Phrases like "alert supervisors" and "human optimization" hint at deeper control by managers.

Parramore enhances her argument through strong language and ironic, sardonic tone: "creepily named," "concocted."

Parramore quotes Humanyze's founder but presents his statement as anything but appealing.

Supports claims with examples from a research study and a case study.

Provides a counter-point offered by the industries that create these technologies.

urine test. Bank of America has started using smart badges that monitor the voice and behavior patterns of call-center workers, partnering with the creepily named Humanyze, a company specializing in "people analytics." Humanyze is the brainchild of the MIT Media Lab, the fancy research institute at the Massachusetts Institute of Technology dedicated to the "betterment of humanity," which, incidentally, receives a quarter of its funding from taxpayers. Humanyze concocted a computer dashboard complete with graphs and pie charts that can display the location of employees (Were you hanging out in the lounge today?) and their "social context" (Do you spend a lot of time alone?).

Humanyze founder Ben Waber points out that companies already spend enormous resources collecting analytics on their customers. Why not their employees?

A growing number of workers are being monitored by GPS, often installed on their smartphones. In the U.S. the Supreme Court ruled that law enforcement officials need a warrant to use GPS devices to track a suspect. But employers don't worry over such formalities in keeping tabs on employees, especially those who are mobile, such as truck drivers. A *Washington Post* report on GPS surveillance noted a 2012 study by the research firm Aberdeen Group, which showed that 62 percent of "field employees"—those who regularly perform duties away from the office—are tracked this way. In May, a California woman filed a lawsuit against her former employer, Intermex Wire Transfer, for forcing her to install a tracking app on her phone, which she was required to keep on 24/7. She described feeling like a prisoner wearing an ankle bracelet. After removing the app, the woman was fired.

Sensitive to Big Brother accusations, the bio-surveillance industry is trying to keep testing and tool evaluations under the radar. Proponents of the technology point to its potential to improve health conditions in the workplace and enhance public safety. Wouldn't it be better, they argue, if nuclear power plant operators, airline pilots, and oil rig operatives had their physical state closely monitored on the job?

Young Americans nurtured in a digital world where their behavior is relentlessly collected and monitored by advertisers may shrug at an employer's demands for a biosurveillance badge. In a world of insecure employment, what choice do they have, anyway? Despite the revelations of alarming National Security Agency spying and increased government and corporate surveillance since 9/11, the young haven't had much experience yet with what's at stake for them personally. What could possibly go wrong?

A lot: Surveillance has a way of dehumanizing workers. It prevents us from experimenting and exercising our creativity on the job because it tends to uphold the status quo and hold back change. Surveillance makes everyone seem suspicious, creating perceptions and expectations of dishonesty. It makes us feel manipulated. Some researchers have found that increased monitoring actually decreases productivity.

Philosopher and social theorist Michel Foucault observed that the relationship between the watcher and the watched is mostly about power. The power of the observer is enhanced, while the person observed feels more powerless. When an employer or manager interprets our personal data, she gets to make categorical judgments about us and determine how to predict our behavior.

What if she uses the information to discriminate? Coerce? Selectively apply the rules? The data she uses to make her judgments may not even be telling the truth: Researchers have warned that big data can produce big errors. People looking at numbers tend to use them to confirm their own biases, cherry-picking the information that supports their beliefs and ditching the rest. And since algorithms are constructed by human beings, they are not immune to human biases, either. A consumer might be labeled "unlikely to pay a credit card bill" because of an ethnic name, thus promulgating a harmful stereotype.

As Americans, we like to tell ourselves that we value freedom and undue interference from authority. But when we are subjected to surveillance, we feel

10   Mentions "Young Americans" as a possible source of opposing argument. "What could go wrong?" Parramore asks.

Parramore answers that question from previous paragraph, first with the word *dehumanizing*.

Applies a well-known philosopher's theory of power to the new context of biosurveillance data.

Considers scenarios of possible discrimination or coercion with bio data and then questions the limits of oversight.

Reminds readers that measurements are prone to error and biases could lead to discriminatory uses of data.

disempowered and disrespected. We may be more inclined to accept the government getting involved because of fears about terrorism—but when it comes to surveillance on the job, our tendency to object may be chilled by weakened worker protections and increased employment insecurity.

Summarizes the potentially harmful outcomes of widespread implementation of biometric surveillance of employees.

Instead of producing an efficient and produc- 15 tive workplace, biosurveillance may instead deliver troops of distracted, apathetic employees who feel loss of control and decreased job satisfaction. Instead of feeling like part of a team, surveilled workers may develop an us-versus-them mentality and look for opportunities to thwart the monitoring schemes of Big Boss.

Concludes by suggesting that those in power most need to be watched "in the name of safety and efficiency"—ostensibly the terms used to justify the practice as applied to workers.

Perhaps what we really need is biosurveillance from the bottom up—members of Congress and CEOs could don devices that could, say, detect when they are lying or how their hormones are behaving. Colorful PowerPoints could display the results of data collection on public billboards for the masses to pore over. In the name of safety and efficiency, maybe we ought to ensure that those whose behavior can do society the most harm do not escape the panopticon.

TOPICS FOR CRITICAL THINKING AND WRITING

1. Do you think biometric measurement by employers is ever justified, or do the privacy and security of one's own body always trump the concerns of employers? Why, or why not?

2. If your teachers or parents could monitor the time you spent, and how you felt, while doing homework and studying, what benefits and drawbacks might result? What types of personal monitoring of children are already in place (or possible) in schools and homes, and are these methods different from biometric surveillance?

3. Do you think Lynn Stuart Parramore fairly portrays the founder of Humanyze and others who see potential in the possibilities for biometric monitoring? Why, or why not? In what other ways might biometric measurements help employees and employers?

4. List some examples of Parramore's use of language, word choice, and phrasing that would influence readers to be suspicious of

biometric monitoring. How does this language make the essay more or less effective or convincing?

5. In what way does Parramore's recommendation in the final paragraph support or contradict her argument about individuals' basic rights to privacy?

EXAMINING ASSUMPTIONS

In Chapter 3, we will discuss **assumptions** in some detail. Here we introduce the topic by emphasizing the importance of *identifying* and *examining* assumptions—those you'll encounter in the writings of others and those you'll rely on in your own essays.

With this in mind, let's again consider some of the assumptions suggested in this chapter's earlier readings. The student who wrote about Stephen Cavanaugh's case pointed out that Nebraska prison officials simply did not see the Church of the Flying Spaghetti Monster as a real religion. Their assumption was that some religions can be more or less "real" than others or can make more sense than others. Assumptions may be *explicit* or *implicit*, stated or unstated. In this case, the prison officials were forthright about their assumptions in their stated claim about the church, perhaps believing their point was obvious to anyone who thought seriously about the idea of a Flying Spaghetti Monster. It didn't occur to them to consider that even major and mainstream religions honor stories, claims, and rituals that seem absurd to others.

An implicit assumption is one that is not stated but, rather, is taken for granted. It works like an underlying belief that structures an argument. In Lynn Stuart Parramore's essay on workplace biometric devices, the unstated assumption is that these sorts of technological monitors in the workplace represent a kind of evil "big brother" intent on subduing and exploiting employees with newer and newer forms of invasion of privacy. Parramore's assumption, while not stated directly, is evident in her choice of language, as we've pointed out above with terms such as *dystopian* and *brave new world*.

Another way to discern her assumption is by looking at the scenarios and selections of examples she chooses. For example, in imagining a company that would seek to know how much time an employee spends in the lounge area or alone, Parramore sees only obsessive monitoring of employees for the purposes of regulating their time. But what if these technologies could enable a company to discover that productivity or worker satisfaction increases in proportion to the amount of time employees spend collaborating in the lounge? Maybe workplace conditions would improve instead of deteriorating (a bigger lounge, more comfortable chairs), and maybe more efforts would be made for team-building and improving interpersonal employee relations. From a position that is skeptical about how employers might use such technologies, biometric surveillance of employees appears to be a dramatic overreach on the part of industries that use them. Biometric devices are seen as an intrusion and perhaps a violation of workers' privacy rights. However, from a business or an organizational strategy perspective, these technologies could be seen as ways to improve workplace heath and productivity.

Assumptions can be powerful sources of ideas and opinions. Understanding our own and others' assumptions is a major part of critical thinking. Assumptions about race, class, disability, sex, and gender are among the most powerful sources of social inequality. The following essay by Helen Benedict was published in 2015, two years after the US Department of Defense lifted the ban on women in combat roles in the armed forces and shortly after Defense Secretary Ashton Carter further lifted exclusions pertaining to women by granting them access to serve in all capacities in combat, including in elite special forces units. One assumption we may make about these developments is that the changed regulations resulted in an equal-access military. However, as Benedict argues, women in the military continue to face obstacles to equality, many of which themselves are based on social assumptions about gender.

✓ A CHECKLIST FOR EXAMINING ASSUMPTIONS

- ☐ Have I identified any of the assumptions presupposed in the writer's argument?
- ☐ Are these assumptions explicit or implicit?
- ☐ Are these assumptions important to the author's argument, or are they only incidental?
- ☐ Does the author give any evidence of being aware of the hidden assumptions in her or his argument?
- ☐ Would a critic be likely to share these assumptions, or are they exactly what a critic would challenge?
- ☐ What sort of evidence would be relevant to supporting or rejecting these assumptions?
- ☐ Am I willing to grant the author's assumptions? Would most readers grant them?

Helen Benedict

Helen Benedict (b. 1952) is a professor at Columbia University's Graduate School of Journalism. She is best known for her journalism on social injustice and the Iraq War as well as her seven novels, most recently Wolf Season, *which received* Publishers Weekly's *Best Contemporary War Novel award in 2018.*

The Military Has a Man Problem

Army Specialist Laura Naylor, a Wisconsin native, spent a year in Baghdad with the 32nd Military Police Company in 2003 and 2004. During that time, she—like all of the more than quarter-million women deployed to Iraq and Afghanistan—was officially banned from ground combat. That technicality didn't slow down Naylor when an IED[1] hit her convoy and it began to take fire from a nearby building. "We had to search this house nearby, thinking they were the ones doing the shooting, and I was the lead person the whole way. I had a flashlight in one hand, a pistol in the other, and I'd kick the door open with my foot, look both ways, give the all clear, go to the next room, do the same thing," she recounted to me a few years later. "We were interchangeable with the infantry."

A friend in her unit, Specialist Caryle Garcia, was wounded when a roadside bomb went off beside her Humvee. Garcia was her team's gunner, her body exposed from the chest up above the Humvee's roof. Their close friend, 20-year-old Specialist Michelle Witmer, became the first National Guardswoman ever killed in action after being shot during another ambush. Witmer's death was a grim marker in a steady march that has seen one woman after another achieve milestones in military service since the September 11, 2001, attacks that would have been unimaginable just a generation ago. During the Vietnam War, female soldiers were not even allowed to carry guns.

In early 2013, outgoing Defense Secretary Leon Panetta, with the backing of the Joint Chiefs of Staff, finally lifted the ban on women serving in ground combat, belatedly admitting they had already been doing so. "Women have shown great courage and sacrifice on and off the battlefield," he said, "and proven their ability to serve in an expanding number of roles." President Barack Obama heralded the move, which remains politically controversial on Capitol Hill, saying, "Valor knows no gender." Since Panetta's decree, the debate has centered on whether, now that women can serve in previously all-male combat units, they have the ability to

---

[1]**IED** improvised explosive device; an unconventional bomb. [Editors' note]

actually do it. The Marine Corps, Army and Special Forces have all been busily, and publicly, putting women to the test, running them through training courses and assessments, and announcing gravely how many have passed or failed.

Yet to many female soldiers and the men who have witnessed their competence in battle over the past 13-plus years, this debate seems like closing the barn door after the horse has bolted—ignoring that the distinction between "rear echelon" and "front line" in these wars is obsolete. Of the roughly 300,000 American women who have deployed to the Afghanistan and Iraq wars since 2001, at least 800 have been wounded, and, as of last count, at least 144 have been killed. Two women have earned Silver Stars, the military's third-highest award.

For generations now, the debate over women in combat has 5 put the onus on women to prove they can handle the infantry and other traditionally all-male units. Yet today's wars have made it clear that the military's problem lies not with its women, their ability or their courage. The military's problem, instead, is with some of its men—and a deeply ingrained macho culture that denigrates, insults and abuses women.

In eight years of covering women at war, I have noticed a pattern in attitudes toward women in the military: The men who have served with women are more than satisfied with their work, while the men who are most resistant to serving alongside women have never done it.

"Oh, it's too rough for women," such men tend to say. Others complain, "Women would ruin our camaraderie" or "We'd be competing for women instead of looking out for ourselves." As retired Gen. Gordon R. Sullivan, a former Army chief of staff, wrote, lifting the combat ban against women would be "confusing" and "detrimental to units."

These attitudes reveal deeply patriarchal, condescending and creaky stereotypes about women, as if they are capable of being nothing more than soft, sexy objects of romance—or sexual prey.

Some of the very same types of prejudiced objections were once raised against black and gay men entering the military, even though they had demonstrated their military prowess long before they were openly welcomed into the ranks. As former chairman of the Joint Chiefs Gen. John Shalikashvili wrote in 2007, many within the military were originally concerned that "letting people who were openly gay serve would lower morale, harm recruitment and undermine unit cohesion."

And yet, even after President Harry Truman forced the racial 10 integration of the military in 1948 and even after the fall of "don't ask, don't tell" in 2011, the military is still standing. And nobody questions any longer whether black or gay people can serve as well as straight white men.

Canada, Denmark and Norway have allowed women to serve in combat since the 1980s. Canadian commanders found no "negative effect on operational performance or team cohesion," according to one report; neither did military leaders in Norway. Israel, which added women to combat units years ago, has found that they "exhibit superior skills" in discipline, shooting and weapons use.

Today's debate about women would be less antediluvian if, instead of questioning whether women can do the job they've already been doing for years, it focused on why so many men in all-male companies still don't want to work with women. To what sort of all-male camaraderie are they clinging, and why?

In some ways, it may seem hard to blame the men who feel this way. Military training inculcates these attitudes deep into their souls. Drill instructors dress down recruits by taunting them with suggestions that their girlfriends and wives are being unfaithful. Military cadences and songs can be astonishingly misogynist. One example from the Naval Academy: *"Who can take a chainsaw / Cut the bitch in two / F--- the bottom half / And give the upper half to you. . . ."*

Long after racist language was banned from training, drill instructors regularly insult male recruits by calling them "ladies," "pussies," "girls" and worse. As an Iraq veteran wrote about his time in Marine boot camp in 2008, "The Drill Instructor's nightly homiletic speeches, full of an unabashed hatred of women, were part of the second phase of boot camp: the process of rebuilding recruits into Marines."

In other words, stoking men's hatred and suspicion of women 15 is a way of firing up those men to kill.

One of the most common objections put forth by men who don't want to work with women is that they would be so concerned with protecting the women in their units that it would risk the mission. That is, they would be too chivalrous to be good soldiers.

But as more data on the military's rampant sexual harassment and abuse come out, this chivalry argument becomes harder to believe. Given that half the women deployed to Iraq and Afghanistan reported being sexually harassed, and one in four reported being sexually assaulted, according to a Department of Veterans Affairs study, evidence of this gallantry is, to say the least, scant.

Former Army Sgt. Rebekah Havrilla, who says she was raped while serving in Afghanistan, testified before the Senate Armed Services Committee: "I had no faith in my chain of command as my first sergeant previously had sexual harassment accusations against him and the unit climate was extremely sexist and hostile in nature towards women."

If the military wants to get serious about inviting female soldiers to play ever-larger roles in war, it will have to find ways to change the attitude of so many of its own soldiers, sailors, airmen and Marines.

Stories from recent years about the depths of the military's misogyny are legendary. In 2013, the head of the Air Force's sexual assault prevention office at the Pentagon, Jeffrey Krusinski, was himself arrested and charged with sexual battery by police in Arlington, Virginia, after allegedly accosting a woman in a parking lot. (He was later acquitted by a jury.) An Army sergeant at Fort Hood who worked as a sexual abuse educator was investigated for running a prostitution ring. The married Army general in charge of Fort Jackson, who oversaw training for many Army recruits, was suspended after allegedly physically attacking his girlfriend.

If these are examples of the people in charge of ensuring 20 respectful treatment of women, is it any surprise that new recruits see women as less than equals? Not long after Krusinski's arrest, West Point's rugby team was disbanded after lewd emails about fellow female cadets surfaced that the school said suggested "a culture of disrespect towards women."

Until the military recognizes women as equal human beings, how can it recognize them as equal soldiers? As Colleen Bushnell, who was sexually assaulted while in the Air Force and now is an advocate for survivors, has said, "This is a predator problem, not a female problem."

Military culture may well be the last bastion of male protectionism in modern society, so it is no surprise that its arguments against admitting women fully are the same as those used whenever women first enter a previously all-male field—whether that is firefighting, policing, politics, sports or voting. Indeed, many of the objections macho military types make to women today mirror those their grandfathers and great-grandfathers made when women were trying to enter public life.

Yet there's precious little evidence that all-male cultures produce anything better than co-ed cultures, just as there is no evidence at all that the presence of women as voters, golfers, politicians, police officers, firefighters — or presidents — ruins anything other than male privilege.

War has changed. It is simply unfeasible to keep women off the front lines. "We're getting blown up right alongside the guys," as one female soldier who served in Iraq told me. "We're in combat! So there's no reason to keep us segregated anymore."

Admitting that the military's problem with female soldiers is 25 actually a man's problem, however, will necessitate stronger military and political leadership than we have yet seen. It will require a wholesale shift in how the military builds respect among its troops. And it means teaching the men who don't want to work with women that they must either respect their female comrades or leave. As Australia's Army chief, David Morrison, put it to his troops in 2013, "Female soldiers and officers have proven themselves worthy of the best traditions of the Australian army. . . . If that does not suit you, then get out. . . . There is no place for you amongst this band of brothers and sisters."

American military leaders, take note.

TOPICS FOR CRITICAL THINKING AND WRITING

1. What purpose do the first two paragraphs of Helen Benedict's essay serve in her overall argument?

2. Identify Benedict's thesis. In your own words, what is she arguing?

3. In the past, what assumptions about women were the basis for excluding them from military combat service? How does Benedict see those assumptions still at work, despite formal recognition that women are capable of combat roles in the service?

4. What examples does Benedict use to make comparisons? How do her comparisons help advance her argument about the "man problem" in the military?

5. What changes or actions may be taken to reduce or eliminate the "man problem" in the military? If you were to make an argument about what can be done to solve the problem, what specific areas of military life could be addressed, and what new procedures might be instituted?

6. Construct an argument to defend your position on this question: Because women are now permitted to serve in all military combat positions, should all women, like all men, have to register for Selective Service and be subject to the military draft, if one were needed?

2

Critical Reading: Getting Started

Some books are to be tasted, others to be swallowed, and some few to be chewed and digested.

—FRANCIS BACON

Read parts of a newspaper quickly or an encyclopedia entry, or a fast-food thriller, but do not insult yourself or a book which has been created with its author's painstakingly acquired skill and effort, by seeing how fast you can dispose of it.

—SUSAN HILL

ACTIVE READING

In the passages that we quote above, two good points are made. The first is that some types of reading do not need to be fully read at all—a taste of what they offer is enough. Some types of reading can be taken in completely and quickly, swallowed whole like a fast-food meal. But some types of reading call for much closer attention. Classical works of literature, for example, may require thoughtful consideration of their language, their meanings, and their relevancy to the present. Similarly, many arguments (usually essays, editorials, articles) require thoughtful deliberation, especially about the ideas they express.

But how do you know the difference between a book (or an essay) that may be read quickly and one that deserves to be read slowly? How can you judge the value of a piece of writing *before* deciding to read it carefully? And if you *do* decide a text is worth reading slowly and carefully, how do you prepare to think critically about it?

Previewing

Even before reading a single word of a text, you may evaluate it to some degree. **Previewing** is a strategy for reading that allows you to use prior knowledge — such as the expectations of your teacher or your understanding of how certain kinds of texts generally work — to help guide your reading. Skilled readers rarely read a text "cold"; instead, they think about it in terms of what they already know. They first examine the text, **skimming** to identify and evaluate the following:

- the author
- the place of publication
- the **genre**, or type of writing
- the table of contents
- headnotes or an abstract (if available)
- the title and subtitle
- section headings
- other information that stands out at a glance (such as images, graphs, and tables)

By previewing and skimming effectively, you can quickly ascertain quite a bit of information about an article or essay. You can detect the author's claims and methods, see the evidence he or she uses (experience, statistics, quotations, etc.), examine the tone and difficulty level, and determine whether the piece of writing offers useful ideas for you. These strategies work well if you're researching a topic and need to review many essays — you can read efficiently to find those that are most important or relevant to you or those that offer different perspectives. Of course, if you do find an essay to be compelling during previewing and skimming, you can begin "chewing and digesting," as Francis Bacon put it — reading more closely and carefully (or else putting it aside for later when you can give it more time).

> **READING TIP** Instead of imagining previewing and slower, more careful reading as two separate stages, think of previewing as an activity that helps you decide — at any time — whether or not you should begin engaging in more careful reading.

One of the first things you can do to begin previewing a piece of writing is to identify the **author**—not just by name but also in terms of any other information you may know or can find out. You might already know, for example, that a work by Martin Luther King Jr. will probably deal with civil rights. You know that it will be serious and eloquent. You know that King's words will likely be related to the social conditions of the 1950s and 1960s and that he will be speaking in a somewhat different language than you are accustomed to. In contrast, if Stephen King is the author, you would change your expectations, probably anticipating the essay to be about fear, the craft of writing, or King's experiences as a horror novelist. You may also know that this King writes for a broad audience, so his essay won't be terribly difficult to understand. But even if you don't know the author, you can often discern something about him or her by looking at biographical information provided in the text or by doing a quick internet search. You can use this information to predict the subject of an essay and its style, as well as its author's possible assumptions and biases.

The **place of publication** may also reveal something about the essay in terms of its subject, style, and approach. For instance, the *National Review* is a conservative journal. If you notice that an essay on affirmative action was published in the *National Review*, you can tentatively assume that the essay will not endorse affirmative action. In contrast, knowing that *Ms.* magazine is a liberal publication, you can guess that an essay on affirmative action published there will probably be an endorsement. You often can learn a good deal about a magazine or journal simply by flipping through it and noticing the kinds of articles in it. The advertisements also tell you what kind of audience the magazine or journal likely has. If you don't know anything about a publication, you can quickly research it on the internet to find out more.

The **title** of an essay, too, may give an idea of what to expect. Of course, a title may announce only the subject and not the author's thesis or point of view ("On Gun Control"; "Should Drugs Be Legal?"). A title may also be opaque or mysterious ("The Chokehold"). Fairly often, though, a title will indicate the thesis (as in "Give Children the Vote" or "We Need Campaign Finance Reform Now"). If you can tell more or less what to expect from a title, you can probably take in some of the major points even on a quick reading. Glancing at subtitles, and any section headings and subheadings, too, can help you map the progression of an argument without fully reading the entire text.

Thesis   Sometimes, you can find the **thesis** (the main point or major claim) of an essay by looking at the first paragraph. Other times, especially if the paragraphs are short, you can locate the thesis within the first several paragraphs. Depending on what you discover while skimming, you can speed up or slow down your reading as needed while you locate the thesis and get a sense of how the argument for it is structured. As we noted, if the essay has sections, pay attention to headings and subheadings to see how the thesis is supported by other minor claims.

Context   When engaging with a text, you also consider the role of **context** — the situational conditions in which a piece was written. Context — literally, "with the text" — can refer to the time period, geographical location, cultural climate, political environment, or any other setting that helps you orient a piece of writing to the conditions surrounding it. Recognizing the context can reveal a lot about how an author treats a subject. For example, an essay about gun control written before the mass shootings of the past ten years might have a less urgent approach and advocate more lenient measures than one written today. An article about transgender identity or police brutality might convey different assumptions about those topics depending on whether it was written before or after the increased recognition of transgender rights or before or after the protests of the Black Lives Matter movement. Social conditions, in short, affect how writers and readers think.

Anything you read exists in at least two broad contexts: the context of its *production* (where and when it was written or published) and the context of its *consumption* (where and when it is encountered and read). One thing all good critical readers do when considering the validity of claims and arguments is to take *both* types of context into account. This means asking questions not only about the approaches, assumptions, and beliefs about certain subjects that were in place when an essay was written, but also about how current events and new trends in thinking that occurred after the original publication date may generate different issues and challenges related to the subject of the essay. The state of affairs in the time and place in which that argument is made *and received* matters to the questions you might ask, the evidence you might consider, and the responses you might produce.

Consider these words, spoken by Abraham Lincoln in his famous debates with Stephen Douglas, when the two campaigned against each other for a US Senate seat in 1858. Douglas had accused Lincoln of holding the then-unpopular view that the black race and white race were equal. Lincoln defended himself against these charges:

> I will say then that I am not, nor ever have been, in favor of bring-ing about in any way the social and political equality of the white and black races [Applause], that I am not nor ever have been in favor of making voters or jurors of negroes, nor of qualifying them to hold office, nor to intermarry with white people; and I will say in addition to this that there is a physical difference between the white and black races which I believe will forever forbid the two races living together on terms of social and political equality. And inasmuch as they cannot so live, while they do remain together there must be the position of superior and inferior, and I as much as any other man am in favor of having the superior position assigned to the white race.

Lincoln's ideas about race in this speech may surprise you. If you saw this quotation somewhere, it might make you think that Abraham Lincoln held racist views despite his reputation as "The Great Emancipator." However, it is crucial to put his words in context to develop a fuller, more mature understanding of them. Historians, for example, read these words in light of common and even "scientific" beliefs about race in the 1850s, informed by the situation at hand (a campaign speech, in which he might feel free to overstate or appeal to popular beliefs), and with knowledge of Lincoln's uncompromising efforts later to abolish slavery. How does consideration of these historical contexts help you under-stand Lincoln's words? How does consideration of the context in which you read it shape your understanding, given your expecta-tions and your prior knowledge about Lincoln?

The "First and Last" Rule   You may apply the "first and last" rule when skimming essays. This rule assumes that somewhere early and late in the writing you can locate the author's key points.

Opening paragraphs are good places to seek out the author's central thesis, and final paragraphs are good places to seek out conclusive statements such as "Finally, then, *it is time that we . . .*" or "Given this evidence, *it is clear that . . .*" Final paragraphs are particularly important because they often summarize the argument and restate the thesis.

The first and last rule works because authors often place main points of emphasis at the beginnings and endings of essays, but they also do the same within individual paragraphs. Authors do not usually bury key ideas in the middle of long essays, and neither do they surround the key ideas of paragraphs with bulky text. Further, authors try not to hide their most important points in the middle of long sentences. Often the main point of a sentence can be found by looking at the elements stated first and last. (Of course, there are always exceptions to the rule.) Consider the following sentences, each of which contains the same basic information arranged in different ways:

Here, the time period and the new smoking prohibitions get the most emphasis:

> Over the past fifteen years, the rate of smoking among New York City residents declined by more than 35% because of new health trends and new tobacco restrictions.

Here, the place and the percentage are most emphasized:

> In New York City, new tobacco restrictions and new health trends helped lower the smoking rate over fifteen years by more than 35%.

WRITING TIP You can arrange elements in a sentence according to the "first and last" rule to control what points you want to emphasize most.

A Short Essay for Previewing Practice

Before skimming the following essay, apply the previewing techniques discussed on pages 41–45 and complete the Thinking Critically: Previewing activity on page 46.

THINKING CRITICALLY PREVIEWING

The following activity lists typical types of questions readers use while previewing. Provide the missing information for Sanjay Gupta and his essay "Why I Changed My Mind on Weed" (below) or another essay of your choosing.

Previewing Strategies	Types of Questions	Answers
Author	Who is the author? What expertise and credibility does the author have? How difficult is the writing likely to be?	
Title	What does the title reveal about the essay's content? Does it give any clues about how the argument will take shape? Do headings or subheadings reveal any further information?	
Place of Publication	How does the place of publication help you understand the argument? What type of audiences will it be likely to target?	
Context	By placing the article in the context of its time — given trends in the conversations about or popular understandings of the subject — what can you expect about the author's position?	
Skimming	As you skim over the first several paragraphs, where do you first realize what the argument of the essay is? What major forms of evidence support the argument?	

Sanjay Gupta

Dr. Sanjay Gupta (b. 1969) is a neurosurgeon and multiple Emmy Award–winning television personality. As a leading public health expert, he is most well known as CNN's chief medical correspondent. In 2011, Forbes magazine named him one of the ten most influential celebrities in the United States. The essay below originally appeared on CNN.com in August 2013.

Why I Changed My Mind on Weed

Over the last year, I have been working on a new documentary called "Weed." The title "Weed" may sound cavalier, but the content is not.

I traveled around the world to interview medical leaders, experts, growers and patients. I spoke candidly to them, asking tough questions. What I found was stunning.

Long before I began this project, I had steadily reviewed the scientific literature on medical marijuana from the United States and thought it was fairly unimpressive. Reading these papers five years ago, it was hard to make a case for medicinal marijuana. I even wrote about this in a *Time* magazine article, back in 2009, titled "Why I Would Vote No on Pot."

Well, I am here to apologize.

I apologize because I didn't look hard enough, until now. I 5 didn't look far enough. I didn't review papers from smaller labs in other countries doing some remarkable research, and I was too dismissive of the loud chorus of legitimate patients whose symptoms improved on cannabis.

Instead, I lumped them with the high-visibility malingerers, just looking to get high. I mistakenly believed the Drug Enforcement Agency listed marijuana as a Schedule 1 substance because of sound scientific proof. Surely, they must have quality reasoning as to why marijuana is in the category of the most dangerous drugs that have "no accepted medicinal use and a high potential for abuse."

They didn't have the science to support that claim, and I now know that when it comes to marijuana neither of those things are true. It doesn't have a high potential for abuse, and there are very legitimate medical applications. In fact, sometimes marijuana is the only thing that works. Take the case of Charlotte Figi, whom I met in Colorado. She started having seizures soon after birth. By age 3, she was having 300 a week, despite being on 7 different medications. Medical marijuana has calmed her brain, limiting her seizures to 2 or 3 per month.

I have seen more patients like Charlotte first hand, spent time with them and come to the realization that it is irresponsible not to provide the best care we can as a medical community, care that could involve marijuana.

We have been terribly and systematically misled for nearly 70 years in the United States, and I apologize for my own role in that.

I hope this article and upcoming documentary will help set the 10 record straight.

On August 14, 1970, the Assistant Secretary of Health, Dr. Roger O. Egeberg, wrote a letter recommending the plant, marijuana, be classified as a Schedule 1 substance, and it has remained that way for nearly 45 years. My research started with a careful reading of that decades-old letter. What I found was unsettling. Egeberg had carefully chosen his words:

"Since there is still a considerable void in our knowledge of the plant and effects of the active drug contained in it, our recommendation is that marijuana be retained within Schedule 1 at least until the completion of certain studies now under way to resolve the issue."

Not because of sound science, but because of its absence, marijuana was classified as a Schedule 1 substance. Again, the year was 1970. Egeberg mentions studies that are under way, but many were never completed. As my investigation continued, however, I realized Egeberg did in fact have important research already available to him, some of it from more than 25 years earlier.

HIGH RISK OF ABUSE

In 1944, New York mayor Fiorello LaGuardia commissioned research to be performed by the New York Academy of Science. Among their conclusions: they found marijuana did not lead to significant addiction in the medical sense of the word. They also did not find any evidence marijuana led to morphine, heroin or cocaine addiction.

We now know that while estimates vary, marijuana leads to 15 dependence in around 9 to 10% of its adult users. By comparison, cocaine, a Schedule 2 substance "with less abuse potential than Schedule 1 drugs," hooks 20% of those who use it. Around 25% of heroin users become addicted.

The worst is tobacco, where the number is closer to 30% of smokers, many of whom go on to die because of their addiction.

There is clear evidence that in some people marijuana use can lead to withdrawal symptoms, including insomnia, anxiety and nausea. Even considering this, it is hard to make a case that it has a high potential for abuse. The physical symptoms of marijuana addiction are nothing like those of the other drugs I've mentioned. I have seen the withdrawal from alcohol, and it can be life threatening.

I do want to mention a concern that I think about as a father. Young, developing brains are likely more susceptible to harm from marijuana than adult brains. Some recent studies suggest that regular use in teenage years leads to a permanent decrease in IQ. Other research hints at a possible heightened risk of developing psychosis.

Much in the same way I wouldn't let my own children drink alcohol, I wouldn't permit marijuana until they are adults. If they are adamant about trying marijuana, I will urge them to wait until they're in their mid-20s, when their brains are fully developed.

MEDICAL BENEFIT

While investigating, I realized something else quite important. 20
Medical marijuana is not new, and the medical community has been writing about it for a long time. There were in fact hundreds of journal articles, mostly documenting the benefits. Most of those papers, however, were written between the years 1840 and 1930. The papers described the use of medical marijuana to treat "neuralgia, convulsive disorders, emaciation," among other things.

A search through the U.S. National Library of Medicine this past year pulled up nearly 20,000 more recent papers. But the majority were research into the harm of marijuana, such as "Bad trip due to anticholinergic effect of cannabis," or "Cannabis induced pancreatitis" and "Marijuana use and risk of lung cancer."

In my quick running of the numbers, I calculated about 6% of the current U.S. marijuana studies investigate the benefits of medical marijuana. The rest are designed to investigate harm. That imbalance paints a highly distorted picture.

THE CHALLENGES OF MARIJUANA RESEARCH

To do studies on marijuana in the United States today, you need two important things.

First of all, you need marijuana. And marijuana is illegal. You see the problem. Scientists can get research marijuana from a special farm in Mississippi, which is astonishingly located in the middle of the Ole Miss campus, but it is challenging. When I visited this year, there was no marijuana being grown.

The second thing you need is approval, and the scientists I inter- 25
viewed kept reminding me how tedious that can be. While a cancer study may first be evaluated by the National Cancer Institute, or a pain study may go through the National Institute for Neurological Disorders, there is one more approval required for marijuana: NIDA, the National Institute on Drug Abuse. It is an organization that has a core mission of studying drug abuse, as opposed to benefit.

Stuck in the middle are the legitimate patients who depend on marijuana as a medicine, oftentimes as their only good option.

Keep in mind that up until 1943, marijuana was part of the United States drug pharmacopeia. One of the conditions for which it was prescribed was neuropathic pain. It is a miserable pain that's tough to treat. My own patients have described it as "lancinating, burning and a barrage of pins and needles." While marijuana has long been documented to be effective for this awful pain, the most common medications prescribed today come from the poppy plant, including morphine, oxycodone and dilaudid.

Here is the problem. Most of these medications don't work very well for this kind of pain, and tolerance is a real problem.

Most frightening to me is that someone dies in the United States every 19 minutes from a prescription drug overdose, mostly accidental. Every 19 minutes. It is a horrifying statistic. As much as I searched, I could not find a documented case of death from marijuana overdose.

It is perhaps no surprise then that 76% of physicians recently 30 surveyed said they would approve the use of marijuana to help ease a woman's pain from breast cancer.

When marijuana became a Schedule 1 substance, there was a request to fill a "void in our knowledge." In the United States, that has been challenging because of the infrastructure surrounding the study of an illegal substance, with a drug abuse organization at the heart of the approval process. And yet, despite the hurdles, we have made considerable progress that continues today.

Looking forward, I am especially intrigued by studies like those in Spain and Israel looking at the anti-cancer effects of marijuana and its components. I'm intrigued by the neuro-protective study by Lev Meschoulam in Israel, and research in Israel and the United States on whether the drug might help alleviate symptoms of PTSD. I promise to do my part to help, genuinely and honestly, fill the remaining void in our knowledge.

Citizens in 20 states and the District of Columbia have now voted to approve marijuana for medical applications, and more states will be making that choice soon. As for Dr. Roger Egeberg, who wrote that letter in 1970, he passed away 16 years ago.

I wonder what he would think if he were alive today.

EXERCISE: THE "FIRST AND LAST" RULE

When writing, you can emphasize main points by using the first and last rule (see pp. 44–45). Try it yourself by considering the following list of observations from Gupta's essay. Rearrange the statements any way you wish to write a single paragraph, using the first and last rule to emphasize the elements that you find most important. (You do not have to include all the details; you might want to add in some others, and feel free to rephrase them.) Next, compare your sentences to your classmates'. How do they compare in terms of emphasis?

- Gupta is one of the most respected voices in public health.
- Gupta argues for the legalization of medical marijuana.
- Gupta's letter was written for CNN News.
- Gupta rejects his previous position on medical marijuana and apologizes for his oversight.
- The article was important because it represented a shift in approach by a leading doctor.

Reading with a Careful Eye: Underlining, Highlighting, Annotating

Once you have a general idea of the work—not only an idea of its topic and thesis but also a sense of the way in which the thesis is argued—you can go back and start reading it carefully.

As you read, **underline** or **highlight** key passages and make **annotations** in the margins. Because you're reading actively, or interacting with the text, you won't simply let your eye rove across the page.

- Highlight the chief points so that later when reviewing the essay you can easily locate the main passages.
- Don't overdo it. If you find yourself highlighting most of a page, you're probably not distinguishing the key points clearly enough.
- Make your marginal annotations brief and selective. They may consist of hints or clues, comments like "doesn't follow," "good," "compare with Jones," "check this," and "really?"
- Highlight key definitions. In the margin you might write "good," "in contrast," or "?" if you think the definition is correct, incorrect, or unclear.
- Use tools to highlight or annotate when using software to read a digital essay. Also consider copying and pasting passages that you would normally highlight into a new document file. Clearly identify these passages as direct quotations to avoid plagiarism, and type your annotations next to them using the review functions.

In all these ways, you interact with the text and lay the groundwork for eventually writing your own essay on what you have read.

What you annotate will depend largely on your **purpose**. If you're reading an essay to see how the writer organizes an argument, you'll annotate one sort of thing. If you're reading to challenge the thesis, you'll annotate other things. Here is a passage from an essay by Charles R. Lawrence titled "On Racist Speech," with a student's rather skeptical, even aggressive, annotations. But notice that the student apparently made at least one of the annotations — "Definition of 'fighting words'" — chiefly to remind herself to locate where the definition of an important term appears in the essay. The essay originally appeared in the *Chronicle of Higher Education* (1989), a publication read chiefly by college and university faculty members and administrators.

Example of such a policy?

University officials who have formulated underlined(policies) to respond to incidents of racial harassment have been characterized in the press as "thought police," but such policies generally do

? nothing more than impose (sanctions) against intentional face-to-face insults. When racist speech takes the form of underlined(face-to-

Example? face insults, catcalls, or other assaultive speech aimed at an individual or small group of persons, it falls directly within the "fighting words" exception to First Amendment protection. The Supreme Court has held that words "which 'by their very utterance inflict injury or tend to incite an immediate breach of the peace"') are not protected by the First Amendment.

What abou sexist speech?

Definition of "fighting words"

If the purpose of the First Amendment is to foster the greatest amount of speech, racial insults disserve that purpose. Assaultive racist speech functions as a preemptive strike. The invective is experienced as a blow, not as a proffered idea, and once the blow is struck, it is unlikely that a dialogue will follow. Racial insults are particularly undeserving of First Amendment protection because the perpetrator's intention is not to discover truth or initiate dialogue but to injure the victim. underlined(In

How does he know? most situations), members of minority groups realize that they are likely to lose if they respond to epithets by fighting and are forced to remain silent and submissive.

Really? Probably depends on the individual.

Why must speech always see "to discove truth"?

Reading: Fast and Slow

Earlier, we recommended skimming as a quick previewing strategy to help you determine the author's purpose, general argument, and major forms of supporting evidence. Then we suggested a way to go a bit deeper, annotating as you read. However, once you determine that a particular text is worth digging into even further, you should alter your strategy so that you can engage with the argument in an even more analytical way. If critical thinking involves "taking apart" a specimen to help you understand it, then doing so with a text is akin to taking apart any complex system to understand better how it works (as with an automobile engine, for example). If you can see how all the parts of an argument work in relation to one another, you can see why they are convincing—or may *sound* convincing even when you disagree with them. But since your task is not just to understand arguments but also to evaluate, judge, and offer possible alternatives to them, you should be alert to areas where improvements can be made, where new questions may be asked, and where new parts can be added to support or challenge the conclusions. To do all this, you must *read more slowly*.

Reading slowly is sometimes called **close reading**, a technique that traces a text's details and patterns. Close reading means, for starters, paying attention to the *language* of an essay. By doing this, you can see how words and their meanings lend support to an argument—but perhaps also reveal assumptions on the part of an author. For example, an author who calls his city's crime problem a "monster" might argue for harsher law enforcement than another who refers to crime as a "sickness," who might argue for investigating the root causes of crime.

To develop new perspectives and solutions related to the issues presented in this book, you must interrogate the readings and test whether or not they hold up to your intellectual scrutiny. The issues raised in this book—and the arguments made about them—require more comment than President Calvin Coolidge supposedly provided when his wife, who hadn't been able to attend church one Sunday, asked him what the preacher talked about in his sermon. "Sin," Coolidge said. His wife persisted: "What did the preacher say about it?" Coolidge's response: "He was against it."

But, again, when we say that most of the arguments in this book require close reading, we don't mean that they are obscure or overly difficult; we mean, rather, that you have to approach them thoughtfully and deliberately, always examining their alternatives.

Some arguments appear convincing simply because all the parts work so well together. Such arguments may appear airtight and indisputable not because they offer the only reasonable or viable position, but just because they are so well constructed, because they appeal to common assumptions or rely on widely shared concepts. To close read effectively, you must employ **analysis**, another word from the Greek: *analusis,* "to loosen; to undo." We like this as a metaphor for close reading analysis because it suggests looking for the ways an argument has been put together and how it might be taken apart again.

When close reading, we often discover areas where an argument can be improved upon or challenged. The following patterns of thought may help you discover those spaces:

- The language in the article is characterized by . . .
- Although the argument is convincing, its assumptions are that . . .
- Although the argument is convincing, it fails to consider *X* alternative perspective . . .
- Although the argument does a good job offering . . . , it could be further improved by offering more of . . .
- The argument, rather than being convincing, instead proves or shows . . .
- Although the author looks at evidence showing . . . , he doesn't attend fully to other evidence showing . . .
- An audience might agree with this argument if they also believed . . .
- An audience might oppose this argument if they believed . . .
- The author's perspective is shaped by the values and interests of . . .
- An opponent's perspective might be shaped by the values and interests of . . .

As these sentence beginnings demonstrate, it takes close reading and analytical skill to decide whether to agree or disagree with an argument, or to draw a different conclusion, or to conceive of a new argument. You must practice disassembling arguments piece by piece, considering words, sentences, and paragraphs thoughtfully, one by one. Above all, go slow! In this vein, recall an episode from Lewis Carroll's *Through the Looking-Glass*:

> "Can you do Addition?" the White Queen asked. "What's one and one and one and one and one and one and one and one and one and one?"

"I don't know," said Alice. "I lost count."

"She can't do Addition," the Red Queen said.

It's easy enough to add one and one and one and so on, and of course Alice can do addition — but not at the pace that the White Queen sets. Similarly, you may find it difficult to perform thorough and thoughtful analysis if you read too quickly. Fortunately, you can set your own pace in reading the essays in this book. Skimming won't work, but slow and close reading—and thinking carefully about what you're reading—will.

Alice with the Red Queen and the White Queen.

When you first pick up an essay, you may indeed want to skim it, but if it is compelling enough, you will have to settle down to read it slowly, and perhaps you will read it more than one time. The effort could be worthwhile.

Defining Terms and Concepts

Writers often attempt to provide a provisional definition of important terms and concepts to advance their arguments. They ask readers, in a way, to accept a definition for the purposes of the argument at hand. Readers may do so, but if they want to argue a different position, they must do so according to the definition offered by the author, or else they must offer their own definition.

Before going further, allow us to define the difference between a **term** and a **concept**. A rule of thumb is that a *term* is more concrete and fixed than a *concept*. You may be able to find an authoritative source (like a federal law or an official policy) to help define a word as a *term*. An author may write, for example, "According to the legal definition, the term 'exploitation' means *A*, *B*, and *C*" (a technical definition). It may be difficult to contend with an author who offers a definition of a term in a strict way such as this. Unless you can find a different standard, you may have to start out on the same basic ground: an agreed-upon definition.

A *concept* is more open-ended and may have a generally agreed-upon definition but rarely a strict or unchanging one. Writers may say, "For the purposes of this argument, let's define 'exploitation' as a moral concept that involves *A*, *B*, and *C*" (a broad definition). Concepts can be abstract but can also function powerfully in argumentation; love, justice, morality, psyche, health, freedom, bravery, masculinity—these are all concepts. You may look up such words in the dictionary, but it won't offer a strict definition and won't say much about how to apply the concept. Arguments that rely predominantly on concepts may be more easily added to or challenged, because concepts are so much more open-ended than terms.

> **WRITING TIP** When defining a term conceptually, you may cite an authoritative person, such as an expert in a field ("Stephen Hawking defines time as . . ."), or you might cite a respected leader or important text ("Mahatma Gandhi defines love as . . ."; "The bible says . . ."). Alternatively, you can combine several views and insert your own provisional definition.

To illustrate how terms and concepts work, suppose you're reading an argument about whether a certain set of images is pornography or art. For the present purpose, let's use a famous example from 1992, when American photographer Sally Mann published *Immediate Family*, a controversial book featuring numerous images of her three children (then ages twelve, ten, and seven) in various states of nakedness during their childhood on a rural Virginia farm. Mann is considered a great photographer and artist ("America's Best Photographer," according to *Time* magazine in 2001), and *Immediate Family* is very well regarded in the art community ("one of the great photograph books of our time," according to the *New Republic*). But some critics couldn't separate the images of Mann's own naked children from the label "child pornography."

If you wished to argue against this position, you might begin by asking, "What is *child pornography*? What is *art*?" If someone were to define child pornography to include *any* images of nude children, that definition would include photographs taken for any reason—medical, sociological, anthropological, scientific—and would include even the innocent photographs taken by proud parents of their children swimming, bathing, and so on. It would also apply to some of the world's great art. Most people do not seriously think the mere image of the naked body, child or adult, is pornography. If you wanted to argue that Mann's photographs are not child pornography, you could draw upon the legal term itself and apply it to the images. You could also offer your own conceptual definition of art and apply that to the images.

Sometimes whether a word is used as a term or a concept has major implications for certain groups and interests. In recent years, for example, the dairy industry has lobbied the Food and Drug Administration to force producers of soy- and almond-based drinks to stop using the word *milk* to describe them. The dairy industry claims that "milk" is a term with a technical definition: a high-fat, high-protein liquid secreted by female animals to nourish their young. It argues that calling soy- and almond-based products "milk" runs the risk of deceiving consumers by suggesting that these drinks are nutritionally equivalent to "real" milk. Obviously, for marketing purposes the producers of the drinks prefer avoiding the term "almond water" or "soy drink." They argue that the word "milk" is more conceptual, commonly used to describe different liquids, such as milk of magnesia, rose milk, and coconut milk. The two sides are fundamentally disagreeing about the definition of the word.

In 2018, the FDA signaled that a legal definition of milk might be on the horizon. It does make us wonder if we will be soon eating "legume paste" instead of peanut butter (given that peanuts are not technically "nuts" and mashed peanuts are not technically "butter").

SUMMARIZING AND PARAPHRASING

After previewing, skimming, and a first reading (maybe even a second one), perhaps the next best step, particularly with a fairly difficult essay, is to reread it (again). Simultaneously, take notes on a sheet of paper, summarizing each paragraph in a sentence or two, and then write an overall summary of the whole argument. Writing a **summary** will help you understand the contents and see the strengths and weaknesses of the piece. It will also help you prepare for writing by providing a snapshot of the argument in your notes.

Don't confuse a summary with a paraphrase. A **paraphrase** is a word-by-word or phrase-by-phrase rewording of a text, a sort of translation of the author's language into your own. A paraphrase is therefore as long as the original or even longer; a summary is much shorter. An entire essay, even a whole book, may be summarized in a page, in a paragraph, even in a sentence. Obviously, a summary will leave out most details, but it will accurately state the essential thesis or claim of the original.

Why would anyone summarize, and why would anyone paraphrase? Because, as we've already said, these two activities—in different ways—help you comprehend an author's ideas and offer ways to introduce those ideas into your arguments in a way that readers can follow. Summaries and paraphrases can help you

- **validate** the basis of your ideas by providing an instance in which someone else wrote about the same topic

- **support** your argument by showing readers where someone else "got it right" (corroborating your ideas) or "got it wrong" (countering your ideas, but giving you a chance to refute that position in favor of your own)

- **clarify** in short order the complex ideas contained in another author's work

- **lend authority** to your voice by showing readers that you have considered the topic carefully by consulting other sources

- **build new ideas** from existing ideas on the topic, enabling you to insert your voice into an ongoing debate made evident by the summary or paraphrase

When you *summarize*, you're standing back, saying briefly what the whole adds up to; you're seeing the forest, as the saying goes, not the individual trees. When you *paraphrase*, you're inching through the forest, scrutinizing each tree—finding a synonym for almost every word in the original in an effort to ensure that you know exactly what the original is saying. (Keep in mind that when you incorporate a summary or a paraphrase into your own essay, you should acknowledge the source and state that you are summarizing or paraphrasing.)

Let's examine the distinction between summary and paraphrase in connection with the first two paragraphs of Paul Goodman's essay "A Proposal to Abolish Grading," excerpted from his book *Compulsory Miseducation and the Community of Scholars* (1966):

> Let half a dozen of the prestigious universities—Chicago, Stanford, the Ivy League—abolish grading, and use testing only and entirely for pedagogic purposes as teachers see fit.
>
> Anyone who knows the frantic temper of the present schools will understand the transvaluation of values that would be effected by this modest innovation. For most of the students,

the competitive grade has come to be the essence. The naïve teacher points to the beauty of the subject and the ingenuity of the research; the shrewd student asks if he is responsible for that on the final exam.

A *summary* of these two paragraphs might read like this:

> If some top universities used tests only to help students learn and not for grades, students would stop worrying about whether they got an A, B, or C and might begin to share the teacher's interest in the beauty of the subject.

Notice that the summary doesn't convey Goodman's style or voice (e.g., the wry tone in his pointed contrast between "the naïve teacher" and "the shrewd student"). That is not the purpose of summary.

Now for a *paraphrase*. Suppose you're not sure what Goodman is getting at, maybe because you're uncertain about the meanings of some words (e.g., *pedagogic* and *transvaluation*), or you just want to make sure you understand the point.

> Suppose some of the top universities — such as Chicago, Stanford, Harvard, Yale, and others in the Ivy League — stopped using grades and instead used tests only to help students learn.
>
> Everyone who is aware of the rat race in schools today will understand the enormous shift in values about learning that would come about by this small change. At present, idealistic instructors talk about how beautiful their subjects are, but smart students know that grades are what count. They only want to know if that subject will be on the exam.

In short, you may decide to paraphrase an important text if you want the reader to see the passage itself but you know that the full passage will be puzzling. In this situation, you offer help, *paraphrasing* before making your own point about the author's claim.

A second good reason to offer a paraphrase is if there is substantial disagreement about what the text says. The Second Amendment to the US Constitution is a good example of this sort of text:

> A well regulated Militia being necessary to the security of a free State, the right of the people to keep and bear Arms shall not be infringed.

Gun control supporters marching in Washington, DC.

Exactly what, one might ask, is a "Militia"? What does it mean for a militia to be "well regulated"? And does "the people" mean each individual or the citizenry as a unified group? After all, elsewhere in the document, where the Constitution speaks of individuals, it speaks of a "man" or a "person," not "the people." To speak of "the people" is to use a term (some argue) that sounds like a reference to a unified group—perhaps the citizens of each of the thirteen states—rather than a reference to individuals. However, if Congress did mean a unified group rather than individuals, why didn't it say, "Congress shall not prohibit the states from organizing militias"?

In fact, thousands of pages have been written about that sentence, and if you're going to write about it, you certainly have to let readers know exactly how you interpret each word. In short, you almost surely will paraphrase the sentence, going word by word, giving readers your own sense of what each word or phrase means. Here is one possible paraphrase:

> Because an independent society needs the protection of an armed force if it is to remain free, the government may not limit the right of the individuals (who may someday form the militia needed to keep the society free) to possess weapons.

In this interpretation, the Constitution grants individuals the right to possess weapons, and that is that.

Other students of the Constitution, however, offer very different paraphrases, usually along these lines:

> Because each state that is now part of the United States may need to protect its freedom (from the new national government), the national government may not infringe on the right of each state to form its own disciplined militia.

✓ A CHECKLIST FOR A PARAPHRASE

☐ Do I have a good reason for offering a paraphrase rather than a summary?

☐ Is the paraphrase entirely in my own words — a word-by-word "translation" — rather than a patchwork of the source's words and my own, with some of my own rearrangement of phrases and clauses?

☐ Do I not only cite the source but also explicitly say that the entire passage is a paraphrase?

This paraphrase says that the federal government may not prevent each state from having a militia; it says nothing about every individual person having a right to possess weapons.

The first paraphrase might be offered by the National Rifle Association or any other group that interprets the Constitution as guaranteeing individuals the right to own guns. The second paraphrase might be offered by groups that seek to limit the ownership of guns.

Why paraphrase? Here are two reasons you might paraphrase a passage:

1. To help yourself understand it. In this case, the paraphrase does not appear in your essay.
2. To help your reader understand a passage that is especially important but that is not immediately clear. In this case, you paraphrase to let the reader know exactly what the passage means. This paraphrase does appear in your essay.

PATCHWRITING AND PLAGIARISM

We have indicated that only rarely will you have reason to paraphrase in your essays. In your notes, you might sometimes copy word for word (quote), paraphrase, or summarize, but if you produce a medley of borrowed words and original words in your essays, you are **patchwriting**, and it can be dangerous: If you submit such a medley, you risk the charge of **plagiarism** *even if you have rearranged the phrases and clauses, and even if you have cited your source.*

Here's an example. First, we give the source: a paragraph from Helen Benedict's essay on the "man problem" in the military reprinted in full beginning on page 35:

> For generations now, the debate over women in combat has put the onus on women to prove they can handle the infantry and other traditionally all-male units. Yet today's wars have made it clear that the military's problem lies not with its women, their ability or their courage. The military's problem, instead, is with some of its men—and a deeply ingrained macho culture that denigrates, insults and abuses women.

Here is a student's patchwriting version:

> Over the past two generations, debates about women's roles in the military have focused on whether or not they can handle the infantry duty. Yet everyday they do. Helen Benedict points out that women are not the problem in the military—the men are, especially those who hold ideas ingrained in a macho culture that is insulting and abusive to women.

As you can see, the student writer has used patchwriting because she followed the source almost phrase by phrase, making small verbal changes here and there, such as substituting new words and key phrases, while at other points using the same vocabulary slightly rearranged. That is, the sequence of ideas and their arrangement, as well as most of the language, are entirely or almost entirely derived from the source, even if some of the words are different. Thus, even if the student cites the source, it is plagiarism.

What the student should have done is either (1) *quote the passage exactly*, setting it off to indicate that it's a quotation and indicating the source, or (2) *summarize it briefly* and credit the source—maybe in a version such as this:

> Helen Benedict points out that arguments used in the past to keep women out of military combat roles were unfounded. Women have proved themselves time and time again since the ban on women in combat roles was lifted. However, Benedict argues, even though women now have the opportunity to serve, they are by no means "equal" in the military. Benedict details the sexist culture in the military—what she calls the military's "man problem"—a problem that subjects women to a deeply hostile environment.

The above example frankly summarizes a source and attributes it to the author, Benedict. The reader knows these ideas are Benedict's, not the writer's. This allows the writer to build on her source's ideas to establish — and distinguish — her own argument.

Citing a source is not enough to protect you from the charge of plagiarism. Citing a source tells the reader that some fact or idea — or some groups of words enclosed within quotation marks or set off by indentation — comes from the named source; it does *not* tell the reader that almost everything in the paragraph is, in effect, someone else's writing with a few words changed, a few words added, and a few phrases moved.

The best way to avoid introducing patchwriting into your final essay is to make certain that when taking notes you indicate, *in the notes themselves*, what sort of notes they are. For example:

- When quoting word for word, put the passage within quotation marks and cite the page number(s) of the source.

- When paraphrasing — perhaps to ensure that you understand the writer's idea or because your readers won't understand the source's highly technical language unless you put it into simpler language — use some sign, perhaps (*par*), to remind yourself later that this passage is a paraphrase and thus is not really *your* writing.

- When summarizing, use a different key, such as (*sum*), and cite the page(s) or online location of the source.

If you have taken notes properly, with indications of the sort we've mentioned, when writing your paper you can say things like the following:

- *X*'s first reason is simple. *X* says, ". . ." (here you quote *X*'s words, putting them within quotation marks).

- *X*'s point can be summarized thus: . . . (here you cite the page).

- *X*, writing for lawyers, uses some technical language, but we can paraphrase her conclusion in this way: . . . (here you give the citation).

For additional information about plagiarism, see the section A Note on Plagiarizing on pages 287–89 in Chapter 7.

STRATEGIES FOR SUMMARIZING

As with paraphrases, summaries can help you establish your understanding of an essay or article. Summarizing each paragraph or each group of closely related paragraphs will enable you to follow the threads of the argument and will ultimately provide a useful map of the essay. Then, when rereading the essay, you may want to underline passages that you now realize are the author's key ideas—for instance, definitions, generalizations, and summaries. You may also want to jot notes in the margins, questioning the logic, expressing your uncertainty, or calling attention to other writers who see the matter differently.

> **WRITING TIP** Your essay is *likely to include brief summaries* of points of view with which you agree or disagree, but it will *rarely include a paraphrase* unless the original is obscure and you feel compelled to present a passage at length in words that are clearer than those of the original. If you do paraphrase, explicitly identify the material as a paraphrase. Never submit patchwriting.

How long should your summaries be? They can be as short as a single sentence or as long as an entire paragraph. Here's a one-sentence summary of Martin Luther King Jr.'s famous essay "Letter from Birmingham Jail," which King wrote after his arrest for marching against racial segregation and injustice in Birmingham, Alabama.

> In his letter, King argues that the time is ripe for nonviolent protest throughout the segregated South, dismissing claims by local clergymen who opposed him and arguing that unjust laws need to be challenged by black people who have been patient and silent for too long.

King's essay, however, is quite long. Obviously, our one-sentence summary cannot convey substantial portions of King's eloquent arguments, sacrificing almost all the nuance of his rationale, but it serves as an efficient summation and allows the writer to move on to his or her own analysis promptly.

A longer summary might try to capture more nuance, especially if, for the purposes of your essay, you need to capture more. How much you summarize depends largely on the *purpose* of your summary (see again our list of reasons to summarize on p. 58). Here is a longer summary of King's letter:

> In his letter, King argues that the time is ripe for nonviolent pro-test in the segregated South despite the criticism he and his fellow civil rights activists received from various authorities, especially the eight local clergymen who wrote a public statement against him. King addresses their criticism point by point, first claiming his essential right to be in Birmingham with his famous statement, "injustice anywhere is a threat to justice everywhere," and then saying that those who see the timing of his group's nonviolent direct action as inconvenient must recognize at least two things: one, that his "legitimate and unavoidable impatience" resulted from undelivered promises by authorities in the past; and two, that African Americans had long been told over and over again to wait for change with no change forthcoming. "This 'wait' has almost always meant 'never,'" King writes. For those who criticized his lead-ership, which encouraged people to break laws prohibiting their march, King says that breaking *unjust* laws may actually be con-strued as a *just* act. For those who called him an extremist, he rev-els in the definition ("was not Jesus an extremist in love?" he asks) and reminds them of the more extremist groups who call for vio-lence in the face of blatant discrimination and brutality (and who will surely rise, King suggests, if no redress is forthcoming for the peaceful southern protestors he leads). Finally, King rails against "silence," saying that to hold one's tongue in the face of segrega-tion is tantamount to supporting it — a blow to "white moderates" who believe in change but do nothing to help bring it about.

This summary, obviously much longer than the first, raises numer-ous points from King's argument and preserves through quotation some of King's original tone and substance. It sacrifices much, of course, but seeks to provide a thorough account of a long and com-plex document containing many primary and secondary claims.

If your instructor asks for a summary of an essay, most often he or she won't want you to include your own thoughts about the content. Of course, you'll be using your own words, but try to "put yourself in the original author's shoes" and provide a summary that reflects the approach taken by the source. It should *not* contain ideas that the original piece doesn't express. If you use exact words and phrases drawn from the source, enclose them in quotation marks.

Summaries may be written for exercises in reading comprehension, but the point of summarizing when writing an essay is to assist your own argument. A faithful summary—one without your own ideas interjected—can be effective when using a source as an example or showing another writer's concordance with your argument. Consider the following paragraph written by a student who wanted to use Henry David Thoreau's 1849 essay, "Resistance to Civil Government," to make a point in her paper on sweatshops and other poor labor conditions in the supply chains of our everyday products. Thoreau famously argued that many northerners who objected to slavery in the United States did not always realize how economically tied up in slavery they were. He argued that true opposition to slavery meant withdrawing fully from all economic activity related to it. The student was arguing that if a person today purchases goods manufactured in sweatshops or under other inadequate labor conditions, he or she is in a sense just as responsible for the abuses of labor as the companies who operate them. Thoreau provided a convenient precedent. Notice how the student offers a summary (underlined) along the way and how it assists her argument.

> Americans today are so disconnected from the source and origins of the products they buy that it is entirely possible for them one day to march against global warming and the next to collect a dividend in their 401k from companies that are the worst offenders. It is possible to weep over a news report on child labor in China and then post an emotional plea for justice on Facebook using a mobile device made by Chinese child laborers. <u>In 1849, Henry David Thoreau wrote in "Resistance to Civil Government" how ironic it was to see his fellow citizens in Boston opposed to slavery in the South, yet who read the daily news and commodity prices and "fall asleep over them both," not recognizing their own investments in, or patronage of, the very thing that offends their consciences. To Thoreau, such "gross inconsistency" makes even well-intentioned people "agents of injustice."</u> Similarly, today we do not see the connections between our consumer habits and the various kinds of oppression that underlie our purchases — forms of oppression we would never support directly and outright.

The embedded short summary addresses only one point of Thoreau's original essay, but it shows how summaries may serve in an integrative way—as analogy, example, or illustration—to support an argument even without adding the writer's own commentary or analysis.

Critical Summary

When writing a longer summary that you intend to integrate into your argument, you may interject your own ideas; the appropriate term for this writing is **critical summary**. It signifies that you're offering more than a thorough and accurate account of an original source, because you're adding your evaluation of it as well. Think of it as weaving together your neutral summary with your own argument so that the summary meshes seamlessly with your overall writing goal. Along the way, during the summary, you may appraise the original author's ideas, commenting on them as you go—even while being faithful to the original.

How can you faithfully account for an author's argument while commenting on its merits or shortcomings? One way is to offer examples from the original. In addition, you might assess the quality of those examples or present others that the author didn't consider. Remember, being critical doesn't necessarily mean refuting the author. Your summary can refute, support, or be more balanced, simply recognizing where the original author succeeds and fails.

> **WRITING TIP** When writing a critical summary, you can problematize by examining areas not considered by the author. Ask: What has the author missed? What evidence or examples have been misinterpreted?

A Strategy for Writing a Critical Summary   Follow these five steps when writing a critical summary:

1. **Introduce** the summary. You don't have to provide all these elements, but consider offering the *author's name* and *expertise*, the *title* of the source, the *place* of publication, the *year* of publication, or any other relevant information. You may also start to explain the author's main point that you are summarizing:

> Pioneering feminist <u>Betty Friedan</u>, in her landmark book <u>*The Feminine Mystique* (1963</u>), argued that . . .

Don't overdo it. Select the most important details carefully and work toward concision. Remember that this is a summary, so "get in and get out." That is, move quickly back to your analysis.

2. **Explain** the major point the source makes. Here you have a chance to tell your readers what the original author is saying, so be faithful to the original but also highlight the point you're summarizing:

> Pioneering feminist Betty Friedan, in her landmark book *The Feminine Mystique* (1963), argued that <u>women of the early 1960s were falling victim to a media-created image of ideal femininity that pressured them to prioritize homemaking, beauty, and maternity above almost all other concerns.</u>

Here you can control the readers' understanding through simple adjectives such as *pioneering* and *landmark*. (Compare how "*stalwart* feminist Betty Friedan, in her *provocative* book" might dispose the reader to interpret your material differently.)

3. **Exemplify** by offering one or more representative examples or evidence on which the original author draws. Feel free to quote if needed, although it is not required in a summary.

> Friedan examines post–World War II trends that included <u>the lowering of the</u> <u>marriage age,</u> <u>the rise of the mass media,</u> and what she calls <u>"the problem that has no name"</u>—that of feminine unfulfillment, or what we might today call "depression."

Feel free to use a short quotation or utilize signature terms, phrases, or concepts from the source.

4. **Problematize** by placing your assessment, analysis, or question into the summary.

> Although the word *depression* never comes up in Friedan's work, <u>one could assume</u> that terms like *malaise, suffering*, and *housewives' fatigue* <u>signal an emerging understanding of the relationship between stereotypical media representations of social identity and mental health.</u>

If you're working toward a balanced critique or rebuttal, here is a good place to insert your ideas or those of someone with a slightly different view. Consider utility phrases that help tie these elements of critical summary together. More adjectives

Visual Guide: Writing a Critical Summary

1 INTRODUCE

Who is the *author*? What is his or her expertise or significance?

What type of *source* is it? When was it published?

2 EXPLAIN

What (and how) is the author arguing? What is the author trying to achieve?

3 EXEMPLIFY

What evidence does the author use to support the argument, thesis, and/or perspective in this essay?

What examples or descriptions of the author's evidence can you include in your summary?

4 PROBLEMATIZE

What are your concerns about the author's interpretation, approach, methodology, or conclusions?

Do you notice any assumptions and predispositions that might have affected the author's interpretations?

What perspectives were left out? What further evidence (or contrary evidence) was overlooked?

5 EXTEND

What the author has done well? Not so well? What more could have been done, if anything?

What might further research reveal?

What other perspectives might have informed or improved the analysis?

What new directions could be opened in light of the author's analysis or your own critical summary?

If your source's ideas were implemented or acted upon, what might be the consequences or implications?

and strong verbs can help indicate your critique and judgment. For example:

> In her *careful* analysis of contemporary horror films, Simpson looks at movies like *X, Y,* and *Z,* showing how *inadequately* women are represented as *weak, vulnerable* victims in need of rescue, mostly by men. Nevertheless, while her analysis is *convincing,* her examples *ignore* films such as *A, B,* and *C,* and this glaring omission shows . . .

5. **Extend** by tying the summary to your argument, helping transition out of the critical summary and back into your own analysis. Imagine your final task as saying (without saying) something like, *And this summary is important to my overall thesis because it shows . . .*

> Friedan's work should raise questions about <u>how women are portrayed in the media today and about what mental health consequences are attributable to the ubiquitous and consistent messages given to women about their bodies, occupations, and social roles.</u>

It is possible to use this method — **Introduce, Explain, Exemplify, Problematize,** and **Extend** — in many ways, but essentially it is a way of providing a critical summary, any element of which can be enhanced or built upon as needed. When you're writing your own critical summary, refer to the Visual Guide (p. 69) for reference.

WRITING TIP Use strong adjectives to establish your assessment or judgments on the value, worth, or quality of the writer's argument, thesis, presentation, or sources (e.g., *landmark* essay, *controversial* book, *blunt* critique).

A Short Essay for Summarizing Practice

The following piece by Susan Jacoby is annotated to provide a "rough summary" in the margins, more or less paragraph by paragraph, the kind you might make if you are outlining an essay or argument.

Susan Jacoby

Susan Jacoby (b. 1946), a journalist since the age of seventeen, is well known for her feminist writings. "A First Amendment Junkie" (our title) appeared in the Hers column in the New York Times *in 1978. Notice that her argument zigs and zags, not because Jacoby is careless but because in building a strong case to support her point of view, she must consider some widely held views that she does* not *accept; she must set these forth and then give her reasons for rejecting them.*

A First Amendment Junkie

It is no news that many women are defecting from the ranks of civil libertarians on the issue of obscenity. The conviction of Larry Flynt, publisher of *Hustler* magazine — before his metamorphosis into a born-again Christian — was greeted with unabashed feminist approval. Harry Reems, the unknown actor who was convicted by a Memphis jury for conspiring to distribute the movie *Deep Throat*, has carried on his legal battles with almost no support from women who ordinarily regard themselves as supporters of the First Amendment. Feminist writers and scholars have even discussed the possibility of making common cause against pornography with adversaries of the women's movement — including opponents of the Equal Rights Amendment and "right-to-life" forces.

> Paragraph 1: Although feminists usually support the First Amendment, when it comes to pornography many feminists take the position of opposing the Equal Rights Amendment, abortion, and other causes of the women's movement.

All of this is deeply disturbing to a woman writer who believes, as I always have and still do, in an absolute interpretation of the First Amendment. Nothing in Larry Flynt's garbage convinces me that the late Justice Hugo L. Black was wrong in his opinion that "the Federal Government is without any power whatsoever under the Constitution to put any type of burden on free speech and expression of ideas of any kind (as distinguished from conduct)." Many women I like and respect tell me I am wrong; I cannot remember having become involved in so many heated discussions of a public issue since the end of the Vietnam

> Paragraph 2: Larry Flynt produces garbage, but Jacoby thinks his conviction represents an unconstitutional limitation of freedom of speech.

War. A feminist writer described my views as those of a "First Amendment junkie."

Many feminist arguments for controls on pornography carry the implicit conviction that porn books, magazines, and movies pose a greater threat to women than similarly repulsive exercises of free speech pose to other offended groups. This conviction has, of course, been shared by everyone—regardless of race, creed, or sex—who has ever argued in favor of abridging the First Amendment. It is the argument used by some Jews who have withdrawn their support from the American Civil Liberties Union because it has defended the right of American Nazis to march through a community inhabited by survivors of Hitler's concentration camps.

If feminists want to argue that the protection of the Constitution should not be extended to *any* particularly odious or threatening form of speech, they have a reasonable argument (although I don't agree with it). But it is ridiculous to suggest that the porn shops on 42nd Street are more disgusting to women than a march of neo-Nazis is to survivors of the extermination camps.

The arguments over pornography also blur the vital 5 distinction between expression of ideas and conduct. When I say I believe unreservedly in the First Amendment, someone always comes back at me with the issue of "kiddie porn." But kiddie porn is not a First Amendment issue. It is an issue of the abuse of power—the power adults have over children—and not of obscenity. Parents and promoters have no more right to use their children to make porn movies than they do to send them to work in coal mines. The responsible adults should be prosecuted, just as adults who use children for back-breaking farm labor should be prosecuted.

Susan Brownmiller, in *Against Our Will: Men, Women, and Rape*, has described pornography as "the undiluted essence of antifemale propaganda." I think this is a fair description of some types of pornography, especially of the brutish subspecies that equates sex with death and portrays women primarily as objects of violence.

Paragraphs 3, 4: Feminists who want to censor pornography argue that it poses a greater threat to women than similar repulsive speech poses to other groups. They can make this case, but it is absurd to say that pornography is a "greater threat" to women than "neo-Nazi . . . extermination camps."

Paragraph 5: Trust in the First Amendment is not refuted by kiddie porn; kiddie porn is an issue of child abuse.

Paragraphs 6, 7, 8: Some feminists think censorship of pornography can be more "rational" than other kinds of censorship, but a picture of a nude woman strikes some women as base and others as "lovely." There is no unanimity.

The equation of sex and violence, personified by some glossy rock record album covers as well as by *Hustler*, has fed the illusion that censorship of pornography can be conducted on a more rational basis than other types of censorship. Are all pictures of naked women obscene? Clearly not, says a friend. A Renoir nude is art, she says, and *Hustler* is trash. "Any reasonable person" knows that.

But what about something between art and trash—something, say, along the lines of *Playboy* or *Penthouse* magazines? I asked five women for their reactions to one picture in *Penthouse* and got responses that ranged from "lovely" and "sensuous" to "revolting" and "demeaning." Feminists, like everyone else, seldom have rational reasons for their preferences in erotica. Like members of juries, they tend to disagree when confronted with something that falls short of 100 percent vulgarity.

In any case, feminists will not be the arbiters of good taste if it becomes easier to harass, prosecute, and convict people on obscenity charges. Most of the people who want to censor girlie magazines are equally opposed to open discussion of issues that are of vital concern to women: rape, abortion, menstruation, contraception, lesbianism—in fact, the entire range of sexual experience from a woman's viewpoint.

Paragraphs 9, 10: If feminists censor girlie magazines, they are unwittingly helping opponents of the women's movement censor discussions of rape, abortion, and so on.

Feminist writers and editors and filmmakers have 10 limited financial resources: Confronted by a determined prosecutor, Hugh Hefner[1] will fare better than Susan Brownmiller. Would the Memphis jurors who convicted Harry Reems for his role in *Deep Throat* be inclined to take a more positive view of paintings of the female genitalia done by sensitive feminist artists? *Ms.* magazine has printed color reproductions of some of those art works; *Ms.* is already banned from a number of high school libraries because someone considers it threatening and/or obscene.

Paragraphs 11, 12: Like other would-be censors, feminists want to use the power of the state to achieve what they have not achieved in "the marketplace of ideas." They lack faith in "democratic persuasion."

Feminists who want to censor what they regard as harmful pornography have essentially the same motivation as other would-be censors: They want to use

---

[1] **Hugh Hefner**   Founder and longtime publisher of *Playboy* magazine.

the power of the state to accomplish what they have been unable to achieve in the marketplace of ideas and images. The impulse to censor places no faith in the possibilities of democratic persuasion.

It isn't easy to persuade certain men that they have better uses for $1.95 each month than to spend it on a copy of *Hustler*. Well, then, give the men no choice in the matter.

Paragraphs 13, 14: This attempt at censorship reveals a "desire to shift responsibility from individuals to institutions." The responsibility is properly the parents'.

I believe there is also a connection between the impulse toward censorship on the part of people who used to consider themselves civil libertarians and a more general desire to shift responsibility from individuals to institutions. When I saw the movie *Looking for Mr. Goodbar*, I was stunned by its series of visual images equating sex and violence, coupled with what seems to me the mindless message (a distortion of the fine Judith Rossner novel) that casual sex equals death. When I came out of the movie, I was even more shocked to see parents standing in line with children between the ages of ten and fourteen.

I simply don't know why a parent would take a child to see such a movie, any more than I understand why people feel they can't turn off a television set their child is watching. Whenever I say that, my friends tell me I don't know how it is because I don't have children. True, but I do have parents. When I was a child, they did turn off the TV. They didn't expect the Federal Communications Commission to do their job for them.

Paragraph 15: We can't have too much of the First Amendment.

I am a First Amendment junkie. You can't OD on 15 the First Amendment, because free speech is its own best antidote.

Summarizing Jacoby   If we want to present a *brief summary* in the form of one coherent paragraph—perhaps as part of an essay arguing for or against—we might write something like the one shown in the paragraph below. (Of course, we would introduce it with a lead-in along these lines: "Susan Jacoby, writing in the *New York Times*, offers a forceful argument against censorship of pornography. Jacoby's view, briefly, is . . .")

When it comes to censorship of pornography, some feminists take a position shared by opponents of the feminist movement.

They argue that pornography poses a greater threat to women than other forms of offensive speech offer to other groups, but this interpretation is simply a mistake. Pointing to kiddie porn is also a mistake, for kiddie porn is an issue involving not the First Amendment but child abuse. Feminists who support censorship of pornography will inadvertently aid those who wish to censor discussions of abortion and rape or censor art that is published in magazines such as *Ms.* The solution is not for individuals to turn to institutions (i.e., for the government to limit the First Amendment) but for individuals to accept the responsibility for teaching young people not to equate sex with violence.

In contrast, a *critical summary* of Jacoby—an evaluative summary in which we introduce our own ideas and examples—might look like this:

Susan Jacoby, writing for the *New York Times* in 1978, offers a forceful argument against censorship of pornography, but one that does not have foresight of the internet age and the new availability of extreme and exploitative forms of pornography. While she dismisses claims by feminists that pornography should be censored because it constitutes violence against women, what would Jacoby think of such things as "revenge porn" and "voyeuristic porn" today or the array of elaborate sadistic fantasies readily available to anyone with access to a search engine? Jacoby says that censoring pornography is a step toward censoring art, and she proudly wears the tag "First Amendment junkie," ostensibly to protect what she finds artistic (such as images of female genitalia in *Ms.* magazine). However, her argument does not help us account for these new forms of exploitation and violence disguised as art or "free speech." Perhaps she would see revenge porn and voyeur porn in the same the way she sees kiddie porn—not so much as an issue of free speech but as an issue of other crimes. Perhaps she would hold her position that we can avoid pornography by just "turning off the TV," but the new internet pornography is intrusive, entering our lives and the lives of our children whether we like it or not. Education is part of the solution, Jacoby would agree, but we could also consider . . .

Introduces author, source, and year and characterizes the argument as "forceful"

Problematizes Jacoby's claims by introducing present-day contexts

Explains Jacoby's argument

Problematizes Jacoby's claim by pointing out its omissions in the current context

Extends Jacoby's argument to a new issue related to today's media environment

This example not only summarizes and applies the other techniques presented in this chapter (e.g., accounting for context and questioning definitions of terms and concepts) but also weaves them together with a central argument that offers a new response and a practicable solution.

✓ A CHECKLIST FOR A SUMMARY

- ☐ Have I adequately previewed the work?
- ☐ Can I state the thesis?
- ☐ If I have written a summary, is it accurate?
- ☐ Does my summary mention all the chief points?
- ☐ If there are inconsistencies, are they in the summary or the original selection?
- ☐ Will my summary be clear and helpful?
- ☐ Have I considered the audience for whom the author is writing?

ESSAYS FOR ANALYSIS

Gwen Wilde

This essay was written for a composition course at Tufts University.

Why the Pledge of Allegiance Should Be Revised (Student Essay)

All Americans are familiar with the Pledge of Allegiance, even if they cannot always recite it perfectly, but probably relatively few know that the *original* Pledge did *not* include the words "under God." The original Pledge of Allegiance, published in the September 8, 1892, issue of the *Youth's Companion,* ran thus:

> I pledge allegiance to my flag, and to the Republic for which it stands: one Nation indivisible, with Liberty and justice for all. (Djupe 329)

In 1923, at the first National Flag Conference in Washington, DC, it was argued that immigrants might be confused by the words "my Flag," and it was proposed that the words be changed to "the Flag of the United States." The following year it was changed again, to "the Flag of the United States of America," and this wording became the official — or, rather, unofficial — wording, unofficial because no wording had ever been nationally adopted (Djupe 329).

In 1942, the United States Congress included the Pledge in the United States Flag Code (4 USC 4, 2006), thus for the first time officially sanctioning the Pledge. In 1954, President Dwight D. Eisenhower approved adding the words "under God." Thus, since 1954 the Pledge reads:

> I pledge allegiance to the flag of the United States of America, and to the Republic for which it stands: one nation under God, indivisible, with Liberty and Justice for all. (Djupe 329)

In my view, the addition of the words "under God" is inappropriate, and they are needlessly divisive — an odd addition indeed to a nation that is said to be "indivisible."

Very simply put, the Pledge in its latest form requires all 5 Americans to say something that some Americans do not believe. I say "requires" because although the courts have ruled that students may not be compelled to recite the Pledge, in effect peer pressure does compel all but the bravest to join in the recitation. When President Eisenhower authorized the change, he said, "In this way we are reaffirming the transcendence of religious faith in America's heritage and future; in this way we shall constantly strengthen those spiritual weapons which forever will be our country's most powerful resource in peace and war" (Sterner).

Exactly what did Eisenhower mean when he spoke of "the transcendence of religious faith in America's heritage" and when he spoke of "spiritual weapons"? I am not sure what "the transcendence of religious faith in America's heritage" means. Of course, many Americans have been and are deeply religious — no one doubts it — but the phrase certainly goes far beyond saying that many Americans have been devout. In any case, many Americans have *not* been devout, and many Americans have *not* believed in "spiritual weapons," but they have nevertheless been patriotic Americans. Some of them have fought and died to keep America free.

In short, the words "under God" cannot be uttered in good faith by many Americans. True, something like 70 or even 80% of Americans say they are affiliated with some form of Christianity, and approximately another 3% say they are Jewish. I don't have the figures for persons of other faiths, but in any case we can surely all agree that although a majority of Americans say they have a religious affiliation, nevertheless several million Americans do *not* believe in God.

If one remains silent while others are reciting the Pledge, or even if one remains silent only while others are speaking the words "under God," one is open to the charge that one is unpatriotic, is "unwilling to recite the Pledge of Allegiance." In the Pledge, patriotism is connected with religious belief, and it is this connection that makes it divisive and (to be blunt) un-American. Admittedly, the belief is not very specific: one is not required to say that one believes in the divinity of Jesus, or in the power of Jehovah, but the fact remains, one is required to express belief in a divine power, and if one doesn't express this belief one is — according to the Pledge — somehow not fully an American, maybe even un-American.

Please notice that I am not arguing that the Pledge is unconstitutional. I understand that the First Amendment to the Constitution says that "Congress shall make no law respecting an establishment of religion, or prohibiting the free exercise thereof." I am not arguing that the words "under God" in the Pledge add up to the "establishment of religion," but they certainly do assert a religious doctrine. Like the words "In God We Trust," found on all American money, the words "under God" express an idea that many Americans do not hold, and there is no reason why these Americans — loyal people who may be called upon to defend the country with their lives — should be required to say that America is a nation "under God."

It has been argued, even by members of the Supreme Court, 10 that the words "under God" are not to be taken terribly seriously, not to be taken to say what they seem to say. For instance, Chief Justice Rehnquist wrote:

> To give the parent of such a child a sort of "heckler's veto" over a patriotic ceremony willingly participated in by other students, simply because the Pledge of Allegiance contains the descriptive phrase "under God," is an unwarranted extension of the establishment clause, an extension which would have the unfortunate effect of prohibiting a commendable patriotic observance. (qtd. in Stephens et al. 104)

Chief Justice Rehnquist here calls "under God" a "descriptive phrase," but descriptive of *what*? If a phrase is a "descriptive phrase," it describes something, real or imagined. For many Americans, this phrase does *not* describe a reality. These Americans may perhaps be mistaken—if so, they may learn of their error at Judgment Day—but the fact is, millions of intelligent Americans do not believe in God.

Notice, too, that Chief Justice Rehnquist goes on to say that reciting the Pledge is "a commendable patriotic observance." Exactly. That is my point. It is a *patriotic* observance, and it should not be connected with religion. When we announce that we respect the flag—that we are loyal Americans—we should not also have to announce that we hold a particular religious belief, in this case a belief in monotheism, a belief that there is a God and that God rules.

One other argument defending the words "under God" is often heard: The words "In God We Trust" appear on our money. It is claimed that these words on American money are analogous to the words "under God" in the Pledge. But the situation really is very different. When we hand some coins over, or some paper money, we are concentrating on the business transaction, and we are not making any affirmation about God or our country. But when we recite the Pledge—even if we remain silent at the point when we are supposed to say "under God"—we are very conscious that we are supposed to make this affirmation, an affirmation that many Americans cannot in good faith make, even though they certainly can unthinkingly hand over (or accept) money with the words "In God We Trust."

Because I believe that *reciting* the Pledge is to be taken seriously, with a full awareness of the words that is quite different from when we hand over some money, I cannot understand the recent comment of Supreme Court Justice Souter, who in a case said that the phrase "under God" is "so tepid, so diluted, so far from compulsory prayer, that it should, in effect, be beneath the constitutional radar" (qtd. in "Guide"). I don't follow his reasoning that the phrase should be "beneath the constitutional radar," but in any case I am willing to put aside the issue of constitutionality. I am willing to grant that this phrase does not in any significant sense signify the "establishment of religion" (prohibited by the First Amendment) in the United States. I insist, nevertheless, that the phrase is neither "tepid" nor "diluted." It means what it says—it *must* and *should* mean what it says, to everyone who utters it—and, since millions of loyal Americans cannot say it, it should not be included in a statement in which Americans affirm their loyalty to our great country.

In short, the Pledge, which ought to unite all of us, is divi- 15 sive; it includes a phrase that many patriotic Americans cannot bring themselves to utter. Yes, they can remain silent when others recite these two words, but, again, why should they have to remain silent? The Pledge of Allegiance should be something that *everyone* can say, say out loud, and say with pride. We hear much talk of returning to the ideas of the Founding Fathers. The Founding Fathers did not create the Pledge of Allegiance, but we do know that they never mentioned God in the Constitution. Indeed, the only reference to religion, in the so-called establishment clause of the First Amendment, says, again, that "Congress shall make no law respecting an establishment of religion, or prohibiting the free exercise thereof." Those who wish to exercise religion are indeed free to do so, but the place to do so is not in a pledge that is required of all schoolchildren and of all new citizens.

WORKS CITED

Djupe, Paul A. "Pledge of Allegiance." *Encyclopedia of American Religion and Politics*. Edited by Paul A. Djupe and Laura R. Olson, Facts on File, 2003.

"Guide to Covering 'Under God' Pledge Decision." *ReligionLink*, 17 Sept. 2005, religionlink.com/database/guide-to-covering -under-god/.

Stephens, Otis H., et al., editors. *American Constitutional Law*. 6th ed., vol. 1, Cengage Learning, 2014.

Sterner, Doug. "The Pledge of Allegiance." *Home of Heroes*, homeofheroes.com/hallofheroes/1st_floor/flag/1bfc_pledge_ print.html. Accessed 13 Apr. 2016.

TOPICS FOR CRITICAL THINKING AND WRITING

1. Summarize the essay in a paragraph.

2. What words are defined in this essay? Are they defined more as terms or as concepts? Explain *how* the author, Gwen Wilde, defines one word or phrase.

3. Does Wilde give enough weight to the fact that no one is compelled to recite the Pledge of Allegiance? Explain your answer.

4. What arguments does Wilde offer in support of her position?

5. Does Wilde show an adequate awareness of counterarguments? Identify one place where she raises and refutes a counterargument.

6. What is Wilde's strongest argument? Are any of her arguments notably weak? If so, how could they be strengthened?

7. What assumptions — tacit or explicit — does Wilde make? Do you agree or disagree with them? Explain your response.

8. What do you take the words "under God" to mean? Do they mean "under God's special protection"? Or "acting in accordance with God's rules"? Or "accountable to God"? Or something else? Explain.

9. Chief Justice Rehnquist wrote that the words "under God" are a "descriptive phrase." What do you think he meant by this?

10. What is the purpose of the Pledge of Allegiance? Does the phrase "under God" promote or defeat that purpose? Explain your answer.

11. What do you think about substituting "with religious freedom" for "under God"? Set forth your response, supported by reasons, in about 250 words.

12. Wilde makes a distinction between the reference to God on US money and the reference to God in the Pledge of Allegiance. Do you agree with her that the two cases are not analogous? Explain.

13. What readers might *not* agree with Wilde's arguments? What values do they hold? How might you try to persuade an audience who disagrees with Wilde to consider her proposal?

14. Putting aside your own views on the issue, what grade would you give this essay as a work of argumentative writing? Support your evaluation with reasons.

15. Consider how you would summarize a photograph such as this one by following the steps of introducing, explaining, exemplifying, problematizing, and extending it (see pp. 67–70).

Spencer Platt/Getty Images News/ Getty Images

Zachary Shemtob and David Lat

Zachary Shemtob, formerly editor in chief of the Georgetown Law Review, *is a clerk in the US District Court for the Southern District of New York. David Lat is a former federal prosecutor. Their essay originally appeared in the* New York Times *in 2011.*

Executions Should Be Televised

Earlier this month, Georgia conducted its third execution this year. This would have passed relatively unnoticed if not for a controversy surrounding its videotaping. Lawyers for the condemned inmate, Andrew Grant DeYoung, had persuaded a judge to allow the recording of his last moments as part of an effort to obtain evidence on whether lethal injection caused unnecessary suffering.

Though he argued for videotaping, one of Mr. DeYoung's defense lawyers, Brian Kammer, spoke out against releasing the footage to the public. "It's a horrible thing that Andrew DeYoung had to go through," Mr. Kammer said, "and it's not for the public to see that."

We respectfully disagree. Executions in the United States ought to be made public.

Right now, executions are generally open only to the press and a few select witnesses. For the rest of us, the vague contours are provided in the morning paper. Yet a functioning democracy demands maximum accountability and transparency. As long as executions remain behind closed doors, those are impossible. The people should have the right to see what is being done in their name and with their tax dollars.

This is particularly relevant given the current debate on 5 whether specific methods of lethal injection constitute cruel and unusual punishment and therefore violate the Constitution.

There is a dramatic difference between reading or hearing of such an event and observing it through image and sound. (This is obvious to those who saw the footage of Saddam Hussein's hanging in 2006 or the death of Neda Agha-Soltan during the protests in Iran in 2009.) We are not calling for opening executions completely to the public—conducting them before a live crowd—but rather for broadcasting them live or recording them for future release, on the web or TV.

When another Georgia inmate, Roy Blankenship, was executed in June, the prisoner jerked his head, grimaced, gasped, and lurched, according to a medical expert's affidavit. The *Atlanta Journal-Constitution* reported that Mr. DeYoung, executed in the same manner, "showed no violent signs in death." Voters should not have to rely on media accounts to understand what takes place when a man is put to death.

Cameras record legislative sessions and presidential debates, and courtrooms are allowing greater television access. When he was an Illinois state senator, President Obama successfully pressed for the videotaping of homicide interrogations and confessions. The most serious penalty of all surely demands equal if not greater scrutiny.

Opponents of our proposal offer many objections. State lawyers argued that making Mr. DeYoung's execution public raised safety concerns. While rioting and pickpocketing occasionally marred executions in the public square in the eighteenth and nineteenth centuries, modern security and technology obviate this concern. Little would change in the death chamber; the faces of witnesses and executioners could be edited out, for privacy reasons, before a video was released.

Of greater concern is the possibility that broadcasting exe- 10 cutions could have a numbing effect. Douglas A. Berman, a law professor, fears that people might come to equate human executions with putting pets to sleep. Yet this seems overstated. While public indifference might result over time, the initial broadcasts would undoubtedly get attention and stir debate.

Still others say that broadcasting an execution would offer an unbalanced picture—making the condemned seem helpless and sympathetic, while keeping the victims of the crime out of the picture. But this is beside the point: the defendant is being executed precisely because a jury found that his crimes were so heinous that he deserved to die.

Ultimately the main opposition to our idea seems to flow from an unthinking disgust—a sense that public executions are archaic, noxious, even barbarous. Albert Camus related in his essay "Reflections on the Guillotine" that viewing executions turned him against capital punishment. The legal scholar John D. Bessler suggests that public executions might have the same effect on the public today; Sister Helen Prejean, the death penalty abolitionist, has urged just such a strategy.

That is not our view. We leave open the possibility that making executions public could strengthen support for them; undecided viewers might find them less disturbing than anticipated.

Like many of our fellow citizens, we are deeply conflicted about the death penalty and how it has been administered. Our focus is on accountability and openness. As Justice John Paul Stevens wrote in *Baze v. Rees*, a 2008 case involving a challenge to lethal injection, capital punishment is too often "the product of habit and inattention rather than an acceptable deliberative process that weighs the costs and risks of administering that penalty against its identifiable benefits."

A democracy demands a citizenry as informed as possible about   15
the costs and benefits of society's ultimate punishment.

Topics for Critical Thinking and Writing

1. In paragraphs 9–13, Zachary Shemtob and David Lat discuss objections to their position. Are you satisfied with their responses to the objections, or do you think they do not satisfactorily dispose of one or more of the objections? Explain.

2. In paragraph 4, the authors say that "[t]he people should have the right to see what is being done in their name and with their tax dollars." But in terms of *rights*, should the person being executed have a right to die in privacy? Articulate a position that weighs the public's right to see what is being done with its tax dollars against death row prisoners' rights to privacy.

3. In the concluding paragraph, the authors imply that their proposal, if enacted, will help inform citizens "about the costs and benefits of society's ultimate punishment." Do you agree? Why, or why not? What reasons do the authors offer to support their proposal?

4. In your view, what is the strongest argument the authors give on behalf of their proposal? What is the weakest? Explain why you made these choices.

3

Critical Reading: Getting Deeper into Arguments

Not everything that is faced can be changed, but nothing can be changed until it is faced.

— JAMES BALDWIN

PERSUASION, ARGUMENT, AND RHETORICAL APPEALS

When we think seriously about an argument, not only do we encounter ideas that may be unfamiliar, but also we are forced to examine our own cherished opinions — and perhaps for the first time really see the strengths and weaknesses of what we believe. As the philosopher John Stuart Mill put it, "He who knows only his own side of the case knows little."

It is useful to distinguish between **persuasion** and **argument**. Persuasion has the broader meaning. To **persuade** is to convince someone else to accept or adopt your position. To be persuasive does not necessarily mean your argument is sound. Persuasion can be accomplished

- by giving reasons (i.e., by argument, by logic);
- by appealing to the emotions; or
- by bullying, lying to, or threatening someone.

Argument, we mean to say, represents only one form of persuasion, but a special one: one that elevates the cognitive or intellectual capacity for reason. Rhetoricians often use the Greek word *logos*, which means "word" or "reason," to denote this aspect of persuasive writing. An appeal to reason may by conducted by using such things as

- physical evidence, data, and facts;
- the testimony of experts, authorities, or respected persons;
- common sense; or
- probability.

Visual Guide: Evaluating Persuasive Appeals

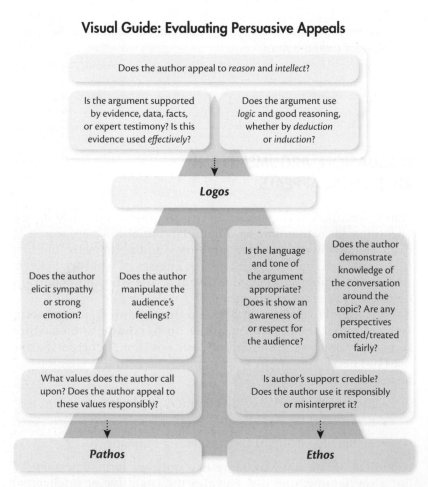

Does the author appeal to *reason* and *intellect*?

Is the argument supported by evidence, data, facts, or expert testimony? Is this evidence used *effectively*?

Does the argument use *logic* and good reasoning, whether by *deduction* or *induction*?

Logos

Does the author elicit sympathy or strong emotion?

Does the author manipulate the audience's feelings?

Is the language and tone of the argument appropriate? Does it show an awareness of or respect for the audience?

Does the author demonstrate knowledge of the conversation around the topic? Are any perspectives omitted/treated fairly?

What values does the author call upon? Does the author appeal to these values responsibly?

Is author's support credible? Does the author use it responsibly or misinterpret it?

Pathos

Ethos

Put it this way: The goal of *argument* is to convince by demonstrating the truth (or probable truth) of an assertion, whereas the goal of *persuasion* is simply to convince by any means whatsoever. **Logos**, the root word of *logic*, means appealing to the intellect to make rational claims and reasoned judgments.

An appeal to the emotions is known as **pathos**, which is Greek for "feeling," and elicits the sym*path*ies (note the root word here) in one form or another. Appeals to the sympathies may call upon any number of emotions, such as anger, fear, pity, or envy, or they may call upon passionate feelings about honor, duty, family, or patriotism. In critical thinking, we may be tempted to privilege the mind (*logos*) over the heart (*pathos*), but we must note that emotions inform decision-making in important ways, too, and most arguments use *logos* and *pathos*, reason and passion, in different degrees. Most of this book is about argument in the sense of presenting reasonable support of claims, but reason is not the whole story.

If an argument is to be effective, it must be presented persuasively, and writers may convincingly call upon readers' feelings to make a sound argument. Consider two broad arguments that were made in 2018 about the Department of Homeland Security's policy of separating families of illegal immigrants at the US–Mexico border. Many conservatives argued by appealing to reason: The law requires all illegal immigrants to be detained and processed, and children need special accommodations and, therefore, separate detention centers. However, many liberals argued by appealing primarily to emotions, using heart-rending images and stories of incarcerated children separated from their parents to inspire public outcry. In response, just over a month after it started, President Donald Trump signed an executive order stopping the practice of separating families at the border.

Images of children held in detention centers, such as this one from 2014, appealed to the emotions of Americans in 2018. What aspects of this photograph make it particularly convincing as an appeal to emotions and values?

John Moore/Getty Images News/Getty Images

In short, emotion won the day over reason—yet in no way can we say that feelings led us astray. Emotions can, in fact, guide us toward wise choices because emotions are often closely connected to values, ideals, morals, ethics, and principles. Feelings can impassion us to make rash decisions, sure, but they can also inspire bold ones. And reason, a powerful tool of the intellect, can just as soon lead us toward the dark rather than the light. As the poet Emily Dickinson wrote, "Much madness is divinest sense / To a discerning eye / Much sense the starkest madness." To conduct our lives strictly according to pure reason *or* pure feeling would lead, we think, to an intolerable existence in either case. We rely upon both of these faculties, and we need both kinds of appeals.

Because of this, most arguments do not divide easily along the lines of *logos* and *pathos*. Nor do arguments always imply two opposing speakers and positions. Of course, arguments *may* put reason and passion in opposition and present clearly opposing positions, but it is not a *requirement* that arguments do so, nor that they contain any special degree of *logos* or *pathos*. For example, the Declaration of Independence is an argument, one that sets forth the colonists' reasons for declaring their independence (*logos*) but also includes powerful language that condemns tyranny and appeals to "Life, Liberty, and the Pursuit of Happiness," words that evoke strong emotion (*pathos*). Even everyday arguments utilize both kinds of appeals. If you were explaining to your parents why you are changing your major, you might supply reasons and justifications for your decision (perhaps by comparing statistics about overall costs, future income potential, and job prospects), thus constructing a *rational* argument based on *logos*, but you may also be appealing to your family's passionate beliefs about happiness, using emotional persuasion to convince them you are making the right choice.

> **WRITING TIP** An argument doesn't require two opposing positions. Even when writing only for oneself, trying to clarify one's thinking by setting forth reasons and justifications for an idea, the result is an argument.

In addition to *logos* and *pathos*, the Greek philosopher Aristotle (384–322 BCE) defined a third type of rhetorical appeal. **Ethos**, the Greek word for "character," involves the careful presentation of self, what Aristotle called "the speaker's personal character when the speech is so spoken as to make us think him credible" (*Rhetoric* 1.2.1356a.4-15). Aristotle emphasized the importance of impressing upon the audience that the speaker is a person of authority, good sense, and moral integrity. When writers convey their *ethos*, their trustworthiness or good character, they may

- establish authority and credibility (e.g., by demonstrating or stating expertise, credentials, or experience),
- use language appropriate to the setting (e.g., by avoiding vulgar language, slang, and colloquialism),
- demonstrate familiarity with their audience (e.g., by achieving the right tone and level of complexity),
- show fair-mindedness (e.g., by offering other points of view in goodwill and by recognizing that contrary points of view may have some merit), or
- show attention to detail (e.g., by citing relevant statistics and careful interpretation of evidence).

THINKING CRITICALLY IDENTIFYING ETHOS

For each method listed, locate a sentence in one of the readings in this book. Provide a quotation that shows the author establishing *ethos*.

Method	Examples	Your Turn
Use personal experience or credentials to establish authority.	"As a student who works and attends school full-time, I can speak firsthand about . . ."	
Acknowledge weaknesses, exceptions, and complexities.	"Although I have shown that X is important, investigation into Y is also necessary to truly understand . . ." "Understandably, my solution may be seen as too simple or reductive, but it may work as a starting point for . . ."	
Mention the qualifications of any sources as a way to boost your own credibility.	"According to X, author and noted professor of Y at Z University, . . ."	

In short, writers who are concerned with *ethos* — and all writers should be — employ devices that persuade readers that they are reliable, intelligent persons in whom their readers can have confidence.

REASON, RATIONALIZATION, AND CONFIRMATION BIAS

We know that if we set our minds to a problem, we can often find reasons (not always necessarily sound ones) for almost anything we want to justify. In an entertaining example from Benjamin Franklin's *Autobiography*, Franklin tells of being hungry and wrestling with his vegetarianism on a voyage from Boston while watching his fellow passengers hauling in cod from the sea:

> Hitherto I had stuck to my resolution of not eating animal food, and on this occasion, I considered with my master Tryon the taking of every fish as a kind of unprovoked murder, since none of them had or ever could do us any injury that might justify the slaughter. All this seemed very reasonable.

However, once the fish was fried,

> it smelt admirably well. I balanced some time between principle and inclination, till I recollected that when the fish were opened I saw smaller fish taken out of their stomachs. Then thought I, if you eat one another, I don't see why we mayn't eat you. So I dined upon cod very heartily and continued to eat with other people, returning only now and then occasionally to a vegetable diet. So convenient a thing it is to be a *reasonable creature*, since it enables one to find or make a reason for everything one has a mind to do.

Franklin is being playful in commenting on how rationalizations work, but he touches on a truth: If necessary, we can find reasons to justify whatever we want. That is, instead of reasoning, we may *rationalize* (a self-serving but dishonest form of reasoning), like the fox in Aesop's fables who, finding the grapes he desired were out of reach, consoled himself with the thought that they were probably sour.

Another aspect of rationalization is **confirmation bias**. Confirmation bias is a type of cognitive bias that describes the tendency to seek out, find, and employ evidence that reinforces our inclinations or preexisting beliefs. In this process, only *confirmatory* ideas, information, and data are accounted for and taken seriously while disconfirming data are ignored or treated with skepticism. In other words, whether consciously or unconsciously, we ignore the full picture, disregard other perspectives without first listening to them, and search only for support for our position, no matter how credible or representative it is. Cognitive bias occurs most when deeply ingrained beliefs or views impede our ability to interpret information fairly. It also occurs when students write papers and research only tidbits of sources—easy quotes or factoids—that support their thesis, rather than fully reading the source material to get the full picture of what the source's argument is. (Be careful of this in your own writing; cherry-picking evidence from sources often leads to misinterpretation, which will damage your own *ethos*.)

Perhaps we can never be certain that we aren't rationalizing or falling victim to confirmation bias, except when being playful like Franklin. But we can think critically about how our own reasoning process can be affected by our own self-interest, beliefs, and worldviews. The more we can be alert to the ways these shape our thinking, the more fairly we can reason.

TYPES OF REASONING

Reason may not be the only way of finding the truth, but it is a way on which we often rely when making arguments, whether we are making them to ourselves or others. Traditionally, arguments are often said to be **inductive** or **deductive**; that is, to proceed along two different pathways toward their conclusions. (We spend some time discussing logical reasoning here, but a more in depth discussion can also be found in Chapter 9, A Logician's View: Deduction, Induction, and Fallacies.)

Induction

Inductive reasoning, or *induction*, is essentially a process of thinking in which patterns of evidence and examples accumulate until the thinker draws a reasonable conclusion from what has been observed. Onc might say, for example: "In my experience, the subway always arrives promptly at 6:00 a.m., so I infer from this evidence that it will also run promptly today at 6:00 a.m." Induction uses information about observed cases to reach a conclusion about unobserved cases.

The word *induction* comes from the Latin *in ducere,* "to lead into" or "to lead up to." In inductive reasoning, we draw from the specific to make generalizations about reality. We discern patterns and expand toward an explanation or a theory. If, on a fishing trip, a green-eyed horsefly bites you (specific incident), you may reasonably conclude that other flies like it in the area will also bite you (generalization). Although it seems obvious, you used induction to infer a conclusion. Your inferences might be even broader: You may be tempted to generalize that these green-eyed horseflies are native to the area and that other fishing streams in the area are likely to have them. Induction has taken your reasoning from a specific example to a general theory of reality.

> **WRITING TIP** By far the most common way to test the adequacy of an inductive argument is to consider one or more **counterexamples**. If the counterexamples are numerous, genuine, and reliable, the generalization can be challenged.

Deduction

In Latin, the term *deduction* means "lead down from," the opposite of induction's tendency "to lead up to." *Deductive reasoning* is the mental process of moving down from one given, true statement through another true statement to produce a reasonable conclusion. That is to say, the generalizations come first, and the specific conclusion is, because of them, therefore proven true.

One of the best ways to think through an argument, especially a deductive argument, is to use a syllogism, so in the next section we examine more closely how syllogisms work.

Premises and Syllogisms

In classical argument, a **syllogism** — Latin for "a reckoning together" — is often used to show the truth or factuality of a conclusion. A syllogism shows two or more propositions called **premises** that are given, or assumed to be true. The word *premise* comes from a Latin word meaning "to set in front." A deductive argument is said to be **valid** if its internal logic is so strong that it makes it impossible for the premises to be true and the conclusion nevertheless to be false. A classical syllogism therefore joins the premises with a third statement presented as a logical conclusion. Thus, premises are set down before the argument begins.

The classic example of a syllogism is this:

Premise: All human beings are mortal.
Premise: Socrates is a human being.
Conclusion: Socrates is mortal.

The purpose of a syllogism is simply to present reasons that establish the truth of a conclusion. Truth can be demonstrated if the argument satisfies both of two independent criteria:

1. All of the premises *must be true*.
2. The syllogism *must be valid*.

If each premise is *true* and the syllogism is *valid*, then the argument is said to be **sound**.

Sound Arguments: True and Valid   But how do we tell in any given case if an argument is sound? We can perform two different tests, one for the *truth* of each of the premises and another for the overall *validity* of the conclusions drawn from the premises.

The basic test for the **truth** of a premise is to determine whether what it asserts corresponds with reality; if it does, then it is true, and if it doesn't, then it is false. The truth of a premise depends on its content—what it asserts—and the evidence provided for it.

The basic test for **validity** is different. A valid argument is one in which the conclusion *necessarily follows* from the premises, so that if all the premises are true, then the conclusion must be true, too. Consider this syllogism:

Extracting oil from the Arctic Wildlife Refuge would adversely affect the local ecology.

Adversely affecting the local ecology is undesirable unless there is no better alternative fuel source.

Therefore, extracting oil from the Arctic Wildlife Refuge is undesirable unless there is no better alternative fuel source.

Here, if we grant the premises to be true and the conclusion necessarily follows from the premises, then the argument is valid.

Valid but Not Sound   Part of being a good critical thinker is the ability to analyze the premises and determine the validity and soundness of an argument. The problem is that arguments can have many premises, or premises that are quite complex, making it difficult to ascertain their truth. Suppose that one or more of a syllogism's premises are false but the syllogism itself is valid. What does that indicate about the truth of the conclusion? Consider this example:

> All Americans prefer vanilla ice cream to other flavors.
>
> Jimmy Fallon is an American.
>
> Therefore, Jimmy Fallon prefers vanilla ice cream to other flavors.

The first (or major) premise in this syllogism is false. Yet the argument passes our formal test for validity: If one grants both premises, then one must accept the conclusion. So we can say that the conclusion *follows from* its premises, even though the premises *do not prove* the conclusion. This is not as paradoxical as it may sound. For all we know, the argument's conclusion may in fact be true; Jimmy Fallon may indeed prefer vanilla ice cream, and the odds are that he does because consumption statistics show that a majority of Americans prefer vanilla. Nevertheless, if the conclusion in this syllogism is true, it's not because this argument proved it.

Alex Segre/Shutterstock.com

The great fictional detective Sherlock Holmes was credited with having unusual powers of deduction. Holmes could see the logical consequences of many and apparently disconnected premises.

True but Not Valid   Some arguments may have true premises yet nevertheless have false conclusions. This occurs when the premises are not related to one another, or when conclusions do not *necessarily* follow from the premises. Consider this syllogism:

> *X* minority group is disadvantaged in schools.
>
> John Doe is a member of *X* minority group.
>
> Therefore, John Doe is disadvantaged in school.

Here, let's grant that the premises are true. Let's also grant that the conclusion may well be true: John Doe could indeed be disadvantaged. But it's also possible that the conclusion is false. Suppose you were to argue that minority groups aren't the only ones who are disadvantaged. Consider, for example, how a learning disability may affect a student's success. In short, the truth of the two premises is no guarantee that the conclusion is also true.

Chemists may use litmus paper to determine instantly whether the liquid in a test tube is an acid or a base; unfortunately, we cannot subject most arguments to a litmus test like this to determine their reasonability. Logicians beginning with Aristotle have developed techniques to test any given argument, no matter how complex or subtle, for centuries; we cannot hope to express the results of their labor in a few pages. Apart from advising you to consult Chapter 9, A Logician's View: Deduction, Induction, and Fallacies, all we can do here is reiterate the core questions you must always ask when evaluating any argument:

- Is it vulnerable to criticism on the grounds that one (or more) of its premises is false?

- Does one of the premises not necessarily relate to another premise?

- Even if all the premises were true, would the conclusion still not necessarily follow?

Enthymemes   Much reasoning that occurs in writing happens in a form of a special form called an **enthymeme**, an incomplete or abbreviated syllogism in which a conclusion is drawn without stating one or more of the premises. To use the classical example, we might say

Socrates is mortal because he is human.

Here, the unstated premise is that all humans are mortal; the premise is missing but remains operative.

We can reason better about what we read and write by thinking about the things that "go without saying." The rhetoric of advertisers and politicians, for example, can sometimes be dismantled by thinking about how enthymemes work to hide the implicit premises. Consider the following claim:

You will improve your complexion by using Clear-Away.

The premises and conclusion here might be presented as a syllogism:

Unstated premise:	All people who use Clear-Away improve their complexion.
Premise:	You use Clear-Away.
Conclusion:	You will improve your complexion.

Bob Mankoff/Cartoon Stock

Or consider this example:

> Jim Hartman doesn't know accurate statistics on crime in his state; therefore, he is unqualified to be governor.

This might be stated as this syllogism:

> People who do not know accurate statistics about crime in their states are unqualified to be governor.
>
> Jim Hartman doesn't know accurate statistics.
>
> Jim Hartman is unqualified to be governor.

Occasionally, it is not the premises that are unstated in an enthymeme, but the conclusions that are left out. Consider this example:

> Lucky Charms breakfast cereal is fortified with vitamins!

The premises and conclusion might be stated this way:

> All food fortified with vitamins is healthy.
>
> Lucky Charms cereal is a food fortified with vitamins.
>
> Lucky Charms cereal is healthy.

Just these few examples should indicate that our alertness to the unstated premises or conclusions of an enthymeme can be valuable.

A Word on Weak and Invalid Arguments   Inductive and deductive arguments can both be critically examined and challenged by searching for weaknesses in their premises or weaknesses in the inferences that lead to their conclusions. Below, for example, you will see an inductive argument presented as a syllogism. (Inductive arguments are not typically presented as such; when they are, they are called "statistical" or "nondeductive" syllogisms.) Working inductively, however, we can present two premises based on observations and draw a generalization:

> Every fish we have taken from the harbor has a fungus.
>
> Every fish we observed with the fungus has died.
>
> All the fish in the harbor are dying of a fungus.

Now, examine the probability of this conclusion. It may well be true that all the fish in the harbor are dying, yet this is still not a *valid* conclusion. It is not valid because the conclusion does not *necessarily follow* from the premises. In fact, inductive arguments are not referred to as valid or invalid at all, or sound or unsound, but as *strong* or *weak* depending on the probability of the conclusion. The example above has *weak induction* because we do not have information about *how many or what types of fish were sampled* or further *what other factors might have contributed to the deaths of the sampled fish*.

When we reason inductively, weaknesses frequently lie in the size and the quality of the **sample**. If we're offering an argument concerning the political leanings of sorority and fraternity members at our campus, we cannot interview *every* member, so instead we select a sample. But we must ask if the sample is a fair one: Is it representative of the larger group? We may interview five members of Alpha Tau Omega and find that all five are Republicans, yet we cannot conclude that all members of fraternities at our school are Republicans. To get a more *representative sample*, we would measure opinions from across the various sororities and fraternities.

> **WRITING TIP** An argument that uses samples ought to tell the reader how the samples were chosen. If it doesn't provide this information, the reader should treat the argument with suspicion.

A larger sample doesn't necessarily mean a *representative* one, however. A poll of the political leanings of college students would tell us very little if it included only students at small private colleges. We could not use that data to extrapolate about *all* college students. Ask yourself: Why not?

Inductive arguments are susceptible to challenges because they tend to generalize, or "lead up" from observations to a conclusion. They are always contingent upon new observations and new data and are susceptible to overgeneralization (which occurs when we extend the application or relevancy of the observed cases too far). Deductive arguments, on the other hand, which "lead down" from their premises toward a conclusion, often posit facts or principles as their premises. Therefore, because deduction can (although it does not always) produce incontrovertible truths, deductive arguments tend to be more reliable than inductive arguments, which can be very strong but never attain 100 percent certainty. When they are sound, deductive arguments based on incontrovertibly true premises provide an *absolutely* necessary conclusion.

SOME PROCEDURES IN ARGUMENT

Definitions

In our current discussion, we are primarily analyzing the logic of arguments—the *logos*—and prioritizing the procedures of thinking and argument that emphasize reason. Another important element to this kind of thought is *definition*. Earlier, in the section Defining Terms and Concepts in Chapter 2 (pp. 55–57), we discussed how definitions of key terms and concepts underpin arguments. As to whether or not a local stream is "polluted," for example, you may use a strict (terminological) or loose (conceptual) definition of the word *pollution* to argue either way. You might define the word *pollution* as a term set forth by your state's environmental protection agency, which perhaps requires that water contains a minimum threshold of toxins, or you might describe *pollution* according to your own concept of having a lot of garbage lying alongside of it. Either definition may help you argue for a state cleanup effort. When we define key words, we're answering the question "What is it?" and setting out our definition for the purposes of the argument at hand. In answering this question as precisely as we can, we can then find, clarify, and develop ideas accordingly.

Trying to decide the best way to define key terms and concepts is often difficult—and sometimes controversial. Consider one of the most contentious debates in our society: abortion rights. Many arguments about abortion depend on a definition of "life." Traditionally, human life has been seen as beginning at birth.

Nowadays, most people see "life" as something that begins at least at viability (the capacity of a fetus to live independently of the uterine environment). But modern science has made it possible to see the beginning of "life" in different ways. Some who want abortion to be prohibited by law define life as beginning with *brain birth*, the point at which "integrated brain functioning begins to emerge." Still others see life beginning as early as fertilization. Whatever the merits of these definitions, the debate itself is convincing evidence of just how important it can be to define your important terms and concepts when making arguments.

Stipulation   When you are writing, you may define your terms and concepts by **stipulating** definitions. The word *stipulate* comes from the Latin verb *stipulari*, meaning "to bargain" or "to secure a guarantee." When you stipulate, you ask the reader to agree with a certain definition for the sake of the argument at hand (although, of course, a reader may not want to make that bargain). For example, you may write one of the following:

- If we can agree the definition of *X* is *Y*, then . . .
- If we can agree the strict definition of *X* does not include *Y*, then . . .

Establishing your definition then allows the reader to consider and evaluate your argument according to your definition.

In contracts, you can often find stipulated definitions made very explicitly because, in a legal context, key terms need to be precisely defined and agreed upon by all parties to avoid disputes. For example, consider this language from a portion of a California home insurance policy covering damage caused by an earthquake:

> For the purposes of this policy . . . the term Earthquake shall mean seismic activity, including earth movement, landslide, mudslide, sinkhole, subsidence, volcanic eruption, or Tsunami, as defined herein. . . . The term Tsunami shall mean a wave or series of waves caused by underwater earthquakes and/or seismic activity, including, but not limited to, volcanic eruptions, landslides, earth movement, mudslide, sinkhole, or subsidence. In no event shall this Company be liable for any loss caused directly or indirectly by fire, explosion or other excluded perils as defined herein.

Parties mutually agree to certain definitions by signing the contract itself. Other forms of writing also require comprehensive definitions. For instance, if you were a legislator writing a law to limit "internet gambling" in your state, you must have a very precise definition of what that means. (The actual legal definition of internet gambling in the US legal code is more than 1,000 words!)

You do not have to be writing a contract or a law to make stipulative definitions. In your arguments, you may stipulate a definition in the following cases:

- when you are seeking to secure a shared understanding of the meaning of a term or concept
- when no fixed or standard definition is available

If you are call something *undemocratic*, you must define what you mean by *democratic*. If you call a painting or a poem a *masterpiece*, you may want to try to define that word, perhaps by offering criteria art must meet to be called a masterpiece. What is your definition of what it means for a nation to *advance*? What definition of *cruel and unusual punishment* will you use in your argument about solitary confinement? How are you defining *food insecurity* in your call to end hunger on campus? Not everyone may accept your stipulative definitions, and there will likely be defensible alternatives. However, when you stipulate a definition, your audience knows what *you* mean by the term.

Consider the opening paragraph of a 1975 essay by Richard B. Brandt titled "The Morality and Rationality of Suicide." Notice that the author does two things:

- He first stipulates a definition.
- Then, aware that the definition may strike some readers as too broad and therefore unreasonable or odd, he offers a reason on behalf of his definition.

"Suicide" is conveniently defined, for our purposes, as doing something which results in one's death, either from the intention of ending one's life or the intention to bring about some other state of affairs (such as relief from pain) which one thinks it certain or highly probable can be achieved only by means of death or will produce death. It may seem odd to classify an act of heroic self-sacrifice on the part of a soldier as suicide. It is simpler, however, not to try to define "suicide" so that an act of suicide is always irrational or immoral in some way; if we adopt a neutral definition like the above we can still proceed to ask when an act of suicide in that sense is rational, morally justifiable, and so on, so that all evaluations anyone might wish to make can still be made. (61)

Sometimes, a definition that at first seems extremely odd can be made acceptable by offering strong reasons in its support. Sometimes, in fact, an odd definition marks a great intellectual leap forward. For instance, in 1990 the US Supreme Court recognized that *speech* includes symbolic nonverbal expressions such as protesting against a war by wearing armbands or by flying the American flag upside down. Such actions—although they are nonverbal—are considered speech because they express ideas or emotions. More controversially, in 2010 the Supreme Court ruled in *Citizens United vs. Federal Election Commission* that corporate spending in the form of campaign contributions constitutes speech and cannot be limited under the First Amendment. This decision spurred unprecedented spending on elections by corporations and today remains a divisive definition of speech.

Our object with these examples is to make one overall point clear: An argument will be most fruitful if the participants first share an understanding of the concepts they are talking about.

Synonym   One way to define a term or concept is through **synonym**. For example, *pornography* can be defined, at least roughly, as "obscenity" (something indecent). But definition by synonym is usually only a start; you then have to define or explain the synonym, too, because, in fact, *pornography* and *obscenity* are not exact synonyms. Imagine writing, "This company's strategy is essentially a *con game*" or "Spanking children is *child abuse*." In each case, synonyms were provided to help define the terms of the argument, but now the synonyms need to be explained.

Example   Another way to define a word is to point to an example (sometimes called an **ostensive definition**, from the Latin *ostendere*, "to show"). This method can be very helpful, ensuring that both writer and reader are talking about the same thing—and adding not only clarity but vivid detail. If you are reviewing a movie and you want to define "tween movies," you could point to specific examples of the kinds of films you mean. You could say that "tween movies" are those films marketed to a certain age demographic—young people between eight and sixteen years old—but the definition may be made concrete and visible by quickly surveying such films: "Tween movies include films that feature plots developed around preteen or teenage characters, such as *The Sandlot* (1993) and *High School Musical* (2006)." Or imagine you are attempting to define American folk heroes as those characters, whether based on real people or wholly invented, whose stories have been exaggerated and transformed in various genres, such as *Johnny Appleseed*, *John Henry*, and *Casey Jones*.

Definitions by example also have their limitations, so choosing the right examples, ones that have all the central or typical characteristics and that will best avoid misinterpretation, is important to using this method of definition effectively. A few decades ago, many people pointed to James Joyce's *Ulysses* and D. H. Lawrence's *Lady Chatterley's Lover* as examples of obscene novels. Today these books are regarded as literary masterpieces. It's possible that they can be obscene and also be literary masterpieces. (Joyce's wife is reported to have said of her husband, "He may have been a great writer, but . . . he had a very dirty mind.")

Establishing Sufficient and Necessary Conditions   A final way to define a term or concept is by establishing its *sufficient and necessary conditions*. For writers, this just means controlling definitions by offering certain preconditions. For example, if you say a "sport" is defined as any activity meeting *sufficient* conditions of competition and physical endurance, you can also argue that video gaming, which meets those criteria, may be called a sport. If you were to argue vaping should not be subject to the same rules on your campus as smoking, you could define "smoking" as an activity requiring

"It all depends on how you define 'chop.'"

the *necessary* conditions of combustion and smoke, neither of which is a feature of a vaporizer.

One common way in formal logic to distinguish between sufficient and necessary conditions is to imagine them phrased as conditional propositions. Sufficient conditions are usually presented as "if, then" propositions, whereas necessary conditions are usually presented as "*if and only if,* then . . ." propositions. Suppose we want to define the word *circle* and are conscious of the need to keep circles distinct from other geometric figures such as rectangles and spheres. We might express our definition by citing sufficient and necessary conditions as follows: "Anything is a circle *if and only if* it is a closed plane figure and all points on the circumference are equidistant from the center." Using the connective "if and only if" between the definition and the term being defined helps make the definition neither too exclusive (too narrow) nor too inclusive (too broad). Of course, for most ordinary purposes we don't require such a formally precise definition.

EXERCISE: DEFINITIONS

1. Read the selections below and (a) identify the term or concept being defined; (b) explain which type of definition it is (stipulation, synonym, example); and (c) use details from the examples to support your answer.

> Marriage is primarily an economic arrangement, an insurance pact. It differs from the ordinary life insurance agreement only in that it is more binding, more exacting. Its returns are insignificantly small compared with the investments. In taking out an insurance policy one pays for it in dollars and cents, always at liberty to discontinue payments. If, however, woman's premium is a husband, she pays for it with her name, her privacy, her self-respect, her very life, "until death doth part."
> — Emma Goldman, *Marriage and Love* (1911)

> Pentagon spending is reaching into areas of American life previously neglected: entertainment, popular consumer brands, sports. Rick and Donna's home is full of this incursion. As they putter around the kitchen, getting ready for the day ahead, they move from the wall cabinets (purchased at DoD contractor Lowe's Home Center) to the refrigerator (from defense contractor Maytag), choosing their breakfast from a cavalcade of products made by Pentagon contractors. These companies that, quite literally, feed the Pentagon's war machine, are the same firms that fill the shelves of America's kitchens. . . . No part of the hours of the day will be lacking in products produced by Pentagon

contractors . . . 3M Post-It notes, Microsoft Windows software, Lexmark printers, Canon Photocopiers, AT&T telephones, Maxwell House coffee from Altria.

— Nicholas Turse, *The Complex* (2008)

A slander is a spoken defamation, whether that act of speech is public and one-time or recorded and redistributed. Slander also includes defamation by gesture, which could include making a gesture that suggests professional incompetence or mental illness. Slander carries the additional burden for a plaintiff of having to prove that they suffered actual loss due to the false statement.

— Mitch Ratcliffe, *How to Prevent Against Online Libel and Defamation* (2009)

When considering a subject as abstract and intangible as peace, it is important to define the term itself. In the context of this discussion, peace may be defined as it is in Webster's dictionary as a community's "freedom from civil disturbance, or a state of security or order provided for by law or custom."

— Kincaid Fitzgerald, *Peace in the Global Neighborhood* [student paper at Leiden University] (2018)

Assumptions

Even the longest and most complex chains of reasoning or proof, and even most carefully constructed definitions, are fastened to assumptions — one or more *unexamined beliefs*. These taken-for-granted, hidden, or neglected beliefs affect how writers and readers make inferences and draw conclusions. If you attend a birthday party, you might *assume* that cake will be served. If the ceiling is wet, you may *assume* that the roof is leaking.

However, false assumptions can be dangerous. If you assume that a person of a certain race, class, or gender will behave in predictable ways, you may be stereotyping that individual and making guesses about that person's actions without evidence. If you assume that traffic will stop at a red light and you proceed through an intersection without looking, you could end up in a car crash. Suppose a business executive assumes that sales are down because of poor marketing and not the quality of her company's product; she could end up ignoring the real problem and wasting time and money on a new advertising campaign instead of improving the product.

Assumptions are sometimes deeply embedded in our value systems and therefore hard to recognize. Consider this case: When education researchers questioned race and class disparities on the

SAT exam in the early 2000s, they found it odd that minorities and other economically disadvantaged students performed worse than their white, middle-class counterparts on the *easier* verbal and math questions, *not* the more difficult ones. That is, some basic vocabulary words like *horse* and *canoe* were likely to be mis-identified by minority and lower-income students than more challenging words like *anathema* and *intractable*. (Colloquially, *horse* could be a verb, as in "play around," or it could refer to heroin. *Canoe*, meanwhile, describes what happens to a cigar when one side burns faster than another.) Researchers found that the problem was the assumptions made by the test designers, not the student test-takers. The more "difficult" words typically learned in school or in textbooks were understood more uniformly among all students. The test designers had assumed that persons of all socioeconomic groups hear language the same way and therefore that their proficiency could be measured using the same linguistic standards. By challenging the assumptions of the exam, researchers were able to challenge the disparities in exam results. As a result, college admissions boards began to regard the SAT as a weaker indicator of academic potential for some groups, while test designers began to address other deeply embedded assumptions in the exam.

Sometimes assumptions may be stated explicitly, especially when writers feel confident that readers share their values. Benjamin Franklin, for example, argued against paying salaries to the holders of executive offices in the federal government on the grounds that men are moved by ambition (love of power) and by avarice (love of money) and that powerful positions conferring wealth incite men to do their worst. These assumptions he stated, although he felt no need to argue them at length because he also guessed that his readers shared them.

"Let me guess. You want French and you want ranch?"

Matthew Diffee/The New Yorker Collection/The Cartoon Bank

Assumptions may also be unstated. Writers, painstakingly arguing specific points, may choose to keep one or more of their argument's assumptions tacit, or unspoken. Or they may be completely unaware of an underlying assumption they hold. For example, Franklin didn't even bother to state two other assumptions:

- Persons of wealth who accept an unpaying job (after all, only persons of wealth could afford to hold unpaid government jobs) will have at heart the interests of all classes of people, not only the interests of their own class.
- Those wealthy government servants will be male.

Probably Franklin didn't state these assumptions because he thought they were perfectly obvious. But if you think critically about the first assumption listed above, you may find reasons to doubt that people who attain wealth will no longer be motivated by self-interest. The second assumption runs even more deeply: Although women could not vote in Franklin's time, there were no legal restrictions on women running for office, yet the assumption Franklin shared with his audience was that politics was a male domain. Both of these assumptions have now shifted to a great extent: We now assume that paying legislators ensures that the government does not consist only of people whose incomes may give them an inadequate view of the needs of others, and our society now assumes that people who are not (or who do not identify as) male can also hold government positions. After the midterm elections of 2018, more than 100 women occupied seats in the US House of Representatives for the first time in history.

Good critical thinking involves sharpening your ability to identify assumptions, especially those that seem so self-evident, or commonsensical, that they hardly need to be stated. When you are evaluating arguments or writing your own, you should question the basic ideas upon which a writer's claims rest and ask yourself if there are other, contradictory, or opposed ideas that could be considered. If there are, you can explore the alternative forms of understanding—alternative assumptions—to test or to critique an argument and perhaps offer a different analysis or a different possibility for action. When you are hunting for assumptions (your own and others'), try the following:

- **Identify** the ideas, claims, or values that are presented as obvious, natural, or given (so much so that they are sometimes not even stated).

- **Examine** those ideas to test for their commonality, universality, and necessity. Are other ways of thinking possible?

- **Determine** whether or not contradictory ideas, claims, or values provide a fruitful new way of interpreting or understanding the information at hand.

Exercise: Assumptions

Read the following sentences and identify the assumptions that are embedded in them. State the assumptions and then challenge the claims of each sentence.

- Jamaican Blue Mountain coffee is expensive; therefore, it must be high-quality coffee.

- All students were given a syllabus detailing the policies and procedures for this course, so they all know the absence policy.

- If you do not vote, you have no right to complain about politicians.

- Someday Joseph will ask Jill to marry him.

- It's hard to believe the president is wasting time golfing when there is an economic crisis at hand.

- After decades of increasing divorce rates in the United States, the divorce rate has dropped by 18 percent in the past ten years; clearly, staying married is more popular now than it was in the past.

- Although my downtown apartment is close to my workplace, crime has been on the rise in the city, so I am moving to the suburbs where I am safer.

Evidence: Experimentation, Examples, Authoritative Testimony, and Numerical Data

In a courtroom, evidence bearing on the guilt of the accused is introduced by the prosecution, and evidence to the contrary is introduced by the defense. Not all evidence is admissible (e.g., hearsay is not, even if it's true), and the law of evidence is a highly developed subject in jurisprudence. In daily life, the sources of evidence are less disciplined. Daily experience, a memorable observation, or an unusual event — any or all of these may serve as evidence for (or against) some belief, theory, hypothesis, or explanation a person develops.

In making arguments, people in different disciplines use different kinds of evidence to support their claims. For example:

- In literary studies, texts (works of literature, letters, journals, notes, and other kinds of writing) are the chief forms of evidence.

- In the social sciences, field research (interviews, observations, surveys, data) usually provides the evidence.

- In the hard sciences, reports of experiments are the usual evidence; if an assertion cannot be tested—if one cannot show it to be false—it is an *opinion*, not a scientific hypothesis.

When you are offering evidence to support your arguments, you are drawing on the specific information that makes your claims visible, concrete, *evident*. For example, in arguing that the entertainment industry needs to address the problem of sexual harassment among powerful male celebrities, you could point to the many men who have been accused of these behaviors. Each instance constitutes **evidence** for the problem. If you are arguing that bump stocks (devices that allow semiautomatic guns to operate like automatic ones) should be banned, you will point to specific cases in which bump stocks were used to commit crimes in order to show the need for regulation. Evidence can take many forms. Here, we discuss three broad categories of evidence.

Experimentation   Often, the forms of evidence that scientists use, whether in the natural and mathematical sciences or in the social sciences, is the result of **experimentation**. Experiments are deliberately contrived situations, often complex in their methodology or the technologies they use, that are designed to yield particular observations. What the ordinary person does with unaided eye and ear, the scientist does much more carefully and thoroughly, often in controlled situations and with the help of laboratory instruments. For example, a natural scientist studying the biological effects of a certain chemical might expose specially bred rodents to carefully monitored doses of the chemical and then measure the effects. A health scientist might design a study in which people who exercise regularly are compared to people who do not in order to argue the beneficial effects of consistent exercise on heart health.

A psychologist might introduce a certain type of therapy to a group of people and then compare the results to other treatment methods.

It's no surprise that society attaches much more weight to the findings of scientists than to the corroborative (much less the contrary) experiences of ordinary people. No one today would seriously argue that the sun really does go around the earth just because it looks that way, nor would we argue that the introduction of carcinogens to the human body through smoking does not increase the risk for cancers. Yet because some kinds of scientific validation (such as repeatability) produce unarguable fact, we sometimes assume that all forms of experimentation are equal in their ability to point to truth. However, we should also be skeptical, since experiment designs can also be flawed—by bad design, bad samples, measurement error, or a host of other problems. Moreover, the results of experimentation can also be used to make different kinds of arguments. Consider that the same scientific data are used by people who argue that humans are the primary cause of climate change as well as by people who deny that humans play a significant role in climate change.

Examples   Unlike the hard sciences, the variety, extent, and reliability of the evidence obtained in the humanities—and in daily life—are quite different from those obtained in the laboratory. In all forms of writing, examples constitute the primary evidence. We follow here with an explanation of examples and a description of several common forms of examples.

Nearly all arguments use examples. Suppose we argue that a candidate is untrustworthy and shouldn't be elected to public office. We may point to episodes in his career—his misuse of funds in 2008 and the false charges he made against an opponent in 2016—as examples of his untrustworthiness. Or if we're arguing that President Harry Truman ordered the atom bomb dropped to save American (and, for that matter, Japanese) lives that otherwise would have been lost in a hard-fought invasion of Japan, we could point to the fierce resistance of the Japanese defenders in battles on the islands of Saipan, Iwo Jima, and Okinawa, where Japanese soldiers fought to the death rather than surrender. These examples indicate that the Japanese defenders of the main islands would have fought to their deaths without surrendering, even though they knew defeat was certain.

An *example* is a type of *sample*. These two words come from the same Old French word, *essample*, from the Latin *exemplum*, which means "something taken out" — that is, a selection from the group, something held up as indicative. A Yiddish proverb shrewdly says, "'For example' is no proof," but the evidence of well-chosen examples can go a long way toward helping a writer convince an audience.

In arguments, three sorts of examples are especially common:

- real events
- invented instances (artificial or hypothetical cases)
- analogies

We will treat each of these briefly.

REAL EVENTS   In referring to Truman's decision to drop the atom bomb, we touched upon examples drawn from real events — the various named battles — to demonstrate our claim that it was ultimately the best option. Yet an example drawn from reality may not be as clear-cut as we would like. We used the Japanese army's behavior on Saipan and on Iwo Jima as evidence for our claim that the Japanese later would have fought to the death in an American invasion of Japan. This, we argued, would therefore have inflicted terrible losses on the Japanese and on the Americans. Our examples could be countered by evidence that in June and July 1945 certain Japanese diplomats sent out secret peace feelers to Switzerland and offered to surrender if the Emperor Hirohito could retain power so that in August 1945, when Truman authorized dropping the bomb, the situation was very different. If we were to argue that Truman should not have dropped the bomb, we could cite those peace feelers specifically, indicating a Japanese willingness to end the war without such destruction.

But most arguments using real events require further support. Some may argue that we are not currently under threat of a nuclear war, and they may offer examples of various agreements made among nuclear-armed nations as evidence. But such an argument needs more support because of the weight of counterexamples. As much as nations have sought to reduce the nuclear threat, arguing that the threat does not exist ignores many examples showing that nuclear war remains a possibility: The continuation of some nuclear programs, the development of new nuclear weapons systems, and documented attempts by terrorists to acquire nuclear material on the black market—all these real events provide counterexamples that could challenge the claim that nuclear war is no longer a possibility.

In short, *real* events are often so entangled in historical circumstances that they might not be adequate or fully relevant evidence in the case being argued. When using real events as examples (a perfectly valid strategy), the writer must

- demonstrate that they are representative,
- anticipate counterexamples, and
- argue against counterexamples, showing that one's own examples can be considered outside of other contexts.

Thus, in our earlier argument against Truman's use of the atomic bomb, we might raise the facts of the fierceness of Japanese resistance in specific earlier battles but then argue that they are not relevant because our examples show that the Japanese were seeking peace. Similarly, if others were arguing that Truman did the right thing, they could mention the peace feelers, but argue that it would not have been desirable to permit the emperor to retain power.

INVENTED INSTANCES   An **invented instance** is an **artificial** or **hypothetical** example. Take this case: A writer poses a dilemma in his argument that "Stand Your Ground" laws are morally indefensible. (These laws allow individuals the right to protect themselves against threats of bodily harm, to the point of using lethal force in self-defense.) In his discussion, he raises the most famous of these cases, involving the death of unarmed Florida teenager Trayvon Martin, who was killed in 2012 by a self-appointed neighborhood watchman named George Zimmerman, who mistook the African American youth as a threat. He writes: "If Trayvon Martin had been of age and legally armed, in fact, he would have had the right to kill Zimmerman when Zimmerman approached him in a hostile way." By imagining this scenario, the writer asks readers to apply the principles of justice underlying the law to the reverse scenario: What happens when neither party is clear about which of them is standing his ground? Even though the example isn't "real"—although it alters the details of a real event—it sets forth the problem in a clear way.

Offering an invented instance is something like a drawing of the parts of an atom in a physics textbook. It is admittedly false, but by virtue of its simplification it sets forth the relevant details very clearly. Thus, in a discussion of legal rights and moral obligation, the philosopher Charles Frankel says:

> It would be nonsense to say, for example, that a nonswimmer has a moral duty to swim to the help of a drowning man.

If Frankel were talking about a real event and a real person, he could get bogged down in details about the actual person and the circumstances of the event, losing his power to put the moral dilemma forward in its clearest terms.

When an example is invented, it is almost certain to support the writer's point — after all, the writer is making it up, so it is bound to be the ideal example. That said, invented instances have drawbacks. First and foremost, they cannot serve as the highest quality of evidence. A purely hypothetical example can illustrate a point, but it cannot substitute for actual events. Sometimes, hypothetical examples are so fanciful that they fail to convince the reader. Here is — what else? — an example of what we mean: The philosopher Judith Jarvis Thomson, in the course of an argument entitled "A Defense of Abortion," asks you to imagine waking up one day and finding that against your will a celebrated violinist has been hooked up to your body for life support. She then asks: Do you have the right to unplug the violinist? Whatever you answer, you have to agree that such a scenario is not exactly the same as asking whether or not a woman has a right to an abortion.

But we add one point: Even a highly fanciful invented case can have the valuable effect of forcing us to see where we stand. A person may say that she is, in all circumstances, against torture — but what would she say if a writer proposed a scenario in which the location of a ticking bomb were known only by one person and extracting that information through torture could save hundreds or thousands of lives? Artificial cases of this sort can help us examine our beliefs; nevertheless, they often create exceptional scenarios that may not be generalized convincingly to support an argument.

ANALOGIES   The third sort of example, **analogy**, is a kind of comparison. Here's an example:

> Before the Roman Empire declined as a world power, it exhibited a decline in morals and in physical stamina; our society today shows a decline in both morals (consider the high divorce rate

and the crime rate) and physical culture (consider obesity in children). America, like Rome, will decline as a world power.

Strictly speaking, an analogy is an extended comparison in which different things are shown to be similar in several ways. Thus, if one wants to argue that a head of state should have extraordinary power during wartime, one can offer an analogy that, during wartime, the state is like a ship in a storm: The crew is needed to lend its help, but the major decisions are best left to the captain. Notice that an analogy like this compares things that are relatively *un*like, similar to metaphor and simile. Simply comparing the plight of one state to another is not an analogy; it's merely an inductive inference from one case of the same sort to another such case.

Let's consider another analogy. We have already glanced at Judith Thomson's hypothetical case in which the reader wakes up to find herself hooked up to a violinist in need of life support. Thomson uses this situation as an analogy in an argument about abortion. The reader stands for the mother; the violinist, for the unwanted fetus. You may want to think about whether this analogy holds up: Is a pregnant woman really like a person hooked up to such a machine? Is an embryo or fetus really equivalent to a celebrated violin player?

The problem with argument by analogy is this: Because different things are similar in some ways does not mean they are similar in all ways. Thomson's argument is basically developed on the premise that being the reader hooked up to a violinist is like being the pregnant mother hooked up to a fetus. But those two things are obviously quite different. Similarly, a state is not a ship in a storm. The government is not a business. As Bishop Butler is said to have remarked in the early eighteenth century, "Everything is what it is, and not another thing."

Analogies can be convincing, however, when they simplify complex issues. "Don't change horses in midstream" isn't

"Do you mind if I use yet another sports analogy?"

Gahan Wilson, The New Yorker Collection/The Cartoon Bank

a statement about riding horses across a river but, rather, about changing a course of action in critical times. Still, in the end, analogies don't necessarily prove anything. What may be true about riding horses across a stream may not be true about, say, choosing a new leader in troubled times. What is true for one need not be true for the other.

Analogies can be helpful in developing our thoughts and in helping listeners or readers understand a point we're trying to make. It is sometimes argued, for instance, that newspaper and television reporters and their confidential sources should share the right to confidential privilege, like the doctor–patient, attorney–client, or priest–confessor relationship. The analogy is worth thinking about: Do the similarities run deep enough, or are there fundamental differences in the types of confidentiality we should expect between journalists and their sources and between people and their doctors, lawyers, or priests?

Authoritative Testimony   Another form of evidence is **testimony**, the citation or quotation of authorities. In daily life, we rely heavily on authorities of all sorts: We get a doctor's opinion about our health, we read a book because an intelligent friend recommends it, we see a movie because a critic gave it a good review, and we pay at least a little attention to the weather forecaster.

In setting forth an argument, one often tries to show that one's view is supported by notable figures — perhaps Jefferson, Lincoln, Martin Luther King Jr., or scientists who won a Nobel Prize — but authorities do not have to be figures of such a high stature. You may recall that when talking about medical marijuana legalization in Chapter 2, we presented an open letter by Sanjay Gupta. To make certain that you were impressed by his ideas, we described him as CNN's chief medical correspondent and a leading public health expert. In our Chapter 2 discussion of Sally Mann, we qualified our description of her controversial photographs by noting that *Time* magazine called her "America's Best Photographer" and the *New Republic* called her book "one of the great photograph books of our time." But heed some words of caution:

- Be sure that the authority, however notable, is *an authority on the topic in question.* (A well-known biologist might be an authority on vitamins but not on the justice of war.)

THINKING CRITICALLY AUTHORITATIVE TESTIMONY

Locate one authority on each issue and use the table to examine whether or not that person is an adequate authority. In the last box, explain why this is a reliable testimony.

Issue	Expert Name and Qualifications	Time Period	Place of Publication	Your Explanation
Recreational marijuana				
Spanking children				
How to manage test anxiety				
Restoring voting rights to felons				
The quality of the latest Academy Award–winning Best Picture				

- Be sure that the authority is *unbiased.* (A chemist employed by the tobacco industry isn't likely to admit that smoking may be harmful, and a producer of violent video games isn't likely to admit that playing those games stimulates violence.)

- Beware of *nameless* authorities: "a thousand doctors," "leading educators," "researchers at a major medical school." (If possible, offer at least one specific name.)

- Be careful when using authorities who indeed were great authorities in their day but *who now may be out of date.* (Examples include Adam Smith on economics, Julius Caesar on the art of war, Louis Pasteur on medicine.)

- Cite authorities *whose opinions your readers will value.* (William F. Buckley Jr.'s conservative/libertarian opinions mean a good deal to readers of the magazine that he founded, the *National Review*, but probably not to most liberal thinkers. Gloria Steinem's liberal/feminist opinions carry weight with readers of the magazines that she cofounded, *New York* and *Ms.* magazine, but probably not with most conservative thinkers.)

One other point: *You* may be an authority. You probably aren't nationally known, but on some topics you might have the authority of personal experience. You may have been injured on a motorcycle while riding without wearing a helmet, or you may have escaped injury because you wore a helmet. You may have dropped out of school and then returned. You may have tutored a student whose native language isn't English, you may be such a student who has received tutoring, or you may have attended a school with a bilingual education program. In short, your personal testimony on topics relating to these issues may be invaluable, and a reader will probably consider it seriously.

Numerical Data   The last sort of evidence we discuss here is data based on math or collections of numbers, also referred to as **quantitative** or **statistical** evidence. Sometimes quantitative evidence offers firm answers. Suppose the awarding of honors at graduation from college is determined based on a student's cumulative grade-point average (GPA). The undisputed assumption is that the nearer a student's GPA is to a perfect record (4.0), the more deserving he or she is of highest honors. Consequently, a student with a GPA of 3.9 at the end of her senior year is a stronger candidate for honors than another student with a GPA of 3.6. When faculty members determine the academic merits of graduating seniors, they know that these quantitative, statistical differences in student GPAs will be the basic (if not the only) kind of evidence under discussion.

Here, numbers prove to be reliable evidence, used to justify the argument that one student deserves honors more than another. However, in many cases, numbers do not simply speak for themselves. Numerical information can be presented in many forms. Graphs, tables, and pie charts are familiar ways of presenting quantitative data in an eye-catching manner, but how the numbers are organized, interpreted, and presented can make a difference in how well they support an argument's claims. (See the section Visuals as Aids to Clarity: Maps, Graphs, and Pie Charts on pp. 170–72 in Chapter 4 for more on graphs.)

Let's look how some different kinds of numbers are commonly used as evidence.

PRESENTING NUMBERS   In an argument, you may need to evaluate whether it is more persuasive to present numbers in percentages or real numbers. For example, arguing that the murder rate increased by 30 percent in one city sounds more compelling than saying there were thirteen murders this year compared to ten last year (only three more, but a technical increase of 30 percent). Should an argument examining the federal budget say that it (1) underwent a *twofold increase* over the decade, (2) increased by *100 percent*, (3) *doubled*, or (4) was *one-half of its current amount ten years ago*? As you can see, these are equivalent ways of saying the same thing, but by making a choice among them, a writer can play up or play down the increase to support different arguments in more or less dramatic ways.

Other kinds of choices may be made in interpreting numbers: Suppose in a given city in 2017, 1 percent of the victims in fatal automobile accidents were bicyclists. In the same city in 2018, the percentage of bicyclists killed in automobile accidents was 2 percent. Was the increase 1 percent (not an alarming figure), or was it 100 percent (a staggering figure)? The answer is both, depending on whether we're comparing (1) bicycle deaths in automobile accidents *with all deaths in automobile accidents* (that's an increase of 1 percent) or (2) bicycle deaths in automobile accidents *only with other bicycle deaths in automobile accidents* (an increase of 100 percent). An honest statement would say that bicycle deaths due to automobile accidents doubled in 2018, increasing from 1 to 2 percent. But here's another point: Although every such death is lamentable, if there was only one such death in 2017 and two in 2018, the increase from one death to two—an increase of 100 percent!— hardly suggests a growing problem that needs attention. No one would be surprised to learn that in the following years there were no deaths at all, or only one or two.

Consider how different calculations can impact the meaning of numerical data. Here are some statistics that pop up in conversations about wealth distribution in the United States. In 2017, the Census Bureau calculated that the **median** household income in the United States was $61,372, meaning that half of households earned less than this amount and half earned above it. However, the **average**—technically, the **mean**—household income in the same year was $86,220, or $24,848 (or 40 percent) higher. Which number more accurately represents the typical household income? Both are "correct," but both are calculated with different measures (median and mean). If a politician wanted to argue that the United States has a strong middle class, he might use the average (mean) income as evidence, a number calculated by dividing the total income of all households by the total number of households. If another politician wished to make a rebuttal, she could point out that the average income paints a rosy picture because the wealthiest households skew the average higher. The median income (representing the number above and below which two halves of all households fall) should be the measure we use, the rebutting politician could argue, because it helps reduce the effect of the limitless ceiling of higher incomes and the finite floor of lower incomes at zero.

Our point: This just shows how different methods of calculating— or how writers may use the results of those different methods—can produce different understandings of an issue.

UNRELIABLE STATISTICAL EVIDENCE   Because we know that 90 percent is greater than 75 percent, we're usually ready to grant that any claim supported by 90 percent of cases is more likely to be true than an alternative claim supported in only 75 percent of cases. The greater the difference, the greater our confidence. Yet statistics often get a bad name because it's so easy to misuse them (unintentionally or not) and so difficult to be sure that they were gathered correctly in the first place. (One old saying goes, "There are lies, damned lies, and statistics.") Every branch of social science and natural science needs statistical information, and countless decisions in public and private life are based on quantitative data in statistical form. It's therefore important to be sensitive to the sources and reliability of the statistics and to develop a healthy skepticism when you confront statistics whose parentage is not fully explained. Always ask: Who gathered the statistics? For what purpose?

Consider this example of statistics, from the self-described "culture jammer" Kalle Lasn, the founder of AdBusters, a group that commonly criticizes aspects of consumer society:

> Advertisements are the most prevalent and toxic of the mental pollutants. From the moment your radio alarm sounds in the

morning to the wee hours of late-night TV, microjolts of commercial pollution flood into your brain at the rate of about three
thousand marketing messages per day. (Kalle Lasn, *Culture Jam*
[1999], 18–19)

Lasn's book includes endnotes as documentation, so, being curious
about the statistics, we turned to the appropriate page and found
this information concerning the source of his data:

"three thousand marketing messages per day." Mark Landler,
Walecia Konrad, Zachary Schiller, and Lois Therrien, "What
Happened to Advertising?" *BusinessWeek*, September 23, 1991,
page 66. Leslie Savan in *The Sponsored Life* (Temple University
Press, 1994), page 1, estimated that "16,000 ads flicker across
an individual's consciousness daily." I did an informal survey in
March 1995 and found the number to be closer to 1,500 (this
included all marketing messages, corporate images, logos, ads,
brand names, on TV, radio, billboards, buildings, signs, clothing,
appliances, in cyberspace, etc., over a typical twenty-four hour
period in my life). (219)

Well, this endnote is odd. In the earlier passage, the author asserted
that about "three thousand marketing messages per day" flood into
a person's brain. In the documentation, he cites a source for that
statistic from *BusinessWeek*—although we haven't the faintest idea
how the authors of the *BusinessWeek* article came up with that figure. Oddly, he goes on to offer a very different figure (16,000 ads)
and then, to our confusion, offers yet a third figure (1,500) based
on his own "informal survey."

Probably the one thing we can safely say about all three figures is that none of them means very much. Even if the compil-
ers of the statistics explained exactly how they counted—let's say
that among countless other criteria they assumed that the average
person reads one magazine per day and that the average magazine
contains 124 advertisements—it would be hard to take them seriously. After all, in leafing through a magazine, some people may
read many ads and some may read none. Some people may read
some ads carefully—but perhaps just to enjoy their absurdity. Our
point: Although Lasn said, without implying any uncertainty, that
"about three thousand marketing messages per day" reach an individual, it's evident from the endnote that even he is confused about
the figure he gives.

We'd like to make a final point about the unreliability of some statistical information—data that looks impressive but that is, in fact, insubstantial. Consider Marilyn Jager Adams's book *Beginning to Read: Thinking and Learning about Print* (1994), in which she pointed out that poor families read to their preschool children only 25 hours per year over a five-year period, whereas in the same period middle-income families read to their preschool children 1,000 to 1,700 hours. The figures were much quoted in newspapers and by children's advocacy groups. Adams could not, of course, interview every family in these two groups; she had to rely on samples. What were her samples? For poor families, she selected twenty-four children in twenty families, all in Southern California. (Ask yourself: Can families from only one geographic area provide an adequate sample for a topic such as this?) And how many families constituted Adams's sample of middle-class families? Exactly one—her own. We leave it to you to judge the validity of her findings.

> **WRITING TIP** When writing, consider presenting your numerical data in ways that have the most impact. A quarter, 25%, and 1 out of 4 are all the same but may resonate differently with your audience. But be ethical; don't try to manipulate your reader.

Sometimes the definition of what is being counted can affect the statistical results. Sociologist Joel Best notes in his book *Stat Spotting* an interesting case: When research several years ago showed that "one-fifth [20 percent] of college students practice self-injury," the dramatic statistic attracted journalists and news media who published all kinds of worrying articles. But a closer look at the study revealed not only that the survey was limited to two Ivy League universities (a sampling problem), but also that it *defined* self-injury in a very broad way, to include minor acts that most psychologists would consider to be within the range of normal behavior—such as pinching, scratching, or hitting oneself. In actuality, as another analysis showed, only 1.6 percent of college students reported injuring themselves to the point of needing medical treatment—quite a lot fewer than 20 percent.

We are not suggesting that everyone who uses statistics is trying to deceive (or is unconsciously being deceived by them). We suggest only that statistics are open to widely different interpretations and that often those columns of numbers, which appear to be so precise with their decimal points and their complex formulas, may actually be imprecise and possibly worthless if they're based on insufficient samples, erroneous methodologies, or biased interpretation.

> ✓ A CHECKLIST FOR EVALUATING STATISTICAL EVIDENCE
>
> Regard statistical evidence (like all other evidence) cautiously and don't accept it until you have thought about these questions:
>
> ☐ Was the evidence compiled by a disinterested (impartial) source? The source's name doesn't always reveal its particular angle (e.g., People for the American Way), but sometimes it lets you know what to expect (e.g., National Rifle Association, American Civil Liberties Union).
>
> ☐ Is it based on an adequate sample?
>
> ☐ What is the definition of the thing being counted or measured?
>
> ☐ Is the statistical evidence recent enough to be relevant?
>
> ☐ How many of the factors likely to be relevant were identified and measured?
>
> ☐ Are the figures open to a different and equally plausible interpretation?
>
> ☐ If a percentage is cited, is it the average (or *mean*), or is it the median?

NONRATIONAL APPEALS

In talking about induction and deduction, definitions, and types of evidence, we've been talking about means of rational persuasion, things normally falling under the purview of *logos*. However, as mentioned earlier, there are also other means of persuasion. Force is an example. If Stacey kicks Janée, and threatens to destroy Janée's means of livelihood, and threatens Janée's life, Staccy may persuade Janée to cooperate or agree with her. Writers, of course, cannot use such kinds of force on their readers (nor would they want to, we hope). But they do have at their disposal forms of persuasion that are more associated with *pathos*. These types of appeals do not rely on rational logic or inference (*logos*), but predominantly on the feeling—the emotions—of readers.

Satire, Irony, Sarcasm

One form of irrational but sometimes highly effective persuasion is **satire**—that is, witty ridicule. A cartoonist may persuade viewers that a politician's views are unsound by caricaturing (thus ridiculing) her appearance or by presenting a grotesquely distorted (funny, but unfair) picture of the issue she supports.

Roger Cracknell 01/classic/Alamy Stock Photo

How does this mural by street artist Banksy use visual irony?

Satiric artists often use caricature; satiric writers, also seeking to persuade by means of ridicule, often use **verbal irony**. This sort of irony contrasts what is said and what is meant. For instance, words of praise may actually imply blame (when Shakespeare's Cassius says, "Brutus is an honorable man," he wants those who hear him to think that Brutus is dishonorable). Occasionally, words of modesty may actually imply superiority ("Of course, I'm too dumb to understand this problem"). Such language, when heavy-handed, is **sarcasm** ("You're a great guy," someone who is actually criticizing you says). If it's witty and clever, we call it irony rather than sarcasm.

Although ridicule isn't a form of reasoning, passages of ridicule, especially verbal irony, sometimes appear in argument essays. These passages, like reasons or like appeals to the emotions, are efforts to persuade the reader to accept the writer's point of view. The key to using humor in an argument is, on the one hand, to avoid wisecracking like a smart aleck and, on the other hand, to avoid mere clownishness. In other words, if you get too silly, acerbic, or outright insulting, you may damage your *ethos* and alienate your audience.

Emotional Appeals

It is sometimes said that good argumentative writing appeals only to reason, never to emotion, and that any emotional appeal is illegitimate and irrelevant. "Tears are not arguments," the Brazilian writer Machado de Assis said. Logic textbooks may even stigmatize with Latin labels the various sorts of emotional appeal—for instance, *argumentum ad populam* (appeal to the prejudices of the mob, as in "Come on, we all know that schools don't teach anything anymore") and *argumentum ad misericordiam* (appeal to pity, as in "No one ought to blame this poor kid for stabbing a classmate because his mother was often institutionalized").

Learning from Shakespeare True, appeals to emotion may distract from the facts of the case; they may blind the audience by, in effect, throwing dust in its eyes or by provoking tears. A classic example occurs in Shakespeare's *Julius Caesar*, when Marc Antony addresses the Roman populace after Brutus, Cassius, and Casca have conspired to assassinate Caesar. The real issue is whether Caesar was becoming tyrannical (as the assassins claim). Antony turns from the evidence and stirs the crowd against the assassins by appealing to its emotions. Shakespeare drew from an ancient Roman biographical writing, Plutarch's *Lives of the Noble Grecians and Romans*. Plutarch says this about Antony:

> [P]erceiving that his words moved the common people to compassion, . . . [he] framed his eloquence to make their hearts yearn [i.e., grieve] the more, and, taking Caesar's gown all bloody in his hand, he laid it open to the sight of them all, showing what a number of cuts and holes it had upon it. Therewithal the people fell presently into such a rage and mutiny that there was no more order kept.

Here's how Shakespeare reinterpreted the event in his play:

> Friends, Romans, countrymen, lend me your ears;
> I come to bury Caesar, not to praise him.

After briefly offering insubstantial evidence that Caesar gave no signs of behaving tyrannically (e.g., "When that the poor have cried, Caesar hath wept"), Antony begins to play directly on his hearers' emotions. Descending from the platform so that he may be in closer contact with his audience (like a modern politician, he wants to work the crowd), he calls attention to Caesar's bloody toga:

> If you have tears, prepare to shed them now.
> You all do know this mantle; I remember
> The first time ever Caesar put it on:
> 'Twas on a summer's evening, in his tent,
> That day he overcame the Nervii.
> Look, in this place ran Cassius' dagger through;
> See what a rent the envious Casca made;
> Through this, the well-belovèd Brutus stabbed . . .

In these few lines, Antony accomplishes the following:

- He prepares the audience by suggesting to them how they should respond ("If you have tears, prepare to shed them now").
- He flatters them by implying that they, like Antony, were intimates of Caesar (he credits them with being familiar with Caesar's garment).
- He then evokes a personal memory of a specific time ("a summer's evening") — the day that Caesar won a battle against the Nervii, a particularly fierce tribe in what is now France. (In fact, Antony was not at the battle and did not join Caesar until three years later.)

Antony doesn't mind being free with the facts; his point here is not to set the record straight but to stir people against the assassins. He goes on, daringly but successfully, to identify one particular slit in the garment with Cassius's dagger, another with Casca's, and a third with Brutus's. Antony cannot know which dagger made which slit, but his rhetorical trick works.

Notice, too, that Antony arranges the three assassins in climactic order, since Brutus (Antony claims) was especially beloved by Caesar:

Judge, O you gods, how dearly Caesar loved him!
This was the most unkindest cut of all;
For when the noble Caesar saw him stab,
Ingratitude, more strong than traitor's arms,
Quite vanquished him. Then burst his mighty heart.

Nice. According to Antony, the noble-minded Caesar — Antony's words have erased all thought of the tyrannical Caesar — died not from wounds inflicted by daggers but from the heartbreaking perception of Brutus's ingratitude. Doubtless there wasn't a dry eye in the crowd. Let's all hope that if we are ever put on trial, we'll have a lawyer as skilled in evoking sympathy as Antony.

Are Emotional Appeals Fallacious? Antony's oration was obviously successful in the play and apparently was successful in real life, but it is the sort of speech that prompts logicians to write disapprovingly of attempts to stir feeling in an audience. (As mentioned earlier, the evocation of emotion in an audience is **pathos**, from the Greek word for "emotion" or "suffering.") There is nothing inherently wrong in stimulating an audience's emotions when attempting to establish a claim, but when an emotional appeal confuses the issue being argued or shifts attention away from the facts, we can reasonably speak of the emotional appeal as a fallacy.

No fallacy is involved, however, when an emotional appeal heightens the facts, bringing them home to the audience rather than masking them. In talking about legislation that would govern police actions, for example, it's legitimate to show a photograph of the battered, bloodied face of an alleged victim of police brutality. True, such a photograph cannot tell the whole truth; it cannot tell if the subject threatened the officer with a gun or repeatedly resisted an order to surrender. But it can demonstrate that the victim was severely beaten and (like a comparable description in words) evoke emotions that may properly affect the audience's decision about the permissible use of police violence. Similarly, an animal rights activist who argues that calves are cruelly confined might reasonably talk about the inhumanely small size of their pens, in which they cannot turn around or even lie down. Others may

THINKING CRITICALLY NONRATIONAL APPEALS

Identify the emotion summoned by the following nonrational appeals and explain how the claim may be countered by logic or reason.

Nonrational Appeal	Emotion	Logical Counter
Football players and other athletes should not be allowed to kneel for the National Anthem to protest police violence because it disrespects the American flag and all those people who died defending it.		
Nowadays, it seems anything goes on television, and even primetime shows feature foul language, sex, and violence. Don't they realize children are watching?		
The Powerball jackpot this week is more than $500 million. Even if you don't normally play the lottery, it's time to buy a ticket!		

argue that calves don't care about turning around or have no right to turn around, but the evocative verbal description of their pens, which makes an emotional appeal, cannot be called fallacious or irrelevant.

In appealing to emotions, then, keep in mind these strategies:

- Do not falsify (especially by oversimplifying) the issue.
- Do not distract attention from the facts of the case.
- Do think ethically about how emotional appeals may affect the audience.

You should focus on the facts and offer reasons (essentially, statements linked with "because"), but you may also legitimately bring the facts home to your readers by seeking to provoke appropriate emotions. Your words will be fallacious only if you stimulate emotions that aren't connected with the facts of the case.

DOES ALL WRITING CONTAIN ARGUMENTS?

Our answer to the question in the heading is no—however, *most* writing probably *does* contain an argument of sorts. The writer wants to persuade the reader to see things the way the writer sees them—at least until the end of the essay. After all, even a recipe for a cherry pie in a food magazine—a piece of writing that's primarily expository (how to do it) rather than argumentative (how a reasonable person ought to think about this topic)—probably starts out with a hint of an argument, such as "*Because* [a sign that a *reason* will be offered] this pie can be made quickly and with ingredients (canned cherries) that are always available, give it a try. It will surely become one of your favorites." Clearly, such a statement cannot stand as a formal argument—a discussion that addresses counterarguments, relies chiefly on logic and little if any emotional appeal, and draws a conclusion that seems irrefutable.

Still, the statement is technically an argument on behalf of making a pie with canned cherries. In this case, we can identify a claim (the pie will become a favorite) and two *reasons* in support of the claim:

- It can be made quickly.
- The chief ingredient—because it is canned—can always be at hand.

There are two underlying *assumptions*:

- Readers don't have a great deal of time to waste in the kitchen.
- Canned cherries are just as tasty as fresh cherries—and even if they aren't, no one who eats the pie will know the difference.

When we read a lead-in to a recipe, then, we won't find a formal argument, but we'll probably see a few words that seek to persuade us to keep reading. And most writing does contain such material—sentences that engage our interest and give us a reason to keep reading. If the recipe is difficult and time consuming, the lead-in may say this:

> Although this recipe for a cherry pie, using fresh cherries that you will have to pit, is a bit more time consuming than the usual recipes that call for canned cherries, once you have tasted it you will never go back to canned cherries.

✓ **A CHECKLIST FOR ANALYZING AN ARGUMENT**

Thesis and Claims

☐ Is the author's claim or thesis clear?

☐ Are any parts of the argument based on *logos*, *pathos*, or *ethos*?

☐ Are any premises false or questionable?

☐ Is the logic — deductive or inductive — valid?

☐ Are important terms and concepts defined satisfactorily?

☐ Does the writer make assumptions that are problematic for his or her argument?

Support and Evidence

☐ Does the writer use evidence to support his or her claims?

☐ Are the examples — imagined, invented, or hypothetical — relevant and convincing?

☐ Are the statistics (if any) relevant, accurate, and complete?

☐ Are other interpretations of evidence possible?

☐ Can authorities who offer evidence be considered impartial?

Fairness

☐ Are alternative viewpoints and counterexamples adequately considered?

☐ Is there any evidence of dishonesty or of a discreditable attempt to manipulate the reader?

☐ Is the writer's tone and use of language appropriate to the subject and the audience?

Again, although the logic is scarcely compelling, the persuasive element is evident. The assumption is that readers have a discriminating palate; once they've tasted a pie made with fresh cherries, they'll never again enjoy the canned stuff. The writer isn't making a formal argument with abundant evidence and detailed refutation of counterarguments, but we know where he stands and how he wishes us to respond.

In short, almost all writers are trying to persuade readers to see things *their* way. As you read the essays in this chapter, keep in mind the questions in the checklist for analyzing an argument. They can help you take apart an argument and discover where strengths and weakness lie and perhaps find new points to make (and things to say) in important discussions and debates.

AN EXAMPLE: AN ARGUMENT AND A LOOK AT THE WRITER'S STRATEGIES

The following essay, "The Reign of Recycling" by John Tierney, concerns the efficacy of recycling — whether or not it is help-ing the environment in significant ways or if it has gone beyond its originally good intentions to become an unsustainable or even counterproductive measure. We follow Tierney's essay with some comments about the ways in which he constructs his argument.

John Tierney

John Tierney (b. 1953) is an award-winning journalist for the New York Times *who publishes frequently on issues related to science, environmen-talism, and politics. He has also published extensively in magazines such as the* Atlantic, Rolling Stone, Newsweek, Discover, *and* Esquire. *Known for his skepticism toward climate science and big government, Tierney is regarded as a conservative critic. This essay appeared in the* New York Times *in 2015.*

Reign in the title suggests that recycling is a pow-erful, perhaps even tyrannical, trend.

The Reign of Recycling

If you live in the United States, you probably do some form of recycling. It's likely that you separate paper from plastic and glass and metal. You rinse the bottles and cans, and you might put food scraps in a container destined for a composting facility. As you sort everything into the right bins, you probably assume that recycling is helping your community and protecting the environment. But is it? Are you in fact wasting your time?

In 1996, I wrote a long article[1] for *The New York Times Magazine* arguing that the recycling process as we carried it out was wasteful. I presented plenty of evidence that recycling was costly and ineffectual, but its defenders said that it was unfair to rush to judgment. Noting that the modern recycling movement had really just begun just a few years earlier, they predicted it would flourish as the industry matured and the public learned how to recycle properly.

So, what's happened since then? While it's true that the recycling message has reached more people than ever, when it comes to the bottom line, both economically and environmentally, not much has changed at all.

Despite decades of exhortations and mandates, it's still typically more expensive for municipalities to recycle household waste than to send it to a landfill. Prices for recyclable materials have plummeted because of lower oil prices and reduced demand for them overseas. The slump has forced some recycling companies to shut plants and cancel plans for new technologies. The mood is so gloomy that one industry veteran tried to cheer up her colleagues this summer with an article in a trade journal titled, "Recycling Is Not Dead!"[2]

While politicians set higher and higher goals, the   5 national rate of recycling has stagnated in recent years. Yes, it's popular in affluent neighborhoods like Park Slope in Brooklyn and in cities like San Francisco, but residents of the Bronx and Houston don't have the same fervor for sorting garbage in their spare time.

The future for recycling looks even worse. As cities move beyond recycling paper and metals, and into glass, food scraps and assorted plastics, the costs rise

> Tierney presents a common assumption — recycling is helping — but questions it.

> Establishes *ethos*: he has long been familiar with (and right about) the central issues and questions.

> Tierney's thesis:
> *Premise*: Recycling was costly and ineffectual in 1996.
> *Premise*: Not much has changed since 1996.
> *Conclusion*: Recycling remains costly and ineffectual.

> Tierney gestures toward evidence, but he does not present concrete examples.

[1]John Tierney, "Recycling Is Garbage," *New York Times*, June 30, 1996, nyti.ms /2kqksIS. [All citations in this selection are the editors'; they appeared as hyperlinks in the original publication.]

[2]Patty Moore, "Recycling Is Not Dead," *Resource Recycling*, July 1, 2015, resource-recycling.com/node/6130.

Notice Tierney quotes an expert authority for corroborating evidence. Why would a Waste Management executive agree with Tierney?

sharply while the environmental benefits decline and sometimes vanish. "If you believe recycling is good for the planet and that we need to do more of it, then there's a crisis to confront," says David P. Steiner, the chief executive officer of Waste Management, the largest recycler of household trash in the United States. "Trying to turn garbage into gold costs a lot more than expected. We need to ask ourselves: What is the goal here?"

Recycling has been relentlessly promoted as a goal in and of itself: an unalloyed public good and private virtue that is indoctrinated in students from kindergarten through college. As a result, otherwise well-informed and educated people have no idea of the relative costs and benefits.

They probably don't know, for instance, that to reduce carbon emissions, you'll accomplish a lot more by sorting paper and aluminum cans than by worrying about yogurt containers and half-eaten slices of pizza. Most people also assume that recycling plastic bottles must be doing lots for the planet. They've been encouraged by the Environmental Protection Agency, which assures the public that recycling plastic results in less carbon being released into the atmosphere.

Tierney suggests the EPA itself may not be trustworthy. Note that the EPA is commonly a target of pro-business conservatives.

But how much difference does it make? Here's some perspective: To offset the greenhouse impact of one passenger's round-trip flight between New York and London, you'd have to recycle roughly 40,000 plastic bottles, assuming you fly coach. If you sit in business- or first-class, where each passenger takes up more space, it could be more like 100,000.

Even those statistics might be misleading. New 10 York and other cities instruct people to rinse the bottles before putting them in the recycling bin, but the E.P.A.'s life-cycle calculation doesn't take that water into account. That single omission can make a big difference, according to Chris Goodall, the author of "How to Live a Low-Carbon Life." Mr. Goodall calculates that if you wash plastic in water that was heated by coal-derived electricity, then the net effect of your recycling could be *more* carbon in the atmosphere.

Proposes that people who think they are doing good for the environment are actually doing worse. How ironic!

To many public officials, recycling is a question of morality, not cost-benefit analysis. Mayor Bill de Blasio of New York declared that by 2030 the city would no longer send any garbage to landfills. "This is the way of the future if we're going to save our earth," he explained[3] while announcing that New York would join San Francisco, Seattle and other cities in moving toward a "zero waste" policy, which would require an unprecedented level of recycling.

> Begins to address "zero waste" proposals, implicitly criticizing New York's decision to pursue such a goal.

The national rate of recycling rose during the 1990s to 25 percent, meeting the goal set by an E.P.A. official, J. Winston Porter. He advised state officials that no more than about 35 percent of the nation's trash was worth recycling, but some ignored him and set goals of 50 percent and higher. Most of those goals were never met and the national rate has been stuck around 34 percent in recent years.

"It makes sense to recycle commercial cardboard and some paper, as well as selected metals and plastics," he says. "But other materials rarely make sense, including food waste and other compostables. The zero-waste goal makes no sense at all—it's very expensive with almost no real environmental benefit."

> Tierney cites another authority, J. Winston Porter, but he may be shifting the issue; Porter actually says some forms of recycling are good.

One of the original goals of the recycling movement was to avert a supposed crisis because there was no room left in the nation's landfills. But that media-inspired fear was never realistic in a country with so much open space. In reporting the 1996 article I found that all the trash generated by Americans for the next 1,000 years[4] would fit on one-tenth of 1 percent of the land available for grazing. And that tiny amount of land wouldn't be lost forever, because landfills are typically covered with grass and converted to parkland, like the Freshkills Park being created on Staten Island. The United States Open tennis tournament is played on the site of an old landfill—and one that never had the linings and other environmental safeguards required today.

> Tierney undermines assumptions that landfills are bad.

Though most cities shun landfills, they have been welcomed in rural communities that reap large 15

---

[3]Jill Jorgensen, "Bill de Blasio Calls for the End of Garbage by 2030," *Observer*, April 22, 2015, observer.com/2015/04/bill-de-blasio-calls-for-the-end-of-garbage-by-2030/.

[4]A. Clark Wiseman. *U.S. Wastepaper Recycling Policies: Issues and Ethics* (1990; *Google Books*), books.google.com/books/about/U_S_Wastepaper_Recycling_Policies .html?id=m9YsAQAAMAAJ.

economic benefits (and have plenty of greenery to buffer residents from the sights and smells). Consequently, the great landfill shortage has not arrived, and neither have the shortages of raw materials that were supposed to make recycling profitable.

With the economic rationale gone, advocates for recycling have switched to environmental arguments. Researchers have calculated that there are indeed such benefits to recycling, but not in the way that many people imagine.

Most of these benefits do not come from reducing the need for landfills and incinerators. A modern well-lined landfill in a rural area can have relatively little environmental impact. Decomposing garbage releases methane, a potent greenhouse gas, but landfill operators have started capturing it and using it to generate electricity. Modern incinerators, while politically unpopular in the United States, release so few pollutants that they've been widely accepted in the eco-conscious countries of Northern Europe and Japan for generating clean energy.

Moreover, recycling operations have their own environmental costs, like extra trucks on the road and pollution from recycling operations. Composting facilities around the country have inspired complaints about nauseating odors, swarming rats, and defecating sea gulls. After New York City started sending food waste to be composted in Delaware, the unhappy neighbors of the composting plant successfully campaigned to shut it down last year.

The environmental benefits of recycling come chiefly from reducing the need to manufacture new products—less mining, drilling and logging. But that's not so appealing to the workers in those industries and to the communities that have accepted the environmental trade-offs that come with those jobs.

Nearly everyone, though, approves of one potential benefit of recycling: reduced emissions of greenhouse gases. Its advocates often cite an estimate by the E.P.A. that recycling municipal solid waste in the United States saves the equivalent of 186 million metric tons of carbon dioxide, comparable to removing the emissions of 39 million cars.

Counterarguments are raised, but Tierney uses them to defend landfills.

Pathos: In arguing against composting facilities, Tierney turns stomachs.

Tierney establishes common ground.

20

According to the E.P.A.'s estimates, virtually all the greenhouse benefits—more than 90 percent—come from just a few materials: paper, cardboard and metals like the aluminum in soda cans. That's because recycling one ton of metal or paper saves about three tons of carbon dioxide, a much bigger payoff than the other materials analyzed by the E.P.A. Recycling one ton of plastic saves only slightly more than one ton of carbon dioxide. A ton of food saves a little less than a ton. For glass, you have to recycle three tons in order to get about one ton of greenhouse benefits. Worst of all is yard waste: it takes 20 tons of it to save a single ton of carbon dioxide.

Once you exclude paper products and metals, the total annual savings in the United States from recycling everything else in municipal trash—plastics, glass, food, yard trimmings, textiles, rubber, leather—is only two-tenths of 1 percent of America's carbon footprint.

> Tierney mixes a fraction and a percentage to present his numerical data. But America still has a huge carbon footprint. Is Tierney downplaying the impact of recycling here?

As a business, recycling is on the wrong side of two long-term global economic trends. For centuries, the real cost of labor has been increasing while the real cost of raw materials has been declining. That's why we can afford to buy so much more stuff than our ancestors could. As a labor-intensive activity, recycling is an increasingly expensive way to produce materials that are less and less valuable.

Recyclers have tried to improve the economics by automating the sorting process, but they've been frustrated by politicians eager to increase recycling rates by adding new materials of little value. The more types of trash that are recycled, the more difficult it becomes to sort the valuable from the worthless.

In New York City, the net cost of recycling a ton 25 of trash is now $300 more than it would cost to bury the trash instead. That adds up to millions of extra dollars per year—about half the budget of the parks department—that New Yorkers are spending for the privilege of recycling. That money could buy far more valuable benefits, including more significant reductions in greenhouse emissions.

So what is a socially conscious, sensible person to do?

It would be much simpler and more effective to impose the equivalent of a carbon tax on garbage, as Thomas C. Kinnaman has proposed after conducting what is probably the most thorough comparison of the social costs[5] of recycling, landfilling and incineration. Dr. Kinnaman, an economist at Bucknell University, considered everything from environmental damage to the pleasure that some people take in recycling (the "warm glow" that makes them willing to pay extra to do it).

He concludes that the social good would be optimized by subsidizing the recycling of some metals, and by imposing a $15 tax on each ton of trash that goes to the landfill. That tax would offset the environmental costs, chiefly the greenhouse impact, and allow each municipality to make a guilt-free choice based on local economics and its citizens' wishes. The result, Dr. Kinnaman predicts, would be a lot less recycling than there is today.

Then why do so many public officials keep vowing to do more of it? Special-interest politics is one reason — pressure from green groups — but it's also because recycling intuitively appeals to many voters: It makes people feel virtuous, especially affluent people who feel guilty about their enormous environmental footprint. It is less an ethical activity than a religious ritual, like the ones performed by Catholics to obtain indulgences for their sins.

Religious rituals don't need any practical justifica-   30
tion for the believers who perform them voluntarily. But many recyclers want more than just the freedom to practice their religion. They want to make these rituals mandatory for everyone else, too, with stiff fines for sinners who don't sort properly. Seattle has become so aggressive that the city is being sued by residents who maintain that the inspectors rooting through their trash are violating their constitutional right to privacy.

It would take legions of garbage police to enforce a zero-waste society, but true believers insist that's the

> Tierney claims his source is "the most thorough" study without defining his criteria. The source title indicates that it is a study of Japan. Does this use of evidence effectively support Tierney's claim?

> Definition by synonym: Recycling is a religion.

---

[5]Thomas C. Kinnaman et al., "The Socially Optimal Recycling Rate: Evidence from Japan," *Journal of Environmental Economics and Management*, vol. 68, no. 1 (2014): 54–70, digitalcommons.bucknell.edu/fac_journ/774/.

future. When Mayor de Blasio promised to eliminate garbage in New York, he said it was "ludicrous" and "outdated" to keep sending garbage to landfills. Recycling, he declared, was the only way for New York to become "a truly sustainable city."

But cities have been burying garbage for thousands of years, and it's still the easiest and cheapest solution for trash. The recycling movement is floundering, and its survival depends on continual subsidies, sermons and policing. How can you build a sustainable city with a strategy that can't even sustain itself?

Tierney ends by proposing a solution: the status quo.

TOPICS FOR CRITICAL THINKING AND WRITING

1. What kinds of claims make John Tierney's essay persuasive? How might he be more convincing?

2. What assumptions are at work in Tierney's essay? For example, what are some of the assumptions about environmentalism that he challenges?

3. In paragraph 29, Tierney defines environmentally conscious behaviors as a "religious ritual." What kind of definition is this? How do you know? (For a refresher, see pp. 98–104.)

4. What does Tierney identify as the main problem, and what solution is he proposing? Provide a summary of his solution, tracing his line of reasoning.

5. Find at least three places where Tierney offers examples to support his claims. What kind of examples are they? Do they stand up to scrutiny?

6. Does Tierney rely more on *logos*, *pathos*, or *ethos*? How and where? In your opinion, should he have relied on one (or more) of these appeals more heavily than he did? Explain your answer.

4

Visual Rhetoric: Thinking about Images as Arguments

"What is the use of a book," thought Alice, *"without pictures or conversations?"*

—LEWIS CARROLL

All photographs are accurate. None of them is the truth.

—RICHARD AVEDON

USES OF VISUAL IMAGES

Most visual materials that accompany written arguments serve one of several functions. One of the most common is to appeal to the reader's emotions (e.g., a photograph of a sad-eyed calf in a narrow pen assists an argument against eating veal by inspiring sympathy for the animal). Pictures can also serve as visual evidence, offering proof that something occurred or appeared in a certain way at a certain moment (e.g., a security photograph shows the face of a bank robber to a jury). Pictures can help clarify numerical data (e.g., a graph shows five decades of law school enrollment by males and females). They can also add humor or satire to an essay (a photograph of an executive wearing a blindfold made of dollar bills supports an argument that companies are blinded by their profit motives). In this chapter, we concentrate on thinking critically about visual images. This means reading images in the same way we read print (or electronic) texts: by looking closely at them and discerning not only *what* they show but also *how* and *why* they show what they do and how they convey a particular message or argument.

When we discussed the appeal to emotion, **pathos**, in Chapter 3 (see Persuasion, Argument, and Rhetorical Appeals, pages 85–90), we explained how certain words and ideas can muster the emotions of an audience. Images can do the same without words or with minimal, carefully selected, and thoughtfully displayed words. In a very immediate way, they can make us laugh, cry, or gasp. Furthermore, when used as evidence, some images, graphs, and visuals have an additional advantage over words: They carry a high level of what communications scholars call *indexical value*, meaning that they seem to point to what is true and indisputable.

In courtrooms today, trial lawyers and prosecutors help stir the audience's emotions when they

- hold up a murder weapon for jurors to see,
- introduce victims of crime as witnesses, or
- exhibit images of a bloody corpse or a crime scene.

Whether presented sincerely or gratuitously, visuals can have a significantly persuasive effect. Visuals may be rationally connected to an argument: A gruesome image of a diseased lung in an anti-smoking ad makes a reasonable claim, as does a photograph of crime scene that establishes the veracity of the locations of evidence. But the immediate impact of a photograph is more often on the viewer's heart (*pathos*) rather than mind (*logos*). Speaking of those appeals, we can also say that images can help establish *ethos*: Think about how lawyers might present to the jury images of defendants portrayed in wholesome contexts—receiving an award, hugging a family member—in order to bolster their character or credibility (even if their defendants are actually lacking these qualities).

Like any kind of evidence, images make statements and support arguments. When the US Congress debated whether to allow drilling in the Arctic National Wildlife Refuge (ANWR), opponents and supporters both used images to support their verbal arguments:

- *Opponents* of drilling showed beautiful pictures of polar bears frolicking, wildflowers in bloom, and caribou on the move, arguing that such a landscape would be despoiled.
- *Proponents* of drilling showed bleak pictures of what they called "barren land" and "a frozen wasteland," pointing to a useless and barely habitable environment.

Both sides knew very well that images are powerfully persuasive, and they didn't hesitate to use them as supplements to words.

US Fish and Wildlife Service/Getty Images

David Howells/Corbis Historical/Getty Images

These two photographs, both of the Arctic National Wildlife Refuge, show different uses of images to argue about the value and use of land.

We invite you to reflect upon the appropriateness of using such images in arguments. Was either side manipulating the "reality" of the ANWR? Both images were *real*, after all. Each side selected a particular *kind* of image for a specific **purpose**—to support its position on drilling in the ANWR. Neither side was being dishonest, and both were showing true pictures, but both were also appealing to emotions.

EXERCISE: RESPONDING TO IMAGES

In a paragraph, discuss how these images of the ANWR offer reasonable support (*logos*) and emotional support (*pathos*) for an argument. Go further: Examine the source of the photographs and also discuss how *ethos* is established.

Types of Emotional Appeals

After reading Chapter 3, you understand much about how arguments appeal to reason through induction and deduction, by definitions and examples, by drawing conclusions, and so forth. You also learned something about *persuasion*, which is a broad term that can include appeals to various kinds of emotions—for example, an **appeal to pity**, such as the image of a sad-eyed calf mentioned at the beginning of this chapter. You might be moved emotionally by such an image and say, "Well, I am never eating meat again because doing so implies the inhumane treatment of helpless animals," and regard the image as both *reasonable* and *emotionally powerful*. Or you might say, "Although it's emotionally powerful, this image doesn't describe the condition of every calf. Some are treated humanely, slaughtered humanely, and eaten ethically." In your argument, you might include an alternative image of a pasture-raised calf on an organic, locally owned farm (although you too would be appealing to emotions).

The point is that images can be persuasive even if they don't make good or complete arguments. The gangster Al Capone famously said, "You can get a lot more done with a kind word and a gun than with a kind word alone." A threat of violence—do this *or else*—is actually a *kind* of an argument, just one that appeals exclusively to the emotions—specifically, to fear.

Although they do not threaten violence, advertisers commonly use the **appeal to fear** as a persuasive technique. The appeal to fear is a threat of sorts. Showing a scary burglary, a visceral car crash, embarrassing age spots, or a nasty cockroach infestation can successfully convince consumers to buy a product—a home security system, a new car insurance policy, an age-defying skin cream, a pesticide. Such images generate fear and anxiety at the same time they offer the solution for it.

However, appeals to fear—like all the appeals we will discuss—are not confined to the world of advertising. Appeals to fear often drive political arguments, especially during a campaign season. Even arguments about art and culture can utilize fear to support an argument. In 1985, the Parents Music Resource Center (PMRC), founded by Tipper Gore (then wife of politician Al Gore), argued that some popular music was undermining society by promoting occult beliefs, precocious sexuality, and drug and alcohol use. After a US Senate hearing was convened, the PMRC successfully lobbied the recording industry to require "Parental Advisory" warnings on all music deemed inappropriate for children.

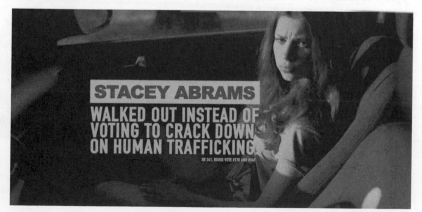

What fears are evoked by this political video ad from Georgia, distributed during the 2018 midterm elections?

There are different kinds of fear to which writers can appeal. Appeals to fear are at work in a recently named phenomenon called FOMO, or Fear of Missing Out, which occurs when someone adopts the latest trends, attends events, or otherwise engages in some activity because they worry about not being part of it. FOMO occurs too when we are hurried to take advantage of a scarce or limited-time opportunity.

Violence and fear can also support arguments made to end acts of terror and cruelty. Images played a crucial role in the antislavery movement in the nineteenth century. The collection shown below offers three different types of visuals and three depictions of the slave experience. The first is a diagram showing how human cargo was packed into a slave ship; it was distributed with Thomas Clarkson's *Essay on the Slavery and Commerce of the Human Species* (1804), one of the first antislavery treatises. Following is Civil War surgeon Frederick W. Mercer's photograph (April 2, 1863) of Gordon, a "badly lacerated" runaway slave. Images such as the slave ship and the runaway slave worked against slave owners' claims that slavery was a humane institution—claims that also were supported by illustrations, such as the woodcut *Attention Paid to a Poor Sick Negro* from Josiah Priest's *In Defence of Slavery* (1843). Examine each picture closely and consider whether you think they make appeals to reason or emotion.

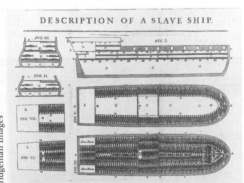

Description of a Slave Ship, 1789 (print)/ English School (18th century)/Wilberforce House Museum/Wilberforce House, Hull City Museums and Art Galleries, UK/ Bridgeman Images

Diagram "Description of a Slave Ship," distributed with Thomas Clarkson's *Essay on the Slavery and Commerce of the Human Species* (1804).

Frederick W. Mercer's photograph (April 2, 1863) of Gordon, a "badly lacerated" runaway slave.

Attention Paid to a Poor Sick Negro, a woodcut from Josiah Priest's *In Defense of
Slavery* (1843).

Appeal to self-interest is another persuasive tactic that
speakers and writers can use. Consider these remarks, which use
the word *interest* in the sense of "self-interest":

Would you persuade, speak of Interest, not Reason.

—BENJAMIN FRANKLIN

There are two levers for moving men—interest and fear.

—NAPOLEON BONAPARTE

Appeals to self-interest may be quite persuasive because
they speak directly to what benefits *you* the most, not necessarily
what benefits others in the community, society, or world. Such
appeals are also common in advertising. "You can save bundles
by shopping at Maxi-Mart," a commercial might claim, without making reference to third-world sweatshop labor conditions
in the supply chain, the negative impact of global commerce, or
other troublesome aspects of what you see only as a great savings for yourself. Maxi-Mart would never say, "Maxi-Mart offers
low prices by buying products made cheaply on the other side of
the world and shipping them to the United States on inefficient
fuel-guzzling cargo ships."

You may be familiar with other types of advertising that speak to the senses more than reason. These kinds of appeals don't necessarily make *good* arguments for the products in question, but they can be highly persuasive — sometimes affecting us subconsciously — because they speak so much to our individual feelings and interests. Of course, as with all appeals, those made to self-interest can be seen in all kinds of arguments, but the appeals of advertisements are often so blunt and obvious that they help us highlight their effects. Thinking critically about appeals in advertisements can be helpful then in developing our ability to analyze other basic kinds of appeals in words and other kinds of images.

Here is a list of some other emotional appeals commonly used in advertising:

- sexual appeals (e.g., a bikini-clad model standing near a product)
- bandwagon appeals (e.g., crowds of people rushing to a sale)
- humor appeals (e.g., a cartoon animal drinking *X* brand of beverage)
- celebrity appeals (e.g., a famous person driving *X* brand of car)
- testimonial appeals (e.g., a doctor giving *X* brand of vitamins to her kids)
- identity appeals (e.g., a "good family" going to *X* restaurant)
- prejudice appeals (e.g., a "loser" drinking *X* brand of beer)
- lifestyle appeals (e.g., a jar of *X* brand of mustard on a silver platter)
- stereotype appeals (e.g., a Latinx person enjoying *X* brand of salsa)
- patriotic appeals (e.g., *X* brand of mattress alongside an American flag)

EXERCISE: EMOTIONAL APPEALS IN VISUAL ARGUMENTS

Select two of the appeals listed above and think of another real-life instance outside advertising in which the type of appeal occurs, either in words or images. For example, images of former pro football quarterback Colin Kaepernick have been used to appeal to the patriotism of audiences in arguments about the appropriateness of his dissent: kneeling on the football field during the national anthem to protest police violence against African Americans.

SEEING VERSUS LOOKING: READING ADVERTISEMENTS

Advertising is one of the most common forms of visual persuasion we encounter in everyday life. The influence of advertising in our culture is pervasive and subtle. Part of its power comes from our habit of internalizing the intended messages of words and images without thinking deeply about them. Once we begin decoding the ways in which advertisements are constructed—once we view them critically—we can understand how (or if) they work as arguments. We may then make better decisions about whether to buy particular products and what factors convinced us or failed to convince us. Further, by sharpening our critical skills, we can approach images in all their forms with a more careful and skeptical approach.

To read any image critically, it helps to consider some basic rules from the field of **semiotics**, the study of signs and symbols. Fundamental to semiotic analysis is the idea that visual signs have shared meanings in a culture. If you approach a sink and see a red faucet and a blue faucet, you can be pretty sure which one will produce hot water and which one will produce cold water. Thus, one of the first strategies we can use in reading advertisements critically is **deconstructing** them, taking them apart to see what makes them work.

For starters, it's helpful to remember that advertisements are enormously expensive to produce and disseminate, so nothing is left to chance. Teams of people typically scrutinize every part of an advertisement to ensure it communicates the intended message—although this doesn't imply that viewers must accept those messages. Taking apart an advertisement (or any image) means examining each visual element carefully in order to understand its purpose, its strategy, and effect.

Consider a 2007 advertisement for Nike shoes featuring basketball star LeBron James, shown on page 144. Already, you should see the celebrity appeal—an implicit claim that Nike shoes help make James a star player. The ad creates an association between the shoes and the sports champion. But look closer, paying attention to how the elements work together to make meaning.

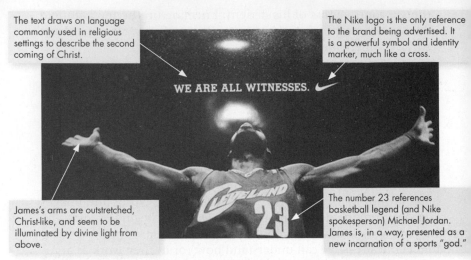

The text draws on language commonly used in religious settings to describe the second coming of Christ.

The Nike logo is the only reference to the brand being advertised. It is a powerful symbol and identity marker, much like a cross.

WE ARE ALL WITNESSES.

James's arms are outstretched, Christ-like, and seem to be illuminated by divine light from above.

The number 23 references basketball legend (and Nike spokesperson) Michael Jordan. James is, in a way, presented as a new incarnation of a sports "god."

A Nike advertisement featuring basketball star Lebron James, annotated to show a deconstruction of the image.

Let's also consider this advertisement in the context of James's 2014 return to the Cleveland Cavaliers, his hometown team, after leaving the team abruptly to play four seasons with the Miami Heat. James's own "second coming" resonated with themes of forgiveness, redemption, and salvation among Cleveland sports fans. In 2018, James signed with the Los Angeles Lakers in free agency. In one of his first public statements about his decision, James said, "I believe the Lakers is a historical franchise, we all know that, but it's a championship franchise and that's what we're trying to get back to. And I'm happy to be part of the culture and be a part of us getting back to that point." Considering these comments, we wonder if this same image of James in a Lakers jersey would have the same resonance.

In the ad, all these associations work together to elevate James, Jordan, and Nike to exalted status. Of course, our description here is tongue in cheek. We're not gullible enough to believe this literally, and the ad's producers don't expect us to be; but they do hope that such an impression will be powerful enough to make us think of Nike the next time we shop for athletic shoes. If sports gods wear Nike, why shouldn't we?

This kind of analysis is possible when we recognize a difference between *seeing* and *looking*. **Seeing** is a physiological process involving light, the eye, and the brain. **Looking**, however, is a social process involving the mind. It suggests apprehending an image in terms of symbolic, metaphorical, and other social and cultural meanings. To do this, we must think beyond the *literal* meaning of an image or image element and consider its *figurative* meanings. If you look up *apple* in the dictionary, you'll find its literal, **denotative** meaning—a round fruit with thin red or green skin and a crisp flesh. But an apple also communicates figurative, **connotative** meanings. Connotative meanings are the cultural or emotional associations that an image suggests.

The connotative meaning of an apple in Western culture dates back to the biblical story of the Garden of Eden, where Eve, tempted by a serpent, eats the fruit from the forbidden tree of knowledge and brings about the end of paradise on earth. Throughout Western culture, apples have come to represent knowledge and the pursuit of knowledge. Think of the ubiquitous Apple logo gracing so many mobile phones, tablets, and laptops: With its prominent bite, it symbolizes the way technology opens up new worlds of knowing. Sometimes, apples represent forbidden knowledge, temptation, or seduction—and biting into one suggests giving in to desires for new understandings and experiences. The story of Snow White offers just one example of an apple used as a symbol of temptation.

How do the DKNY and Bulova advertisements use the symbolic, connotative meanings of the apple to make an argument about their products?

When you are looking—and not just seeing in the simplest sense—you are attempting to discern the ways in which symbolic meanings are used to communicate a message. Take, for example, the following advertisement for Play-Doh, one of the most enduring and popular toys of the past century. First developed in 1930s, Play-Doh has sold billions of canisters around the world. Today, Play-Doh competes with a wide array of technological toys for children, such as smartphones and video game systems.

An advertisement for the timeless toy, Play-Doh, that takes on its digital competitors. The text at the bottom reads, "No In-App Purchases."

The ad for Play-Doh featured here makes an argument with just a single line of text: "No In-App Purchases." These words are set below the image of a shopping cart with a plus sign made of Play-Doh, which has come to be an almost universally recognized symbol for an electronic shopping cart online. Both the words and the icon are textured and look a little rough at the edges, suggesting that they are also made of Play-Doh. In a blue open space suggesting three-dimensionality, the advertisement seems to make a case for the role of real-life, non-digital play in the development of children. It presents Play-Doh as a traditional, value-based proposition without manipulative sales tactics, something trustworthy and honest. The way children play has changed dramatically since the 1930s, but by fashioning the electronic icon and text out of a nearly century-old product, the ad implies that just because a toy — or anything else — is new and high-tech, that does not make it inherently better than old-fashioned things. After all, the product being advertised has stood the test of time; how long will an app on a smartphone or tablet last until it is replaced with a newer version requiring a new update?

✔ A CHECKLIST FOR ANALYZING IMAGES

☐ What is the overall effect of the design (e.g., colorful and busy, quiet and understated, old-fashioned or cutting-edge)?

☐ Is color (or the lack of it) used for a particular purpose? Do colors signify any cultural meaning?

☐ Does the image evoke a particular emotional response? Which elements contribute to that response?

☐ Is the audience for the image apparent? Does the image successfully appeal to this audience?

☐ Is there an argument present? If so, does it appeal to reason (*logos*) — perhaps using statistics, charts, or graphs — or to feelings (*pathos*) — evoking emotional responses or deeply held values? Or is it both?

☐ If there is an appeal to character or credibility (*ethos*), suggesting good sense, trustworthiness, or prudence, is it effective?

☐ Is there any text? If so, what is its relation to the image?

Visual Guide: Analyzing Images

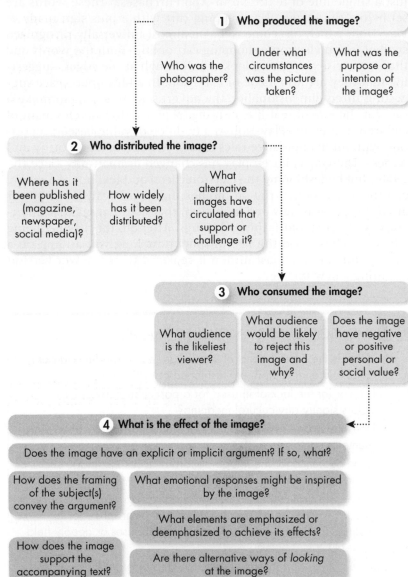

1 Who produced the image?

Who was the photographer?

Under what circumstances was the picture taken?

What was the purpose or intention of the image?

2 Who distributed the image?

Where has it been published (magazine, newspaper, social media)?

How widely has it been distributed?

What alternative images have circulated that support or challenge it?

3 Who consumed the image?

What audience is the likeliest viewer?

What audience would be likely to reject this image and why?

Does the image have negative or positive personal or social value?

4 What is the effect of the image?

Does the image have an explicit or implicit argument? If so, what?

How does the framing of the subject(s) convey the argument?

What emotional responses might be inspired by the image?

What elements are emphasized or deemphasized to achieve its effects?

How does the image support the accompanying text?

Are there alternative ways of *looking* at the image?

LEVELS OF IMAGES

One helpful way of deriving the meanings of images by *looking* at them is to use *seeing* first as a way to define what is plainly or literally present in them. You can begin by *seeing*—identifying the elements that are indisputably "there" in an image (the denotative level). In a sense, you are merely taking an inventory of what is visible and evident. Then you move on to *looking*—interpreting the meanings suggested by the elements that are present (the connotative level). Arguably, when we *see*, we pay attention only to the denotative level—that is, we observe just the explicit elements of the image. We aren't concerned with the meaning of the image's elements yet, just with the fact that they're present.

When we *look*, we move to the connotative level—that is, we speculate on the elements' deeper meanings: what they suggest figuratively, symbolically, or metaphorically in our cultural system. We may also consider the relationship of different elements to one another.

Seeing	Looking
Denotation	Connotation
Literal	Figurative
What is present	What it means
Understanding/Textual	Interpreting/Subtextual/Contextual

Further questions we can ask have to do with the contexts in which they are created, disseminated, and received. Within each of those, other questions arise.

EXERCISE: SEEING VERSUS LOOKING

Examine the images on page 150 and do the following:

1. *See* the image. Thoroughly describe the image. Write down as many elements as possible that you see: colors, shapes, text, people, objects, lighting, framing, perspective, and so forth.

2. *Look* at the image. Take the elements you have observed and relate what they suggest by considering their figurative meanings, their meanings in relation to one another, and their meanings in the context of the images' production and consumption.

Cattle grazing in a California pasture near a wind farm in 1996. A rainbow crosses the sky in the background.

Moms Demand Action, a national public safety advocacy group against gun violence, published this advertisement in 2013. The text reads, "One child is holding something that's been banned in America to protect them. Guess which one."

DOCUMENTING REALITY: READING PHOTOGRAPHS

As we learned with the uses of images relating to the Arctic National Wildlife Refuge (see p. 138), photographs can serve as evidence but have a peculiar relationship to the truth. We must never forget that images are constructed, selected, and used for specific purposes.

When advertisers use images, we know they're trying to convince consumers to purchase a product or service. But when images serve as documentary evidence, we often assume that they're showing the "truth" of the matter at hand. When we see an image in the newspaper or a magazine, we may assume that it captures a particular event or moment in time *as it really happened*. Our level of skepticism may be lower than when we are looking at images designed to persuade us.

But these kind of images—historical images, images of events, news photographs, and the like—are not free from the potential for manipulation or for (conscious or unconscious) bias. Consider how liberal and conservative media sources portray the nation's president in images: One source may show him proud and smiling in bright light with the American flag behind him, whereas another might show him scowling in a darkened image suggestive of evil intent. Both are "real" images, but the framing, tinting, setting, and background can inspire significantly different responses in viewers.

As we saw with the image of LeBron James, certain postures, facial expressions, and settings can contribute to a photograph's interpretation. Martin Luther King Jr.'s great speech of August 28, 1963, "I Have a Dream," still reads very well on the page, but part of its immense appeal derives from its setting: King spoke to some 200,000 people in Washington, DC, as he stood on the steps of the Lincoln Memorial. That setting, rich with associations of slavery and freedom, strongly

Martin Luther King Jr. delivering his "I Have a Dream" speech on August 28, 1963, from the steps of the Lincoln Memorial.

Bettmann/Getty Images

assists King's argument. In fact, images of King delivering his speech are nearly inseparable from the very argument he was making. The visual aspects—the setting (the Lincoln Memorial with the Washington Monument and the Capitol in the distance) and King's gestures—are part of the speech's persuasive rhetoric.

Derrick Alridge, a historian, examined dozens of accounts of Martin Luther King Jr. in history books, and he found that images of King present him overwhelmingly as a messianic figure—standing before crowds, leading them, addressing them in postures reminiscent of a prophet. Although King is an admirable figure, Alridge asserts, history books err by presenting him as more than human. Doing so ignores his personal struggles and failures and makes a myth out of the real man. This myth suggests he was the epicenter of the civil rights movement, an effort that was actually conducted in different ways via different strategies on the part of many other figures whom King eclipsed. We may even get the idea that the entire civil rights movement began and ended with King alone. When history books present King as a holy prophet, Alridge argues, it becomes easier to focus on his gospel of love, equality, and justice and not on the specific policies and politics he advocated—his avowed socialist stances, for instance. In short, while photographs of King seek to help us remember, they may actually portray him in a way that causes us to forget other things—for example, that his approval rating among whites at the time of his death was lower than 30 percent and among blacks lower than 50 percent.

Martin Luther King Jr. on "Chicken Bone Beach" in Atlantic City.

A Word on "Alternative Facts"

All this discussion of "seeing and looking" is intended to underscore how much photographs that seem to provide a clear window into reality are not absolute guarantors of truth. How images are selected, created, and circulated has much to do with their meaning and value. Furthermore, in the digital age, it's remarkably easy to alter photographs. Because of this, we have become more suspicious of photographs as direct evidence of reality. We retain our skepticism when we encounter images of celebrities on the internet who have been obviously "Photoshopped." However, we sometimes do not anticipate the degree to which all kinds of published images may be altered for persuasive purposes. When those purposes are the result of political or ideological bias, we are particularly vulnerable to misinformation because of our assumptions about the reality or truth-value of images.

One memorable moment brings to light how disputes over the truth of images matter. During the inauguration of President Donald Trump, some media outlets were accused by the president of deliberately downplaying the crowd size by comparing images of that day to images of larger crowds at the 2009 Obama inaugural. "[W]e caught them [the media] in a real beauty," the president said. Probably referring to a tweet by the *New York Times* showing side-by-side images of the two inaugurals, White House Press Secretary Sean Spicer said that the photographs "were intentionally framed . . . to minimize the enormous support that had gathered on the National Mall."

Spicer's claim may or may not have been true, but he insisted that "this was the largest audience ever to witness an inauguration, period." He referred to what his colleague Kellyanne Conway now famously called "alternative facts": his calculations of the crowd size, the ridership levels on the DC Metro system, and images of the inauguration

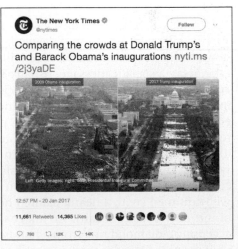

A *New York Times* tweet comparing the crowd sizes at the Obama and Trump inaugurals in 2009 and 2017 drew the ire of the White House, which accused the media of bias.

AP Photo/Patrick Semansky

Empty spaces were cropped out of this image produced by the National Park Service at the White House's request for more flattering images of the crowd size at the 2017 inauguration. These images were subsequently released to media outlets.

ceremony produced by the National Park Service, which had been cropped in such a way as to depict a larger crowd size.

We think this story gets us to the heart of what is meant by alternative facts. To be blunt, the phrase simply means alternative *beliefs* or alternative *forms of evidence* that people present as facts. Although two contradictory facts can't be true, two depictions of the same event may be presented, and therefore seen and interpreted, as factual. To counteract our own tendency to think that "seeing is believing," we can be more critical about images by approaching them through three broad frameworks: accommodation, resistance, and negotiation.

ACCOMMODATING, RESISTING, AND NEGOTIATING THE MEANING OF IMAGES

Most images are produced, selected, and published so as to have a specific effect on readers and viewers. This dominant meaning of an image supposes that the audience will react in a predictable way or take away a specific message, usually based on the widespread **cultural codes** that operate within a society. Images of elegant women in designer dresses, rugged men driving pickup trucks, stodgy teachers, cutthroat CEOs, hipster computer programmers, and so on speak to generally accepted notions of what certain types of people are like. An image of a suburban couple in an automobile advertisement washing their new car subconsciously confirms and perpetuates a certain ideal of middle-class suburban life (a heterosexual couple, a well-trimmed lawn, a neatly painted house and picket fence—and a brand-new midsize sedan). An image of a teary-eyed young woman accepting a diamond ring from a handsome man will likely touch the viewer in a particular way, in part because of our society's cultural codes about the rituals of romantic love and marriage, gender roles, and the diamond ring as a sign of love and commitment.

These examples demonstrate that images can be constructed according to dominant connotations of gender, class, and racial, sexual, and political identity. When analyzing an image, ask yourself what cultural codes it endorses, what ideals it establishes as natural, and what social norms or modes of everyday life it idealizes or assumes.

As image consumers, we often **accommodate** (i.e., passively accept) those messages and cultural codes promoted by media images. For example, in the hypothetical advertisement featuring a marriage proposal—a man kneeling, a woman crying sentimentally—you might not decide to buy a diamond, but you might accept the messages that diamond rings are the appropriate objects to represent love and commitment. Further, you might accept the cultural codes about the rituals of romantic love, marriage, and gender roles, sharing the assumption that men should propose to women and that women are more emotional than men.

When you *accommodate* cultural codes without understanding them critically, you allow the media that perpetuate these codes to interpret the world for you. That is, you accept their interpretations without questioning the social and cultural values implicit in their assumptions, many of which may actually run counter to your own or others' social and cultural values. When analyzing an image, ask yourself what cultural codes it endorses, what ideals it establishes as natural, and what social norms it assumes or idealizes.

If you **resist** the cultural codes of an image, you actively criticize its message and meaning. Suppose you (1) question how the ad presents gender roles and marriage, (2) claim that it idealizes heterosexual marriage, and (3) point out that it confirms and extends traditional gender roles in which men are active and bold and women are passive and emotional. Moreover, you (4) argue that the diamond ring represents a misguided commodification of love because diamonds are kept deliberately scarce by large companies and, as

What cultural codes does this ad accommodate?

such, are overvalued and overpriced; meanwhile, you say, the ad prompts young couples to spend precious money at a time when their joint assets might be better saved, and because many diamonds come from third-world countries under essentially slave labor conditions, the diamond is more a symbol of oppression than of love. If your analysis follows such paths, you *resist* the dominant message of the image in question. Sometimes, this is called an *oppositional reading*.

Negotiation, or a *negotiated reading*, the most useful mode of reading and viewing, involves a middle path — a process of revision that seeks to recognize and change the conditions that give rise to certain negative aspects of cultural codes. Negotiation implies a practical intervention into common viewing processes that help construct and maintain social conditions and relations. A negotiated reading enables you to emphasize the ways in which individuals, social groups, and others relate to images and their dominant meanings and how different personal and cultural perspectives can challenge those meanings. This intervention can be important when inequalities or stereotypes are perpetuated by cultural codes. Without intervention, there can be no revision, no positive social or cultural change. You *negotiate* cultural codes when:

- you understand the underlying messages of images and accept the general cultural implications of these codes, *but*
- you acknowledge that in some circumstances the general codes do not apply.

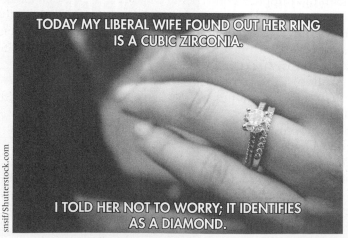

Memes often use humor to present oppositional ideas. However, in doing so, they sometimes reaffirm other cultural codes and assumptions.

EXERCISE: ACCOMMODATING, RESISTING, AND NEGOTIATING IMAGES

Examine the image shown here of an advertisement for Lego building blocks or choose your own ad, PSA, or other image. Provide brief examples of how a viewer could accommodate, resist, or negotiate the images in the ad.

Image Courtesy of The Advertising Archives

ARE SOME IMAGES NOT FIT TO BE SHOWN?: POLITICS AND PICTURES

Images of suffering—either human or animal—can be immensely persuasive. In the nineteenth century, for instance, the antislavery movement made extremely effective use of images in its campaign. We reproduced two antislavery images earlier in this chapter, as well as a counterimage that sought to assure viewers that slavery was a beneficent system (pp. 140–41). But are there some images not fit to print?

Until recently, many newspapers did not print pictures of lynched African Americans, hanged and burned and maimed. The reasons for not printing such images probably differed between South and North: Southern papers may have considered the images to be discreditable to whites, and northern papers may have deemed the images too revolting. Even today, when it's commonplace for newspapers and television news to show pictures of dead victims of war, famine, or traffic accidents, one rarely sees bodies that are horribly maimed. (For traffic accidents, the body is usually covered, and we see only the smashed car.) The US government refused to release photographs showing the bodies of American soldiers killed in the war in Iraq, and it was most reluctant to show pictures of dead Iraqi soldiers and civilians. Only after many Iraqis refused to believe that former Iraqi president Saddam Hussein's two sons had been killed did the US government reluctantly

AP Photo/Nick Ut

Huynh Cong (Nick) Ut, *The Terror of War: Children on Route 1 near Trang Bang*, 1972.

AP Photo/Eddie Adams

Eddie Adams, *Execution of Viet Cong Prisoner, Saigon*, 1968.

release pictures showing the two men's blood-spattered faces—and some American newspapers and television programs refused to use the images.

There have been notable exceptions to this practice, such as Huynh Cong (Nick) Ut's 1972 photograph of children fleeing a napalm attack in Vietnam (top), which was widely reproduced in the United States and won the photographer a Pulitzer Prize in 1973. It's impossible to measure the influence of this particular photograph, but many people believe that it played a substantial role in increasing public pressure to end the Vietnam War. Another widely reproduced picture of horrifying violence is Eddie Adams's 1968 picture (bottom) of a South Vietnamese chief of police allied with the United States firing a pistol into the head of a Viet Cong prisoner.

The issue remains: Are some images unacceptable? For instance, although capital punishment—by methods including lethal injection, hanging, shooting, and electrocution—is legal in parts of the United States, every state prohibits the publication of pictures showing the execution.

An Argument on Publishing Images

A twenty-first-century example concerning the appropriateness of showing certain images arose early in 2006. In September 2005, a Danish newspaper, accused of being afraid to show political cartoons that were hostile to Muslim terrorists, responded by publishing twelve cartoons. One cartoon showed the prophet Muhammad wearing a turban that looked like a bomb. The images at first didn't arouse much attention, but when they were reprinted in Norway in January 2006, they attracted worldwide attention and outraged Muslims, most of whom regard any depiction of Muhammad as blasphemous. Some Muslims in various Islamic nations burned Danish embassies and engaged in other acts of violence. Most non-Muslims agreed that the images were in bad taste, and, apparently in deference to Islamic sensibilities (but possibly also out of fear of reprisals), very few Western newspapers reprinted the cartoons when they covered the news events. Most newspapers (including the *New York Times*) merely described the images. The editors of these papers believed that readers should be told the news, but that because the drawings were so offensive to some persons, they should be described rather than reprinted. A controversy then arose: Do readers of a newspaper deserve to *see* the evidence for themselves, or can a newspaper adequately fulfill its mission by offering only a verbal description? These questions arose again after the 2007 bombing of the French satirical newspaper *Charlie Hebdo* and then after another mass shooting at the same newspaper in 2015 that claimed the lives of twelve editors and staff members.

Persons who argued that the images should be reproduced in the media generally made these points:

- Newspapers should yield neither to the delicate sensibilities of some readers nor to threats of violence.

- Jews for the most part do not believe that God should be depicted (the prohibition against "graven images" appears in Exodus 20.3), but they raise no objections to such Christian images as the ceiling of the Sistine Chapel. Further, when Andres Serrano (a Christian) in 1989 exhibited a photograph of a small plastic crucifix submerged in urine, it outraged a wider public (several US senators condemned it because the artist had received federal funds), but virtually all newspapers showed the image, and many even printed its title, *Piss Christ*. The subject was judged to be newsworthy, and the fact that some viewers would regard the image as blasphemous was not considered highly relevant.

- Our society values freedom of speech, and newspapers should not be intimidated. When certain pictures are a matter of news, readers should be able to see them.

In contrast, opposing voices made these points:

- Newspapers must recognize deep-seated religious beliefs. They should indeed report the news, but there is no reason to *show* images that some people regard as blasphemous. The images can be adequately *described* in words.

- The Jewish response to Christian images of God, and even the tolerant Christians' response to Serrano's image of the crucifix immersed in urine, are irrelevant to the issue of whether a Western newspaper should represent images of the prophet Muhammad. Virtually all Muslims regard depictions of Muhammad as blasphemous, and that's what counts.

- Despite all the Western talk about freedom of the press, the press does *not* reproduce all images that become matters of news. For instance, news items about the sale of child pornography do not include images of the pornographic photos.

EXERCISES: THINKING ABOUT IMAGES

1. In June 2006, two American soldiers were captured in Iraq. Later their bodies were found, dismembered and beheaded. Should newspapers have shown photographs of the mutilated bodies? Why, or why not? (In July 2006, insurgents in Iraq posted images on the internet showing a soldier's severed head beside his body.)

2. Hugh Hewitt, an Evangelical Christian, offered a comparison to the cartoon of Muhammad wearing a bomb-like turban. Suppose, he asked, an abortion clinic were bombed by someone claiming to be an Evangelical Christian. Would newspapers publish "a cartoon of Christ's crown of thorns transformed into sticks of TNT"? Do you think they would? If you were the editor of a newspaper, would you? Why, or why not?

3. A week after the 2015 attack on *Charlie Hebdo*, and in response to media hesitancy to republish the offending images of Muhammad, the Index on Censorship and several other journalistic organizations called for all newspapers to publish them simultaneously and globally on January 8, 2015. "This unspeakable act of violence has challenged and assailed the entire press," said Lucie Morillon of Reporters Without Borders. "Journalism as a whole is in mourning. In the name of all those who have fallen in the defense of these fundamental values, we must continue *Charlie Hebdo*'s fight for the right to freedom of information." Evaluate this position.

4. Examine the image shown here by photojournalist Paul Fusco of the November 22, 2003, funeral for Sgt. Scott C. Rose, who was killed in Iraq. In an argumentative essay of about 500 words, argue your view on this photograph. Is such a photograph so intimately personal that it should not be made public? What possible uses of this photograph can you imagine?

© Paul Fusco/Magnum Photos

WRITING ABOUT POLITICAL CARTOONS

Most editorial pages print political cartoons as well as editorials. Like the writers of editorials, cartoonists seek to persuade, but they rarely use words to *argue* a point. True, they may use a few words in speech balloons or in captions, but generally the drawing does most of the work. Because their aim usually is to convince the viewer that some person's action or proposal is ridiculous, cartoonists almost always **caricature** their subjects: They exaggerate the subject's distinctive features to the point at which the subject becomes grotesque and ridiculous—absurd, laughable, contemptible.

We agree that it's unfair to suggest that because, say, a politician who proposes a new law dresses in outdated clothes and has a distinctive jawline, his proposal is ridiculous, but that's the way cartoonists work. Further, cartoonists are concerned with producing a striking image, not with exploring an issue, so they almost always oversimplify, implying that there really is no other sane view.

In the course of saying that (1) the figures in a cartoon are ridiculous and *therefore* their ideas are contemptible and (2) there is only one side to the issue, cartoonists often use **symbolism**. Here's a list of common symbols:

- symbolic figures (e.g., the US government as Uncle Sam)
- animals (e.g., the Democratic Party as donkey and the Republican Party as elephant)
- buildings (e.g., the White House as representing the nation's president)
- things (e.g., a bag with a dollar sign on it as representing a bribe)

For anyone brought up in American culture, these symbols (like the human figures they represent) are obvious, and cartoonists assume that viewers will instantly recognize the symbols and figures, will get the joke, and will see the absurdity of whatever issue the cartoonist is seeking to demolish.

In writing about the argument presented in a cartoon, normally you will discuss the ways in which the cartoon makes its point. Caricature usually implies, "This is ridiculous, as you can plainly see by the absurdity of the figures depicted" or "What *X*'s proposal adds up to, despite its apparent complexity, is nothing more than . . ." As we have said, this sort of persuasion, chiefly by ridicule, probably is unfair: Almost always the issue is more complicated than the cartoonist indicates. But cartoons work largely by ridicule and the omission of counterarguments, and we shouldn't reject the possibility that the cartoonist has indeed highlighted the absurdity of the issue.

In analyzing the cartoon and determining the cartoonist's attitude, consider the following elements:

- the relative size of the figures in the image
- the quality of the lines (e.g., thin and spidery, thick and seemingly aggressive)
- the amount of empty space in comparison with the amount of heavily inked space (a drawing with lots of inky areas conveys a more oppressive tone than a drawing that's largely open)
- the degree to which text is important, as well as its content and tone (e.g., witty, heavy-handed)

Your essay will likely include an *evaluation* of the cartoon. Indeed, the *thesis* underlying your analytic/argumentative essay may be that the cartoon is effective (persuasive) for such-and-such reasons but unfair for such-and-such other reasons.

The cartoon by Pulitzer Prize–winning cartoonist Walt Handelsman responds to recent breaches of political decorum. It depicts a group of Washington, DC, tourists being driven past what the guide calls "The Museum of Modern American Political Discourse," a building in the shape of a giant toilet. The toilet as a symbol of the level of political discussion dominates the cartoon, effectively driving home the point that Americans are watching our leaders sink to new lows as they debate the future of our nation. By drawing the toilet on a scale similar to that of familiar monuments in Washington, Handelsman may be pointing out that today's politicians, rather than being remembered for great achievements like those of George Washington or Abraham Lincoln, will instead be remembered for their rudeness and aggression. If you were accommodating the meaning of this cartoon, you might agree with Handelsman, but if you were resisting its message, you could point out that it blames politicians solely for the state of political discourse and portrays the "people" as separate from it (or subject to it); however, as we must recognize, political discourse is also in bad shape among the people themselves, too.

Walt Handelsman/Chicago Tribune/TNS

THINKING CRITICALLY ANALYSIS OF A POLITICAL CARTOON

Find a recent political cartoon to analyze, pulled from a print or online news publication. For each Type of Analysis section in the chart below, provide your own answer based on the cartoon.

Type of Analysis	Questions to Ask	Your Answer
Context	Who is the artist? Where and when was the cartoon published? What situations, issues, or political conditions does it respond to?	
Description	What do you see in the cartoon? What elements does it include?	
Analysis	Looking more closely at the images and considering their meanings, how does the cartoon make its point? Is it effective? How could you accommodate, resist, or negotiate the meanings of this image?	

✓ A CHECKLIST FOR ANALYZING POLITICAL CARTOONS

☐ Is there a lead-in?

☐ Is there a brief but accurate description of the drawing?

☐ Is the source of the cartoon cited (perhaps with a comment by the cartoonist)?

☐ Is there a brief report of the event or issue that the cartoon is targeting, as well as an explanation of all the symbols?

☐ Is there a statement of the cartoonist's claim (thesis)?

☐ Is there an analysis of the evidence, if any, that the image offers in support of the claim?

☐ Is there an analysis of the ways in which the drawing's content and style help convey the message?

☐ Is there adequate evaluation of the drawing's effectiveness?

☐ Is there adequate evaluation of the effectiveness of the text (caption or speech balloons) and of the fairness of the cartoon?

AN EXAMPLE: A STUDENT'S ESSAY ANALYZING IMAGES

Ryan Kwon

Professor Carter

English 101

17 September 2018

The American Pipe Dream?

Visual arguments are powerful tools used by photographers, advertisers, and artists to persuade an audience. Two powerful examples of visual arguments about a shared subject, the so-called American Dream, occur in two different types of images, yet they both point to important questions about the attainability of the dream in two different contexts. The first is Margaret Bourke-White's 1937 photograph of flood victims, and the second is Mike Keefe's 2012 political cartoon from InToon .com. Both images, although seventy-five years apart, aim to persuade the audience that the ideology of the American Dream is unattainable in reality. While Bourke-White does so through the use of appeals to irony, juxtaposition, and color contrast, Keefe does so through heavy symbolism and carefully selected text. By comparing these two images, we can see how the American dream is — and always was — elusive.

Thesis: Two visual arguments from different contexts reveal the irony of the American Dream.

Bourke-White's photo of flood victims waiting in a bread line in 1937 (Fig. 1) is not a staged photo like an advertisement, but on closer inspection, it utilizes visual framing to undermine the ideology of the American Dream through appeals

Kwon 2

Margaret Bourke-White/Time & Life Pictures/Getty Images

Fig. 1. Margaret Bourke-White, *Kentucky Flood* (1937).

Makes use of an "inventory" of elements in the photograph—billboard, words, clothing, smiles, car, dog, empty baskets.

to irony, juxtaposition, and color contrast. The billboard is loaded with emotive, powerful phrases like, "World's Highest Standard of Living" and "There's no way like the American Way." The family in the billboard image is nicely dressed, smiling, and driving a shiny, new car. This billboard presents the good life that the American Dream is known to give its citizens.

However, the juxtaposition of this billboard with the line of flood victims beneath it creates an appeal to irony. The American good life is physically above the heads of the people in line, as if it were nothing more than a dream. The family on the billboard is "free" in the sense that they are on the open road. Even the dog appears to be smiling. Meanwhile, the flood victims, stuck in line, are not moving at all. Unlike the family, they do not appear to be enjoying the privileges of ownership: their baskets are (literally and figuratively) empty. The billboard

Kwon recognizes visual metaphor: Being stuck in line is a symbol for social immobility.

Kwon 3

creates the illusion that all American citizens can live the good life simply by being a citizen, but the realities of the flood victims in this photograph say otherwise.

The audience must also take into account that in 1937, racism and segregation of blacks from whites was heavily prominent. Since the billboard pictures a white family, it excludes minorities from the American Dream. Therefore, this photograph demonstrates specifically that minorities are unable to attain the American Dream. The color contrast in this photo further emphasizes the division between light and dark, black people and white people. The billboard is bright, white, and promising, in a dreamlike world above the heads the real individuals who are shadowed and dark, demonstrating that the American Dream is nothing more than an unattainable dream for some.

Keefe's more recent political cartoon (Fig. 2) also demolishes the attainability of the American Dream, but adds

Placing the photograph in historical context helps interpret meaning.

More on how the form and visual details of the photograph add meaning.

Fig. 2.   Mike Keefe, "The American Pipe Dream with Attached Mirage . . ." (2012).

a more modern perspective through the use of symbolism and carefully selected text. The description of the cartoon reads, "The American Pipe Dream with Attached Mirage . . ." Since political cartoons are meant to be read in a matter of seconds by the audience, it is important for the cartoonist to get his or her message across quickly. Keefe manages to do so by setting the tone with this description. A white family, like the one in Bourke-White's photo, is drawn struggling to climb up a desert mountain, demonstrated by their wide eyes, their open mouths, and the beads of sweat surrounding the man's head. They are struggling because they are weighed down by four objects: a prison ball named "Underemployment"; a treasure chest of "Credit Card Debt"; a big bag of "Student Loans"; and a wide-eyed infant. The prison ball weighs the man down because without steady income from a secure job, he cannot support his family. Credit card debt is represented as a treasure chest because a credit card can buy lots of material items, but one must pay off the bill. Leaving the bill unpaid means all of the so-called treasures are taken away. The woman is literally carrying baggage, and that baggage is the amount of student loans that add into the credit card debt. Finally, having a child without a job and with heavy debt is an extra expense. With all of these items weighing the family down, it is no surprise they are struggling to achieve the American Dream, represented by the floating mirage of a suburban home.

> Again, author shows how visual details can be interpreted as metaphors.

The American Dream is floating above the struggling family in Keefe's image, much like the billboard in Bourke-White's photo. This time, however, it is a white family who is struggling to achieve the American Dream, the same kind of family who, ironically, were once the face of it. Thus, Keefe's cartoon manages to express the modern unattainability of the American Dream for all to its audience in a matter of moments, in a way that is just as effective as Bourke-White's photograph.

Author uses evidence from the image to establish the American Dream as something unreachable — always an ideal, but not a reality for all.

Clearly, visuals are powerful tools that can persuade an audience to take a stance on a certain political ideology, such as the American Dream. Both Bourke-White and Keefe make their stances about the unattainability of the American Dream clear, and even build off of each other to make the message stronger, despite their works being created in two different contexts. While textual arguments are certainly accredited more for their persuasion, visual arguments play a powerful role with the ability to persuade an audience.

Works Cited

Bourke-White, Margaret. *Kentucky Flood. Life,* Time Inc., 1937, images.google.com/hosted/life/bdb4f71a5f11cf96.html.

Keefe, Mike. "American Pipe Dream." *InToon.com,* The Association of American Editorial Cartoonists, 13 Apr. 2012, editorialcartoonists.com/cartoon/display .cfm/110032/. Accessed 20 Sep. 2018.

VISUALS AS AIDS TO CLARITY: MAPS, GRAPHS, AND PIE CHARTS

Often, writers use visual aids that are not images but still present information or data graphically in order to support a point. Maps were part of the argument in the debate over drilling in the Arctic National Wildlife Refuge we discussed at the beginning of this chapter.

- Advocates of drilling argued that it would take place only in a tiny area. Their drawn map showed the entire state of Alaska, with a smaller inset showing a much smaller part of the state that was the refuge. The map points out the drilling area with an arrow, implying it is too insignificant of an area to matter because it is too miniscule to show.

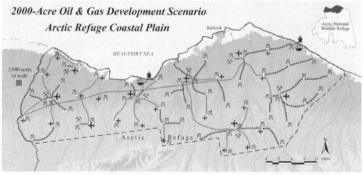

Maps showing the refuge in different ways for different purposes: advocates of drilling used the map on the top to emphasize size, and opponents used the map on the bottom to emphasize industrial transformation.

- Opponents utilized a close-up image to show the extent of industrial sprawl and roads that would have to be constructed across the refuge for drilling to take place. The map uses many icons to show how intrusive the drilling would be to this green natural area. The inset Alaska map is much smaller, deemphasizing the size of the refuge relative to the state.

By changing the scale and orienting viewers to the information in different ways, maps of the same area support different arguments.

Graphs, tables, and pie charts usually present quantitative data in visual form, helping writers clarify dry, statistical assertions. For instance, a line graph may illustrate how many immigrants came to the United States in each decade of the twentieth century.

A bar graph (with bars running either horizontally or vertically) offers similar information. In the Coming to America graph below, we can see at a glance that, say, the second bar on the lower left is almost double the height of the first, indicating that the number of immigrants almost doubled between 1850 and 1860.

A pie chart is a circle divided into wedges so that we can see, literally, how a whole comprises its parts. We can see, for instance, in the From Near and Far chart on page 172, an entire pie representing the regions of foreign-born US immigrants: 32 percent were born in Central America and Mexico, 40 percent in Asia, 9 percent in Europe, and so on.

COMING TO AMERICA . . .

Both the percentage and number of foreign-born people in the United States dropped during much of the twentieth century, but after 1970, the tide was turning again.

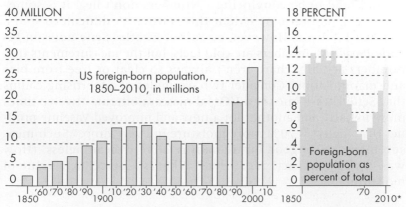

*Most recent estimate

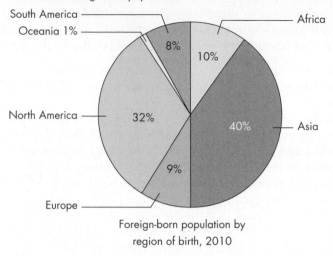

. . . FROM NEAR AND FAR

Central America, Mexico, and Asia contribute
most to the foreign-born population.

Foreign-born population by
region of birth, 2010

Data from U.S. Department of Homeland Security

A Word on Misleading or Manipulative Visual Data

Because maps, charts, tables, and graphs offer empirical data to support arguments, they communicate a high degree of reliability and tend to be convincing. "Numbers don't lie," it is sometimes said, and to some extent this is true. It's difficult to spin a fact like 1 + 1 = 2. However, as author Charles Seife notes in his book *Proofiness*, numbers are cold facts, but the measurements that numbers actually chart aren't always so clear or free from bias and manipulation. Consider two examples of advertising claims that Seife cites—one for a L'Oréal mascara offering "twelve times more impact" and another for a new and improved Vaseline product that "delivers 70% more moisture in every drop." Such measurements *sound* good but remain relatively meaningless. (How was eyelash "impact" measured? What is a percentage value of moisture?)

✓ A CHECKLIST FOR CHARTS AND GRAPHS

☐ Is the source authoritative?

☐ Is the source cited?

☐ Will the chart or graph be intelligible to the intended audience?

☐ Is the caption, if any, clear and helpful?

Another way data can be relatively meaningless is when it addresses only part of the question at stake. In 2013, a Mayo Clinic study found that drinking coffee regularly lowered participants' risk of the liver disease known as primary sclerosing cholangitis (PSC). But PSC is already listed as a "rare disease" by the Centers for Disease Control and Prevention, affecting fewer than 1 in 2,000 people. So even if drinking coffee lowered the risk of PSC by 25 percent, a person's chances would improve only slightly from 0.0005 percent chance to 0.0004 percent chance—hardly a change at all, and hardly a rationale for drinking more coffee. Yet statistical information showing a 25 percent reduction in PSC sounds significant, even more so when provided under a headline proclaiming "Drinking coffee helps prevent liver disease."

Consider other uses of numbers that Seife shows in his book to constitute "proofiness" (his title and word to describe the misuse of numbers as evidence):

- In his 2006 State of the Union Address, George W. Bush declared No Child Left Behind (NCLB) a success: "[B]ecause we acted," he said, "students are performing better in reading and math." (True, fourth to eighth graders showed improved scores, but other grade levels declined. In addition, fourth- to eighth-grade reading and math scores had been improving at an unchanged rate both before and after the NCLB legislation.)

- In 2000, the *New York Times* reported "Researchers Link Bad Debt to Bad Health" (the "dark side of the economic boom"). The researchers claimed that debt causes more illness, but in doing so they committed the correlation-causation fallacy: Just because two phenomena are correlated does not mean they are causally related. (Example: More people wear shorts in the summer and more people eat ice cream in the summer than during other seasons, but wearing shorts does not *cause* higher ice cream consumption.)

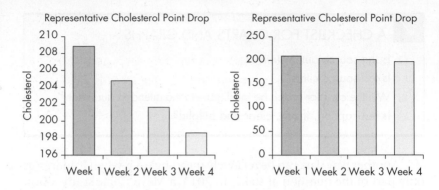

Finally, consider the graph above showing that eating Quaker Oats decreases cholesterol levels after just four weeks of daily servings. The bar graph suggests that cholesterol levels will plummet. But a careful look at the graph reveals that the vertical axis doesn't begin at zero. In this case, a relatively small change has been (mis)represented as much bigger than it actually is.

A more accurate representation of cholesterol levels after four weeks of eating Quaker Oats, using a graph that starts at zero, would look more like the second graph—showing essentially unchanged levels.

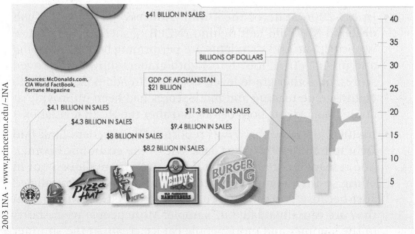

In this graph, McDonald's $41 billion in sales are shown to be about 3.5 times higher than the revenues of its next closest competitor, Burger King (at $11.3 billion), but the McDonald's logo graphic is about 13 times larger than Burger King's.

Be alert to common ways in which graphs can be misleading:

- Vertical axis doesn't start at zero or skips numbers.
- Scale is given in very small units to make changes look big.
- Pie charts don't accurately divide on scale with percentages shown.
- Oversized graphics don't match the numbers they represent.

EXERCISE: MISLEADING VISUALS

Examine these two graphs and describe how the way data from the Bureau of Labor Statistics is visualized presents two different stories about the declining unemployment rate in the United States.

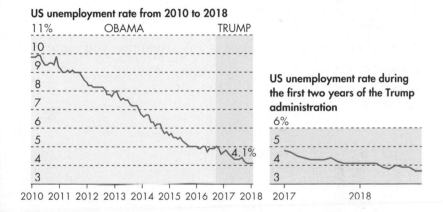

USING VISUALS IN YOUR OWN PAPER

Every paper uses some degree of visual persuasion, merely in its appearance. Consider these elements of a paper's "look": title page; margins (ample, but not so wide that they indicate the writer's inability to produce a paper of the assigned length); double-spaced text for the reader's convenience; headings and subheadings that indicate the progression of the argument; paragraphing; and so on. But you may also want to use visuals such as pictures, graphs, tables, or pie charts to provide examples, help readers digest statistical data more quickly, or simply liven up your essay or presentation. Keep a few guidelines in mind as you work with visuals, "writing" them into your own argument with as much care as you would read them in others' arguments:

- Consider your audience's needs and attitudes and select the type of visuals—graphs, drawings, photographs—likely to be most persuasive to that audience.

- Consider the effect of color, composition, and placement within your document. Because images are most effective when they appear near the text that they supplement, do not group all images at the end of the paper.

Remember especially that images are almost never self-supporting or self-explanatory. They may be evidence for your argument (e.g., Ut's photograph of napalm victims is *very* compelling evidence of suffering), but they aren't arguments themselves.

- Be sure to explain each visual that you use, integrating it into the verbal text that provides the logic and principal support behind your thesis.

- Be sure to cite the source of any visual that you paste into your argument.

5

Writing an Analysis of an Argument

*To expect truth to come from thinking signifies that we mistake
the need to think with the urge to know. Thinking can and must
be employed in the attempt to know, but in the exercise of this
function it is never itself; it is but the handmaiden of an altogether
different enterprise.*

—HANNAH ARENDT

*I don't wait for moods. You accomplish nothing if you do that.
Your mind must know it has got to get down to work.*

—PEARL S. BUCK

Fear not those who argue but those who dodge.

—MARIE VON EBNER-ESCHENBACH

ANALYZING AN ARGUMENT

Most of your writing in other courses will require you to write an
analysis of someone else's writing. In a political science course, you
may have to analyze, say, an essay first published in *Foreign Affairs*,
perhaps reprinted in your textbook, that argues against raising tar-
iffs on foreign goods. A course in sociology may require you to analyze a report on the correlation between fatal accidents and drunk
drivers under the age of twenty-one. In much of your college writing, you will be asked to set forth reasoned responses to your reading as preparation for making arguments of your own.

Examining the Author's Thesis

Obviously, you must understand an essay before you can analyze it thoughtfully. You must read it several times—not just skim it—and (the hard part) you must think critically about it. You'll find that your thinking is stimulated if you take notes and if you ask yourself questions about the material. Are there any websites or organizations dedicated to the material you are analyzing? If there are, visit some to see what others are saying about the material you are reviewing. Notes will help you keep track of the writer's thoughts and also of your own responses to the writer's thesis. The writer probably *does* have a **thesis**—a main claim or point—and if so, you must try to locate it. Perhaps the thesis is explicitly stated in the title, in a sentence or two near the beginning of the essay, or in a concluding paragraph, or perhaps it is not directly stated and you will have to infer it from the essay as a whole.

Notice that we said the writer *probably* has a thesis, stated or unstated. Much of what you read will indeed be primarily an **argument:** a writer explicitly or implicitly trying to support some thesis and to convince readers to agree with it. But some of what you read will be relatively neutral, with the argument just faintly discernible—or even with no argument at all. A work may, for instance, chiefly be a report: Here is the data, or here is what X, Y, and Z said; make of it what you will. A report might simply state how various ethnic groups voted in an election, for example. In a report of this sort, of course, the writer hopes to persuade readers that the facts are correct, but no thesis is advanced—at least not consciously; the writer is not evidently arguing a point and trying to change readers' minds. Such a document differs greatly from an essay by a political analyst who presents those same findings to persuade a candidate to sacrifice the votes of one ethnic bloc to get more votes from other blocs.

If you are looking for evidence that what you are reading is an argument, look for the presence of two elements:

- transitions implying the drawing of a conclusion (such as *therefore, because, for the reason that,* and *consequently*)

- verbs implying proof (such as *confirms, verifies, accounts for, implies, proves, disproves, is [in]consistent with, refutes,* and *it follows that*)

Keep your eye out for such terms and examine their role whenever they appear. If the essay does not seem to be advancing a clear thesis, think of one it might support or some conventional belief it might undermine. That could be the implicit thesis. (See also Thinking Critically: Examining Language to Analyze an Author's Argument on p. 191.)

Examining the Author's Purpose

While reading an argument, try to form a clear idea of the author's **purpose**. A first question is this: Judging from the essay or the book, is the purpose to persuade, or is it to report? An analysis of a persuasive argument requires more investment in the analysis of language and rhetoric, whereas an analysis of a pure report (a work apparently without a thesis or argumentative angle) calls for dealing chiefly with the accuracy of the report. (The analysis must also consider whether the report really has an argument built into it, consciously or unconsciously.)

Purpose can mean many things because people write for many reasons. We write notes and emails sometimes with a purpose to persuade:

> Dear Professor, please forgive my absence from class this morning. I hit a deer on the way to class. Thankfully, only my car got damaged. I do hope I can make up the exam.

Such an email seems simple enough, but this note is a pretty carefully constructed argument. It establishes *ethos* (in a polite and formal tone) and appeals to *pathos* (by pointing to a sympathetic circumstance). It reasons, without really stating it, that the unforeseeable nature of the event is a good excuse to allow a make-up exam. If necessary, it could feasibly be underwritten by evidence (such as an accident report or an image of the damaged car).

In formal writing, purposes may vary. Sometimes, writers are trying to change an opinion, arguing that a certain perspective or interpretation of events is the correct one. A historian may assemble evidence from the past to argue that something occurred a certain way or that one event bore a relationship to some other events. A literary scholar might examine a novel and argue that some constellation of details amounts to something significant. In the sciences, the interpretation of data could be an effort to persuade. In opinion columns, blogs, and newspapers, people routinely write editorials sharing their perspectives and interpretations of the world. Whether the purpose is to change minds, challenge common assumptions, criticize institutionalized ideas, or argue that people should take some specific action, all arguments have a purpose.

When you are analyzing arguments, you will have a specific purpose. Perhaps you want simply to inform, attempting to convey someone else's argument as accurately as you can as if it were a report. Or perhaps you want to affirm (or challenge) the argument, making another argument (or counterargument) or your own. You might also satirize the argument, the writer, or the kind of thinking it represents. Whenever you analyze an argument, you are paying special attention to the author, context, language, medium—everything about the setting of an argument—and how those details and choices help the author achieve his or her purpose.

Examining the Author's Methods

If the essay advances a thesis to achieve a clear purpose, you will want to analyze the strategies or **methods** of argument that allegedly support the thesis.

- Is the argument aimed at a particular audience? Do the author's chosen methods work for that particular audience?

- Does the writer quote authorities? What publications does the writer draw from? Are these authorities competent in this field? Does the writer consider equally competent authorities who take a different view?

- Does the writer use statistics? If so, who compiled them, and are they appropriate to the point being argued? Can they be interpreted differently?

- Does the writer build the argument by using examples or analogies? Are they satisfactory?

- Does the writer include images (photos, graphs, charts, screenshots)? Are the image sources reliable? Do they support the writer's argument well, perhaps by an appeal to *logos* or *pathos*?

- Are the writer's assumptions acceptable?

- Does the writer consider all relevant factors? Has he or she omitted some points that you think should be discussed? For instance, should the author recognize certain opposing positions and perhaps concede something to them?

- Does the writer seek to persuade by means of humor or ridicule? If so, is the humor or ridicule fair? Is it supported also by rational argument?

Examining the Author's Persona

You will probably also want to analyze something a bit more elusive than the author's explicit arguments: the author's self-presentation. Does the author seek to persuade readers partly by presenting himself or herself as conscientious, friendly, self-effacing, authoritative, or in some other light? Most writers, while they present evidence, also present themselves (or, more precisely, they present the image of themselves that they wish us to behold). In persuasive writing, this **persona** — this presentation of self, which can often be discerned from *language, voice,* and *tone* of the author — may be no less important than the presentation of evidence. In some cases, the persona may not much matter, but the point is that you should look at the author's self-presentation to consider if it's significant.

In establishing a persona, writers adopt various rhetorical strategies, ranging from the level of vocabulary they use, to their specific word choices, to the way they approach or organize their argument. The author of an essay may be polite, for example, and show fair-mindedness and open-mindedness, treating the opposition with great courtesy and expressing interest in hearing other views. Such a tactic is itself a persuasive device. Another author may use a technical vocabulary and rely on a range of hard evidence such as statistics. This reliance on a scientific tone and seemingly objective truths is itself a way of seeking to persuade — a rational way, to be sure, but a mode of persuasion nonetheless.

Consider these further examples:

- A writer who speaks of an opponent's "gimmicks" instead of "strategy" probably is trying to downgrade the opponent and also to convey the self-image of a streetwise person.

- A writer who uses legalistic language and cites numerous court cases is seeking to reveal her fluency in the law and her research capabilities to convince readers she is authoritative.

- A writer who seems professorial or pedantic, referencing a lot of classical figures and citing intellectual sources, is hoping to present himself as a person of deep knowledge and wisdom.

- A writer who draws a lot of examples from daily life in their ordinary neighborhood is wanting to be seen as a regular, commonsense person.

On a larger scale, then, consider not only the language, voice, and tone of the author, but also the *kind* of evidence that is used and the *ways* in which it is organized and presented. One writer may first bombard the reader with facts and then spend relatively little time drawing conclusions. Another may rely chiefly on generalizations, waiting until the end of the essay to bring the thesis home with a few details. Another may begin with a few facts and spend most of the space reflecting on these. All such devices deserve comment in your analysis.

The writer's persona may color the thesis and help it develop in a distinctive way. If we accept the thesis, it is no doubt partly because the writer has won our goodwill by persuading us of his or her good character or *ethos*. Good writers present themselves not as know-it-alls, wise guys, or bullies, but as decent people whom the reader presumably would like to invite to dinner.

In short, the author's self-presentation usually matters. A full analysis of an argument must recognize its effect, whether positive or negative.

Examining the Author's Audience

Another key element in understanding an argument lies in thinking about the intended audience — how the author perceives the audience and what strategies the author uses to connect to it. We have already said something about the creation of the author's persona. An author with a loyal following is, almost by definition, someone who in earlier writings has presented an engaging persona, a persona with a trustworthy *ethos*. A trusted author can sometimes cut corners and can perhaps adopt a colloquial tone that would be unacceptable in the writing of an unknown author. The acclaimed mythologian Joseph Campbell once said, "You can always tell an author who is still working under the authorities by the number of footnotes he provides in his text."

Authors who want to convince their audiences need to think about how they present information and how they present themselves. Consider how you prefer people to talk to you. What sorts of language do you find engaging? Much, of course, depends on the circumstances, notably the topic, the audience, and the place. A joke may be useful in an argument about whether the government should regulate junk food, but almost surely a joke will be inappropriate — will backfire, will alienate the audience — in an argument about abortion. The *way* an author addresses the reader (through an invented persona) can have a significant impact on the reader's perception of the author, which is to say perception of the author's *views* and *argument*. A slip in tone or an error of fact, however small, may be enough for the audience to dismiss the author's argument. When you write your own arguments, understanding audience means thinking about all the possible audiences who may come into contact with your writing or your message and thinking about the consequences of what you write and where it is published.

Consider the impact of President Donald Trump's frequent use of Twitter to share his opinions and ideas. In that venue, he commonly castigates his political opponents (and sometimes his friends) and rails against policies and people he disagrees with. For many people, including some Republicans, not only does he generalize and oversimplify—after all, he is limited to a special number of characters—but his curious uses of capitalization and common misspellings are seen to detract from his *ethos*. For others, who may argue that Twitter is only one limited channel of communication where misspellings and solecisms are common, Trump's *ethos* is not damaged. Regardless of whether you think Trump strengthens or weakens his *ethos* through his tweets, they are on public record and will doubtlessly be analyzed long into the future; as the ancient Roman poet Horace said, *"Nescit vox missa reverti"* ("The word once spoken can never be recalled"), or, in plain proverbial English, "Think twice before you speak."

Our point is that we must consider the author's persona in conjunction with the publication type or venue in which an argument occurs in order to fully analyze the argument—whether it is occurring in a tweet, an editorial, a magazine article, a review, or a scholarly essay—because each publication context has a specific intended audience to whom the author is appealing.

Consider your own social media usage. Have you ever seen something posted by a friend or influencer on Facebook, Instagram, or Twitter and then swiftly taken down again? Have you ever received a text message or email not intended for you? Just as you must consider the purposes of the authors in those cases, when you are reading more formal essays it is equally important to think about who wrote them (author and author's persona) and for whom they were intended (audience). These factors can help you

A tweet from Donald Trump claiming that Barack Obama ordered surveillance in Trump Tower during the 2016 US presidential campaign.

better discern the perspective and intentions of the author, which can significantly inform the ways evidence was gathered, interpreted, and represented.

✓ **A CHECKLIST FOR ANALYZING AN AUTHOR'S INTENDED AUDIENCE**

☐ Where did the piece appear? Who published it? Why, in your view, might someone have found it worth publishing?

☐ In what technological format does this piece appear? Print journal? Online magazine? Blog? What does the technological format say about the piece, the author, or the audience?

☐ Is the writing relatively informal — for instance, a tweet or a Facebook status update? Why is this medium good or bad for the message?

☐ Who is the intended audience? Are there other audiences who may also have an interest but whom the author has failed to consider?

☐ If *you* are the intended audience, what shared values do you have with the author?

☐ What strategies does the writer use to create a connection with the audience?

Organizing Your Analysis

In writing an analysis of an argument, it is usually a good idea at the start of your analysis—if not in the first paragraph, then in the second or third—to let the reader know the purpose (and thesis, if there is one) of the work you are analyzing and then to summarize the work briefly, noting its main points.

Throughout the essay, you will want to analyze the strategies or methods of argument that allegedly support the thesis. Thus, you will probably find it useful (and your readers will certainly find it helpful) to write out *your* thesis (your evaluation or judgment). You might say, for instance, that the essay is impressive but not conclusive, or is undermined by convincing contrary evidence, or relies too much on unsupported generalizations, or is wholly admirable. It all depends on what you conclude as you go through the process of analyzing the argument at hand.

And then, of course, comes the job of setting forth your analysis and the support for your thesis. There is no one way of going about this work, and the organization of your analysis may or may not follow the organization of the work you are analyzing. (The Visual Guide: Organizing Your Analysis graphic shows some options, but there are, of course, others that may better suit your argument.)

Especially in analyzing a work in which the author's persona, ideas, and methods are blended, you will want to spend some time commenting on the persona. Whether you discuss it near the beginning of your analysis or near the end will depend on how you want to construct your essay, and this decision will partly depend on the work you are analyzing. For example, if the author's persona is kept in the background and is thus relatively invisible, you may want to make that point fairly early to get it out of the way and then concentrate on more interesting matters. If, however, the persona is interesting—and perhaps seductive, whether because it seems so scrupulously objective or so engagingly subjective—you may want to hint at this quality early in your essay and then develop the point while you consider the arguments.

Visual Guide: Organizing Your Analysis

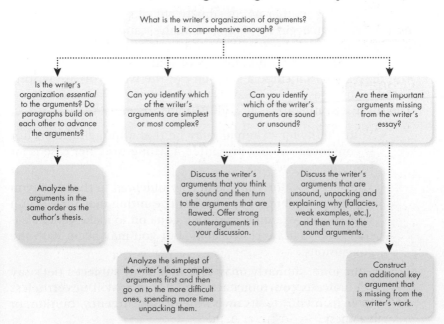

A good conclusion for an analysis of an argument might offer a reassessment of the major points made by the author and a final statement about the validity or viability of the argument. You also have a chance in the conclusion to test the author's argument further, perhaps applying it to new or different situations that highlight its effectiveness or show where it falls short. If readers were to accept or reject the argument, what would be the implications? What other arguments would gain or lose currency by accepting or rejecting this one? Does the argument represent a new kind of potential or a new kind of threat—in a general sense, does it disrupt or attempt to disrupt current thinking, and, if so, is that a good or bad thing?

Summary Versus Analysis

In the last few pages, we have tried to persuade you that, in writing an analysis of a reading

- most of the nonliterary material that you will read is designed to argue, to report, or to do both; read and reread thoughtfully, and take careful notes, and
- most of this material also presents the writer's personality, or voice, and this voice usually merits attention in an analysis.

There is yet another point, equally obvious but often neglected by students who begin by writing an analysis and end up by writing only a summary, a shortened version of the work they have read: Although your essay is an analysis of someone else's writing and you may have to include a summary of the work you are writing about, your essay is *your* essay, your analysis, not a mere summary. The thesis, the organization, and the tone are yours.

- Your thesis, for example, may be that although the author is convinced she has presented a strong case, her case is far from proved because . . .
- Your organization may be deeply indebted to the work you are analyzing, but it need not be. The author may have begun with specific examples and then gone on to make generalizations and to draw conclusions, but you may begin with the conclusions.
- Your tone, similarly, may resemble your subject's (let's say the voice is courteous academic), but it will nevertheless have its own ring, its own tone of, say, urgency, caution, or coolness.

Most of the essays that we have included thus far are written in an intellectual if not academic style, and indeed several are by students and by professors. But argumentative writing is not limited to intellectuals and academics. Arguments occur everywhere—in academic articles and newspaper editorials and on the backs of cereal boxes. Being able to analyze arguments is essential to being a wise citizen, a skeptical consumer, and a competent member of any field or profession. If it weren't all these things (and probably more), colleges would not require so many people to take a course in the subject.

✓ **A CHECKLIST FOR ANALYZING A TEXT**

Have I considered all the following matters?

☐ Does the author have a self-interest in writing this piece?

☐ Is there evidence in the author's tone and style that enables me to identify anything about the intended audience? Is the tone appropriate?

☐ Given the publication venue (or any other contexts), can I tell if the audience is likely to be neutral, sympathetic, or hostile to the argument?

☐ Does the author have a thesis? Does the argument ask the audience to accept or to do anything?

☐ Does the author make assumptions? Does the audience share those assumptions? Do I?

☐ Is there a clear line between what is factual information and what is interpretation, belief, or opinion?

☐ Does the author appeal to reason (*logos*), to the emotions (*pathos*), or to our sense that the speaker is trustworthy (*ethos*)?

☐ Is the evidence provided convincing? If visual materials such as graphs, pie charts, or pictures are used, are they persuasive?

☐ Are significant objections and counterevidence adequately discussed?

☐ Is the organization of the text effective? Are the title, the opening paragraphs, and the concluding paragraphs effective?

☐ Is the overall argument correct in its conclusions? Or is there anything missing that I could use to add to or challenge the argument?

☐ Has the author convinced me?

AN ARGUMENT, ITS ELEMENTS, AND A STUDENT'S ANALYSIS OF THE ARGUMENT

In many types of media, we are exposed to the opinions and judgments of others, often capable writers, who argue their positions clearly, reasonably, and convincingly. We want to think carefully before we accept an argument, so we encourage skepticism but not entrenchment in your own position. You must be willing to hear and seriously consider different positions. Consider the following argument by columnist Nicholas Kristof, published in the *New York Times* in 2005. Analyze the essay and, after you do, examine our analysis of Kristof's argument, as well as the analysis provided by student Theresa Carcaldi, to see how it matches your own.

Nicholas D. Kristof

Nicholas D. Kristof (b. 1959), a two-time Pulitzer Prize winner, grew up on a farm in Oregon. After graduating from Harvard, he was awarded a Rhodes scholarship to Oxford, where he studied law. In 1984, he joined the New York Times *as a correspondent, and since 2001 he has written as a columnist. The editorial that follows first appeared in the* New York Times *in 2005.*

For Environmental Balance, Pick Up a Rifle

Here's a quick quiz: Which large American mammal kills the most humans each year?

It's not the bear, which kills about two people a year in North America. Nor is it the wolf, which in modern times hasn't killed anyone in this country. It's not the cougar, which kills one person every year or two.

Rather, it's the deer. Unchecked by predators, deer populations are exploding in a way that is profoundly unnatural and that is destroying the ecosystem in many parts of the country. In a wilderness, there might be ten deer per square mile; in parts of New Jersey, there are up to 200 per square mile.

One result is ticks and Lyme disease, but deer also kill people more directly. A study for the insurance industry estimated that deer kill about 150 people a year in car crashes nationwide and cause $1 billion in damage. Granted, deer aren't stalking us, and they come out worse in these collisions—but it's still true that in a typical year, an American is less likely to be killed by Osama bin Laden[1] than by Bambi.

If the symbol of the environment's being out of whack in the 5
1960s was the Cuyahoga River in Cleveland catching fire, one such symbol today is deer congregating around what they think of as salad bars and what we think of as suburbs.

So what do we do? Let's bring back hunting.

Now, you've probably just spilled your coffee. These days, among the university-educated crowd in the cities, hunting is viewed as barbaric.

The upshot is that towns in New York and New Jersey are talking about using birth control to keep deer populations down. (Liberals presumably support free condoms, while conservatives back abstinence education.) Deer contraception hasn't been very successful, though.

Meanwhile, the same population bomb has spread to bears. A bear hunt has been scheduled for this week in New Jersey — prompting outrage from some animal rights groups (there's also talk of bear contraception: make love, not cubs).

As for deer, partly because hunting is perceived as brutal and 10
vaguely psychopathic, towns are taking out contracts on deer through discreet private companies. Greenwich, Connecticut, budgeted $47,000 this year to pay a company to shoot eighty deer from raised platforms over four nights — as well as $8,000 for deer birth control.

Look, this is ridiculous.

We have an environmental imbalance caused in part by the decline of hunting. Humans first wiped out certain predators — like wolves and cougars — but then expanded their own role as predators to sustain a rough ecological balance. These days, though, hunters are on the decline.

According to "Families Afield: An Initiative for the Future of Hunting," a report by an alliance of shooting organizations, for every hundred hunters who die or stop hunting, only sixty-nine hunters take their place.

I was raised on *Bambi* — but also, as an Oregon farm boy, on venison and elk meat. But deer are not pets, and dead deer are as natural as live deer. To wring one's hands over them, perhaps after polishing off a hamburger, is soggy sentimentality.

[1.]The Al-Qaeda leader and mastermind of the 9/11 attack who was still at large at Kristof's writing. [Editors' note]

What's the alternative to hunting? Is it preferable that deer die 15 of disease and hunger? Or, as the editor of *Adirondack Explorer* magazine suggested, do we introduce wolves into the burbs?

To their credit, many environmentalists agree that hunting can be green. The New Jersey Audubon Society this year advocated deer hunting as an ecological necessity.

There's another reason to encourage hunting: it connects people with the outdoors and creates a broader constituency for wilderness preservation. At a time when America's wilderness is being gobbled away for logging, mining, or oil drilling, that's a huge boon.

Granted, hunting isn't advisable in suburban backyards, and I don't expect many soccer moms to install gun racks in their minivans. But it's an abdication of environmental responsibility to eliminate other predators and then refuse to assume the job ourselves. In that case, the collisions with humans will simply get worse.

In October, for example, Wayne Goldsberry was sitting in a home in northwestern Arkansas when he heard glass breaking in the next room. It was a home invasion—by a buck.

Mr. Goldsberry, who is six feet one inch and weighs two hun- 20 dred pounds, wrestled with the intruder for forty minutes. Blood spattered the walls before he managed to break the buck's neck.

So it's time to reestablish a balance in the natural world—by accepting the idea that hunting is as natural as bird-watching.

Topics for Critical Thinking and Writing

1. What is Nicholas Kristof's chief thesis? (State it in one sentence.)

2. Does Kristof make any assumptions — tacit or explicit — with which you agree or disagree? Why?

3. Is the slightly humorous tone of Kristof's essay inappropriate for a discussion of deliberately killing wild animals? Why, or why not?

4. What kind of evidence does Kristof offer to justify his claim that more hunting is needed? What interpretations of Kristof's evidence could be made if you were trying to challenge him?

5. Do you agree that "hunting is as natural as bird-watching" (para. 21)? In any case, do you think that an appeal to what is "natural" is a good argument for expanding the use of hunting? Why, or why not?

6. To whom is Kristof talking? How do you know?

THINKING CRITICALLY EXAMINING LANGUAGE TO ANALYZE AN AUTHOR'S ARGUMENT

Look at Nicholas D. Kristof's essay on page 188. Provide two examples of sentences from Kristof's essay that use each type of conclusion or proof.

Language	Examples	Two Examples from Kristof's Essay
Transitions that imply the drawing of a conclusion	*therefore, because, for the reason that, consequently*	
Verbs that imply proof	*confirms, verifies, accounts for, implies, proves, disproves, is (in)consistent with, refutes, it follows that*	

The Essay Analyzed

By now you have read and begun to analyze Kristof's essay. Now let's examine his argument with an eye to identifying those elements we mentioned earlier in this chapter that deserve notice when examining *any* argument: the author's *thesis, purpose, methods, persona,* and *audience* (see Analyzing an Argument, pp. 177–87). It is important to point out that analysis does not always (or even usually) happen in a linear way.

When analyzing, we always consider the author, the publication type, and the context in which the argument was written. We knew that Kristof is a self-described progressive but is also known to take provocative positions somewhat out of step with typical liberal attitudes (for example, Kristof argued elsewhere in several *New York Times* editorials that sweatshops in foreign countries could be a good thing, a necessary stage on the way to progress). Thus, we could better interpret his argument about hunting deer: Although it involves guns and the killing of animals, it presents ethical and ecological reasons likely to be valued by liberals. We also knew that the essay appeared in a newspaper, the *New York Times*, where paragraphs are customarily very short, partly to allow for easy reading. Taking all this information together, we can assume that Kristof's intended audience was a commonsense, urban (or suburban) moderate who might hold typical liberal values about guns and hunting. This assumption allows us to read Kristof's tone — funny and acerbic but not cutting or insulting—as one suitable to the writer's purpose: to challenge a relatively sympathetic audience and at the same time gently ridicule their more "bleeding-heart" brethren.

THESIS   Kristof does not *announce* the thesis in its full form until paragraph 6 ("Let's bring back hunting"); instead he begins with evidence that builds up to the thesis. (It's worth noting that his paragraphs are very short, and if the essay were published in a book instead of a newspaper, Kristof's first two paragraphs probably would be combined, as would the third and fourth.)

PURPOSE   He wants to *persuade* readers to adopt his view. Kristof does not show that his essay is argumentative by using key terms that normally mark argumentative prose: *in conclusion, therefore,* or *because of this.* Almost the only traces of the language of argument are "Granted" (para. 18) and "So" (i.e., *therefore*) in his final paragraph. But the argument is clear—if unusual—and he wants readers to accept his argument as *true.* Possibly, part of his purpose is that he wants to make this argument specifically to a liberal audience unlikely to assume that hunting or guns could be a solution.

METHODS   Kristof offers evidence identifying the problem of deer overpopulation, pointing out the annual number of deaths, and comparing that number—with a reference to a global terrorist—to the number of deaths from terrorism. He also points out other hazards such as Lyme disease and the economic impact of deer overpopulation. Kristof's methods of presenting evidence include providing **statistics** (paras. 3, 4, 10, and 13), giving **examples** (paras. 10, 19–20), and citing **authorities** (paras. 13 and 16).

PERSONA   Kristof presents himself as a confident, no-nonsense fellow, a newspaper columnist. A folksy tone ("Here's a quick quiz") and informal, humorous language establish a good relationship with readers. A well-known columnist, Kristof is a progressive who often takes nontypical views and presents a voice of "common sense." His readers probably know what to expect, and they read him with pleasure.

AUDIENCE   Kristof is known to be progressive, and he knows his audience is, too ("Now you've probably just spilled your coffee," he says when he proposes hunting as a solution). But he also mocks the "the university-educated crowd in the cities, [for whom] hunt-ing is viewed as barbaric" (para. 7). So he is mocking liberal dogmas even though his audience is presumable of the same ilk. But he is not conservative (in fact, he spoofs them, too). Ordinarily, it is a bad idea to make fun of persons, whether they're you're intended audience or not; impartial readers rarely want to align themselves with someone who mocks others. In the essay we are looking at, however, Kristof gets away with this smart-guy tone because he not only has loyal readers but also has written the entire essay in a highly informal or playful manner.

Let's now turn to a student's written analysis of Kristof's essay and then to our own analysis of the student's analysis.

Carcaldi 1

Theresa Carcaldi

Professor Markle

ENG 120

13 July 2018

For Sound Argument, Drop the Jokes:

How Kristof Falls Short in Convincing His Audience

In recent years, the action of hunting wild animals has become controversial. However, the *New York Times* columnist Nicholas D. Kristof attempts to argue for the necessity of hunting deer in America in his piece, "For Environmental Balance, Pick up a Rifle." Kristof certainly engages his audience in this newspaper column, especially progressive-minded readers who might believe any expansion of guns or hunting is abhorrent. He presents evidence that at first seems convincing; however, it is clear that the soundness of his argument falls short as a result of replacing his arguments with jokes, failing to provide adequate evidence, and including lines that are both

Carcaldi examines the paradox of the title—for a liberal goal, use a gun.

Note in Carcaldi's thesis her primary critique of Kristof's argument.

Carcaldi 2

incapable of relating to a majority of the population as well as disbelieving.

Before describing why Kristof's essay falls short of being sound, it is first important to concede the fact that Kristof's essay appeared in a newspaper column that is meant to be read in a quick manner, so the tone of his essay as well as its length and lack of evidence and full development of ideas is

Analyzes how Kristof establishes ethos*.*

to be expected. His sarcastic, conversational tone is layered with occasional jokes and creates a friendly relationship with the audience that sets the stage for trust between author and reader. Therefore, some initial evidence sets out the problems of deer overpopulation in a way likely to be accepted, including dramatic statistics about human highway deaths caused by deer and the incident rates of Lyme disease spread by deer. By

Points out Kristof's persuasive strategy.

doing this, Kristof appeals to fear in the basic structure of his argument: the drastic rise in the deer population is wreaking havoc across America, and the solution to this problem is to hunt more deer.

Accounts for the fact that there is a problem, but takes issue with how that problem is overdramatized.

No doubt, deer do cause serious problems. As Kristof says, deer "kill people more directly" each year than any other mammal (para. 4). However, the evidence is mostly unconvincing. By showing the deer threat to be more significant than the threat of terrorism, Kristof intends to highlight the often irrationality of his audience's anxieties. However, his sample is

Carcaldi reinterprets and challenges the evidence Kristof uses.

too small: just because deaths caused by deer in a single year exceed that of terrorism in America, that does not mean that a major terrorist attack will not happen in the future.

Carcaldi 3

Even with the threats deer do pose, the idea of hunting being the best solution is unconvincing. While Kristof states in paragraph 16 that the New Jersey Audubon Society "advocated deer hunting as an ecological necessity," this is only convincing if the audience is aware of what the New Jersey Audubon Society advocates for — which Kristof fails to explain. To add, Kristof proposes that the present alternative to deer hunting is to let the deer perish from natural causes like "disease and hunger" (para. 15). While this appeal to the audience's sensitivities about animal cruelty is good evidence for supporting deer hunting, Kristof does not fully explain why other solutions, such as deer birth control, are inadequate; instead, he just jokes about it, poking fun at the oversensitive "make love, not cubs" crowd. Rather than giving an argument, in other words, he makes a joke, then adds a further one that "Liberals presumably support free condoms, while conservatives back abstinence education" (para. 8). While this may make the audience laugh, it also suggests that people's political attitudes often prevent them from using common sense. This is an appeal to humor and to common sense, but is certainly not a fully stated reason for why deer contraception is not a solution. Kristof once states, "Deer contraception hasn't been very successful" (para. 8), yet does not explain why — he merely makes a statement without evidence, which does not contribute to a sound argument.

In addition, Kristof ends his essay with unbelievable statements. First, he claims hunting "connects people with the outdoors and creates a broader constituency for wilderness

Suggests that the argument Kristof makes is presented as one (although not the only or best) solution.

Acknowledges other types of appeals Kristof makes.

Carcaldi 4

preservation" (para. 17). This statement contradicts his previous statement that "Humans first wiped out certain predators — like wolves and cougars" (para. 12). After stating the negative effects hunting has had on wildlife preservation, it is difficult to claim that hunting nowadays would be any different. Finally, Kristof ends with "hunting is as natural as bird-watching" (para. 21). While hunting in the wild is certainly natural, it goes without saying that hunting with manmade weapons is far from being natural. Thus, with these two statements, not only does Kristof contradict himself, but he jeopardizes his audience's trust. While Kristof may use transitions of argumentation, such as "Granted" (para. 3), "Meanwhile" (para. 9), and "To their credit" (para. 16), his writing is primarily based on unsupported statements and jokes rather than sound reasoning. Ultimately, his essay is left labeled as an unsound argument.

Carcaldi concludes by reiterating her own thesis and main points.

Clearly, Kristof has written an engaging article about a controversial topic and has written it well for the medium in which it was produced and for the audience he sought. However, this does not mean his argument is logical and sound. As a result of his lack of evidence, his often overconfident statements, and the logical fallacies ridden throughout the piece, his argument is left unsound, and his audience is left utterly unconvinced that the only solution to the deer issue across America is to hunt them.

An Analysis of the Student's Analysis

Carcaldi's essay seems to us to be excellent, doubtless the product of a good deal of thoughtful revision. She does not cover every possible aspect of Kristof's essay—she concentrates on Kristof's reasoning and says very little about his style—but we think Carcaldi does a good job in a short space. What makes her essay effective?

- She has a strong title ("For Sound Argument, Drop the Jokes: How Kristof Falls Short in Convincing His Audience") that is of at least a little interest; it picks up Kristof's method of using humor, and it gives a hint of what is to come.

- She promptly identifies Kristof's subject and gives us a hint of where she will be going, telling us outright that it is "clear that the soundness of his essay falls short."

- She recognizes Kristof's audience at the start and analyzes his use of language and his assumptions with that knowledge in mind.

- She uses a few brief quotations to give us a feel for Kristof's essay and to let us hear the evidence for itself, but she does not pad her essay with long quotations.

- She considers all Kristof's main points.

- She organizes her essay reasonably, letting us hear Kristof's thesis, letting us know the degree to which she accepts it, and finally letting us know her specific reservations about Kristof's essay.

- She concludes without the formality of "in conclusion" but structures her analysis in such a way as to account for the charm or effectiveness of Kristof's essay but not agree with his solutions.

- Notice, finally, that she sticks closely to Kristof's essay. She does not go off on a tangent about the virtues of vegetarianism or the dreadful politics of the *New York Times*, the newspaper that published Kristof's essay. She was asked to analyze the essay, and she has done so.

✓ **A CHECKLIST FOR WRITING AN ANALYSIS OF AN ARGUMENT**

☐ Have I accurately stated the writer's thesis (claim) and summarized his or her supporting reasons?

☐ Have I indicated early in the essay where I will be taking my reader (i.e., have I indicated my general response to the essay I am analyzing)?

☐ Have I called attention to the strengths, if any, and the weaknesses, if any, of the essay?

☐ Have I commented on the ways *logos* (logic, reasoning), *pathos* (emotion), and *ethos* (character of the writer) are presented in the essay?

☐ Have I explained any disagreements I might have about definitions of important terms and concepts?

☐ Have I examined the chief uses of evidence in the essay and offered supporting or refuting evidence or interpretation?

☐ Have I used occasional brief quotations to let my reader hear the author's tone and to ensure fairness and accuracy?

☐ Is my analysis effectively organized?

☐ Have I taken account of the author's audience(s)?

☐ Does my essay, perhaps in the concluding paragraphs, indicate my agreement or disagreement with the writer but also my view of the essay as a piece of argumentative writing?

☐ Is my tone appropriate?

6

Developing an Argument of Your Own

The difficult part in an argument is not to defend one's opinion but to know what it is.

— ANDRÉ MAUROIS

No greater misfortune could happen to anyone than that of developing a dislike for argument.

— PLATO

PLANNING AN ARGUMENT

First, hear the wisdom of Mark Twain: "When the Lord finished the world, He pronounced it good. That is what I said about my first work, too. But Time, I tell you, Time takes the confidence out of these incautious early opinions."

All of us, teachers and students, have our moments of confidence, when we feel certain that our thoughts and judgments are settled. However, for the most part we know too that new information and new experiences can always change our early opinions on matters. To execute a well-informed, well-reasoned argument takes time and effort, and most of all a willingness to revise: to revise our thinking as we learn, and our writing as we produce it. Clear, thoughtful, seemingly effortless prose is not common on the first try. Good writing requires rethinking and revision. In a live conversation we can always claim ignorance and cover ourselves with such expressions as "Well, I don't know, but I sort of think . . . ," and we can always revise our words instantly

("Oh, well, I didn't mean it that way"). However, once we have had the chance to learn about and reason through an issue, and are committed to writing down our thoughts—and once we have handed in the final version of our writing—we are helpless. We are (putting it strongly) naked to our enemies.

Producing the strongest arguments requires good planning—but that can be difficult when you do not yet know what to think about something. Thus, planning your argument starts with developing it.

Getting Ideas: Argument as an Instrument of Inquiry

In Chapter 1, we quoted Robert Frost, "To learn to write is to learn to have ideas," and we offered strategies about generating ideas, a process traditionally called **invention**. A moment ago we said that we often improve our ideas when explaining them to someone else. Partly, of course, we're responding to questions or objections raised by our companion in the conversation. But in writing we must respond to other writers and also to ourselves: Almost as soon as we think we know what we have to say, we may find that it won't do. If we're lucky, we may find a better idea surfacing. One of the best ways of getting ideas is to talk things over.

When it comes to writing, the process of "talking things over" usually begins with a dialogue between yourself and a text that you're reading: Your notes, your summary, and your annotations are a kind of dialogue between you and the author. You can also have a dialogue with classmates and friends about your topic to try out and develop ideas. You may be arguing, but not chiefly to persuade; rather, you're using argument to find the truth—testing ideas, playing the devil's advocate, speaking hypothetically. Through reading, taking notes, and talking, you may find that you have developed some clear ideas that can be put into writing. So you take up a sheet of blank paper, but then a paralyzing thought suddenly strikes: "I have ideas but just can't put them into words." The blank white page (or screen) stares back at you.

All writers, even professional ones, are familiar with this experience. Good writers know that waiting for inspiration is usually not the best strategy. You may be waiting a long time. The best thing to do is begin. Recall some of what we said in Chapter 1: *Writing is a way of thinking*. It's a way of *getting and developing ideas*. *Argument* is an instrument of inquiry as well as persuasion. It is an important *method* of *critical thinking*. It helps us clarify what we think. One reason we have trouble writing is our fear of putting ourselves on record, but another reason is our fear that we have no ideas worth putting down. However, by writing notes—or even free associations—and by writing a draft, no matter how weak, we can begin to think our way toward good ideas.

When you are planning an argument, talking with others can help, but sometimes there isn't time to chat live. Take advantage of the tools at your disposal. Use the internet, including your email, social media, search engines, blogs, and wikis, to involve yourself in the conversation. Posting on social media or writing a blog entry in a public space about your topic can foster conversations about the topic and help you discover what others think—and your own opinions. Using the internet to uncover and refine a topic is common practice, especially early in the brainstorming process.

Three Brainstorming Strategies: Freewriting, Listing, and Diagramming

If you are facing an issue, debate, or topic and don't know what to write, it is likely because you don't yet know what you think. If, after talking about the topic with yourself (via your reading notes) and others (via any means), you are still unclear on what you think, try one of three strategies: freewriting, listing, or diagramming.

Freewriting   Write for five or six minutes, nonstop, without censoring what you produce. You may use what you write to improve your thinking. You may even dim your computer screen so you won't be tempted to look up and fiddle too soon with what you've just written. Once you have spent the time writing out your ideas, you can use what you've written to look further into the subject at hand.

Freewriting should be totally free. As a topic, let's imagine the writer below is thinking about how children's toys are constructed for different genders. The student is reflecting on the release of the Nerf Rebelle, a type of toy gun made specifically for girls. A good freewrite might look like this:

> FREEWRITING: Nerf released a new toy made for girls, the Nerf
> Rebelle gun. It was an attempt the company made to offer toys
> for girls that have been traditionally made for boys. This seems
> good — showing an effort toward equality between the sexes. Or is

Nerf just trying to broaden its market and sell more toys (after all, boys are only half the population)? Or is it both? That could be my central question. But it is not like the gun is gender-neutral. It is pink and purple and has feminine-looking designs on it. And with its "elle" ending the gun sounds small, cute, and girly. Does this toy represent true equality between the sexes, or does it just offer more in the way of feminine stereotypes? It shoots foam arrows, unlike the boys' version of the gun, which shoots bullets. This suggests Cupid, maybe — a figure whose arrows inspire love. A stereotype that girls aren't saving the world with their weapons but seeking love and marriage. What kind of messages does this send to young girls? Is it the same message suggested by the gun? How does this work in other areas of life, like business and politics?

Notice that the writer here is jumping around, generating and exploring ideas while writing. Later she can return to the freewriting and begin organizing her ideas and observations. Notice that right in the middle of the freewriting she made a connection between the toy and Cupid, and by extension to the larger culture in which forms of contemporary femininity can be found. This connection seems significant, and it may help the student to broaden her argument from a critique of the company's motives early on, to a more evidence-based piece about assumptions underlying certain trends in consumer and media culture. The point is that freewriting in this case led to new paths of inquiry and may have inspired further research into different kinds of toys and media.

Listing   Writing down keywords, just as you do when making a shopping list, is another way of generating ideas. When you make a shopping list, you write *ketchup*, and the act of writing it reminds you that you also need hamburger rolls — and *that* in turn reminds you that you also need tuna fish. Similarly, when preparing a list of ideas for a paper, just writing down one item will often generate another. Of course, when you look over the list, you'll probably drop some of these ideas — the dinner menu will change — but you'll be making progress. If you have a smartphone or tablet, use it to write down your thoughts. You can even email these notes to yourself so you can access them later, or you can store them digitally in the cloud.

Here's an example of a student listing questions and making associations that could help him focus on a specific argument within a larger debate. The subject here is whether prostitution should be legalized. Key terms are underlined.

LIST: Prostitutes & Law

What types of <u>prostitutes</u> exist?

How has the law traditionally <u>policed</u> sex in history and in different places?

How many prostitutes are arrested every year?

<u>Individual rights</u> vs. <u>public good</u>?

Why shouldn't people be allowed to <u>sell</u> sex?

Could prostitution be <u>taxed</u>?

Who gains or suffers most from <u>enforcement</u>? From legalization?

If it were legal, could its negative effects be better <u>controlled</u>?

Aren't "escort services" really <u>prostitution rings</u> for people with <u>more money</u>?

Who goes into the "oldest business" and why?

Notice that the student doesn't really know the answers yet but is asking questions by free-associating and seeing what turns up as a productive line of analysis. The questions range from the definition of prostitution to its effects, and they might inspire the student to do some basic internet research or even deeper research. Once you make a list, see if you can observe patterns or similarities among the items you listed or if you invented a question worthy of its own thesis statement (e.g., "The enforcement of prostitution laws hurts *X* group unequally, and it uses a lot of public money that could better be used in other areas or toward regulating the trade rather than jailing people").

Diagramming   Sketching a visual representation of an essay is a kind of listing. Three methods of diagramming are especially common.

CLUSTERING   As we discuss on pages 10–11, you can make an effective cluster by writing, in the middle of a sheet of paper, a word or phrase summarizing your topic (e.g., *fracking*, the process of forcing high pressure into rock to extract natural resources; see diagram), circling it, and then writing down and circling a related word or idea (e.g., *energy independence*). You then circle these phrases and continue jotting down ideas, making connections, and indicating relationships. Here, the economic and environmental impacts of fracking seem to be the focus. Whether you realize it or not, an argument is taking shape.

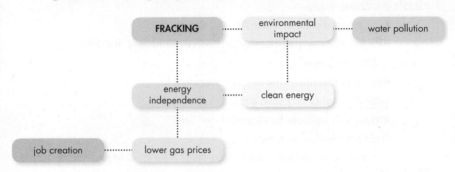

BRANCHING Some writers find it useful to draw a tree, moving from the central topic to the main branches (chief ideas) and then to the twigs (aspects of the chief ideas).

COMPARING IN COLUMNS Draw a line down the middle of the page and then set up two columns showing oppositions. For instance, if you are concerned with the environmental and economic impacts of fracking, you might produce columns that look something like this:

Environmental	Economic
water pollution	employment
chemicals used	independence from unstable oil-producing countries
gas leaks	cheaper fuel
toxic waste	cheaper electricity

All these methods can, of course, be executed with pen and paper, but you may also be able to use them on your computer, depending on the capabilities of your software. You might also find templates from a good website helpful.

EXERCISE: BRAINSTORMING

Consider these topics by using freewriting, listing, or diagramming:

- What is the biggest threat to national security today?
- Should your college require students to study a foreign language?
- Should monuments to Confederate leaders be removed from public spaces?

Revision as Invention

Whether you're using a computer or a pen, you may put down some words and almost immediately see that they need improvement, not simply a little polishing but a substantial overhaul. You write, "Race should be counted in college admissions for two reasons," and as soon as you write those words, a third reason comes to mind. Or perhaps one of those "two reasons" no longer seems very good. As E. M. Forster said, "How can I know what I think till I see what I say?" We have to see what we say—we have to get something down on the page—before we realize that we need to make it better.

Writing, then, is really **rewriting**—that is, **revising**—and a revision is a *re-vision*, a second look. The essay that you submit—whether as hard copy or as digital file—should be clear and may appear to be effortlessly composed, but in all likelihood the clarity and apparent ease are the result of a struggle with yourself during which you refined your first thoughts. You begin by putting down ideas, perhaps in random order, but sooner or later comes the job of looking at them critically, developing what's useful in them and removing what isn't. If you follow this procedure, you will be in the company of Picasso, who said that he "advanced by means of destruction." Any passages that you cut or destroy can be kept in another file in case you want to revisit those deletions later. Sometimes, you end up restoring them and developing what you discarded into a new essay with a new direction.

Whether you advance bit by bit (writing a sentence, revising it, writing the next, etc.) or whether you write an entire first draft and then revise it and revise it again and again is chiefly a matter of temperament. Probably most people combine both approaches, backing up occasionally but trying to get to the end fairly soon so that they can see rather quickly what they know, or think they know, and can then start the real work of thinking, of converting their initial ideas into something substantial.

Asking Questions with Stasis Theory

Generating ideas, we said when talking about **topics** and invention strategies in Chapter 1 (p. 20), is mostly a matter of asking (and then thinking about) questions. In this book, we include questions at the end of each argumentative essay not to torment you, but to help you think about the arguments—for instance, to turn your attention to especially important matters. If your instructor asks you to write an answer to one of these questions, you are lucky: Examining the question will stimulate your mind to work in a specific direction.

Another method of using your own questions is to use **stasis theory**, an invention process used by ancient rhetoricians like Aristotle and Cicero to work through a topic and find what facts and judgments "hold." (*Stasis* means something like "stability," so you can image the process as leading you to what is true about a topic or issue.) If your instructor doesn't assign a topic for an argumentative essay, you'll find that some ideas may be generated by applying the four key questions of stasis theory. These four questions, for the ancients, sought to establish the facts, the meaning, the importance, and the action needed in a given situation. We present an example of using stasis theory below.

First, consider these questions in general:

1. What is *X*? (*definition*)
2. What is the value or seriousness of *X*? (*quality*)
3. What are the causes (or the consequences) of *X*? (*fact*)
4. What should (or could or must) we do about *X*? (*policy*)

Let's spend a moment looking at each of these questions.

1. *What is* X?   Suppose your topic was capital punishment; *defining* what that is could be its own argument, although you would certainly want to go beyond saying simply, "Capital punishment is the legally authorized killing of a person." That does not need to be argued. Similarly, we can hardly argue about which states utilize capital punishment and which do not, or about how many people have been sentenced to death in the United States in the past ten years—a glance at the appropriate reports will answer those questions. You might instead define the uses, limits, evolution, or means of capital punishment as administered in the United States. Which uses might constitute cruel and unusual punishment? How has the death penalty changed over time, and what does that say about a changing society? Is the death penalty discriminatory? Your definition does not necessarily have to argue that it should or should not be abolished, or that it should or should not be applied fairly. You might be doing enough just by establishing a clear definition of the topic and its problems. An argument about abortion, for example, might concentrate strictly on the definition of a "person" or of the "viability" of a fetus, or even the definition of "when life begins." Arguments of this sort may make a claim—and may take a stand—but they do not also have to argue for an action. You may establish a clear definition of the problem and leave it to others for possible responses.

2. *What is the value or seriousness of X?* Assessing the value of a topic or issue is thinking about its meaning and how it reflects or relates to a larger significance, whether personal, social, political, religious, and so on. Why should a general audience of American readers care about your examination of the death penalty? Why should your target audience—lawyers, Catholics, general voters, or whomever—care? What is the *seriousness* of discrimination in the criminal justice system? What morals, values, or principles are at stake? An essay offering this kind of evaluation normally has two purposes:

- to set forth an assessment
- to convince readers that the assessment is reasonable

In writing an evaluation, you have to rely on criteria, and these will vary depending on your topic. What criteria serve best in making an evaluation? Probably some or all of the following:

- testimony of authorities
- inductive evidence
- appeals to logic ("it follows, therefore, that . . .")
- appeals to emotion

> **WRITING TIP** College courses often call for arguments about art and literature. In writing an evaluation, you have to rely on criteria particular to literature. For instance, in comparing the artistic merit of plays by Tennessee Williams and Arthur Miller, you may want to talk about the quality of the characterization, the importance of the theme, and so on.

3. *What are the causes (or the consequences) of* X?   When you ask about the causes and consequences of an issue, you are assessing the real or conjectured facts of the matter. Think about this in relation to the topic of capital punishment: You might look at what the actual or probable effects are (or would be) for various groups of people either personally affected or professionally interested in this aspect of our justice system.

Consider also this example concerning the academic performance of girls in single-sex schools. It is pretty much agreed (based on statistical evidence) that the graduates of these schools do better, as a group, than girls who graduate from coeducational schools. But why? What is the *cause*? Administrators of girls' schools usually attribute the success to the fact that their classrooms offer an atmosphere free from male intimidation: Girls allegedly gain confidence and become more expressive without the presence of boys. This may be the answer, but skeptics have attributed the graduates' success to two other causes:

- Most single-sex schools require parents to pay tuition, and it is a documented fact that the children of well-to-do parents do better, academically, than the children of poorer parents.

- Most single-sex schools are selective private schools whose students are chosen based upon academic promise — that is, students who have *already done well academically*.

The lesson? Be cautious in attributing a cause. There may be multiple causes and factors.

The kinds of support that usually accompany claims of consequence and cause include the following:

- factual data, especially statistics
- analogies ("The Roman Empire declined because of *X* and *Y*; our society exhibits *X* and *Y*; therefore . . .")
- inductive evidence

4. *What should (or could or must) we do about* X?   Whether you end up arguing that a problem exists to identify it, diagnose its larger importance, or demonstrate its unfortunate consequences, you may find yourself in a position to recommend a partial or full solution to the problem. What action should be taken, and by whom? Continuing our example, should the death penalty be abolished? Should parents change the ways they discipline their children? Should the law allow eighteen-year-olds to drink alcohol? Should eighteen-year-old women be required to register for Selective Service? Should steroid use by athletes be banned? These questions involve conduct and policy; how you answer them will reveal your values and principles.

(See the Visual Guide: Organizing Your Argument on p. 224 for an example of how an argument of policy might be structured.)

Support for claims of policy usually include the following:

- statistics
- testimony of authorities
- appeals to common sense and to the reader's moral sense

Again, an argument may be entirely based on one, two, three, or all of the four basic questions discussed in this section. Someone interested in analyzing the debate over censorship of fake news may construct the argument exclusively about what fake news *is* (a question of definition); about the *seriousness* of fake news in a democratic society (a question of quality); about how efforts to curb fake news limit free speech (a question of fact); or that some entity or institution, such as the US government or Facebook, should act to limit fake news (a question of policy). Of course, all of these questions could also be combined in a more comprehensive argument.

As you work through various questions and discover your argument, keep in mind that other elements of critical thinking and argument we have discussed up to this point are still relevant. You should still address different perspectives and possible objections to your ideas—counterarguments—and refute them if possible. Most of all, you should be careful to support your ideas with carefully selected evidence and examples.

WRITING TIP If a question seems relevant or a piece of evidence inspires new questions and answers in your mind, it's a good idea to start writing — even just fragmentary sentences if necessary. You'll probably find that one idea leads to another and that new questions and issues begin to appear. Even if your ideas seem weak as you write them, don't be discouraged; you will have put something on paper, and returning to these words, perhaps in five minutes or even the next day, you'll probably find that some ideas aren't at all bad and may stimulate even better ones.

The Thesis or Main Point

Let's assume that you are writing an argumentative essay — perhaps an evaluation of an argument in this book — and you have what seems to be a pretty good draft or at least a collection of notes that are the result of hard thinking. You really do have ideas now, and you want to present them effectively. How will you organize your essay? No one formula works best for every essayist and for every essay, but it is usually advisable to formulate a basic **thesis** (a claim, a central point, a chief position) and to state it early. Every essay that is any good, even a book-length one, has a thesis (a main point), which can be stated briefly, usually in one sentence. Remember Calvin Coolidge's alleged remark to his wife on the preacher's sermon on sin: "He was against it." Don't confuse the **topic** (sin) with the thesis (sin is bad). The thesis is the argumentative theme, the author's primary claim or contention, the proposition that the rest of the essay will explain and defend. Of course, the thesis may sound commonplace, but the book or essay or sermon ought to develop it in an interesting and convincing way.

When you formulate a thesis and ask questions about it — such as who the readers are, what they believe, what they know, and what they need to know — you also begin to get ideas about how to organize the material (or, at least, you realize that you'll have to work out some sort of organization). The thesis may be clear and simple, but the reasons (the argument) may take many pages. The thesis is the point; the argument sets forth the evidence that supports the thesis.

Raising the Stakes of Your Thesis   Imagine walking across campus and coming upon a person ready to perform on a tightrope suspended between two buildings. He is wearing a glittering leotard and is eyeing up his challenge very seriously. Here's the thing, though: His tightrope is only *one foot off the ground*. Would you stop and watch him walk across it? Maybe, maybe not. Most people are likely to take a look and move on. If you did spend a few minutes watching, you wouldn't be very worried about the performer falling. If he lost his balance momentarily, you wouldn't gasp in horror. And if he walked across the tightrope masterfully, you might be somewhat impressed but not enraptured.

Now imagine the rope being *a hundred feet off the ground*. You and many others would almost certainly stop and witness the feat. The audience would likely be captivated, nervous about the performer potentially falling, "oohing" if he momentarily lost his balance, and cheering if he crossed the rope successfully.

Considering thesis statements as tightropes strung at different heights can help you consider the stakes of your argument.

Consider the tightrope as your thesis statement, the performer as writer, and the act of crossing as the argument. What we call "low-stakes" thesis statements are comparable to low tightropes: A low-stakes thesis statement itself may be interesting, but not much about it is vital to any particular audience. Low-stakes thesis statements lack a sense of importance or relevance. They may restate what is already widely known and accepted, or they may make a good point but not discuss any consequences. Some examples:

Good nutrition and exercise can lead to a healthy life.

Our education system focuses too much on standardized tests.

Children's beauty pageants are exploitative.

Students can write well-organized, clear, and direct papers on these topics, but if the thesis is "low stakes" like these, the performance would be similar to that of an expert walking across a tightrope that is only one foot off the ground. The argument may be well executed, but few in the audience will be inspired by it.

However, if you raise the stakes by "raising the tightrope," you can compel readers to *want* to read and keep reading. There are several ways to raise the tightrope. First, *think about what is socially, culturally, or politically important* about your thesis statement and argument. Some writing instructors tell students to ask themselves "So what?" about the thesis, but this can be a vague directive. Here are some better questions:

- Why is your thesis important?
- What is the impact of your thesis on a particular group or demographic?
- What are the consequences of what you claim?
- What could happen if your position were *not* recognized?
- How can your argument benefit readers or compel them to action (by doing something or adopting a new belief)?
- What will readers *gain* by accepting your argument as convincing?

In formulating your thesis, keep in mind the following points.

- *Different thesis statements may speak to different target audiences.* An argument about changes in estate tax laws may not thrill all audiences, but for a defined group—accountants, lawyers, or the elderly, for instance—it may be quite controversial and highly relevant.

- *Not all audiences are equal—or equally interested in your thesis or argument.* In this book, we generally select topics of broad importance. However, in a literature course, a film history course, or a political science course, you'll calibrate your thesis statements and arguments to an audience that is invested in those fields. In writing about the steep decline in bee populations, your argument might look quite different if you're speaking to ecologists as opposed to gardeners. (We will discuss audience more in the following section.)

- *Be wary of compare-and-contrast arguments.* One of the most basic approaches to writing is to compare and contrast, a maneuver that produces a low-tightrope thesis. It normally looks like this: "*X* and *Y* are similar in some ways and different in others." But if you think about it, *anything* can be compared and contrasted in this way, and doing so doesn't necessarily *tell* anything important. So, if you're writing a compare-and-contrast paper, make sure to include the reasons why it is important to compare and contrast these things. What benefit does the comparison yield? What significance does it have to some audience or some issue?

THINKING CRITICALLY "WALKING THE TIGHTROPE"

Examine the low-stakes thesis statements provided below and expand each one into a high-stakes thesis by including the importance of asserting it and by proposing a possible response. The first one has been done as an example.

Low-Stakes Thesis	High-Stakes Thesis
Good nutrition and exercise can lead to a healthy life.	One way to help solve the epidemic obesity problem in the United States is to remind consumers of a basic fact accepted by nearly all reputable health experts: Good nutrition and exercise can lead to a healthy life.
Every qualified American should vote.	
Spanking children is good/bad.	
Electric cars will reduce air pollution.	

A CHECKLIST FOR A THESIS STATEMENT

☐ Does the statement make an arguable assertion rather than (1) merely assert an unarguable fact, (2) merely announce a topic, or (3) declare an unarguable opinion or belief?

☐ Is the statement broad enough to cover the entire argument that I will be presenting, and is it narrow enough for me to cover the topic in the space allotted?

☐ Does the thesis have consequences beneficial to some audience or consequences that would be detrimental if it were not accepted? (In other words, are there stakes?)

Imagining an Audience

Raising the tightrope of your thesis will also require you to imagine the *audience* you're addressing. The questions that you ask yourself in generating thoughts on a topic will primarily relate to the topic, but additional questions that consider the audience are always relevant:

- Who are my readers?
- What do they believe?
- What common ground do we share?
- What do I want my readers to believe?
- What do they need to know?
- Why should they care?

Let's think about these questions. The literal answer to the first probably is "my teacher," but (unless you receive instructions to the contrary) you should not write specifically for your teacher. Instead, you should write for an audience that is, generally speaking, like your classmates. In short, your imagined audience is literate, intelligent, and moderately well informed, but its members don't know everything that you know, and they don't know your response to the problem being addressed. Your audience needs more information along those lines to make an intelligent decision about the issue.

For example, in writing about how children's toys shape the minds of young boys and girls differently, it may not be enough to simply say, "Toys are part of the gender socialization process." ("Sure they are," the audience might already agree.) However, if you raise the stakes based on who your intended audience is and the audience's level of intelligence, you have an opportunity to direct a more complex argument that results from this observation: You frame the questions, lay out the issues, identify the problems, and note the complications that arise because of your basic thesis. You could point out that toys have a significant impact on the interests, identities, skills, and capabilities that children develop and carry into adulthood. Because toys are so significant, is it important to ask questions about whether they perpetuate gender-based stereotypes? Do toys help perpetuate social inequalities between the sexes? Most children think toys are "just fun," but they may be teaching kids to conform unthinkingly to the social expectations of their sex, to accept designated sex-based social roles, and to cultivate talents differently based on sex. What we want you to see is that asking broader questions about the implications of your argument extends it further and gives it social importance to make it relevant to your audience.

> **WRITING TIP** If you wish to persuade, finding premises that you share with your audience can help establish common ground, a function of *ethos*.

What audiences should be concerned with your topic? Maybe you're addressing the general public who buys toys for children at least some of the time. Maybe you're addressing parents who are raising young children. Maybe you're addressing consumer advocates, encouraging them to pressure toy manufacturers and retailers to produce more gender-neutral offerings. The point is that your essay should contain (and sustain) an assessment of the impact of your high-stakes thesis, and it should set out a clear course of action for a particular audience.

That said, if you know your audience well, you can argue for different courses of action that are most likely to be persuasive. You may not be very convincing if you argue to parents in general that they should avoid all Disney-themed toys. Perhaps you should argue simply that parents should be conscious of the gender messages that toys convey, offer their kids diverse toys, and talk to their children while playing with them about alternatives to the stereotypical messages that the toys convey. However, if you're writing for a magazine called *Radical Parenting* and your essay is titled "Buying Toys the Gender-Neutral Way," your audience and its expectations—therefore, your thesis and argument—may look far different. The bottom line is not just to know your audience but to define it.

The essays in this book are from many different sources with many different audiences. An essay from the *New York Times* addresses educated general readers; an essay from *Ms.* magazine targets readers sympathetic to feminism. An essay from *Commonweal*, a Roman Catholic publication for nonspecialists, is likely to differ in point of view or tone from one in *Time*, even though both articles may advance approximately the same position. The *Commonweal* article may, for example, effectively cite church fathers and distinguished Roman Catholic writers as authorities, whereas the *Time* article would probably cite few or none of these figures because a non-Catholic audience might be unfamiliar with them or, even if familiar, might be unimpressed by their views.

The tone as well as the gist of the argument is in some degree shaped by the audience. For instance, popular journals, such as *National Review* and *Ms.* magazine, are more likely to use ridicule than are journals chiefly addressed to, say, an academic audience.

Instructors sometimes tell students to imagine their audience as their classmates. What they probably mean is that your argument should be addressed to people invested in the world of ideas, not just your literal classmates. Again, ask yourself the following questions:

- What do my readers need to know?
- What do I want them to believe?

EXERCISE: IMAGINING YOUR AUDIENCE

Consider one of the four topics below and write your responses to each question for your chosen topic.

Animal intelligence / Free college tuition / Screen time / Minimum wage

1. Who are my readers?
2. What do they believe?
3. What common ground do we share?
4. What do I want my readers to believe?
5. What do they need to know?
6. Why should they care?

Addressing Opposition and Establishing Common Ground

Presumably, your imagined audience does not share all your views. But why? By putting yourself into your readers' shoes—and your essay will almost surely summarize the views that you're going to speak against—and by thinking about what your audience knows or thinks it knows, you will also generate ideas. Ask yourself:

- Why does your audience not share your views? What views do they hold?
- How can these readers hold a position that to you seems unreasonable?

You may also spend time online reviewing websites dedicated to your topic to discover facts and assess common views and opinions.

Let's assume that you believe the minimum wage should be raised, but you know that some people hold a different view. Why do they hold it? Try to state their view *in a way that would be satisfactory to them*. Having done so, you may perceive that your conclusions and theirs differ because they're based on different premises—perhaps different ideas about how the economy works—or different definitions, concepts, or assumptions about fairness or employment. Examine the opposition's premises carefully and explain, first to yourself (and ultimately to your readers), why you see things differently.

A protest for a higher minimum wage.

Perhaps some facts are in dispute, such as whether or not an oil pipeline poses a serious threat to the local ecology. The thing to do, then, is to check the facts. If you search online on a reputable website or in a database and find that environmental harms have not been common in cases of other pipelines, yet you are still against one in your own area, you can't premise your argument on the harm the pipeline is likely to cause. You'll have to develop an argument that takes account of the facts and interprets them reasonably.

Among the relevant facts there surely are some that your audience or your opponent will not dispute. The same is true of the values relevant to the discussion; both sides very likely believe in some of the same values. These areas of shared agreement are crucial to effective persuasion in argument.

There are two good reasons for identifying and isolating the areas of agreement:

- There is no point in disputing facts or values on which you and your readers already agree.

- It usually helps establish goodwill between yourself and your opponent when you can point to shared beliefs, assumptions, facts, and values.

Recall that in composing college papers it's usually best to write for a general audience, an audience rather like your classmates but without the specific knowledge that they all share as students enrolled in one course. If the topic is raising the minimum wage, the audience presumably consists of supporters and nonsupporters, as well as people who hold no opinion at all (*yet*, perhaps, until they read your ideas). Thinking "What do readers need to know?" may prompt you to give statistics about the rising cost of living and the number of people who make just the minimum wage. Or if you're arguing against raising the minimum wage, it may prompt you to cite studies showing how doing so increases the cost of goods and the rate of unemployment. If you are writing for a general audience, asking "What does the audience believe?" is important because many people will not be familiar with the basic facts about the minimum wage and the implications of raising it. You will likely be painting with broad strokes, arguing from the widest possible perspectives. But if the audience is specialized, such as a group of economists, a union group, or a sector of small business owners who fear that rate hikes will interfere with their business, an effective essay will have to address their special beliefs.

In addressing the beliefs of your likely opponents, you must try to establish some common ground. If you advocate for the minimum wage hike, you should recognize the possibility that this represents a threat to some proprietors of small businesses. But perhaps you can argue that increases in the minimum wage typically result in more spending at small businesses, which would be good for small business owners in the long run. This is how your thoughts in imagining an audience can prompt you to think of other kinds of evidence — perhaps testimony or statistics on this issue, for example.

✓ A CHECKLIST FOR IMAGINING AN AUDIENCE

- ☐ Have I identified my readers as a general or more specific audience?
- ☐ Do I understand how much my readers need to be told based on what I believe they already know?
- ☐ Have I provided necessary background (including definitions of special terms) if the imagined readers probably are not especially familiar with the topic?
- ☐ Am I able to identify whether or not my readers are likely to be neutral, sympathetic, or hostile to my views?

  - ☐ For neutral audience members, have I offered good reasons to persuade them?

  - ☐ If they're sympathetic, have I done more than merely reaffirm their present beliefs? That is, have I perhaps enriched their views or encouraged them to act?

  - ☐ If they're hostile, will they nevertheless feel respected and informed by my position? Have I taken account of their positions and recognized their strengths but also called attention to their limitations? Have I offered a position that might persuade them to modify their position?

DRAFTING AND REVISING AN ARGUMENT

There is no one way to begin writing. As we have suggested earlier in this chapter, sometimes the best way to get started writing is just to start writing, building ideas, and seeing where your pen (or keyboard) takes you. But, alas, at a certain point, you will want to begin organizing your essay more deliberately, considering your purpose, audience, language, and the organization of your ideas.

The Title

One of the first things you might do in planning an argument is invent a **title**, where you can announce the thesis or topic explicitly, or simply attract the attention of readers in a unique or imaginative way. If you examine the titles of essays in this book, you can see titles that announce their positions and topics both more and less explicitly than others:

> "We Must Make Public Colleges and Universities Tuition-Free" (announces thesis)
>
> "The Boston Photographs" (announces topic)
>
> "A First Amendment Junkie" (invites readers' curiosity)

Be prepared to rethink your title *after* completing the last draft of your paper. A working title can help guide your inquiry, but do not hesitate to rethink your title after you have written your argument to ensure it accurately represents your position and analysis.

> **WRITING TIP** It's better to invent a simple, direct, informative title than a strained, puzzling, or overly cute one. You want to engage readers, not turn them off.

The Opening Paragraphs

Opening paragraphs are difficult to write, so don't worry about writing an effective opening when you're drafting. Just get some words down on paper and keep going. But when you revise your first draft, you should begin to think seriously about the effect of your opening.

A good introduction arouses readers' interest and prepares them for the rest of the paper. How? One convenient method of writing an introduction is to offer a "hook" first—something to simultaneously attract the reader and set the stage for the essay. The following table lists some strategies for opening paragraphs.

Hook	Description	Example
Anecdote	A brief story or vignette	I was having lunch recently in the newly built food court, and I noticed the word *organic* on my package of carrots, and I began to wonder . . .
Statistic	A relevant (sobering, shocking, attention-grabbing) number	According to a 2017 Common Sense Media report, American children between the ages of 0 and 8 spend an average of 2.25 hours per day of "screen time" . . .
Noteworthy event	A recent news story, real-life account, or interesting illustration of the current situation	When the president said this year in his State of the Union address that more must be done for the nation's infrastructure, he touched on an issue that . . .
Analogy	A case similar in structure but different in detail from the point being established	When a leopard stalks its prey, it can spend a full day establishing a prime ambush position, then all at once dart at over 35 miles per hour and jump over 20 feet to close the deal. This is something like . . .
Quotation	Wise, poignant, or landmark words framing your discussion	In 1903, W. E. B. Du Bois said in *The Souls of Black Folk* that "the problem of the twentieth century is the problem of the color line." In the twenty-first century, . . .
Historical account	A brief account of the background or evolution of the topic	The evolution of the monster movie extends from early films such as *Nosferatu* (1922) and *The Hunchback of Notre Dame* (1923) to today's renditions such as *The Babadook* (2014) and *Slenderman* (2018). In that evolution, we can see . . .

You may set your hook quickly, provide a more elaborate version, or even combine the strategies listed in the table. In addition to grabbing readers' attention, opening paragraphs also usually do at least one (and often all) of the following:

- prepare readers for the topic (naming the topic, giving some idea of its importance, noting conventional beliefs about it, or relaying in brief what people are saying about it)
- provide readers with definitions of key terms and concepts (stipulating, quoting an authority, etc.)
- establish a context for your argument by linking your subject, topic, and views to relevant social issues, debates, and trends
- reveal the thesis
- provide readers a map of the argument (giving a sense of how the essay will be organized)

You may not wish to announce your thesis in the title, but if you don't announce it there, you should set it forth early in the argument, in the introductory paragraph or paragraphs. Although it is possible for the thesis to be blurted out in the first line, usually writers spend some time preparing the argument before providing the thesis. And although it is possible never to state the thesis directly but only imply it throughout the argument, thesis statements may also be bold and daring.

Another thing you can do in an introduction is spend some time outlining the general subject into which your topic fits. The subject is the general area in which your questions and research reside, whereas your specific topic might be narrower. For example, the subject of your paper may be workers' rights, or immigration, or national security, but your topic will usually be something that falls within that subject — the minimum wage, or the border wall, or WikiLeaks, for example. You may go to great lengths to frame your topic within a subject, or you may just mention it, but it usually helps to position your discussion in a larger framework.

> **WRITING TIP** If your argument will be written or published online, you might establish a context for your argument by linking to a news video that outlines the topic, or you might offer your thesis and then link to a news story that supports your claim. (Remember that using any videos, images, or links also requires a citation of some kind.)

After announcing the topic, giving the necessary background and context, and stating your position in as engaging a manner as possible, you will do well to give the reader an idea of *how* you will proceed — that is, how the essay will be organized. It is not a requirement that all writers must state exactly what they will be doing in each part of their essay — and in fact, it may not be an effective strategy for certain audiences and purposes. Nevertheless, at any point in your introduction, you may announce that there are, say, four common objections to your thesis and that you will take them up one by one. You could add that you will move from the weakest (or most widely held) to the strongest (or least familiar), after which you will advance your own view in greater detail. Or you might announce that three primary views of an issue exist, and you will spell them out before moving on.

Not every writer states plans like this outright. But if your analysis is methodical and perhaps complex, you can tell readers where you will be taking them and by what route. In effect, you are giving them a look at your own outline. How far you go to clue the reader in to your method of analysis is up to you, just as it is up to you to decide how much background, context, definition, and so on you include. Ultimately, these decisions will impact the length and style of your introduction and set the foundations for the rest of your argument.

It is important to note that all the elements of introductions we have laid out so far do not have to be included categorically or in a formulaic way. You might do more background work, you might provide a very detailed account of competing perspectives in order to position yourself within a debate, you might offer both an anecdote and a statistic, or you might combine some elements and leave out others. The following introduction has been annotated to show the writer's choices.

Hooks reader with a dramatic statistic.

According to a 2017 Common Sense Media report, American children between the ages of 0 and 8 spend an average of 2.25 hours per day involved in "screen time," a term used to denote the total time a child spends in front of any visual electronic media, whether television, video game, or internet. If that is correct, then children are spending a whopping 34 days — a full month and then some — each year on "screens." The debate over how much screen time is appropriate for children, and what its ultimate effects are on children's development, has been lively in the fully connected digital world. But since the advent of the iPhone

Defines a ke term.

Author inserts her own voice to express concern.

Contextualizes the debate abou screen time

in 2007, the debate has heated up even more. One group of investors, JANA Partners, recently worried about the "toxic" effects of the current levels of screen time on children, and others have correlated increasing levels of anxiety and depression in children with high levels of internet usage. To understand the potential impact of screen time on children, and what may be done about it, it is important first to examine what kinds of screen time might be positive or negative. As I will show, some kinds of screen time act as positive influences in children's life, increasing children's creativity and in some instances sociability. While there may be negative impacts to some kinds of "screen time" or too much "screen time" (even with positive or educational media), if parents and educators understand more about how to select and control children's media usage, we can work toward a practical solution in a society where these kinds of technologies are not likely to disappear.

-ovides a ¬ap" of how ╌e analysis ╌ll proceed.

Concedes to possible counter-points, but enters into the conversation with a relevant, impactful thesis.

Organizing the Body of the Essay

We begin with a wise remark by a newspaper columnist, Robert Cromier: "The beautiful part of writing is that you don't have to get it right the first time—unlike, say, a brain surgeon."

In drafting an essay, you will, of course, begin with an organization that seems appropriate, but you may find, in rereading the draft, that some other organization is better. For a start, in the Visual Guide: Organizing Your Argument, we offer three types of organization that are common in argumentative essays. Please note, however, that we do not mean to suggest that essays should be formulaic. These general structures need to be considered alongside your argument's needs to present counterpoints at the appropriate times, to relate an anecdote in the middle of things, or to introduce shorter summaries of others' arguments. Occasionally, these items warrant new paragraphs. The best writers know how to manage structure and how to go down little rabbit holes to explore a point further (perhaps with an analogy, anecdote, or example) but without being *digressive*, departing too far from the main point.

Even if you were to adhere closely to the patterns, you have a lot of room for variation. But let's assume that in the introductory paragraphs you have sketched the topic (and have shown, or implied, that the reader doubtless is interested in it) and have fairly and courteously set forth the opposition's view, recognizing its merits ("I grant that," "admittedly," "it is true that") and indicating the

Visual Guide: Organizing Your Argument

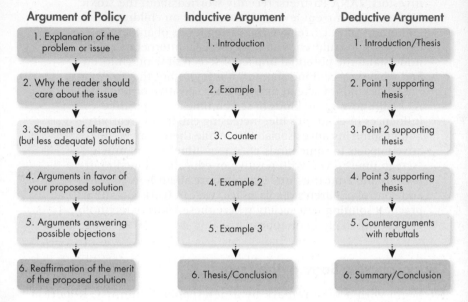

Argument of Policy	Inductive Argument	Deductive Argument
1. Explanation of the problem or issue	1. Introduction	1. Introduction/Thesis
2. Why the reader should care about the issue	2. Example 1	2. Point 1 supporting thesis
3. Statement of alternative (but less adequate) solutions	3. Counter	3. Point 2 supporting thesis
4. Arguments in favor of your proposed solution	4. Example 2	4. Point 3 supporting thesis
5. Arguments answering possible objections	5. Example 3	5. Counterarguments with rebuttals
6. Reaffirmation of the merit of the proposed solution	6. Thesis/Conclusion	6. Summary/Conclusion

degree to which you can share part of that view. You now want to set forth arguments explaining why you differ on some essentials.

In presenting your own position, you can begin with either your strongest or your weakest reasons. Each method of organization has advantages and disadvantages.

- If you begin with your strongest examples or reasons, your essay could impress your readers and then peter out, leaving them asking, "Is that all?"

- If you begin with your weakest material, you build to a climax, but readers may not still be with you because they may have felt that the beginning of the essay was frivolous or irrelevant.

The obvious solution is to ensure that even your weakest argument demonstrates strength. Yet because we are not always so fortunate to have equally strong reasons, you can always assure your readers explicitly how you are going to proceed. For example, you may go ahead and say that stronger points will soon follow and you offer this point first to show that you are aware of it and that, slight though it is, it deserves some attention. The body of the essay, then, is devoted to arguing a position in whatever ways you need to explain yourself best.

> **WRITING TIP** By acknowledging arguments other than your own — and possible objections to your points — you let readers know that you've done your homework and build their trust. You also have a chance to preempt critiques of your ideas, which helps you be more persuasive.

Doubtless you'll sometimes be uncertain, while drafting an essay, whether to present a given point before or after another point, or when you should explain why you are proceeding the way you are. When you write, and certainly when you revise, try to put yourself into the reader's shoes: Which point do you think the reader needs to know first? Which point *leads to* which further point? Your argument should not be a mere list of points; rather, it should clearly integrate one point with another in order to develop an idea and transition smoothly from one idea to the next. However, in all likelihood you won't have a strong sense of the best organization until you have written a draft and have reread it.

Checking Transitions   Make sure, in revising, that the reader can move easily from the beginning of a paragraph to the end and from one paragraph to the next. Transitions help signal the connections between units of the argument. For example ("For example" is a transition, indicating that an illustration will follow), they may illustrate, establish a sequence, connect logically, amplify, compare, contrast, summarize, or concede (see Thinking Critically: Using Transitions in Argument). Transitions serve as guideposts that enable the reader to move easily through your essay.

Bill Watterson/Universal Uclick

When writers revise an early draft, they chiefly do these tasks:

- They **unify** the essay by eliminating irrelevancies.
- They **organize** the essay by keeping in mind the imagined audience.
- They **clarify** the essay by fleshing out thin paragraphs, by ensuring that the transitions are adequate, and by making certain that generalizations are adequately supported by concrete details and examples.

We are not talking here about polish or elegance; we are talking about fundamental matters. Be especially careful not to abuse the logical connectives (*thus, as a result*, and so on). If you write several sentences followed by *therefore* or a similar word or phrase, be sure that what you write after the *therefore* really *does follow* from what has gone before. Logical connectives are not mere transitional devices that link disconnected bits of prose. They are supposed to mark a real movement of thought, which is the essence of an argument.

THINKING CRITICALLY USING TRANSITIONS IN ARGUMENT

Fill in examples of the types of transitions listed below, using topics of your choice. The first one has been done as an example.

Type of Transition	Type of Language Used	Example of Transition
Illustrate	*for example, for instance, consider this case*	"Many television crime dramas contain scenes of graphic violence. For example, in an episode of *Law and Order* . . ."
Establish a sequence	*a more important objection, a stronger example, the best reason*	
Connect logically	*thus, as a result, therefore, so, it follows*	
Amplify	*further, in addition to, moreover*	
Compare	*similarly, in a like manner, just as, analogously*	
Contrast	*on the one hand . . . on the other hand, but, in contrast, however*	
Summarize	*in short, briefly*	
Concede	*admittedly, granted, to be sure*	

The Ending

What about concluding paragraphs, in which you summarize the main points and reaffirm your position? A conclusion—the word comes from the Latin *claudere*, "to shut"—ought to provide a sense of closure, but it can be much more than a restatement of the writer's thesis. It can, for instance, make a quiet, emotional appeal by suggesting that the issue is important and that the ball is now in the reader's court.

If you can look back over your essay and add something that both enriches it and wraps it up, fine; but don't feel compelled to say, "Thus, in conclusion, I have argued *X*, *Y*, and *Z*, and I have refuted Jones." After all, *conclusion* can have two meanings: (1) ending, or finish, as the ending of a joke or a novel; or (2) judgment or decision reached after deliberation. Your essay should finish effectively (the first sense), but it need not announce a judgment (the second).

If the essay is fairly short, so that a reader can keep its general gist in mind, you may not need to restate your view. Just make sure that you have covered the ground and that your last sentence is a good one. Notice that the student essay presented later in this chapter (p. 237) doesn't end with a formal conclusion, although it ends conclusively, with a note of finality.

By "a note of finality" we do *not* mean a triumphant crowing. It's far better to end with the suggestion that you hope you have by now indicated why those who hold a different view may want to modify it and accept yours.

If you study the essays in this book or the editorials and op-ed pieces in a newspaper, you will notice that writers often provide a sense of closure by using one of the following devices:

- a return to something stated in the introduction
- a glance at the wider implications of the issue (i.e., what would happen if your solution were implemented or not)
- a hint toward unasked or answered questions that the audience might consider in light of the writer's argument (i.e., predict new questions or issues, and let them ring out at the end as guides to further thinking)
- a suggestion that the reader can take some specific action or do some further research (i.e., the ball is now in the reader's court)
- an anecdote that illustrates the thesis in an engaging way (i.e., a brief account, real or imagined, that brings your ideas into a visible form)
- a brief summary (i.e., a recap. But note that this sort of ending may seem unnecessary and tedious if the paper is short and the summary merely repeats what the writer has already said.)

Uses of an Outline

Outlines may seem rigid to many writers, especially to those who compose online, where we're accustomed to cutting, copying, moving, and deleting as we draft. You're probably familiar with the structure known as a **formal outline**. Major points are indicated by I, II, III; points within major points are indicated by A, B, C; divisions within A, B, C are indicated by 1, 2, 3; and so on. Thus:

> I. Arguments for opening all Olympic sports to professionals
>   A. Fairness
>   1. Some Olympic sports are already open to professionals.
>   2. Some athletes who really are not professionals are classified as professionals.
>   B. Quality (achievements would be higher)

However, an outline — whether you write it before drafting or use it to evaluate the organization of something you've already written — is meant to be a guide rather than a straitjacket.

The Outline as a Preliminary Guide   Some writers sketch an outline as soon as they think they know what they want to say, even before writing a first draft. This procedure can be helpful in planning a tentative organization, but remember that in revising a draft you'll likely generate some new ideas and have to modify the outline accordingly. A preliminary outline is chiefly useful as a means of getting going, not as a guide to the final essay.

The Outline as a Way of Checking a Draft   Whether or not you use a preliminary outline, we strongly suggest that after writing what you hope is your last draft, you make an outline of it; there is no better way of finding out whether the essay is well organized.

Go through the draft and write down the chief points in the order in which you make them. That is, prepare a table of contents — perhaps a phrase for each paragraph. Next, examine your notes to see what kind of sequence they reveal in your paper:

- Is the sequence reasonable? Can it be improved?
- Are any passages irrelevant?
- Does something important seem to be missing?

If no coherent structure or reasonable sequence clearly appears in the outline, the full prose version of your argument probably doesn't have any either. Therefore, produce another draft by moving things around, adding or subtracting paragraphs — cutting and pasting them into a new sequence, with transitions as needed — and then make another outline to see if the sequence now is satisfactory.

> ✓ A CHECKLIST FOR ORGANIZING AN ARGUMENT
>
> ☐ Does the introduction let the readers know where the author is taking them?
>
> > ☐ Does the introduction state the problem or issue?
> >
> > ☐ Does it state the claim (the thesis)?
> >
> > ☐ Does it suggest the organization of the essay, thereby helping the reader follow the argument?
>
> ☐ Do subsequent paragraphs support the claim?
>
> > ☐ Do they offer evidence?
> >
> > ☐ Do they face objections to the claim and offer reasonable responses?
> >
> > ☐ Do they indicate why the author's claim is preferable?
> >
> > ☐ Do transitions (signposts such as *Furthermore*, *In contrast*, and *Consider as an example*) guide the reader through the argument?
>
> ☐ Does the essay end effectively, with a paragraph (at most, two paragraphs) bringing a note of closure?

Tone and the Writer's Persona

Although this book is chiefly about argument in the sense of rational discourse — the presentation of reasons in support of a thesis or conclusion — the appeal to reason (*logos*) is only one form of persuasion, as we have shown in earlier chapters. Another form is the appeal to emotion (*pathos*) — to pity, for example — and a third form of persuasion is the appeal to the speaker's character (*ethos*). What Aristotle called the **ethical appeal** is the idea that effective speakers convey the suggestion that they are

- informed,
- intelligent,
- fair minded (persons of goodwill), and
- honest.

Because they are perceived as trustworthy, their words inspire confidence in their listeners. It is a fact that when reading an argument we're often aware of the *person* or *voice* behind the words, and our assent to the argument depends partly on the extent to which we share the speaker's assumptions and see the matter from his or her point of view—in short, the extent to which we can *identify* with the speaker.

How can a writer inspire the confidence that lets readers identify with him or her? First, the writer should possess the virtues Aristotle specified: intelligence or good sense, honesty, and benevolence or goodwill. As a Roman proverb puts it, "No one gives what he does not have." Still, possession of these qualities is not a guarantee that you will convey them in your writing. Like all other writers, you'll have to revise your drafts so that these qualities become apparent; stated more moderately, you'll have to revise so that nothing in the essay causes a reader to doubt your intelligence, honesty, and goodwill. A blunder in logic, a misleading quotation, a snide remark, even an error in spelling—all such slips can cause readers to withdraw their sympathy from the writer.

> **WRITING TIP** Present yourself so that readers see you as knowledgeable, honest, open-minded, and interested in helping them to think about the significance of an issue.

Of course, all good argumentative essays do not sound exactly alike; they do not all reveal the same speaker. Each writer develops his or her own voice, or (as literary critics and instructors call it) **persona**. (We discussed persona in more detail in Chapter 5, Examining the Author's Persona, pp. 181–82.) In fact, one writer may have several voices or personae, depending on the topic and the audience. The president of the United States delivering an address on the State of the Union has one persona; when chatting with a reporter at his summer home, he has another. This change is not a matter of hypocrisy. Different circumstances call for different language. As a French writer put it, there is a time to speak of "Paris" and a time to speak of "the capital of the nation." When Abraham Lincoln spoke at Gettysburg, he didn't say "Eighty-seven years ago"; instead, he intoned "Four score and seven years ago." We might say that just as some occasions required him to be the folksy Honest Abe during election campaigns, the occasion of the dedication of hallowed ground at Gettysburg, where so many Civil War soldiers lost their lives, required him to be formal and solemn—thus, as president of the United States he appropriately used biblical language.

When we talk about a writer's persona, we mean the way in which the writer presents his or her attitudes

- toward *the self,*
- toward *the audience,* and
- toward *the subject.*

Thus, if a writer says:

> I have thought long and hard about this subject, and I can say with assurance that . . .

we may feel that he is a self-satisfied egotist who probably is mouthing other people's opinions. Certainly he's mouthing clichés: "long and hard," "say with assurance."

Let's look at a subtler example of an utterance that reveals certain attitudes:

> President Nixon was hounded out of office by journalists.

The statement above conveys a respectful attitude toward Nixon ("President Nixon") and a hostile attitude toward the press (they are beasts, curs who "hounded" our elected leader). If the writer's attitudes were reversed, she might have said something like this:

> The press turned the searchlight on Tricky Dick's criminal shenanigans.

"Tricky Dick" and "criminal" are obvious enough, but notice that "shenanigans" also implies the writer's contempt for Nixon, and "turned the searchlight" suggests that the press is a source of illumination, a source of truth. The original version and the opposite version both say that the press was responsible for Nixon's resignation, but the original version ("President Nixon was hounded") conveys indignation toward journalists, whereas the revision conveys contempt for Nixon.

These two versions suggest two speakers who differ not only in their view of Nixon but also in their manner, including the seriousness with which they take themselves. Although the passage is very short, it seems to us that the first speaker conveys righteous indignation ("hounded"), whereas the second conveys amused contempt ("shenanigans"). To our ears, the tone, as well as the point, differs in the two versions.

Loaded Words   We are talking now about **loaded words**, which convey the writer's attitude and, through their connotations, seek to win the reader to the writer's side. Compare the words in the left-hand column with those in the right:

freedom fighter	terrorist
pro-choice	pro-abortion
pro-life	antichoice
economic refugee	illegal alien
terrorist surveillance	domestic spying

The words in the left-hand column sound like good things; speakers who use them seek to establish themselves as virtuous people supporting worthy causes. The **connotations** (associations, overtones) of these pairs of words differ, even though the **denotations** (explicit meanings, dictionary definitions) are the same—just as the connotations of *mother* and *female parent* differ, although the denotations are the same. Similarly, although Lincoln's "four score and seven" and "eighty-seven" both denote "thirteen less than one hundred," they differ in connotation.

Tone is not only a matter of connotation (*hounded out of office* versus, let's say, *compelled to resign*, or *pro-choice* versus *pro-abortion*); it is also a matter of such things as the selection and type of examples. A writer who offers many examples, especially ones drawn from ordinary life, conveys a persona different from that of a writer who offers no examples or only an occasional invented instance. The first writer seems friendlier, more honest, more down-to-earth.

Using Tone to Address Opposition   On the whole, when writing an argument, it's advisable to be courteous and respectful of your topic, your audience, and people who hold views opposite to yours. It is rarely good for one's own intellectual development to regard as villains or fools persons who hold views different from one's own, especially if some of them are in the audience. Keep in mind the story of two strangers on a train who, striking up a conversation, found that both were clergymen, although of different faiths. Then one said to the other, "Well, why shouldn't we be friends? After all, we both serve God, you in your way and I in His."

Complacency is all right when telling a joke, but not when offering an argument:

- Recognize opposing views.
- Assume that they are held in good faith.
- State them fairly. If you don't, you do a disservice not only to the opposition but also to your own position because the perceptive reader won't take you seriously.

- Be temperate in arguing your own position: "If I understand their view correctly . . ."; "It seems reasonable to conclude that . . ."; "Perhaps, then, we can agree that . . ."

- Write calmly. If you become overly emotional, readers may interpret you as biased or unreasonable, and they may lose their confidence in you.

We, One, or I?

The use of *we* in the last paragraph brings us to another point: Is it correct to use the first-person pronouns *I* and *we*? In this book, because three of us are writing, we often use *we* to mean the three authors. Sometimes we use *we* to mean the authors and the readers, or *we* the people in general. This shifting use of one word can be troublesome, but we hope (clearly, the *we* here refers only to the authors) that we have avoided ambiguity. But can, or should, or must an individual use *we* instead of *I*? The short answer is no.

If you're simply speaking for yourself, use *I*. Attempts to avoid the first-person singular by saying things like "This writer thinks . . ." and "It is thought that . . ." and "One thinks that . . ." are far more irritating (and wordy) than the use of *I*. The so-called editorial *we* sounds as odd in a student's argument as the royal *we* does. (Mark Twain said that the only ones who can appropriately say *we* are kings, editors, and people with a tapeworm.) It's advisable to use *we* only when you are sure you're writing or speaking directly to an audience who holds membership in the same group, as in "We *students of this university should . . .*" or "We *the members of Theta Chi fraternity need to. . . .*" If the *we* you refer to has a referent, simply refer to what it means: Say "Americans are" rather than "We are," or "College students should" rather than "We should," or "Republicans need to" rather than "We need to."

Many students assume that using *one* will solve the problem of pronouns. But because one *one* leads to another, the sentence may end up sounding, as James Thurber once said, "like a trombone solo." It's best to admit that you are the author and to use *I*. However, there is no need to preface every sentence with "I think." The reader knows that the essay is yours and that the opinions are yours; so use *I* when you must, but not needlessly. Do not write, "I think *X* movie is terrible"; simply say, "*X* movie is terrible." And do not add extra words that say more obvious things, like "*It is my idea that* the company needs a new mission statement." Just write, "*The company needs a new mission statement.*"

THINKING CRITICALLY ELIMINATING *WE, ONE,* AND *I*

Rewrite the following sentences to eliminate unnecessary uses of *we, one, I,* and other gratuitous statements of opinion. (The first row has been completed as an example.)

Original Sentence	Rewritten Sentence
I think fracking is the best way to achieve energy independence and to create jobs.	Fracking is the best way to achieve energy independence and to create jobs.
In our country, we believe in equality and freedom.	
One should consider one's manners at formal dinner parties.	
In my opinion, the government should not regulate the sizes of sodas we can order.	
It is clearly the case that the new policy treats employees unfairly.	

Often you'll see *I* in journalistic writing and autobiographical writing—and in some argumentative writing, too—but in most argumentative writing, it's best to state the facts and (when drawing reasonable conclusions from them) to keep yourself in the background. Why? The more you use *I* in an essay, the more your readers will attach *you* directly to the argument and may regard your position as personal rather than as relevant to themselves.

✓ A CHECKLIST FOR ESTABLISHING TONE AND PERSONA

☐ Do I have a sense of what the audience probably knows or thinks about the issue to best present myself to them?

☐ Have I tried to establish common ground and then moved on to advance my position?

☐ Have I used appropriate language (e.g., defined terms that are likely to be unfamiliar)?

☐ Have I indicated why readers should care about the issue and should accept my views, or at least give them serious consideration?

☐ Have I presented myself as a person who is fair, informed, and worth listening to? In short, have I conveyed a strong *ethos*?

Avoiding Sexist Language

Courtesy—as well as common sense—requires that you respect your readers' feelings. Many people today find offensive the implicit gender bias in the use of male pronouns ("As the reader follows the argument, he will find . . .") to denote not only men but also women or people who use nonbinary gender pronouns such as *ze* or *they*. And sometimes the use of the male pronoun to denote all people is ridiculous ("An individual, no matter what his sex, . . .").

In most contexts, there is no need to use gender-specific nouns or pronouns. One way to avoid using *he* when you mean any person is to use *he or she* (or *she or he*), but the result is sometimes cumbersome—although superior to the overly conspicuous *he/she* and *s/he*. Some people will accept *they*, even when the syntax of a sentence calls for a singular pronoun, to avoid this issue ("When a person enters the exhibit, they will see . . ."), but not everyone accepts this usage in formal writing yet.

Here are two simple ways to solve the problem:

- *Use the plural* ("As readers follow the argument, they will find . . .").
- *Recast the sentence* so that no pronoun is required ("Readers following the argument will find . . .").

Because *man* and *mankind* strike many readers as sexist when used in such expressions as "Man is a rational animal" and "Mankind has not yet solved this problem," consider using such words as *human being, person, people, humanity,* and *we* (e.g., "Human beings are rational animals"; "We have not yet solved this problem").

PEER REVIEW

Your instructor may suggest—or require—that you submit an early draft of your essay to a fellow student or small group of students for comment. Such a procedure benefits both author and readers: You get the responses of a reader, and the student-reader gets experience in thinking about the problems of developing an argument, especially such matters as the degree of detail that a writer needs to offer to a reader and the importance of keeping the organization evident to a reader.

Oral peer reviews allow for the give and take of discussion, but probably most students and most instructors find written peer reviews more helpful because reviewers think more carefully about their responses to the draft, and they help essayists to get beyond a

✓ A CHECKLIST FOR PEER REVIEW

Read through the draft quickly. Then read it again, with the following questions in mind. Remember: You are reading a draft, a work in progress. You're expected to offer suggestions, and you're expected to offer them courteously.

In a sentence, indicate the degree to which the draft shows promise of fulfilling the assignment.

☐ Is the writer's tone appropriate? Who is the audience?

☐ Looking at the essay as a whole, what thesis (main idea) is advanced?

☐ Are the needs of the audience kept in mind? For instance, do some words need to be defined?

☐ Is the evidence (e.g., the examples and the testimony of authorities) clear and effective?

☐ Can I accept the assumptions? If not, why not?

☐ Is any obvious evidence (or counterevidence) overlooked?

☐ Is the writer proposing a solution? If so,

    ☐ Are other equally attractive solutions adequately examined?

    ☐ Has the writer overlooked some unattractive effects of the proposed solution?

Look at each paragraph separately.

☐ What is the basic point?

☐ How does each paragraph relate to the essay's main idea or to the previous paragraph?

☐ Should some paragraphs be deleted? Be divided into two or more paragraphs? Be combined? Be moved elsewhere? (If you outline the essay by writing down the gist of each paragraph, you'll get help in answering these questions.)

☐ Is each sentence clearly related to the sentence that precedes and to the sentence that follows? If not, in a sentence or two indicate examples of good and bad transitions.

☐ Is each paragraph adequately developed? Are there sufficient details, perhaps brief supporting quotations from the text?

☐ Are the introductory and concluding paragraphs effective?

Look at the paper as a whole.

☐ What are the paper's chief strengths?

☐ Make at least two specific suggestions that you think will help the author improve the paper.

knee-jerk response to criticism. Online reviews on a class website, through email, or via another platform such as a file-sharing service or internet-based document tool are especially helpful precisely because they are not face to face; the peer reviewer gets practice *writing*, and the essayist is not directly challenged.

A STUDENT'S ESSAY, FROM ROUGH NOTES TO FINAL VERSION

While we were revising this textbook, we asked the students in one of our classes to write a short essay (500–750 words) on some ethical problem that concerned them. Because this assignment was the first writing assignment in the course, we explained that a good way to generate ideas is to ask oneself some questions, write down responses, question those responses, and write freely for ten minutes or so, not worrying about contradictions. We invited our students to hand in their initial notes along with the finished essay so that we could get a sense of how they proceeded as writers. Not all of them chose to hand in their notes, but we were greatly encouraged by those who did. What encouraged us was the confirmation of an old belief — we call it a fact — that students will hand in a thoughtful essay if before preparing a final version they ask themselves *why* they think this or that, write down their responses, and are not afraid to change their minds as they proceed.

Here are the first notes of a student, Emily Andrews, who elected to write about whether to give money to street beggars. She simply put down ideas, one after the other.

Help the poor? Why do I (sometimes) do it?

I feel guilty, and think I should help them: poor, cold, hungry (but also some of them are thirsty for liquor, and will spend the money on liquor, not on food).

I also feel annoyed by them — most of them.

Where does the expression "the deserving poor" come from?

And "poor but honest"? Actually, that sounds odd. Wouldn't "rich but honest" make more sense?

Why don't they work? Fellow with red beard, always by bus stop in front of florist's shop, always wants a handout. He is a regular, there all day every day, so I guess he is in a way "reliable," so why doesn't he put the same time in on a job?

Or why don't they get help? Don't they know they need it? They *must* know they need it.

Maybe that guy with the beard is just a con artist. Maybe he makes more money by panhandling than he would by working, and it's a lot easier!

Kinds of poor — how to classify??

> drunks, druggies, etc.
> mentally ill (maybe drunks belong here, too)
> decent people who have had terrible luck

Why private charity?

Doesn't it make sense to say we (fortunate individuals) should give something — an occasional handout — to people who have had terrible luck? (I suppose some people might say there's no need for any of us to give anything — the government takes care of the truly needy — but I *do* believe in giving charity. A month ago a friend of the family passed away, and the woman's children suggested that people might want to make a donation in her name to a shelter for battered women. I know my parents made a donation.)

BUT how can I tell who is who, which are which? Which of these people asking for "spare change" really need (deserve???) help, and which are phonies? Impossible to tell.

Possibilities:

> Give to no one.
> Give to no one but make an annual donation, maybe to United Way.
> Give a dollar to each person who asks. This would probably not cost me even a dollar a day.

Occasionally do without something — maybe a new album or a meal in a restaurant — and give the money I save to people who seem worthy.

WORTHY? What am I saying? How can I, or anyone, tell? The neat-looking guy who says he just lost his job may be a phony, and the dirty bum — probably a drunk — may desperately need food. (OK, so what if he spends the money on liquor instead of food? At least he'll get a little pleasure in life. No! It's not all right if he spends it on drink.)

Other possibilities:

Do some volunteer work?
To tell the truth, I don't want to put in the time. I don't feel *that* guilty.

So what's the problem?

Is it, How I can help the very poor (handouts, or through an organization)? or

How I can feel less guilty about being lucky enough to be able to go to college and to have a supportive family?

I can't quite bring myself to believe I should help every beggar who approaches, but I also can't bring myself to believe that I should do nothing, on the grounds that:

a. it's probably their fault
b. if they are deserving, they can get gov't help. No, I just can't believe that. Maybe some are too proud to look for government help, or don't know that they're entitled to it.

What to do?

On balance, it seems best to:

a. give to United Way
b. maybe also give to an occasional individual, if I happen to be moved, without worrying about whether he or she is "deserving" (since it's probably impossible to know)

A day after making these notes Emily reviewed them, added a few points, and then made a very brief selection from them to serve as an outline for her first draft:

Opening para.: "poor but honest"? Deserve "spare change"?

Charity: private or through organizations?

> pros and cons
> guy at bus
> it wouldn't cost me much, but . . . better to give through organizations

Concluding para.: still feel guilty?

> maybe mention guy at bus again?

After writing and revising a draft, Emily submitted her essay to a fellow student for review. She then revised her work in light of the peer's suggestions and her own further thinking.

Emily's final essay appears below. If after reading the final version you reread Emily's early notes, you'll notice that some of her notes never made it into the final version. But without the notes, the essay probably wouldn't have been as interesting as it is. When Emily made the notes, she wasn't so much putting down her ideas as *finding* ideas through the process of writing. (By the way, Emily told us that in her next-to-last draft, the title was "Is It Right to Spare 'Spare Change'?" This title, unlike the revision, introduces the topic but not the author's position.)

Andrews 1

Emily Andrews

Professor Barnet

English 102

January 15, 2019

Title is informative, alerting the reader to the topic and the author's position.

Why I Don't Spare "Spare Change"

"Poor but honest." "The deserving poor." I don't know the origin of these quotations, but they always come to mind

Andrews 2

when I walk through my city, Boston, and encounter "the poor" on the streets asking for money. When I do, I have to face an ethical dilemma — not as to whether or not I *can* spare my spare change, but whether or not I *should*. Panhandlers by definition are people who solicit money for their personal use without providing goods or services. This forces me to consider the behavior I am enabling by giving away money on the street. Many of these people, perhaps through alcohol or drugs, have ruined not only their own lives but also the lives of others in order to indulge in their own habits. Perhaps alcoholism and drug addiction really are "diseases," as many people say, but my own feeling — based, of course, not on any serious study — is that most alcoholics and drug addicts can be classified with the "undeserving poor." And that is largely why I don't distribute spare change to panhandlers.

Surely among street people there are also some who can rightly be called "deserving." Deserving of what? A fair shake in life, or government assistance? Perhaps. But my spare change? It happens that I have been brought up to believe that it is appropriate to make contributions to charity — let's say a shelter for battered women — but if I give some change to a panhandler, I may be helping someone, or, on the contrary, I could just as easily be encouraging someone to continue their alcohol or drug abuse, and not to get help. Maybe even worse: maybe I am supporting a criminal, or con artist, or someone who could use my money to get high and take advantage of someone else. The fact is, I don't know.

Side annotations:

Opening paragraph holds readers' interest by alluding to familiar phrases and an anecdote.

Defines a key term: *panhandler.*

Author presents general outline of argument and thesis.

Voices the reader's probably uneasy response to the opening, showing audience awareness.

Supports her argument with reason.

Andrews 3

Clearly sets forth the alternatives. A reader may disagree with them, but they are stated fairly.

If one believes in the value of private charity, one can give either to needy individuals or to charitable organizations. Money given to panhandlers may indeed help a person badly in need, but it could just as easily be misused and cause greater harm. In giving to an organization such as the United Way, in contrast, one can feel that one's money is likely to be used wisely. True, confronted by a panhandler one may feel that *this* particular unfortunate individual needs help at *this* moment — a cup of coffee or a sandwich — and the need will not be met unless I put my hand in my pocket right now. But I have come to think that the beggars whom I encounter can get along without my spare change. If they choose, they can go to shelters where charitable contributions can be collected and spent wisely. Indeed, panhandlers may actually be better off if people did not give them spare change which they can subsequently use on alcohol or drugs.

Paragraphs 4 and 5 are more personal than the earlier paragraphs. The writer, more or less having stated what she takes to be the facts, now is entitled to offer a highly personal response to them.

It happens that in my neighborhood I encounter a few panhandlers regularly. There is one fellow who is always by the bus stop where I catch the bus to the college, and I never give him anything precisely because he is always there. He is such a regular that, I think, he ought to be able to hold a regular job. Putting him aside, I routinely encounter about three or four beggars in an average week. (I'm not counting street musicians. These people seem quite able to work for a living. If they see their "work" as playing or singing, let persons who enjoy their performances pay them. I do not consider myself among their audience.) The truth of the matter is that since I meet so few

Andrews 4

beggars, I could give each one a dollar and hardly feel the loss.
At most, I might go without seeing a movie some week. But I
know nothing about these people, and it's my impression — based
on what I see — that they simply prefer begging to working.

That's why I usually do not give "spare change," and
I don't think I will in the future. These people will get along
without me, and may get along better without me if their needs
eventually lead them to a shelter or a food bank. Someone else
will have to come up with money for their coffee or their liquor,
or, at worst, they will just have to do without. I will continue
to contribute occasionally to a charitable organization, not
simply (I hope) to salve my conscience but because I believe
that these organizations actually do good work. But I will not
attempt to be a mini-charitable organization, distributing spare
change likely to go to an unworthy cause.

The final
paragraph
nicely
concludes with
a reference to
the title, giving
the reader
a sense of
completeness.

TOPICS FOR CRITICAL THINKING AND WRITING

1. Does the writer establish a good sense of *ethos* in this essay?
   Explain what works best and what works least in terms of establishing credibility or goodwill.

2. Do you think this essay has a strong thesis? A strong argument?
   Explain.

3. What assumptions are made about panhandlers in this essay? If
   you wanted to challenge these assumptions, what kinds of questions could you ask and what evidence could you seek?

4. What are some alternative solutions or counterarguments that the
   writer did not address?

5. Who is the writer's intended audience? Do you think the writer's
   language and tone are appropriate?

7.

Using Sources

Research is formalized curiosity. It is poking and prying with a purpose.

—ZORA NEALE HURSTON

There is no way of exchanging information that does not involve an act of judgment.

—JACOB BRONOWSKI

I have yet to see any problem, however complicated, which, when you looked at it in the right way, did not become still more complicated.

—POUL ANDERSON

A university is just a group of buildings gathered around a library.

—SHELBY FOOTE

WHY USE SOURCES?

We have pointed out that one gets ideas by writing. While prewriting and drafting, ideas form and stimulate further ideas, especially when you question and *think critically* about what you are writing. Of course, when writing about complex, serious questions, nobody is expected to invent all the answers out of thin air. On the contrary, a writer is expected to be familiar with the chief answers already produced by others and to make use of them through selective incorporation and criticism. When you write about an issue, you are not expected to reinvent the wheel; sometimes, simply adding a spoke is enough.

You may be familiar with some directives about research from previous courses. Your instructors may have asked you to locate three sources, or four sources, or six sources, and to use those sources in support of an argument (perhaps with some added requirement that one or more of these be scholarly sources). However, your teachers generally do not want you simply to go out and find a fixed number of sources to plug in to your essay for the sake of it. The goal of research is more idealistic. The point is not that a minimum number of sources is right for every argument, nor is it to send you off on a scavenger hunt for types of sources. Instead, research is intended to encourage learning, thoughtful engagement with a topic, and the production of an informed view.

Entering a Discourse

Kenneth Burke (1887–1993), one of America's most important theorists of rhetoric, wrote:

> Imagine that you enter a parlor. You come late. When you arrive, others have long preceded you, and they are engaged in a heated discussion, a discussion too heated for them to pause and tell you exactly what it is about. In fact, the discussion had already begun long before any of them got there, so that no one present is qualified to retrace for you all the steps that had gone before. You listen for a while, until you decide that you have caught the tenor of the argument; then you put in your oar. Someone answers; you answer him; another comes to your defense; another aligns himself against you, to either the embarrassment or gratification of your opponent, depending upon the quality of your ally's assistance. However, the discussion is interminable. The hour grows late, you must depart. And you do depart, with the discussion still vigorously in progress.[1]

When you are writing, imagine you are entering a discussion, but not a live one as in Burke's analogy. Imagine instead you are entering into a **discourse**. A discourse is a type of discussion, surely. But unlike a live conversation, a discourse takes place over a

---

[1] *The Philosophy of Literary Form* (Baton Rouge: Louisiana State University Press, 1941), 110–11.

longer period of time among many participants in various types of writing and public venues. A discourse is a conversation writ large, one that has gone on before you enter the fray, and one that will likely continue after you leave.

So why are sources important in discourse?

- The first answer is practical: You use sources because they are where conversations about important topics occur.

- The second is more idealistic: It is your responsibility as an intelligent citizen to participate meaningfully in discourses.

From sources, you learn what the facts are, what issues are current, and what positions certain people or groups are taking on the issues. Through sources, you discover new ideas, questions, and answers. When you perform research on a topic, you are *finding*, *evaluating*, and *synthesizing* sources so as to position yourself to speak within that kind of conversation known as a discourse.

Two caveats are important. First, although we will discuss finding, evaluating, and synthesizing sources separately, once you begin researching you will see that these activities are not entirely separable. As you find sources, you will simultaneously be assessing their relevancy and value (evaluating) and placing sources into conversation with one another (synthesizing) while considering ways to integrate them into your own writing.

Second, the boundaries of discourse are not clear-cut. Obviously, many conversations about many different topics occur constantly in a variety of places. We may speak generally of political discourse, scientific discourse, or economic discourse, and we may speak more particularly of discourses on women's rights, environmentalism, or taxation. Any subject at all may be thought of in terms of the discourses (or conversations) that take place about it. Consider, for example, the conversation about security and freedom in the United States. This conversation — this *discourse* — has been ongoing since the nation was founded, and it continues today. In articles, essays, speeches, legal reviews, court opinions, congressional debates, and elsewhere, people continue to weigh the appropriate balance between security and freedom: The country needs to be kept safe, and so law enforcement agencies are granted many powers to investigate, detect, and prevent lawbreaking, yet American citizens are also protected by the US Constitution from unwarranted harassment, search and seizure, and other invasions of privacy. Today, terrorism, illegal immigration, stop-and-frisk practices, and cybersecurity are just a few areas of focus in this conversation-writ-large. Within each of those categories, even narrower conversations occur. Airport security, border security, cell phone searches, facial recognition technology — the list goes on and on. Many combined, overlapping conversations (some very general, some quite specific) may all be said to be part of this *discourse* about freedom and security. Even fictional novels, plays, films, and television shows contribute to the discourse. A television series like *House of Cards* (2013–2018) or a blockbuster superhero movie like *Captain America: Winter Soldier* (2014) can represent and spur discussion about topical issues related to freedom and security — and potentially be a rich source for research and analysis to support your own argument and entry into the conversation.

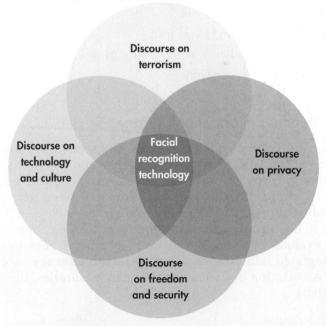

Intersecting discourses

A **discourse community** is any group of people who share general interests, assumptions, and values and who communicate with one another in some form of media, usually adhering to a set of conventions for that communication. For example, imagine a professor of physics who is active in the scientific discourse on thermodynamics, publishing his theories in academic books and articles. In those, he is addressing one discourse community of scientists and experts in a particular type of writing style or genre. But maybe he is also an environmentalist in his hometown who publishes on the Sierra Club blog and posts videos about local ecology. And maybe he is also a fan of X-Men and writes passionately about the Marvel mutants on a listserv dedicated to that series. In those cases, he is addressing narrower discourse communities.

Now, this hypothetical professor would be likely to research and write differently depending on which discourse community he is engaging. Understanding discourse communities is important because it can help you

- focus your own research by determining which types of sources you need to seek,
- evaluate the sources you find,
- define your audience and purpose in writing, and
- write more persuasively.

Understanding Information Literacy

During your college courses — and in work and daily life — you will be reading and listening to ongoing conversations within and among discourse communities. Sometimes, you will want (or need) to participate yourself. You will have to interject, responding to issues by speaking and writing. Thus, when you set out to learn about and contribute to a discourse, how you discover, evaluate, and use your sources is crucial. Together, these are integrated skills known as **information literacy**. According to the Association of College and Research Libraries, these skills encompass

- the thoughtful and reflective discovery of information,

- the understanding of how information is produced and valued, and
- the ethical use of information in creating new ideas by participating in various academic or civic discourses.

Information literacy involves being able to survey what and how knowledge circulates about a topic, thinking critically while you learn. It allows you to see what kinds of questions have been raised and what answers have been provided. As you poke and pry into a topic, you can distinguish between strong and weak sources and separate the wheat from the chaff.

Information literacy skills are necessary to be able to navigate the vast fields of information to which we are exposed constantly in the digital media environment. Even when we are trying to be diligent in our efforts to find quality sources, we face obstacles. Search engines, for example, simply cannot index, curate, and return results from the billions of websites on the ever-expanding internet. This means we need to develop skills on *how* to search: how to use search operators and phrases to limit the results we get and how to search for only certain kinds of websites or file types. But even the best search strategies will not return full-length published books or password-protected content such as subscription-only magazines, newspapers, and journals, many of which are carefully edited and vetted for quality (and are often the best possible sources).

Further, we should also be aware that search engines are not neutral. They commonly return results that are most popular (or most highly paid for), not necessarily those that are most thorough, interesting, or reliable. Some search engines tailor the top results to your previous searches and online activity through "personalized" search results, leading to an information ecosystem susceptible to "filter bubble" and "echo chamber" effects in which people are led to information limited by a single perspective or ideology. If you are searching for a political topic and your search engine knows your political leanings, it will likely return in your top results webpages that reflect your political views. This practice seriously raises the potential for confirmation bias (discussed on pp. 90–91).

Once you narrow in on a topic and adopt a central idea or position on an issue — a thesis — your ability to persuade an audience will depend on the sources you provide, evaluate, and cite. Even one citation of a fraudulent website or one uncritical reference to a highly partisan or narrowly ideological source can undermine your credibility. On the other hand, well-researched and thoughtfully discussed sources show that you are an educated participant in a discourse—or even one small area of it—who is equipped with foundational facts and evidence drawn from reputable sources; you have an argument worth listening to.

CHOOSING A TOPIC

Because of the complexity of discourses—the plurality of topics, issues, ideas, and opinions (in so many different forms and from so many different groups)—the research process isn't straightforward and neat. Research is a form of inquiry that can range from finding answers to simple questions to exploring complex topics, problems, or issues discussed within or among discourse communities. Part of conducting a successful, fruitful research effort is first selecting an area of focus and narrowing the scope of your research to suit the needs of your assignments or interests.

If a topic is not assigned, choose one that

- interests you, and
- can be researched with reasonable thoroughness in the allotted time.

Topics such as censorship, the environment, and sexual harassment obviously impinge on our lives, and it may well be that one such topic is of special interest to you. But the breadth of these topics (like with freedom vs. security, discussed earlier) makes researching them potentially overwhelming. Type the word *censorship* into an internet search engine, and you will be referred to millions of information sources.

This brings us to our second point: getting a manageable topic. Any of the previous topics would need to be refined substantially before you could begin researching in earnest. Similarly, even more specific topics such as "the effects of the Holocaust" can hardly be mastered in a few weeks or argued in a ten-page paper. They are simply too big. (The questions that immediately come to mind are,

What kind of effects do you mean? Political effects? Psychological effects? For whom? Where? When? Where will you find the evidence?) Getting a manageable topic often means working on one area of a larger puzzle, pinpointing the places where you can add your piece. You can do that by

- seeking gaps or areas of conflict within or among discourses (places where you can weigh in) or
- breaking down complex topics, issues, or debates into simpler questions (perhaps focusing on one question informing the larger issue).

By focusing your research on one area within a broader discourse, you can limit the range and types of resources you consult based on your circumstances and goals. As you research, you may find yourself drawn toward even more specific questions. If you were writing about the psychological effects of the Holocaust, for instance, you could focus on an affected ethnic group like Jewish people or focus further on German, French, Russian, or American Jews; you could define a time frame; or you could deal with a specific postwar generation, or consider a group within that generation, such as women, men, children, or second-generation survivors (those born after the war). If you chose to develop your analysis around specific traumatic events, places, or even practices, such as the use of gas chambers, you might seek evidence in psychological studies, memoirs, and testimony or in the arts.

> **WRITING TIP** You may think you have little to contribute to conversations whose participants are illustrious authorities and experts. However, by dint of being a student, you have a unique perspective: You are on the edge of the future, able to apply new questions and issues in the present to those old primary and secondary resources. Or maybe you may have a purpose for writing that is fundamentally different from anyone else's.

One strategy for narrowing your topic is, first, to find your general topic and then apply some basic questions to discover how you might find an entry point into the conversations about it.

Find Relevance

- What are some of the ways people have been discussing this topic recently?
- To whom — that is, to what groups or audiences — is this topic especially important now?
- Is there any data, any evidence, or an example that arguments on this topic have not yet accounted for?

Develop a New Approach

- What is most important or interesting to *me* about this topic?
- Is there a perspective or an application that has been under-reported in the discourses on this topic?
- Can I ask new questions by thinking politically, historically, religiously, scientifically, psychologically, philosophically, culturally — or in some combination of these?

Determine Your Research Goals and Writing Context

- Where do I stand?
- What type of audience do I want to reach most?
- How do I want to position myself in the discourse on this topic (i.e., in what genre, in what format will I make myself heard, including considerations of length and depth)?

EXERCISE: EXPLORING YOUR TOPIC

Once you've narrowed your focus, spend a little time exploring your topic to see if you can locate interesting conversations and manageable topics or issues by taking one or more of these approaches:

- ***Do a web search on the topic.*** You can quickly put your finger on the pulse of popular approaches to a topic by scanning the first page or two of results to see who is talking about it (individuals, groups, etc.) and in what forms (articles, news, blogs, etc.).

- ***Plug the topic into one of the library's article databases.*** Just by scanning the titles in a general database, you can get a sense of what questions have been and are currently being raised about your topic.

- *Browse the library shelves where books on the topic are kept.* A quick check of the tables of contents of recently published books may give you ideas of how to narrow your topic.

- *Ask a librarian to show you where specialized reference books on your topic are found.* Instead of general encyclopedias, try sources like *CQ Researcher* or *Encyclopedia of Science, Technology, and Ethics.*

- *Talk to an expert.* Members of the faculty who specialize in the area of your topic might be able to point you to key sources and discourses.

FINDING SOURCES

Your sources' quality and integrity are crucial to your own credibility and to the strength of your argument. In Chapters 5 and 6, we discussed *ethos* as an appeal that establishes credibility with readers. When you do competent research, you let your audience see that you have done your homework, which thereby increases your *ethos*. Sources, we mean to say, provide evidence in support of your argument, but they also collectively serve as evidence that you are familiar with the discourses on your topic, that you know what you're talking about, and that your interpretation is sound.

To find good sources, you must have a strategy for searching. What strategy you use will depend on your topic. Researching a social problem or a new economic policy may involve reading recent newspaper articles, scanning information on government websites, and locating current statistics. On the other hand, researching the meaning of a pop culture trend, for example, may be best tackled by seeking out books and scholarly journal articles on the sociological nature of fashion and also some popular style magazines or videos to use as evidence. In all your research, you will be attempting to identify the places where conversations on your topic are taking place—in specific academic journals, magazines, websites, annual conferences, and so on. By noting what is common among your sources, what data and evidence are shared, you may find other authoritative sources and get leads on further research.

Visual Guide: Finding Discourse on Your Topic

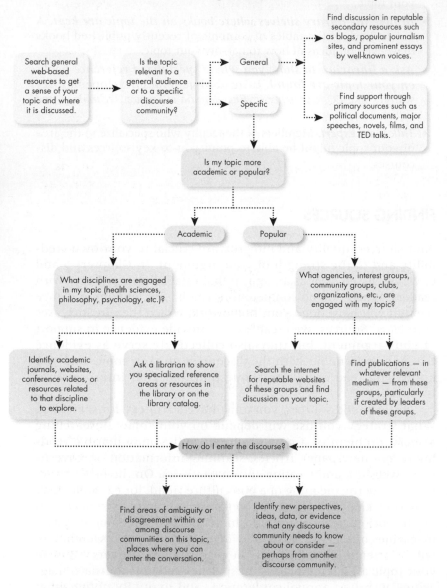

Search general web-based resources to get a sense of your topic and where it is discussed.

Is the topic relevant to a general audience or to a specific discourse community?

General

Specific

Find discussion in reputable secondary resources such as blogs, popular journalism sites, and prominent essays by well-known voices.

Find support through primary sources such as political documents, major speeches, novels, films, and TED talks.

Is my topic more academic or popular?

Academic

Popular

What disciplines are engaged in my topic (health sciences, philosophy, psychology, etc.)?

What agencies, interest groups, community groups, clubs, organizations, etc., are engaged with my topic?

Identify academic journals, websites, conference videos, or resources related to that discipline to explore.

Ask a librarian to show you specialized reference areas or resources in the library or on the library catalog.

Search the internet for reputable websites of these groups and find discussion on your topic.

Find publications — in whatever relevant medium — from these groups, particularly if created by leaders of these groups.

How do I enter the discourse?

Find areas of ambiguity or disagreement within or among discourse communities on this topic, places where you can enter the conversation.

Identify new perspectives, ideas, data, or evidence that any discourse community needs to know about or consider — perhaps from another discourse community.

If your topic warrants it, you may also want to supplement your library or internet research with your own fieldwork. You could conduct surveys or interviews, design an experiment, or visit a museum. You could perform research in an archive or other repository to analyze original documents or artifacts. This kind of research is called **primary research** because you are the one gathering the basic evidence and data. **Secondary research** is the term given to the kind of inquiry that involves your study of research done by others.

One form of research is not necessarily better than the other, although some may be better suited to certain topics or research questions than others. Many types of research projects involve both methods. Whether research is primary or secondary also does not bear on its reliability. Both kinds are subject to biases, omissions, and assumptions that could color the data. Therefore, critical thinking is essential every step of the way, whether you are seeking primary or secondary research or are performing it.

> **RESEARCH TIP** Practice the prewriting and invention strategies we discuss in earlier chapters to help guide your research. Keep your notes on sources in an organized fashion so that you do not end up with a lot of links, digital files, printouts, and books, with no record of what you thought about them.

Finding Quality Information Online

The internet is a valuable source of information for many topics and less helpful for others. In general, if you're looking for information on public policy, popular culture, current events, legal affairs, or any subject of interest to agencies of the federal or state government, the internet is likely to have useful material. If you're looking for literary criticism or scholarly analysis of historical or social issues, you may be better off using library databases, described later in this chapter.

It is important to remember that the research process and the application of critical thinking do not occur separately: You may be jumping around from contemporary to historical sources, databases, and webpages, evaluating them as you proceed. Seek more facts as needed and remain adaptable, flexible, and open-minded all the while. Be prepared to take different perspectives seriously and be on the lookout for areas of ambiguity, unsettled issues, and debatable questions. Again, these are places where you can potentially weigh in. Do not hesitate to modify your search terms. If a path of research is not getting you anywhere, back up and try different terms. Think of your process as an open-ended engagement with information, not as an effort to prove something you already think.

To make good use of the internet, try these strategies:

- Use the most specific terms possible when using a general search engine; put phrases in quotes.

- Use the advanced search option to limit a search by date (such as websites updated in the past week or month).

- Consider which government agencies and organizations might be interested in your topic and go directly to their websites.

- Use clues in URLs to see where sites originate. Delete everything after the first slash in the URL to go to the parent site to see if it provides information about the website's source, origin, or purpose.

- Always bear in mind that the sources you choose must be persuasive to your audience. Avoid sites that may be dismissed as unreliable or biased. (See Evaluating Sources, beginning on p. 262, for more strategies on how to do that.)

A Word about **Wikipedia**   Links to *Wikipedia* often rise to the top of search results. This vast and decentralized site provides nearly six million articles on a wide variety of topics. However, anyone can contribute to the online encyclopedia, so the accuracy of articles varies, and in some cases, the coverage of a controversial issue is one-sided or disputed. In other cases, businesses, political campaigns, and public relations firms patrol *Wikipedia* and manage their own or their clients' "online reputation" by adding and subtracting information from the website. Nevertheless, many articles are accurate, particularly when they are noncontroversial; however, like any encyclopedia, they provide only basic information. *Wikipedia*'s founder, Jimmy Wales, cautions students against using it as a source, except for obtaining general background knowledge: "You're in college; don't cite the encyclopedia."[2]

[2]"Wikipedia Founder Discourages Academic Use of His Creation," *Chronicle of Higher Education Wired Campus*, June 12, 2006, http://www.chronicle.com/wiredcampus /article/1328/wikipedia-founder-discourages-academic-use-of-his-creation.

Wikipedia is most valuable when you use it for basic undisputed facts or to locate bibliographies that will help you conduct further independent research.

Finding Articles Using Library Databases

Your library has a wide range of general and specialized databases available through its website. When you search through a database, you are searching within an electronic index of citations from published sources, both popular and scholarly. Some databases provide references to articles (and perhaps abstracts or summaries), and some provide direct links to the full text of entire articles.

Through your school library, you may have access to general and interdisciplinary databases such as Academic Search Premier (produced by the EBSCOhost company) and Expanded Academic Index (from InfoTrac), which provide access to thousands of publications, including both scholarly and popular sources. LexisNexis or ProQuest Newsstand are particularly useful for newspaper articles that are not available for free online. More specialized databases include PsycINFO (for psychology research) and ERIC (focused on topics in education). Others, such as JSTOR, are fulltext digital archives of scholarly journals. Some databases offer the archives of a single publication, like the *New York Times*, *Wall Street Journal*, or *JAMA* (the *Journal of the American Medical Association*). Others offer scientific, medical, or economic data exclusively (such as Web of Science, MEDLINE, EconLit), and still others are virtual archives (such as African American Newspapers of the Nineteenth Century or The Sixties, a searchable database of independent newspapers and ephemera of that age). Some databases offer art (ArtStor), video (Films on Demand), music (Database of Recorded American Music [DRAM]), or photography (Associated Press Images Collection). Others may offer excellent resources for highly specific material: The Burns Archive, for example, offers one million historic photographs and is recognized by scholars as a primary resource for early medical photography. Look at your library's website and find out where you can browse the databases.

As you can see, databases abound. To navigate them and find the right one for your topic and project, look at your library's offerings and roll your cursor over database titles to get some information about the scope and holdings of each one. Never hesitate to ask a librarian at the reference desk for a quick tutorial on how to use your university databases—after all, you technically pay for these subscriptions through your tuition.

When using databases for research, first choose a topic, then narrow your topic using the strategies outlined earlier in this chapter. List synonyms for your key search terms. As you search, look at words used in titles and descriptors for alternative ideas and make use of the "advanced search" option so that you can easily combine multiple terms. Rarely will you find exactly what you're looking for right away. Try different search terms and different ways to narrow your topic. Consider limiting the date range of your search to find historical sources on your topic or narrowing results to show scholarly journal articles only.

RESEARCH TIP Beware of trying to find the "perfect source." Students often get frustrated with the research process because they have an excellent original idea but cannot find analysis, commentary, or opinion that directly supports it. Although it may not feel like it, not being able to find sources may actually be a *good* thing: It may indicate you have an original perspective or argument, a perfect place to add your voice.

Most databases have an advanced search option that offers fillable forms for combining multiple terms. In Figure 7.1 we show a search field using Boolean operators (AND, OR, and NOT) to seek targeted information on the use of anabolic steroids. Because a simple search of "anabolic steroids" retrieved far too many results, we used this advanced search to combine three concepts: anabolic steroids, legal aspects of their use, and use of them by athletes. Related terms are combined with the word "or": *law* or *legal*. The last letters of a word have been replaced with an asterisk so that any ending will be included in the search. *Athlet** will search for *athlete, athletes,* or *athletics*. Options on both sides of the list of articles retrieved offer opportunities to refine a search by date of publication or to restrict the results to only academic journals, magazines, or newspapers. Notice in Figure 7.2 some further ways to limit your searches.

As with an internet search, when you search through databases, you'll need to make critical choices about which articles are worth pursuing. Some results may not be useful. A title might tell you right away that a source is not exactly about your topic, or

Figure 7.1 A Database Search

you might notice that the publication date is not relevant to your questions. The subject lines may contain some keywords associated with your topic (or not), and if you open the source, you may find an abstract that tells you more about the contents and findings of the source. All these leads can let you know how much further to look into your source.

Figure 7.2 Advanced Search Options

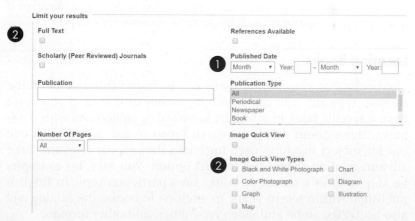

① Drop-down menus specify types of documents, types of publications, languages, and dates.

② Check boxes specify full text, references, cover stories, image types, and file types.

> **RESEARCH TIP** Sources that at first appear to be unrelated to your topic may actually be *relatable* to your topic. If you are writing about poor labor conditions in US clothing companies' supply chains in Asia, and you find an article about the working conditions of agricultural laborers in South America, don't just cast that article aside. Rather, explore the possible overlaps. Determine whether or not you can apply one situation to the other.

Don't forget that your sources need not have links to the full text for you to retrieve them easily. It is the role of a library to get you the information you need. If you cannot link to the full text of an article you want to read, find your library's Interlibrary Loan (ILL) system, which you can use to request books and copies of articles to be sent to your library for you. Often, ILL materials take less than a day for electronic delivery and anywhere from two days to two weeks for physical books.

As you choose and use sources, keep track of them. You can save them in a folder, or you can use your library's system for selecting and saving resources. You can save, email, or print the references you have selected. You may also have an option to export references to a citation management program such as RefWorks or EndNote. These programs allow you to create your own personal database of sources in which you can store your references and take notes. Later, when you're ready to create a bibliography, these programs will automatically format your references in MLA, APA, or another style. Ask a librarian if one of these programs is available to students on your campus.

Locating Books

The books that your library owns can be found through its online catalog. Typically, you can search by author or title or, if you don't have a specific book in mind, by keyword or subject. As with databases, think about different search terms to use, keeping an eye out for subject headings used for books that appear relevant. Take advantage of an "advanced search" option. You may, for example, be able to limit a search to books on a particular topic in English published within recent years. In addition to books, the catalog will also list DVDs, audio and video recordings, and other formats.

Unlike articles, books tend to cover broad topics, so be prepared to broaden your search terms. It may be that a book has a chapter or ten pages that are precisely what you need, but the catalog typically

THINKING CRITICALLY USING SEARCH TERMS

Imagine that your research question is this: Should first-year college students be required to live on campus? Identify useful key issues, terms, and related terms that you can use to search. (The first row has been completed as an example.)

Question	Key Terms	Related Terms	Search Terms
Should first-year college students be required to live on campus?	first-year students required to live on campus	freshmen freshman year residency policies residence hall requirement dorm dormitory	freshman OR first-year student* Residency rules OR residence requirement dorm*
Which schools have a first-year residency requirement, and which do not?			
What are the benefits and drawbacks of living on campus?			
How do alternative on- or off-campus living situations compare?			

doesn't index the contents of books in detail. Think instead of what kind of book might contain the information you need.

Once you've found some promising books in the catalog, note down the call numbers, find them on the shelves, and then browse. Because books on the same topic are shelved together, you can quickly see what additional books are available by scanning the shelves. As you browse, be sure to look for books that have been published recently enough for your purposes. You do not have to read a book from cover to cover to use it in your research. Instead, skim the introduction to see if it will be useful and then use its table of contents and index to pinpoint the sections of the book that are the most relevant.

If you are searching for a very specific name or phrase, you might try typing it into Google Book Search (books.google.com), which searches the contents of more than twenty-five million scanned books. Although it tends to retrieve too many results for most topics and you may only be able to see a snippet of content, it can help you locate a particular quote or identify which books might include an unusual name or phrase. There is a "find in a library" link that will help you determine whether the books are available in your library.

EXERCISE: PRACTICING RESEARCH

Select one of the research questions below or use one you're currently working on. Using the Visual Guide: Finding Discourse on Your Topic as well as the instruction in this chapter, determine the best research strategy: General internet searching? Library databases? Books? Narrow it down: Which websites will you visit? Which databases will you use? What books can you peruse by searching your library's catalog?

> *Research Question 1*: How do children's toys impact the development of gender?
>
> *Research Question 2*: What are the dangers and benefits of nationalism?
>
> *Research Question 3*: Should big college sports programs pay athletes?

Then, find your sources online, in the database, or in your library's catalog. Use words or phrases from the research question and combine them with your own words to search for related information to answer it. Practice maneuvers like limiting results by date range, looking for scholarly and popular sources, searching for images, or seeking only certain kinds of documents.

EVALUATING SOURCES

Each step of the way in your research process, you will be making choices about your sources. As you proceed, from selecting promising items in a database search to browsing the book collection, you will want to use the techniques for previewing and skimming detailed on pages 41–45 in order to make your selections and develop your argument as you research. Begin by asking yourself some basic questions:

- Is this source relevant?
- Is it current enough?

- Does the title or abstract suggest it will address an important aspect of my topic?

- Am I choosing sources that represent a range of ideas, not simply ones that support my opinion?

- Do I have a reason to believe that these sources are trustworthy?

> **RESEARCH TIP** During your research, write down observations and questions. This way, you won't find yourself with a pile of printouts and books and no idea what to say about them. What you have to say will flow naturally out of the prewriting you've already done — and that prewriting will help guide your further research.

Once you have collected a number of likely sources, you will want to do further filtering. Examine each one with these questions in mind:

- *Is this source credible? Does it include information about the author and his or her credentials that can help me decide whether to rely on it?* In the case of books, you might check a database for book reviews for a second opinion. In the case of websites, find out where the site came from and why it has been posted online. Don't use a source if you can't determine its authorship or purpose.

- *Will my audience find this source credible and persuasive?* A story about US politics from the *Washington Post*, whose writers conduct firsthand reporting in the nation's capital, carries more clout than a story from a small-circulation newspaper that is drawing its information from a wire service.

- *Am I using the best evidence available?* Quoting directly from a government report may be more effective than quoting a news story that summarizes the report. Finding evidence that supports your claims in a president's speeches or letters is more persuasive than drawing your conclusions from a page or two of a history textbook.

- *Am I being fair to all sides?* Make sure you are prepared to address alternate perspectives, even if you ultimately take a position. Avoid sources that clearly promote an agenda in favor of ones that your audience will consider balanced and reliable.

- *Can I corroborate my key claims in more than one source?* Compare your sources to ensure that you aren't relying on facts that can't be confirmed. If you're having trouble confirming a source, check with a librarian.

- **Do I really need this source?** It's tempting to use all the books and articles you have found, but if two sources say essentially the same thing, choose the one that is likely to carry the most weight with your audience.

Scholarly, Popular, and Trade Sources

An important part of finding and evaluating the reliability of your sources is determining whether they are **scholarly** or **popular** sources. In the table shown on pages 265–66, we cover some of the basic elements that distinguish these two types of publications. We also examine a third category called **trade** publications.

Scholarly publications are generally considered the gold standard of reliability in the production of knowledge and the circulation of discourse. This is primarily because scholarly publications are generally

- nonprofit;
- built on a mission to advance knowledge in a specific area;
- organized according to disciplinary methodologies, standards, and ethics; and
- peer-reviewed or refereed (meaning that before publication, the articles are reviewed and accepted by a group of experts in that field and in that specific area).

Popular publications—newspapers, magazines, newsletters, websites, blogs—may be more or less reliable sources, but they generally do not carry the academic weight of scholarly ones. Popular sources have relative value: Some have high journalistic and editorial standards—think of the *Los Angeles Times* or the *Economist* magazine—and may contain articles and essays by respected journalists and experts—even scholars. But even intellectual magazines like *Science* or the *New Yorker* are popular publications in the same sense that *Cosmopolitan, Game Informer, Better Homes and Gardens*, or *Car and Driver* are: They are written for a general audience, and they are driven by profit.

Consider the implications. Magazines and newspapers must publish articles that sell to broad audiences; indeed, the goal of any commercial media enterprise is to make money from sales, subscriptions, and sponsors. Therefore, they are not as likely as academic sources to offer the widest range of subjects or perspectives, the same level of complexity, or the deepest, most thorough, and thoughtful forms of analysis.

Trade publications, the third category of sources, are more related to publications in the popular category; however, trade sources are designed for people in particular industries and professional associations. They sometimes appear to be very complex because they assume that readers are familiar with an insider's vocabulary. However, they are not popular because they are not for a general audience, and they are not scholarly because they do not involve a peer review process. Nevertheless, trade publications often utilize the latest field-specific research and expert voices and may be considered reliable resources in many cases. That said, we must remember that industry groups are likely to interpret issues through the lens of their interests—so, for example, *Coal Age* magazine (published by Mining Media International) and *SNLEnergy* (published by the American Coal Council) are much more likely to view coal production and use favorably as compared to *Solar Today Magazine* (published by the American Solar Energy Society).

Remember that just because something is published in a scholarly journal doesn't mean it is peer reviewed. In some journals, a peer-reviewed article may sit side by side with a book review or an editorial. Popular magazines will almost never contain scholarly articles; a respected scholar might contribute an original essay to a popular magazine, but again that doesn't mean the article is "scholarly."

Types of Sources

	Scholarly	Popular	Trade
Publisher	Universities, government agencies, research foundations, and institutions	Media companies, for-profit groups, internet website owners, interest groups	Professional associations, trade groups, unions, business groups, consortiums
Purpose	To report on research, experiments, and theories to expand human knowledge	To inform, entertain, and engage; to expand influence or profit or both	To inform, entertain, and engage; to expand influence in a specific field or industry
Audience	Academics, intellectuals, specialists, researchers	General public	People who have interests in a specific trade or industry

(continued)

Types of Sources (*continued*)

	Scholarly	Popular	Trade
Language	Complex, technical, authoritative	Accessible, conversational	Accessible but with insider-speak such as jargon and acronyms
Sources cited	Always	Sometimes, usually through in-text reference or hyperlinks	Sometimes, usually through in-text reference or hyperlinks
Features and characteristics	Plain style; lots of footnotes or endnotes, long articles; few advertisements (if any); often charts and graphs; longer paragraphs and titles; peer reviewed	Glossy, attractive style; shorter and easier-to-digest articles; many advertisements; simple charts and graphs; shorter paragraphs and titles (if any); not peer reviewed	Various styles ranging from newsprint to glossy styles; technical but easier-to-digest articles, titles indicating industry-specific issues, advertising related to field; not peer reviewed
Frequency	Usually quarterly, semiannually	Usually daily, weekly, biweekly, monthly	Sometimes quarterly or semiannually; most often daily, weekly, monthly, bimonthly
Examples	*American Journal of Sociology, Harvard Asia Pacific Review, Foreign Affairs,* government reports	*Time, New York Times, Vogue, Popular Mechanics, HuffPost, Business Insider*	*AdWeek, Publishers Weekly, Columbia Journalism Review, Chronicle of Higher Education, Comics and Games Retailer*

Evaluating Online Sources

Unlike the information found in a library or published and circulated widely in print, much information online does not go through an evaluative process, as when librarians curate their collections or an editor reviews and selects material for a publication. Thus, one of the first things you must do to determine the quality and reliability of information online is consider the pathway of its publication on the internet. Did the information pass through any review process? Who was doing the reviewing? If the comments section in the *New York Times* shows someone claiming to be a doctor giving advice on some health issue, should you believe it? After all, you too could claim to be a doctor and publish your comments somewhere. At the same time, it may be that the commentator *is* a doctor and *is* reliable — but how would you know? In this hypothetical case, we would recommend corroborating the alleged doctor's claim using a respectable, reviewed medical publication (even if it happens to be openly available online).

Today, most print publications offer their content online in a digital format. However, there are also reliable online resources that are not duplicated in print, from high-quality citizen journalism to TED talks to university lectures online. There may be thoughtful blogs or other publication formats (video, podcast, indexes) created or curated by people who have a high degree of credibility, but you must be cautious. The popularity of a website, blog, or podcast does not automatically confer expertise upon the creators or producers. Neither does the way a website *looks*. Given the ease of entry into the marketplace of ideas via the internet and the relative ease of designing a professional-looking webpage, the popularity and design of a website cannot be considered key criteria in evaluating reliability.

A further problem is caused by the surge in disreputable publication venues that offer open-access publishing in journals that appear to be peer reviewed but really have dramatically lower standards — or none at all. These venues are usually predatory: They project the veneer of a scholarly journal, often with academic-sounding titles to match. For a fee, or sometimes for free (if they are ad revenue–based), these "journals" will publish material with little or no quality control. They are primary locations for fraudulent and hoax papers. Be wary of online journals discovered on the open internet and review them very carefully. It is always safer to use your university databases for scholarly sources.

Nevertheless, it is likely most of us will seek sources on the internet. The best steps you can take to remain a skeptical but open-minded researcher is to apply critical thinking skills. The first thing to do is consider all the contexts that inform your online sources:

- How did they get onto the internet?
- What organizations or individuals are behind their publication?
- Were they originally published elsewhere?
- What are the limitations of this particular kind of online resource?

- Why is this type of source a legitimate form of evidence in the context of your analysis?

- What special authority does the individual or group cited have for speaking on an issue?

With so much information online, you don't always get the basic indicators of authority, such as author credentials or an indication of editorial review. Remember that anyone can publish online with no review process. All that is needed is access to the internet.

You need not discount information available online, though; the internet provides a stunning array of unique perspectives and analyses. It has made it possible for people everywhere to contribute their arguments, opinions, and comments to public discourses.

> **WRITING TIP** You can use (and cite) the information you find on websites, in blogs, in comments, and on social media posts; just make sure you frame that information with a fair accounting of the source. ("One user on YouTube with the handle *SportsTVFan* commented that the latest Super Bowl commercials are '*X*.'" or "Twitter user @DavidScottRedpath, an amateur astronomer with over a million followers, posted a tweet that claimed *X* about black holes.")

Many students have been told to examine the domains of websites to judge the reliability of a source; however, whether a website is a *.com*, *.org*, or *.edu* is a weak marker of a source's reliability. All domain types can host reliable or unreliable information. Similarly, tweets and comments, even when written by experts, may or may not carry much weight depending on the subject and occasion of their tweets or comments.

The information you will look for as you evaluate internet sources is often the same as what you need to record in any citation. Use clues in URLs to see where sites originate. For example, URLs containing *.k12* are hosted at elementary and secondary schools, so they may be intended for a young audience; those ending in *.gov* are government agencies, so they tend to provide official information, but if a *.gov* website is followed by a country code, you must also consider the context of place revealed by that origin. A website with a domain such as *.gov.ca* (Canada) may be more trustworthy than one from a country where freedoms of speech are curtailed, such as *.gov.kp* (North Korea). You can streamline the process of creating a list of works cited by identifying these elements as you

Figure 7.3   A Page from a Government Website

1. URL—Site has a .gov domain.

2. "About NIH" link will explain the mission and role of the government agency.

3. Contact provided for additional verification if needed.

4. Article dateline and title with subtitle descriptions.

5. Article begins by citing authoritative sources.

find and begin to evaluate a source. (See Documentation later in this chapter for more on how to properly cite sources.)

In Figure 7.3, the URL includes the ending *.gov*, meaning it is a government website, an official document that has been vetted. There is an "about" link that will explain the government agency's mission. This appears to be a high-quality source of basic information on the issue. The information you need to cite this report is also on the page; make sure you keep track of where you found the source and when, since websites can change. One way to keep track is by creating an account at a social bookmarking site such as Diigo (diigo.com) where you can store and annotate websites.

Figure 7.4 on page 270 shows how the information on a web page might lead you to reject it as a source. Clearly, although this site purports to provide educational information in a well-meaning way, its primary purpose is to sell services and products. The focus on marketing should send up a red flag.

Figure 7.4 A Page from a Commercial Website

① URL shows that the site is a .com (commercial) site.

② Menu bar offers speaking services, recipes that use sponsored products, and shopping for sponsored products.

③ "About" link tells us that author's qualifications do not include formal education in health science.

④ Additional link to the "news" is actually an advertisement. (We suspect the "free newsletter" will also be ad-driven.)

⑤ Article on "proven" benefits of turmeric is list-based and anecdotal, and it supports the ad nearby.

Exercise: Finding Reliable Websites

Perform an internet search on a topic, and find a more reliable and less reliable website, using the questions below (and continued on the next page) to help you determine the factors that indicate reliability. *Hint*: To get past the most popular results from major news organizations, go deeper in the search results.

- What kind of domain does the website have? Does it impact its reliability? How so?
- Can you follow an "about" link (or delete everything after the first slash in the URL to go to the parent site)? If so, who is behind the website?

- What is the purpose or mission of the individual or organization operating the website?
- Are there advertisements visible on the page? If so, what kind of products are they? Is the content of the website related to the products being advertised? How?
- Is the information on the website reviewed by anyone before it is selected and posted? Who is selecting and reviewing? Is that person (or body) reputable and reliable? Why or why not?

Why Finding Reliable Internet Sources Is So Challenging

With our instant access to so much knowledge, and in the midst of an online cacophony of perspectives and voices, finding dependable, trustworthy sources of information can be difficult. Today, individuals can articulate their views publicly in a variety of online venues. With just a few clicks, individuals can expose poor customer service at a restaurant or abuses of power by police. They can report on news events as they happen, rally like-minded people to causes and activism, and share their opinions about almost anything in videos, blogs, tweets, and comments. This suggests an unprecedented democratic potential: The role of the internet in facilitating Arab Spring, a series of antigovernment protests across the Middle East in 2010–2011, or the #occupy, #blacklivesmatter, and #metoo movements in the United States, is inspiring. The internet's structure gives voice to the voiceless, allowing underrepresented and systematically marginalized people to share experiences and form discourse communities across the globe.

At the same time, this democratic potential is accompanied by serious perils. Hate groups and narrowly ideological activist organizations, for example, sometimes deliberately spread propaganda, promoting shallow conspiracy theories and outright lies. Consider a couple of claims popularized by such groups in recent years: that the Sandy Hook Elementary School shooting was staged by gun-control activists seeking to push through new firearms controls; that Barack Obama was not born in the United States; that the September 11, 2001, attacks on the World Trade Center were an "inside job"; that a secret society called the Illuminati controls the world. These false stories were created and perpetuated by highly partisan, conspiracy-driven, or fraudulent websites and were amplified by individual social media users vulnerable to such misinformation who shared the stories with networks of friends and followers.

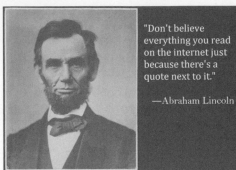

"Don't believe everything you read on the internet just because there's a quote next to it."

—Abraham Lincoln

Sometimes "authority" can be misleading.

Critical thinking can help mitigate the dangers of the media environment, which includes the possibility that lies, hysteria, and even violence can result from the unsafe, uncritical acceptance of information available on the internet. The proliferation of "fake news" stories and websites, viral misinformation campaigns, clickbait articles, and fraudulent websites all complicate our efforts to find quality information online. But not all fake news is created by political operatives, foreign agents, malicious bots, or entrepreneurs seeking to make money from advertising on bogus websites. Some fake news stories are created by everyday individuals. In 2016, Tim Tucker, a Twitter user who photographed a line of buses near a Donald Trump election rally in Austin, Texas, claimed that his photographs were evidence of Democratic Party busing in paid anti-Trump protesters. By his own admission, this claim was false, invented out of thin air, yet although he started with only 40 followers on Twitter, his post was shared 16,000 times on that site and 350,000 times on Facebook in a single day and subsequently was covered by a variety of conservative news outlets. Soon, it was referenced by Trump himself on his Twitter account. In just a few days, one user's incautious post created a national firestorm. ("Anytime you see me in the future," Tucker later said, "I can assure you I am going to try my best to be balanced with the facts and very clear about what is opinion and what is not.")

In sum, the internet gives us unprecedented access to information and to our own assertions of authority, but this empowerment also requires us to examine information carefully and proffer it responsibly. It is important to respect accuracy and reliability when sharing our ideas on the internet, to track the sources of viral stories, and to fact-check as much as possible the claims and details they offer.

A Word on "Fake News"

It has become somewhat fashionable to label as "fake news" any kind of information that does not accord with one's own worldview. For example, politicians often call into question the objectivity and reliability of news outlets that have been the standard-bearers of ethical journalism in the United States for decades—in some cases, more than a century (the *New York Times*, for example). Here we must be emphatic: The mainstream news media, such as the *New York Times*, CNN, FOX, MSNBC, and others, are *not* fake news outlets. These organizations may or may not exhibit political biases and may or may not privilege information likely to attract certain kinds of readers and viewers, but they also carefully demarcate what they consider to be news programs and opinion programs, and they follow the most rigorous standards of verifiable reporting. (Also remember that taking a thoughtful position is not the same as having a bias. In fact, taking a thoughtful position means *overcoming* biases, integrating a range of perspectives, meeting challenges to your own views, and adhering strictly to the goals of fairness and accuracy.)

Whether today's fake news stories are created by nefarious individuals or antagonistic intelligence agencies, their purpose is to sow confusion, doubt, and disorder by promoting falsehoods on the internet. Often these stories play upon base prejudices and superstitions. Their creators are not shy about telling wholesale lies, inventing quotations, and manipulating charts, graphs, and images, for example. They are indiscriminate in their attacks on truth: Liberals and conservatives, celebrities and everyday people have been targeted. Sometimes, fake news stories are built around issues: Unscientific claims denying climate change, the efficacy of vaccinations, and the integrity of elections are just a few instances. Other types of fake news stories are created to further the agendas of activist organizations. Still others are designed merely to be eye-catching, their sole purpose to generate traffic to a website.

Unreliable or misleading news sources also include popular tabloids such as the *National Enquirer*, which blurs the lines between fiction and reality with salacious, screaming headlines like "Muslim Spies in Obama's CIA" and "Ted Cruz's Father Linked to JFK Assassination." Consider, too, satirical publications and programs like *The Onion*, *The Daily Show* (Comedy Central), or *Last Week Tonight* (HBO). Although such programs offer sometimes sharp commentary and analysis, their purpose is largely to entertain, not to inform. As such, they should not be considered quality sources of information.

Anatomy of a Fake News Story   NewsPunch is a fake news website posing as a legitimate news outlet, which you can see in Figure 7.5 on p. 274. It has a respectable title and a "punchy" tagline ("Where Mainstream Fears to Tread"), as well as a clean design and layout characteristic of respectable news websites (a navigation menu of

Figure 7.5 A Fake News Website

1. The title bar features an ad, which is uncommon on most reputable news sites and signals a page that is revenue-driven.

2. The navigation menu looks standard, but "Contact Us" is repeated on both lines, and there is an option for "Advertise," another warning sign.

3. Another ad, higher and more prominent on the page than most articles.

4. The stories mimic the layout of news sites: a photo with a category label ("Health") and a title, publication date, author, and first lines of the article.

relevant topics and lists of recent and popular articles). There is even a headline ticker bar that scrolls between titles as if they were breaking news stories. When we visited the site, clickbait titles appeared such as "Under Obama, US Became World's #1 Hotspot for Pedophilia." Thus, although the site projects some signs of journalistic legitimacy, we knew we needed to look more closely to determine if it was actually reliable.

We looked at the first story on the page and searched for author Sean Adl-Tabatabai to verify his credentials as a writer. We discovered through a quick internet search that the former television producer is the founder of this fake news site, and the site has been flagged by a European Union task force charged with investigating Russian efforts to destabilize Western democracies. We found no information about the second author listed, Niamh Harris.

The first headline, "CDC: 'Statistically Strong Relationship Exists Between MMR and Autism,'" suggests that the Centers for Disease Control and Prevention (CDC), the US government's national health protection agency, makes this claim. In fact, the CDC is *very* clear that MMR vaccines do NOT cause autism—the CDC uses huge letters on its website to emphasize its position—and it has devoted significant resources to debunking dangerous theories that they do. The quotation in the headline is actually attributed to Dr. Brian Hooker of the Children's Health Defense organization, an activist group widely discredited in the medical community for its antivaccine stance and not associated at all with the CDC.

Hooker's findings were first published (the NewsPunch article tells us) in the *Journal of American Physicians and Surgeons*. This publication sounds fairly impressive at first. However, further searching on Google and "source watch" websites such as Beall's List of Predatory Journals and Publications showed us that this journal is published by the Association of American Physicians and Surgeons (AAPS), an ultraconservative activist group advocating a range of scientifically discredited theories, including that HIV does not cause AIDS and that abortion leads to breast cancer. The *Journal of American Physicians and Surgeons* is not listed in reputable academic literature databases like MEDLINE and Web of Science, and the US Library of National Medicine has denied AAPS's requests to index the journal, which has also been listed by watchdog scholars as a predatory open-access journal. As a result of our evaluation of the website plus further research and cross-checking, we concluded this article is fake news and not to be trusted.

The article on MMR vaccines and autism, and the other examples cited earlier, are undoubtedly the strictest forms of fake news (spurious, mendacious, malicious). Websites like NewsPunch contain information mostly from other sources, recycled and reinterpreted through a sensationalistic or ideological lens. Other partisan websites may be less severe but nevertheless project the look of a news organization with none of its integrity.

What we cannot stress enough is that such information sources—and, in fact, *all* types of information sources—demand our most careful critical thinking and information literacy skills. Use the table on page 276 to help identify and evaluate resources that may be unreliable. Use the Checklist for Identifying Fake News on page 278 to ascertain a website's origins, legitimacy, and value and to dig further into the online sources you find to measure their validity.

Types of "Fake News" and Unreliable Content

Type	Creator(s)	Purpose(s)	Features	Example(s)
Propaganda	Government agencies, activist groups, political organizations, corporations	To affect social and political beliefs, attitudes, and behaviors to further an agenda	Widespread, often misleading or biased; one-sided (not objective or neutral)	Advertising, issue-based political messages, public service announcements, recruitment or indoctrination materials
Clickbait	Companies and paid content creators	To entice viewers to navigate to websites designed to generate ad revenue based on traffic volume	Sensational "teaser" headlines with links	"Amazing" health news, discoveries, celebrity gossip, lists, inspirational or revolting personal stories
Sponsored content	Companies and marketing firms	To present advertisements as news or interest stories so as to drive revenue	Designed to look like news, will reference products or services in main text	Articles worked into major news sources and webpages directing users to third-party content; often labeled
Partisan news	Media companies and special-interest groups	To provide perspective-based information to like-minded viewers/readers	Ideological; not impartial (although may claim to be); facts may be present but selective; biased interpretations of facts	Self-identified liberal or conservative information outlets, news personalities; some mainstream networks
Conspiracy theory	Special-interest groups, individuals	To subvert, fool, or entertain (for political or other purposes)	Dismisses experts and authorities; provides simplistic or sensationalistic answers to complex questions; spreads beliefs rooted in paranoia, fear, uncertainty	Material claiming to provide the "real" truth contrary to accepted knowledge or beliefs; claims to expose "hoaxes" perpetuated by powerful persons or interests

Native Advertising and Branded Content

Some magazines, you probably have noticed, contain nearly as many (or even more) pages of advertisements than original content — a sign that the publication's content may be driven by the sponsors. In some publications, content itself can be part of an overall marketing scheme. In the magazine industry, this type of content is known as "ad-friendly copy" or "advertorial," with articles deliberately written to puff up a person, product, or service. On the internet, you have probably seen links to "sponsored content," which is like a digital version of advertorial (see Fig. 7.6). Even reputable news agencies will include links to sponsored content (and will usually indicate as much). These are not good sources because they are not neutral: They are less interested in providing quality information and more interested in selling a product or service.

Figure 7.6 Sponsored Content

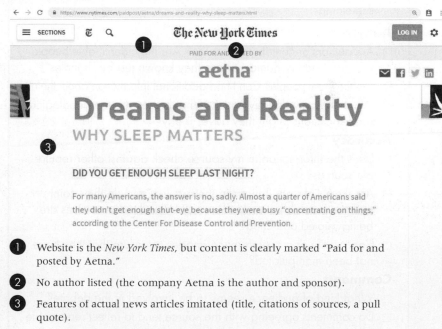

① Website is the *New York Times*, but content is clearly marked "Paid for and posted by Aetna."

② No author listed (the company Aetna is the author and sponsor).

③ Features of actual news articles imitated (title, citations of sources, a pull quote).

✓ A CHECKLIST FOR IDENTIFYING FAKE NEWS

Website

☐ Does my source appear to be on a reputable website? Is it a .com, .edu, .org, or .net?

☐ Is there an "About" link (or a "Who We Are" or "Mission" link)? What individual or organization is behind the website?

☐ Is the content edited, or can users post anything?

☐ Does the website respect intellectual property? What website policies ensure (or compromise) source integrity?

☐ Do errors or misspellings on the website signal a lack of quality or reputability?

☐ How is the website supported (ads, donations, sponsorships)? What kinds of products and services are being sold, directly or indirectly, on the website? Are ads and sponsored content clearly marked as such?

☐ Are there a lot of pop-ups, surveys, or other distractions? Are visitors being asked for personal information or to sign up for something?

Authors

☐ Are authors or contributors named? Are they identifiable people with first and last names, or are they known just by "handles"?

☐ Are they real people? Can I find additional information about them?

☐ What authority do they have? What biases or other ideological predispositions might they have, if any?

Accuracy

☐ Does the information in my source check against other reputable sources?

☐ Are there links or citations in the articles (and do they point to other reputable, timely sources)? What kind of sources are being quoted and cited?

☐ Can I verify or cross-reference images to ensure that they have not been manipulated?

Comments

☐ What kind of audience seems to be involved in the debate?

☐ Do comments agreeing with the source tend to reflect reasonable ideas and common values? What about dissenting comments?

☐ If the site does not allow commenting, why?

Considering How Current Sources Are

Popular sources do have one major advantage in that they are very current. Newspapers and magazines publish frequently enough—daily, weekly, monthly—that they can respond to events as they occur. Although this schedule makes them prone to errors of fact and misreadings of developing situations, they have an indispensable immediacy. Academic journals, on the other hand, usually publish quarterly or semiannually because the peer-review process is so elaborate and the content so rich: Although it takes a longer time to write, review, and publish issues of an academic journal, the content tends not to age as fast. Because academic journals are so deeply researched, analyzed, and reviewed, their findings generally have staying power.

So far, we have been discussing the difference between scholarly, popular, and trade **periodicals**—that is, publications that appear on a regular basis. Whether they are scholarly, popular, or trade publications, or appear frequently or not, reputable publications have strong editorial review processes and abide by the codes of journalistic ethics. Full-length books, too, may be popular or scholarly, published by a university press or a respected organization. Although scholarly books are not always peer reviewed, many academic publishers are overseen by editorial boards who solicit feedback from expert reviewers. Academic books are also subject to a secondary review process in scholarly journals after they are published, so you can always examine how a source has been regarded by other experts if you wanted to verify its credibility. Like with popular and scholarly periodicals, full-length books may also have different levels of continuing relevance. Some books are published quickly and are intended to speak to current events; others take years to write, vet, and publish and may stick around as authoritative sources for a long time, even decades.

Remember, however, that academic books *do* age. Those you find on the library shelves may be much older than the relevant results from an internet or database search. Such books published long ago may be of historical interest, but they are rarely the strongest sources speaking directly to current issues, and they must be regarded in context. A book about juvenile delinquency published by a sociologist in 1955 cannot be used as evidence for a theory of adolescence nowadays, and even a landmark work, like Sigmund Freud's *The Interpretation of Dreams* (1899), may be an interesting book to study in and of itself or may prove to be an excellent background reference in your work, but it would not serve as evidence in an argument that the Oedipal complex — Freud's famous theory of psychosexual development — should inform how parents interact with their children today.

✓ **A CHECKLIST FOR EVALUATING SOURCES**

☐ Can I identify the person or organization who produced the source?

☐ Can I identify the source's purpose?

☐ Are the authors real, reliable, and credentialed?

☐ Do sources cited represent a range of ideas, not simply ones that support one viewpoint?

☐ Are images verifiable from other sources?

☐ Is the source recent? If not, is the information I will be using from it likely or unlikely to change over time?

☐ Does the source treat the topic superficially or in depth?

☐ Does the article speak directly (or relevantly) to my topic and tentative thesis?

☐ If the article is from a scholarly journal, am I sure I understand it?

☐ Is the source titled and marketed as entertainment? If so, have I considered the author's commercial biases?

☐ Is the source targeted at a specific audience likely to be sympathetic to its claims?

☐ Do the arguments in the source seem sound, based on what I have learned about skillful critical reading and writing?

PERFORMING YOUR OWN PRIMARY RESEARCH

Research isn't limited to the world of professors and scientists. In one way or another, everyone does research at some point. If you decided to open your own business, you would want to do market research to persuade the bank that you are likely to be profitable enough to repay a loan. If you wanted to find out how and why a campus monument was erected, you could visit the university library's institutional archives and seek out information on it. If you were reviewing a film or book, you would probably go to the cinema or read in a comfortable place. Doing any of these things is performing primary research. In college, you might find yourself working on primary research alongside faculty members or participating in a class project to collect data. In other circumstances, you may wish to supplement your arguments with primary sources. Here, we touch on several kinds of primary research commonly performed by students.

Interviewing Peers and Local Authorities

For many topics, consider that you are surrounded by experts at your college. You ought to try to consult them—for instance, members of the faculty or other authorities on art, business, law, university administration, and so forth. You can also consult interested laypersons. Remember that experts may have their biases and "ordinary" people may have knowledge that experts lack. When interviewing experts, keep in mind Pablo Picasso's comment: "You mustn't always believe what I say. Questions tempt you to tell lies, particularly when there is no answer."

If you are interviewing your peers, you will probably want to make an effort to get a representative sample. Of course, even within a group not all members share a single view—for example, many African Americans favor affirmative action, but not all do; some lawmakers support capital punishment, but again, many do not. Make an effort to talk to a range of people who might offer varied opinions. You may learn some unexpected things.

You may also collect **testimonial** evidence from professors, students, community members, or family members. If you are writing about the women's rights movement of the 1970s, you might interview a professor or family member who lived through the era or participated in civil rights activities. You may know veterans who can speak to issues surrounding US wars or the experience of military service. Or perhaps an expert on a particular subject is visiting your campus for a lecture or talk, and you can find a way to put some questions of interest to her.

Conducting Observations

Observational research is the process of collecting information by situating yourself in a real-life context and making observations of what is present or what occurs. It may be *structured*, which means that you spend time designing your observation in a systematic way so as to get consistent results. For example, perhaps you want to see

Visual Guide: Conducting Interviews

1 Find subjects for interviews

If you are looking for expert opinions, you may want to start with a faculty member on your campus. Search department and college websites for information about the special interests of the faculty and also about lecturers who will be visiting the campus.

2 Request the interview

Request the interview, preferably in writing, a week in advance.

- Ask for ample time, but respect the interviewee's schedule.

- Indicate whether the material will be confidential and (if relevant) ask if you may record the interview.

If the person accepts the invitation:

- Ask if he or she recommends any reading.
- Establish a suitable time and place.

4 Conduct the interview

- Begin by engaging in brief conversation, without taking notes.

- Come prepared with an opening question or two, but as the interview proceeds, don't hesitate to ask questions that you hadn't anticipated asking.

- Even if your subject has consented to let you record the interview, be prepared to take notes on points that strike you as especially significant.

- Near the end, ask the subject if he or she wishes to add anything, perhaps by way of clarifying some earlier comment.

- Conclude by thanking the interviewee and by offering to provide a copy of the final version of your paper.

3 Prepare thoroughly

- Read any recommended or background material.

- Formulate some questions, keeping in mind that you want detailed answers. Questions beginning with *Why* and *How* will usually require the interviewee to go beyond yes and no answers.

5 Write up the interview

- As soon as possible, type up your notes and observations and clarify them, filling in any abbreviations or shorthand you used while you still remember.

- If you recorded the interview, transcribe it or use a transcription program such as Transcribe. (You can also upload the audio to YouTube and then click on the transcribe button as it plays.)

- Scan the transcription and mark the parts that now strike you as especially significant.

- Be especially careful to indicate which words are direct quotations from your interview and which are your own observations. If in doubt, check with the interviewee.

if male and female children are more likely to select gender-specific toys from a toy chest if they are with peers of the same sex; to prepare, you might code each toy according to its gendered properties and then watch and record while same-sex and mixed-sex groups of children are at play in the toy chest. To aim for consistent results, you might conduct the observation in multiple sittings, but always at the same time with the same number of children in each group.

Observational research may also be *unstructured*, meaning that you simply immerse yourself in a situation and carefully note what you see or experience. If you visited a toy store to gather impressions about how children's toys are segregated according to gender, you would be performing unstructured observational research. The same goes for attending a political convention as an observer (as opposed to a participant) or riding along with a police officer.

However, when you conduct observations, you must be careful to abide by ethical standards; you should not record people without their consent, for example. You must also be aware of observer biases—the notion that people's behavior changes when they know they are being watched, for one thing, and also that you yourself as a researcher may get swept up in what you are observing to a degree that you are not able to be neutral or objective in your observations.

Conducting Surveys

Surveys are excellent ways to ascertain the opinions and beliefs of a certain population. Whether you distribute your surveys via paper or set up an online survey through an online service like Doodle or SurveyMonkey, your college's in-house software such as Qualtrics, or even a Facebook poll, be sure to distribute your survey to the target population. Whether you are trying to collect opinions, values, behaviors, or facts, your survey questions should be constructed carefully to get the data that you want. Here are some other pitfalls of collecting surveys:

- *Not enough respondents/bad sample size:* If only five women responded to your survey on attitudes about fraternities on campus, you shouldn't use just five responses to say "80% of women on campus have a favorable view of fraternities."

- *Leading questions:* Leading questions use language likely to influence respondents' answers, such as "How fast should drivers be allowed to go on our serene campus roads?" As you can see, the language "leads" the respondent: For these questions, respondents are likely to answer lower speeds for "serene" roads. A more appropriate version of this question would be "What in your opinion is a safe driving speed for campus roads?"

- *Loaded questions:* Loaded questions push respondents to answer questions that don't fully or accurately represent their actual opinions. "On a scale of 1 to 5," a loaded question might ask, "how awful do you think it is that our administration is raising tuition?" Such a question forces all respondents to answer in the "awful" range, even if they are somewhat satisfied with the tuition amount overall.

Research in Archives and Special Collections

Archives are collections of material maintained and preserved by organizations such as college and university libraries, public libraries, corporations, governments, churches, museums, and historical societies. Archives generally contain records that are important to an institution's own history and that may be relevant to others. The National Archives in Washington, DC, for example, curates a vast number of resources, including America's founding documents and military service records. Coca-Cola's company archives and the Walt Disney archives are examples of corporate archives that hold a vast array of materials related to those companies' pasts. Your college or university probably keeps its own institutional archives in its library.

Special collections are bodies of original material—including photographs, films, letters, memos, manuscripts of unique interests, and often material artifacts—usually gathered around a specialized topic, theme, or individual. Special collections often include original, rare, and valuable artifacts that may require permission for access or examination. Many libraries and museums offer at least limited access to digital archives and special collections via their websites, and some databases offer access to primary research sources, too (letters, original newspapers, early manuscripts, and so on).

Some special collections are broad and deep: The Library of Congress, the Smithsonian, and other national museums, for example, hold special collections on a variety of subjects in American political, social, and natural history. Other special collections can be quite specific, ranging from collections of science fiction pulp novels of the 1950s; to letters from combat veterans of World War II; to photograph, film, art, and music collections, antique and contemporary. The Blues Archive at the University of Mississippi contains—among other treasures—the musician B.B. King's personal record collection. The popular culture collection at Bowling Green State University holds 10,000 comic books and graphic novels, among other curiosities like a complete Pokémon set and *Star Trek* memorabilia.

Exercises: Conducting Primary Research

1. *Observation*: Visit a location on campus or a local event and report on the subjects or interactions you find there. Try to formulate a question you want answered: Do people tend to eat lunch outside more often when the cafeteria is busy? Do more people dress in

school colors on days when the football team or basketball team is competing?

2. **Survey**: Design three to five survey questions that will help you aggregate data about attitudes, beliefs, opinions, or behaviors of students on your campus. Your survey might be about a specific campus issue or political or social opinions, or you could imagine a demographic you are trying to reach, such as in-state or out-of-state or international students, African American or Latinx students, or students of a particular religion. Reflect on how you might distribute this survey—electronically or using paper—and why.

3. **Archives**: Visit the website of your own school, or another local college or museum, and examine its special collections. Identify the special collections available and choose one that sounds especially interesting. Look further into it: What kinds of materials are in the collection? Is digital access available? If so, select an example of an original artifact (document, image, etc.) and save it or print it out for closer inspection. For what kind of research topics might it be an important or relevant item? If digital access is unavailable, identify an item you would like to get access to and outline the process of doing so.

SYNTHESIZING SOURCES

When you are evaluating sources, consider the words of Francis Bacon, Shakespeare's contemporary:

> Some books are to be tasted, others to be swallowed, and some few to be chewed and digested.

Your instructor will expect you not just to find but to digest your sources. This doesn't mean you need to accept them but only that you need to read them thoughtfully. Your readers will expect you to tell them *what you make of your sources*, which means that you will go beyond writing a summary and will synthesize the material into your own contribution to the discourse. *Your* view is what is wanted, and readers expect this view to be thoughtful—not mere summary and not mere tweeting.

Let's pause for a moment and consider the word **synthesis**. You probably are familiar with *photosynthesis*, the chemical process in green plants that produces carbohydrates from carbon dioxide and hydrogen. Synthesis combines preexisting elements and produces something new. In your writing, you will *synthesize* sources, combining existing material into something new, drawing nourishment from what has already been said (giving credit, of course), and converting it into something new—a view that you think is worth considering. In our use of the word *synthesis*, even a view that you utterly reject becomes a part of your new creation *because it helped stimulate you to formulate your view*; without the idea that you reject, you might not have developed the view that you now hold.

During the process of reading and evaluating sources, and afterward, you will want to listen, think, and say to yourself something like the following:

- "No, no, I see things very differently; it seems to me that . . ."
- "Yes, of course, but on one large issue I think I differ."
- "Yes, sure, I agree, but I would go further and add . . ."
- "Yes, I agree with the conclusion, but I hold this conclusion for reasons different from the ones offered."

> **WRITING TIP** In your final draft, *you must give credit to all your sources.* Let the reader know whether you are quoting (in this case, you will use quotation marks around all material directly quoted), whether you are summarizing (you will explicitly say so), or whether you are paraphrasing (again, you will explicitly say so).

TAKING NOTES

Whether you are performing primary or secondary research, using library special collections or online resources, you should be keeping notes along the way. When it comes to taking notes, all researchers have their own habits that they swear by: We still prefer to take notes on four-by-six-inch index cards; others use a notebook or a computer for note taking. If you use a citation management program such as RefWorks or EndNote, you can store your personal notes and commentary with the citations you have saved. By using the program's search function, you can easily pull together related notes and citations, or you can create project folders for your references so that you can easily review what you've collected.

Whatever method you use, the following techniques should help you maintain consistency and keep organized during the research process:

1. If you use a notebook or index cards, organize them carefully, write in ink (pencil gets smudgy), and write on only

one side of the paper or card to avoid losing track of your material. If you keep notes electronically, consider an online tool such as Microsoft OneNote, a Google Doc, or another cloud-based service so that you will not lose your research in the event of a computer crash or a lost laptop.

2. Summarize, for the most part, rather than quote at length. Quote only passages in which the writing is especially effective or passages that are in some way crucial. Make sure that all quotations are exact.

3. Indicate the source. The author's last name is enough if you have consulted only one work by the author, but if you consult more than one work by an author, you need further identification, such as both the author's name and a short title.

4. Add your own comments about the substance of what you are recording. Such comments as "but contrast with Sherwin" or "seems illogical" or "evidence?" will ensure that you are thinking as well as reading and writing.

5. In a separate computer file, or on a separate card or page, write a bibliographic entry for each source. The information in each entry will vary, depending on whether the source is a book, a periodical, an electronic document, and so forth. The kind of information (e.g., author and title) needed for each type of source can be found in the sections MLA Format: The List of Works Cited (p. 300) and APA Format: The List of References (p. 313).

A NOTE ON PLAGIARIZING

Plagiarism is the unacknowledged use of someone else's work. The word comes from a Latin word for "kidnapping," and plagiarism is indeed the stealing of something engendered by someone else. Your college or your class instructor probably has issued a statement concerning plagiarism. If there is such a statement, be sure to read it carefully.

We won't deliver a sermon on the dishonesty (and folly) of plagiarism; we intend only to help you understand exactly what plagiarism is. The first thing to say is that plagiarism is not limited to the unacknowledged quotation of words.

Paraphrasing   A *paraphrase* is a sort of word-by-word or phrase-by-phrase translation of the author's language into your own language. Unlike a summary, then, a paraphrase is approximately as long as the original.

Paraphrase thus has its uses, but writers often use it unnecessarily, and students who overuse it may find themselves crossing the border into plagiarism. True, if you paraphrase you are using your own words, but you are also using someone else's ideas, and, equally important, you are using this other person's sequence of thoughts.

Even if you change every third word in your source, you are plagiarizing. Here is an example of this sort of plagiarism, based on the previous sentence:

> Even if you alter every second or third word that your source gives, you still are plagiarizing.

Further, even if the writer of this paraphrase had cited a source after the paraphrase, he or she would still have been guilty of plagiarism. How, you may ask, can a writer who cites a source be guilty of plagiarism? Easy. Readers assume that only the gist of the idea is the source's and that the development of the idea—the way it is set forth—is the present writer's work. A paraphrase that runs to several sentences is in no significant way the writer's work: The writer is borrowing not only the idea but also the shape of the presentation, the sentence structure. What the writer needs to do is to write something like this:

> Changing an occasional word does not free the writer from the obligation to cite a source.

And, if the central idea were not a commonplace one, the source would still need to be cited.

Now consider this question: *Why* paraphrase? As we explained in Summarizing and Paraphrasing in Chapter 2 (pp. 57–61), the chief reason to paraphrase a passage is to clarify it—that is, to ensure that you and your readers understand a passage that—perhaps because it is badly written—is obscure. Often there is no good answer for why you should paraphrase. Since a paraphrase is as long as the original, you might as well quote the original, if you think that a passage of that length is worth quoting. Probably it is *not* worth quoting in full; probably you should *not* paraphrase but rather should drastically *summarize* most of it, and perhaps quote a particularly effective phrase or two.

> ✓ A CHECKLIST FOR AVOIDING PLAGIARISM
>
> Ask yourself these questions, first about your notes:
> - ☐ Did I always put quoted material within quotation marks?
> - ☐ Did I summarize *in my own words* and give credit to the source for the idea?
> - ☐ Did I avoid paraphrasing? That is, did I avoid copying, keeping the structure of the source's sentences but using some of my own words?
>
> And then about your paper:
> - ☐ If I set forth a borrowed idea, do I give credit, even though the words and the structure of the sentences are entirely my own?
> - ☐ If I quote directly, do I put the words within quotation marks and cite the source?
> - ☐ Do I *not* cite material that can be considered common knowledge?
> - ☐ If I have the slightest doubt about whether I should or should not cite a source, have I taken the safe course and cited the source?

COMPILING AN ANNOTATED BIBLIOGRAPHY

When several sources have been identified and gathered, many researchers prepare an annotated bibliography. That's a list providing all relevant bibliographic information (just as it will appear in your Works Cited list or References list), as well as a brief descriptive and evaluative summary of each source—perhaps one to three sentences. Your instructor may ask you to provide an annotated bibliography for your research project.

An annotated bibliography serves four main purposes:

1. It helps you master the material contained in any given source. To find the heart of the argument presented in an article or book, to phrase it briefly, and to comment on it, you must understand it fully.

2. It helps you think about how each portion of your research fits into the whole of your project, how you will use it, and how it relates to your topic and thesis.

3. It allows your readers to see quickly which items may be especially helpful in their own research.
4. It gives you hands-on practice at bibliographic format, thereby easing the job of creating your final bibliography (the Works Cited list or References list of your paper).

Following is an example entry for an annotated bibliography in MLA (Modern Language Association) format for a project on the effect of violence in the media. Notice that the entry does three things:

1. It begins with a bibliographic entry — author (last name first), title, and so forth.
2. Then it provides information about the content of the work under consideration.
3. Then it suggests how the source might work to support your argument in the final research paper you are writing.

Clover, Carol J. *Men, Women, and Chain Saws: Gender in the Modern Horror Film*. Princeton UP, 1992. The author focuses on Hollywood horror movies of the 1970s and 1980s. She studies representations of women and girls in these movies and the responses of male viewers to female characters, suggesting that this relationship is more complex and less exploitative than the common wisdom claims. Could use this source to establish a counterpoint to the idea that all women are represented stereotypically in horror films.

Citation Generators   There are many citation generators available online. These generators allow you to enter the information about your source, and, with a click, they will create Works Cited entries in APA or MLA format. But just as you cannot trust spell- and grammar-checkers in Microsoft Word, you cannot trust these generators completely. If you use them, be sure to double-check what they produce before submitting your essay. Always remember that responsible writers take care to cite their sources properly and that failure to do so puts you at risk for accusations of plagiarism.

QUOTING FROM SOURCES

When is it necessary, or appropriate, to quote? Using your notes, consider where the reader would benefit by seeing the exact words of your source. If you are arguing that Z's definition of *rights* is too inclusive, your readers have to know exactly how Z defined *rights*, word for word. If your source material is so pithy and well worded that summarizing it would weaken its force, give your readers the pleasure of reading the original. Of course, readers won't give you credit for writing these words, but they will appreciate your taste and your effort to make their reading experience pleasant. In short, use (but don't overuse) quotations. Don't quote *too often* and don't quote *too much* of the original source (and never use quotations to achieve more length!). Speaking roughly,

- quotations should occupy no more than 10 to 15 percent of your paper;
- they may occupy much less; and
- most of your paper should set forth your ideas, not other people's ideas.

Long and Short Quotations   **Long quotations** (more than four lines of typed prose or three or more lines of poetry) are set off from the text. To set off material, start on a new line, indent one-half inch from the left margin, and type the quotation double-spaced. Do not enclose quotations within quotation marks if you are setting them off.

Short quotations are treated differently. They are embedded within the text; they are enclosed within quotation marks, but otherwise they do not stand out.

All quotations, whether set off or embedded, must be exact. If you omit any words, you must indicate the ellipsis by substituting three spaced periods for the omission; if you insert any words or punctuation, you must indicate the addition by enclosing it within square brackets, not to be confused with parentheses.

Original   The Montgomery bus boycott not only brought national attention to the discriminatory practices of the South, but elevated a twenty-six-year-old preacher to exalted status in the civil rights movement.

Quotation in student paper   "The Montgomery bus boycott . . . elevated [King] to exalted status in the civil rights movement."

Leading into a Quotation   Now for a less mechanical matter: The way in which a quotation is introduced. To say that it is "introduced" implies that one leads into it, although on rare occasions a quotation appears without an introduction, perhaps immediately after the title. Normally one leads into a quotation by giving any one or more of the following (but be aware that using them all at once can get unwieldy and produce awkward sentences):

- the *name of the author* and (no less important) the author's expertise or authority
- an indication of *the source of the quotation*, by title and/or year
- *clues signaling the content of the quotation and the purpose* it serves in the present essay

For example:

William James provides a clear answer to Huxley when he says that ". . ."

In *The Will to Believe* (1897), psychologist William James provides a clear answer to Huxley when he says that ". . ."

Either of these lead-ins work, especially because William James is quite well known. When you're quoting from a lesser-known author, it becomes more important to identify his or her expertise and perhaps the source, as in

Biographer Theodora Bosanquet, author of *Henry James at Work* (1982), subtly criticized Huxley's vague ideas on religion by writing, ". . . ."

Notice that in all these samples, the writer uses the lead-in to signal to readers the general tone of the quotation to follow. The writer uses the phrase "a clear answer" to signal that what's coming is, in fact, clear, uses the terms "subtly criticized" and "vague" to indicate that the following words by Bosanquet will be critical and will point out a shortcoming in Huxley's ideas. In this way, the writer anticipates and controls the meaning of the quotation for the reader. If the writer believed otherwise, the lead-ins might have run thus:

William James's weak response to Huxley does not really meet the difficulty Huxley calls attention to. James writes, ". . . ."

Biographer Theodora Bosanquet, author of *Henry James at Work* (1982), unjustly criticized Huxley's complex notion of religion by writing ". . . ."

In these examples, clearly the words "weak" and "unjustly criticized" imply how the essayist wants the reader to interpret the quotation. In the second one, Huxley's idea is presented as "complex," not vague.

Signal Phrases   Think of your writing as a conversation between you and your sources. As in conversation, you want to be able to move smoothly between different, sometimes contrary, points of view. You also want to be able to set your thoughts apart from those of your sources. Signal phrases make it easy for readers to know where your information came from and why it's trustworthy by pointing to key facts about the source:

According to psychologist Stephen Ceci . . .

A report published by the US Bureau of Justice Statistics *concludes* . . .

Feminist philosopher Sandra Harding *argues* . . .

To avoid repetitiveness, vary your sentence structure:

. . . *claims* Stephen Ceci.

. . . *according to* a report published by the US Bureau of Statistics.

Some useful verbs to introduce sources include the following:

acknowledges	contends	points out
argues	denies	recommends
believes	disputes	reports
claims	observes	suggests

Note that papers written using MLA style refer to sources in the present tense (*acknowledge, argue, believe*). Papers written in APA style use the past tense (*acknowledged, argued, believed*).

Leading Out of a Quotation   You might think of providing quotations as a three-stage process that includes the **lead-in**, the **quotation** itself, and the **lead-out**. The lead-out gives you a chance to interpret the quoted material, further controlling the intended meaning and telling the reader what is most important.

Visual Guide: Integrating Quotations

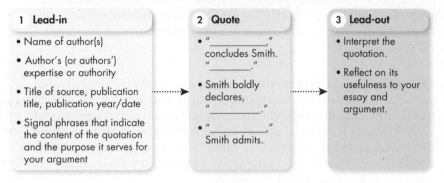

1 Lead-in	2 Quote	3 Lead-out
• Name of author(s)	• "_____," concludes Smith.	• Interpret the quotation.
• Author's (or authors') expertise or authority	"_____."	• Reflect on its usefulness to your essay and argument.
• Title of source, publication title, publication year/date	• Smith boldly declares, "_____."	
• Signal phrases that indicate the content of the quotation and the purpose it serves for your argument	• "_____," Smith admits.	

In the lead-out, you have a chance to reflect on the quotation and to shift back toward your own ideas and analysis. Consider this three-stage process applied in the following two ways:

> In his first book, *A World Restored* (1954), future Secretary of Defense Henry Kissinger wrote the famous axiom "History is the memory of states." It is the collective story of an entire people, displayed in public museums and libraries, taught in schools, and passed on from generation to generation.

> In his first book, *A World Restored* (1954), Nixon's former Secretary of Defense Henry Kissinger wrote glibly, "History is the memory of states." By asserting that history is largely the product of self-interested propaganda, Kissinger's words suggest that the past is maintained and controlled by whatever groups happen to hold power.

Notice the three-step process, and notice especially how the two examples convey different meanings of Kissinger's famous phrase. In the lead-in to the first sample, Kissinger's "future" role suggests hope. It signals a figure whose influence is growing. By using "famous" and "axiom," the author presents the quotation as true or even timeless. In the lead-out, the role of the state in preserving history is optimistic and idealistic.

In the second sample, "former" is used in the lead-in, suggesting Kissinger's later association with the ousted president he served, Richard Nixon. Readers are told that Kissinger "wrote glibly" even before they are told what he wrote, so readers may tend to read the quoted words that way. In the lead-out, the state becomes a more nefarious source of history keeping, one not interested in accommodating marginal voices or alternative perspectives, or remembering events inconvenient to its authority or righteousness.

> **WRITING TIP** In introducing a quotation, it is usually advisable to signal the reader *why* you are using the quotation by means of a lead-in consisting of a verb or a verb and adverb, such as *admits* or *convincingly shows.*

Again, we hope you can see in these examples how the three-step process facilitates a writer's control over the meanings of quotations. Returning to our earlier example, if after reading something by Huxley the writer had merely stated that "William James says . . . ," readers wouldn't know whether they were getting confirmation, refutation, or something else. The essayist would have put a needless burden on the readers. Generally speaking, the more difficult the quotation, the more important is the introductory or explanatory lead-in, but even the simplest quotation profits from some sort of brief lead-in, such as "James reaffirms this point when he says . . ."

THINKING CRITICALLY USING SIGNAL PHRASES

In the space provided, rewrite each signal phrase using a different structure. The first has been done as an example. Use different verbs to introduce each source.

Original Signal Phrase	Revised Signal Phrase
According to political economist Robert Reich . . .	. . . claims Robert Reich.
The National Health Council reports . . .	
The *Harvard Law Review* claims . . .	
As science essayist Jennifer Ackerman suggests . . .	

DOCUMENTATION

In the course of your essay, you will probably quote or summarize material derived from a source. You must give credit, and although there is no one form of documentation to which all scholarly fields subscribe, you will probably be asked to use one of two. One, established by the Modern Language Association (MLA), is used chiefly in the humanities; the other, established by the American Psychological Association (APA), is used chiefly in the social sciences.

We include two papers that use sources. "An Argument for Corporate Responsibility" (p. 320) uses the MLA format. "Does Ability Determine Expertise?" (p. 328) follows the APA format. (You may notice that various styles are illustrated in other selections we have included.)

In some online venues, you can link directly to your sources. If your assignment is to write a blog or some other online text, linking helps the reader look at a note or citation or the direct source quickly and easily. For example, in describing or referencing a scene in a movie, you can link to reviews of the movie, to a YouTube video of the trailer, or to the exact scene you're discussing. These kinds of links can help your audience get a clearer sense of your point. When formatting such a link in your text, make sure the link opens in a new window so that readers won't lose their place in your original text. In a blog, linking to sources usually is easy and helpful.

A Note on Footnotes (and Endnotes)

Before we discuss these two formats, a few words about footnotes are in order. Before the MLA and the APA developed their rules of style, citations commonly appeared in footnotes. Although today footnotes are not so frequently used to give citations, they still may be useful for another purpose. (The MLA suggests endnotes rather than footnotes, but most readers seem to think that, in fact, footnotes are preferable to endnotes. After all, who wants to keep shifting from a page of text to a page of notes at the end?) If you want to include some material that may seem intrusive in the body of the paper, you may relegate it to a footnote. For example, you might translate a quotation given in a foreign language, or you might demote from text to footnote a paragraph explaining why you aren't taking account of such-and-such a point. By putting the matter in a footnote, you signal to the reader that it is dispensable—that it's relevant but not essential, something extra that you are, so to speak, tossing in. Don't make a habit of writing this sort of note, but there are times when it is appropriate to do so.

MLA FORMAT: CITATIONS WITHIN THE TEXT

Brief citations within the body of the essay give credit, in a highly abbreviated way, to the sources for material you quote, summarize, or make use of in any other way. These *in-text citations* are made clear by a list of sources, titled Works Cited, appended to the essay. Thus, in your essay you may say something like this:

> Commenting on the relative costs of capital punishment and life imprisonment, Ernest van den Haag says that he doubts "that capital punishment really is more expensive" (33).

The **citation,** the number 33 in parentheses, means that the quoted words come from page 33 of a source (listed in the Works Cited) written by van den Haag. Without a Works Cited list, a reader would have no way of knowing that you are quoting from page 33 of an article that appeared in the February 8, 1985, issue of the *National Review.*

Usually, the parenthetic citation appears at the end of a sentence, as in the example just given, but it can appear elsewhere; its position will depend chiefly on your ear, your eye, and the context. You might, for example, write the sentence thus:

> Ernest van den Haag doubts "that capital punishment really is more expensive" than life imprisonment (33), but other writers have presented figures that contradict him.

Five points must be made about these examples:

1. *Quotation marks*   The closing quotation mark appears after the last word of the quotation, not after the parenthetic citation. Because the citation is not part of the quotation, the citation is not included within the quotation marks.

2. *Omission of words (ellipsis)*   If you are quoting a complete sentence or only a phrase, as in the examples given, you do not need to indicate (by three spaced periods) that you are omitting material before or after the quotation. But if for some reason you want to omit an interior part of the quotation, you must indicate the omission by inserting an ellipsis, the three spaced dots. To take a simple example, if you omit the word "really" from van den Haag's phrase, you must alert the reader to the omission:

> Ernest van dsen Haag doubts that "capital punishment . . . is more expensive" than life imprisonment (33).

3. *Punctuation with parenthetic citations* In the preceding examples, the punctuation (a period or a comma in the examples) follows the citation. If, however, the quotation ends with a question mark, include the question mark within the quotation, since it is part of the quotation, and put a period after the citation:

> Van den Haag asks, "Isn't it better — more just and more useful — that criminals, if they do not have the certainty of punishment, at least run the risk of suffering it?" (33).

But if the question mark is your own and not in the source, put it after the citation, thus:

> What answer can be given to van den Haag's doubt that "capital punishment really is more expensive" (33)?

4. *Two or more works by an author* If your list of Works Cited includes two or more works by an author, you cannot, in your essay, simply cite a page number—the reader will not know which of the works you are referring to. You must give additional information. You can give it in your lead-in; thus:

> In "New Arguments against Capital Punishment," van den Haag expresses doubt that "capital punishment really is more expensive" than life imprisonment (33).

Or you can give the title, in a shortened form, within the citation:

> Van den Haag expresses doubt that "capital punishment really is more expensive" than life imprisonment ("New Arguments" 33).

5. *Citing even when you do not quote* Even if you don't quote a source directly but instead use its point in a paraphrase or a summary, you will give a citation:

> Van den Haag thinks that life imprisonment costs more than capital punishment (33).

Notice that in all the previous examples, the author's name is given in the text (rather than within the parenthetic citation). But there are several other ways of giving the citation, and we shall look at them now.

AUTHOR AND PAGE NUMBER IN PARENTHESES

It has been argued that life imprisonment is more costly than capital punishment (van den Haag 33).

AUTHOR, TITLE, AND PAGE NUMBER IN PARENTHESES

Doubt has been expressed that capital punishment is as costly as life imprisonment (van den Haag, "New Arguments" 33).

A GOVERNMENT DOCUMENT OR A WORK OF CORPORATE AUTHORSHIP

The Commission on Food Control, in *Food Resources Today*, concludes that there is no danger (37–38).

A WORK BY TWO AUTHORS

There is not a single example of the phenomenon (Christakis and Fowler 293).

Christakis and Fowler insist there is not a single example of the phenomenon (293).

A WORK BY MORE THAN TWO AUTHORS

If there are *more than two authors,* give the last name of the first author, followed by *et al.* (an abbreviation for *et alia,* Latin for "and others")

Gittleman et al. argue (43) that . . .

On average, the cost is even higher (Gittleman et al. 43).

PARENTHETICAL CITATION OF AN INDIRECT SOURCE (CITATION OF MATERIAL THAT ITSELF WAS QUOTED OR SUMMARIZED IN YOUR SOURCE)

Suppose you're reading a book by Jones in which she quotes Smith and you wish to use Smith's material. Your citation must refer the reader to Jones—the source you're using—but of course, you cannot attribute the words to Jones. You will have to make it clear that you are quoting Smith, so after a lead-in phrase like "Smith says," followed by the quotation, you will give a parenthetic citation along these lines:

(qtd. in Jones 324-25).

PARENTHETICAL CITATION OF TWO OR MORE WORKS

The costs are simply too high (Smith 301; Jones 28).

AN ANONYMOUS WORK

For an anonymous work, or for a work where the author is unknown, give the title in your lead-in or give it in a shortened form in your parenthetic citation:

A Prisoner's View of Killing includes a poll taken of the inmates on death row (32).

According to the website for the American Civil Liberties Union . . .

AN INTERVIEW

Vivian Berger, in an interview, said . . .

If you don't mention the source's name in the lead-in, you'll have to give it in the parentheses:

Contrary to popular belief, the death penalty is not reserved for serial killers and depraved murderers (Berger).

AN ONLINE SOURCE

Generally, you can use the same formatting of the entries we've discussed so far for an online source. If the source uses pages or breaks down further into paragraphs or screens, insert the appropriate identifier or abbreviation (*p.* or *pp.* for page or pages; *par.* or *pars.* for paragraph or paragraphs; *screen* or *screens*) before the relevant number:

The growth of day care has been called "a crime against posterity" by a spokesman for the Institute for the American Family (Terwilliger, screens 1-2).

MLA FORMAT: THE LIST OF WORKS CITED

As the previous pages explain, parenthetic documentation consists of references that become clear when the reader consults the list titled Works Cited at the end of an essay. Here are some general guidelines.

FORM ON THE PAGE

The list of Works Cited begins on its own page.

- Continue the pagination of the essay: If the last page of text is 10, then the Works Cited begins on page 11.

- Type the heading Works Cited, centered, one inch from the top, and then double-space and type the first entry.

- Double-space the page; that is, double-space each entry, and double-space between entries.

- Begin each entry flush with the left margin, and indent a half inch for each succeeding line of the entry. This is known as a hanging indent, and you can set most word processing programs to achieve this formatting easily.

- Italicize titles of works published independently (which the MLA also calls *containers*; see below), such as books, pamphlets, and journals.

- Enclose within quotation marks a work not published independently—for instance, an article in a journal or a short story.

- Arrange the list of sources alphabetically by author, with the author's last name first. For anonymous works, use the title, and slot in your list alphabetically. For works with more than one author, and two or more works by one author, see sample entries that follow. If your list includes two or more works by one author, do not repeat the author's name for the second title; instead represent it by three hyphens followed by a period (---.).

- Anonymous works are listed under the first word of the title or the second word if the first is *A*, *An*, or *The* or a foreign equivalent. We discuss books by more than one author, government documents, and works of corporate authorship in the sample entries in this section.

CONTAINERS AND PUBLICATION INFORMATION

When a source being documented comes from a larger source, the larger source is considered a *container* because it contains the smaller source you are citing. For example, a container might be an anthology, a periodical, a website, a television program, a database, or an online archive. The context of a source will help you determine what counts as a container.

In Works Cited lists, the title of a container is listed after the period following the author's name. The container title is generally italicized and followed by a comma, since the information that follows describes the container. Here are some guidelines:

- Capitalize the first word and the last word of the title.

- Capitalize all nouns, pronouns, verbs, adjectives, adverbs, and subordinating conjunctions (e.g., *although, if, because*).

- Do not capitalize articles (e.g., *a, an, the*), prepositions (e.g., *in, on, toward, under*), coordinating conjunctions (e.g., *and, but, or, for*), or the *to* in infinitives, unless it's the first or last word of the title or the first word of the subtitle.

- Disregard any unusual typography, such as the use of all capital letters or the use of an ampersand (&) for *and*.

- Italicize the container title (and subtitle, if applicable; separate them by a colon), but do not italicize the period that concludes this part of the entry.

When citing a source within a container, the title of the source should be the first element following the author's name. The source title should be set within quotation marks with a period inside the closing quotation mark. The title of the container is then listed, followed by a comma, with additional information—including publication information, dates, and page ranges—about the container set off by commas.

The following example cites a story, "Achates McNeil," from an anthology—or container—called *After the Plague: Stories*. The anthology was published by Viking Penguin in 2001, and the story appears on pages 82 through 101.

> Boyle, T. C. "Achates McNeil." *After the Plague: Stories*, Viking
> Penguin, 2001, pp. 82-101.

Notice that the full name of the publisher is listed. Always include the full names of publishers except for terms such as "Inc." and "Company"; retain terms such as "Books" and "Publisher." The only exception is university presses, which are abbreviated thus: *Yale UP, U of Chicago P, State U of New York P.*

On the following pages, you will find more specific information for listing different kinds of sources. Although we have covered many kinds of sources, it's entirely possible that you will come across a source that doesn't fit any of the categories that we have discussed. For greater explanations of these matters, covering the proper way to cite all sorts of troublesome and unbelievable (but real) sources, see the *MLA Handbook,* Eighth Edition (Modern Language Association of America, 2016).

Books

A BOOK BY MORE THAN ONE AUTHOR

The book is alphabetized under the last name of the first author named on the title page. If there are *two authors,* the name of the second author is given in the normal order, *first name first, after the first author's name.*

> Gilbert, Sandra M., and Susan Gubar. *The Madwoman in the Attic: The Woman Writer and the Nineteenth-Century Literary Imagination.* Yale UP, 1979.

If there are *more than two authors,* give the name only of the first, followed by a comma, and then add *et al.* (Latin for "and others").

> Zumeta, William, et al. *Financing American Higher Education in the Era of Globalization.* Harvard Education Press, 2012.

WORKS OF CORPORATE AUTHORSHIP

Begin the citation with the corporate author, even if the same body is also the publisher.

> American Psychiatric Association. *Psychiatric Glossary.* American Psychiatric Association, 1984.

> Human Rights Watch. *World Report of 2018: Events of 2017.* Seven Stories Press, 2018.

A REPRINT

After the title, give the date of original publication (it can usually be found on the reverse of the title page of the reprint you are using), then a period, and then the publisher and date of the edition you are using.

> de Mille, Agnes. *Dance to the Piper.* 1951. Introduction by Joan Acocella, New York Review Books, 2015.

A BOOK WITH AN AUTHOR AND AN EDITOR

> Kant, Immanuel. *The Philosophy of Kant: Immanuel Kant's Moral and Political Writings*. Edited by Carl J. Friedrich, Modern Library, 1949.

A TRANSLATED BOOK

> Ullmann, Regina. *The Country Road: Stories*. Translated by Kurt Beals, New Directions Publishing, 2015.

AN INTRODUCTION, FOREWORD, OR AFTERWORD

Usually, an introduction or comparable material is listed under the name of the author of the book (here Karr) rather than under the name of the writer of the foreword (here Dunham), but if you are referring to the apparatus rather than to the book itself, use the form given.

> Dunham, Lena. Foreword. *The Liars' Club*, by Mary Karr, Penguin Classics, 2015, pp. xi-xiii.

A BOOK WITH AN EDITOR BUT NO AUTHOR

> Horner, Avril, and Anne Rowe, editors. *Living on Paper: Letters from Iris Murdoch*. Princeton UP, 2016.

A WORK WITHIN A VOLUME OF WORKS BY ONE AUTHOR

The following entry indicates that a short work by Susan Sontag, an essay called "The Aesthetics of Silence," appears in a book by Sontag titled *Styles of Radical Will*. Notice that the inclusive page numbers of the short work are cited—not merely page numbers that you may happen to refer to, but the page numbers of the entire piece.

> Sontag, Susan. "The Aesthetics of Silence." *Styles of Radical Will*, Farrar, Straus, and Giroux, 1969, pp. 3-34.

A BOOK REVIEW

> Walton, James. "Noble, Embattled Souls." Review of *The Bone Clocks and Slade House*, by David Mitchell. *The New York Review of Books*, 3 Dec. 2015, pp. 55-58.

If a review is anonymous, list it under the first word of the title or under the second word if the first is *A, An,* or *The.* If an anonymous review has no title, begin the entry with *Review of* and then give the title of the work reviewed; alphabetize the entry under the title of the work reviewed.

AN ARTICLE OR ESSAY IN A COLLECTION

A book may consist of a collection (edited by one or more persons) of new essays by several authors. Here, the essay by Sayrafiezadeh occupies pages 3 to 29 in a collection edited by Marcus.

> Sayrafiezadeh, Saïd. "Paranoia." *New American Stories*, edited by
> Ben Marcus, Vintage Books, 2015, pp. 3-29.

MULTIPLE WORKS FROM THE SAME COLLECTION

You may find that you need to cite multiple sources from within a single container, such as several essays from the same edited anthology. In these cases, provide an entry for the entire anthology (the entry for Marcus below) and a shortened entry for each selection. Alphabetize the entries by authors' or editors' last names.

> Eisenberg, Deborah. "Some Other, Better Otto." Marcus, pp. 94-136.

> Marcus, Ben, editor. *New American Stories.* Vintage Books, 2015.

> Sayrafiezadeh, Saïd. "Paranoia." Marcus, pp. 3-29.

Articles in Periodicals

AN ARTICLE IN A REFERENCE WORK (INCLUDING A WIKI)

For a *signed* article, begin with the author's last name. Provide the name of the article, the publication title, edition number (if applicable), the publisher, and the copyright year. For an unsigned article, begin with the title of the article:

> Robinson, Lisa Clayton. "Harlem Writers Guild." *Africana: The*
> *Encyclopedia of the African and African American Experience.*
> 2nd ed., Oxford UP, 2005.

> "The Ball's in Your Court. " *The American Heritage Dictionary of Idioms.*
> 2nd ed., Houghton Mifflin Harcourt, 2013.

For an online reference work, such as a wiki, include the author name and article name followed by the name of the website, the date of publication or the most recent update, and the URL (without *http://* before it).

> Durante, Amy M. "Finn Mac Cumhail." *Encyclopedia Mythica*, 17 Apr. 2011, www.pantheon.org/articles/f/finn_mac_cumhail.html.

> "House Music." *Wikipedia*, 16 Nov. 2015, en.wikipedia.org/wiki /House_music.

AN ARTICLE IN A SCHOLARLY JOURNAL

The title of the article is enclosed within quotation marks, and the title of the journal is italicized.

> Matchie, Thomas. "Law versus Love in the Round House." *Midwest Quarterly*, vol. 56, no. 4, Summer 2015, pp. 353-64.

Matchie's article occupies pages 353 to 364 in volume 56, which was published in 2015. When available, give the issue number as well.

AN ARTICLE IN A MAGAZINE

Do not include volume or issue numbers, even if given.

> Thompson, Mark. "Sending Women to War: The Pentagon Nears a Historic Decision on Equality at the Front Lines." *Time*, 14 Dec. 2015, pp. 53-55.

AN ARTICLE IN A NEWSPAPER

Because a newspaper usually consists of several sections, a section number or a capital letter may precede the page number. The example indicates that an article appears on page 1 of section C.

> Bray, Hiawatha. "As Toys Get Smarter, Privacy Issues Emerge." *The Boston Globe*, 10 Dec. 2015, p. C1.

AN ARTICLE IN AN ONLINE PERIODICAL

Give the same information as you would for a print article, plus the URL. (See Fig. 7.7.)

Figure 7.7   Citing an Online Magazine

1 URL

2 Title of periodical

3 Title of article

4 Subtitle of article

5 Author

6 Publication date (If the article doesn't have a publication date, include the date you accessed it.)

> Acocella, Joan. "In the Blood: Why Do Vampires Still Thrill?" *New Yorker*,
>> 16 March 2009. www.newyorker.com/magazine/2009/03/16
>> /in-the-blood.

AN UNSIGNED EDITORIAL OR LETTER TO THE EDITOR

Include the label "Editorial" or "Letter" at the end of the entry (and before any database information).

> "The Religious Tyranny Amendment." *New York Times*, 15 Mar. 1998,
>> p. 16. Editorial.

Adrouny, Salpi. "Our Shockingly Low Local Voter Turnout." *AJC*
.*com*, 8 Nov. 2015, www.ajc.com/news/news/opinion/readers
-write-nov-8/npHrS/. Letter.

A DATABASE SOURCE

Treat material obtained from a database like other printed
material, but at the end of the entry add (if available) the title of the
database (italicized) and a permalink or DOI (digital object identifier) if the source has one. If a source does not have that information, include a URL (without the protocol, such as *http://*).

Coles, Kimberly Anne. "The Matter of Belief in John Donne's Holy
Sonnets." *Renaissance Quarterly*, vol. 68, no. 3, Fall 2015,
pp. 899-931. JSTOR, doi:10.1086/683855.

Macari, Anne Marie. "Lyric Impulse in a Time of Extinction."
American Poetry Review, vol. 44, no. 4, July/Aug. 2015,
pp. 11-14. *General OneFile*, go.galegroup.com/.

Government Documents

If the writer is not known, treat the government and the agency as
the author.

United States, Department of Agriculture, Food and Nutrition Service, Child Nutrition Programs. *Eligibility Manual for School
Meals: Determining and Verifying Eligibility*. July 2015, www
.fns.usda.gov/sites/default/files/cn/SP40_CACFP18_SFSP20
-2015a1.pdf.

Interviews

A PUBLISHED OR BROADCAST INTERVIEW

Give the name of the interview subject and the interviewer,
followed by the relevant publication or broadcast information, in
the following format:

Weddington, Sarah. "Sarah Weddington: Still Arguing for *Roe*."
Interview by Michele Kort, *Ms.*, Winter 2013, pp. 32-35.

Tempkin, Ann, and Anne Umland. Interview by Charlie Rose. *Charlie
Rose: The Week*, PBS, 9 Oct. 2015.

AN INTERVIEW YOU CONDUCT

Akufo, Dautey. Personal interview, 11 Apr. 2016.

Online Sources

A WEBSITE AND PARTS OF WEBSITES

Include the following elements: the name of the person who created the site or authored the page (omit if not given, as in Figure 7.8 on p. 310); page title (in quotation marks), if applicable, and site title (italicized); any sponsoring institution or organization (if the title of the site and the sponsor are the same or similar, use the title of the site but omit the sponsor); date of electronic publication or of the latest update (if given; if not, provide the date you accessed the site at the end of the citation); and the URL (without *http://*).

Legal Guide for Bloggers. Electronic Frontier Foundation, www.eff
.org/issues/bloggers/legal. Accessed 5 Apr. 2016.

Bae, Rebecca. Home page. Iowa State U, 2015, www.engl.iastate
.edu/rebecca-bae-directory-page.

Enzinna, Wes. "Syria's Unknown Revolution." *Pulitzer Center on Crisis Reporting*, 24 Nov. 2015, pulitzercenter.org/projects
/middle-east-syria-enzinna-war-rojava.

ENTIRE BLOG

Kiuchi, Tatsuro. Tatsuro Kiuchi: *News & Blog*. tatsurokiuchi.com.
Accessed 3 Mar. 2016.

Ng, Amy. Pikaland. Pikaland Media, 2015, www.pikaland.com.

A SOCIAL MEDIA POST OR COMMENT

Include the name of the social media page (e.g., Facebook, Instagram) on which the post appeared, the name of the post (or the post on which the comment appears), the name of the site, the date, and the URL of the post or comment.

Bedford English. "Stacey Cochran Explores Reflective Writing
in the Classroom and as a Writer: http://ow.ly/YkjVB." *Facebook*, 15 Feb. 2016, www.facebook.com/BedfordEnglish
/posts/10153415001259607.

For Twitter, include the handle of the poster, the content of the tweet (enclosed in quotation marks), the name of the site, the date and time of the post, and the URL.

> Curiosity Rover. "Can you see me waving? How to spot #Mars in the night sky: https://youtu.be/hv8hVvJlcJQ." *Twitter*, 5 Nov. 2015, 11:00 a.m., twitter.com/marscuriosity/status /672859022911889408.

> @grammarphobia (Patricia T. O'Conner and Steward Kellerman). "When Dickens don't use 'doesn't' #English #grammar #usage." *Twitter*, 11 June 2018, 8:10 a.m., twitter.com/grammarphobia.

Figure 7.8   Citing a Blog

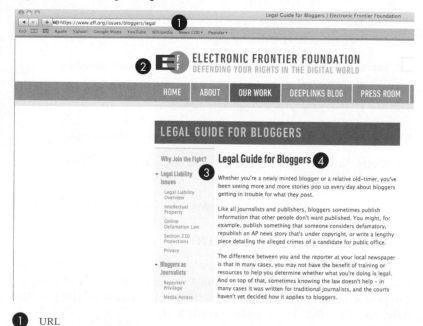

1 URL

2 Sponsor of website

3 No author given; start citation with the title.

4 No date of publication given; include date of access in citation.

Multimedia Sources

WORK OF ART (INCLUDING PHOTOGRAPHS)

Bradford, Mark. *Let's Walk to the Middle of the Ocean*. 2015, Museum
   of Modern Art, New York.

Hura, Sohrab. *Old Man Lighting a Fire*. 2015. *Magnum Photos*, pro.magnum
   photos.com/CS.aspx?VP3=SearchResult&VBID=2K1HZO4
   JVP42X8&SMLS=1&RW=1280&RH=692.

CARTOON OR COMIC

Zyglis, Adam. "City of Light." *Buffalo News*, 8 Nov. 2015, buffalonews
   .com/2015/11/08/city-of-light/. Cartoon.

ADVERTISEMENT

AT&T. *National Geographic*, Dec. 2015, p. 14. Advertisement.

Toyota. *The Root*. Slate Group, 28 Nov. 2015, www.theroot.com.
   Advertisement.

VISUALS (TABLES, CHARTS, GRAPHICS, ETC.)

Add the type of visual at the end, if it's not obvious from the title
or website. This is optional, but good for clarity.

"Number of Measles Cases by Year." *Centers for Disease Control
   and Prevention*, 6 June 2019, www.cdc.gov/measles/cases
   -outbreaks.html. Table.

Brown, Evan. "15 Golden Principles of Visual Hierarchy." *DesignMantic*,
   15 Oct. 2014, www.designmantic.com/blog/infographics/15-golden
   -principles-of-visual-hierarchy. Infographic.

A TELEVISION OR RADIO PROGRAM

Be sure to include the title of the episode or segment (in quotation
marks), the title of the show (italicized), the producer or director of the
show, the network, and the date of the airing. Other information, such
as performers, narrator, and so forth, may be included if pertinent.

"Fast Times at West Philly High." *Frontline*, produced by Debbie
   Morton, PBS, 17 July 2012.

"Federal Role in Support of Autism." *Washington Journal*, narrated
by Robb Harleston, C-SPAN, 1 Dec. 2012.

PODCAST

Include the podcast host(s) and the title of the episode. Then
list the title of the podcast, the network or service, the date, and
the place where you access the episode. If you access the podcast
through an app or a platform such as Spotify, treat the app or platform as a separate container, similar to a database.

McDougall, Christopher. "How Did Endurance Help Early Humans
Survive?" *TED Radio Hour,* NPR, 20 Nov. 2015, www
.npr.org/2015/11/20/455904655/how-did-endurance
-help-early-humans-survive.

FILM

Begin with whatever you are emphasizing in your work: entire
film (first model), director (second model), and so forth.

Birdman or (The Unexpected Virtue of Ignorance). Directed by
Alejandro González Iñárritu, performances by Michael Keaton,
Emma Stone, Zach Galifianakis, Edward Norton, and Naomi
Watts, Fox Searchlight, 2014.

Scott, Ridley, director. *The Martian*. Performances by Matt Damon,
Jessica Chastain, Kristen Wiig, and Kate Mara, Twentieth Century
Fox, 2015.

VIDEO FROM AN ONLINE SOURCE (SUCH AS YOUTUBE)

Nayar, Vineet. "Employees First, Customers Second." *YouTube*,
9 June 2015, www.youtube.com/watch?v=cCdu67s_C5E.

APA FORMAT: CITATIONS WITHIN THE TEXT

The APA style emphasizes the date of publication; the date appears
not only in the list of references at the end of the paper but also
in the paper itself, when you give a brief parenthetic citation of a
source that you have quoted or summarized or in any other way
used. Here is an example:

Statistics are readily available (Smith, 1989, p. 20).

The title of Smith's book or article will be given at the end of your paper in the list titled References. We discuss the form of the material listed in the References after we look at some typical citations within the text of a student's essay.

A SUMMARY OF AN ENTIRE WORK

Smith (1988) holds the same view.

Similar views are held widely (Smith, 1988; Jones & Metz, 1990).

A REFERENCE TO A PAGE OR TO PAGES

Lanier (2018) argues that "to free yourself, to be more authentic . . . delete your accounts" (p. 24).

A REFERENCE TO AN AUTHOR WHO HAS MORE THAN ONE WORK IN THE LIST OF REFERENCES

If in the References you list two or more works that an author published in the same year, the works are listed in alphabetical order, by the first letter of the title. The first work is labeled *a*, the second *b*, and so on. Here is a reference to a second work that Smith published in 1989:

Florida presents "a fair example" of how the death penalty is administered (Smith, 1989b, p. 18).

APA FORMAT: THE LIST OF REFERENCES

Your paper will conclude with a separate page headed References, on which you list all your sources. If the last page of your essay is numbered 10, number the first page of the References 11. Here are some general guidelines.

FORM ON THE PAGE

- Begin each entry flush with the left margin, but if an entry runs to more than one line, indent five spaces for each succeeding line of the entry.
- Double-space each entry and double-space between entries.

ALPHABETICAL ORDER

- Arrange the list alphabetically by author.
- Give the author's last name first and then the initial of the first name and of the middle name (if any).
- If there is more than one author, name all of the authors up to seven, again inverting the name (last name first) and giving only initials for first and middle names. (But do not invert the editor's name when the entry begins with the name of an author who has written an article in an edited book.) When there are two or more authors, use an ampersand (&) before the name of the last author. For example (here, of an article in the tenth volume of a journal called *Developmental Psychology*):

Drabman, R. S., & Thomas, M. H. (1974). Does media violence increase children's tolerance of real-life aggression? *Developmental Psychology, 10,* 418-421.

- For eight or more authors, list the first six followed by three ellipsis dots (. . .) and then the last author.
- If you list more than one work by an author, do so in the order of publication, the earliest first. If two works by an author were published in the same year, give them in alphabetical order by the first letter of the title, disregarding *A, An,* or *The,* and a foreign equivalent. Designate the first work as *a,* the second as *b,* and so forth. Repeat the author's name at the start of each entry.

Donnerstein, E. (1980a). Aggressive erotica and violence against women. *Journal of Personality and Social Psychology, 39,* 269-277.

Donnerstein, E. (1980b). Pornography and violence against women. *Annals of the New York Academy of Sciences, 347,* 227-288.

Donnerstein, E. (1983). Erotica and human aggression. In R. Green & E. Donnerstein (Eds.), *Aggression: Theoretical and empirical reviews* (pp. 87-103). New York, NY: Academic Press.

FORM OF TITLE

- In references to books, capitalize only the first letter of the first word of the title (and of the subtitle, if any) and capitalize proper nouns. Italicize the complete title (but not the period at the end).

- In references to articles in periodicals or in edited books, capitalize only the first letter of the first word of the article's title (and subtitle, if any) and all proper nouns. Do not put the title within quotation marks or italicize it. Type a period after the title of the article.

- In references to periodicals, give the volume number in arabic numerals, and italicize it. Do not use *vol.* before the number and do not use *p.* or *pg.* before the page numbers.

Sample References

For a full account of the APA method of dealing with all sorts of unusual citations, see the sixth edition (2010) of the APA manual, *Publication Manual of the American Psychological Association.*

Books

A BOOK BY ONE AUTHOR

Pavlov, I. P. (1927). *Conditioned reflexes* (G. V. Anrep, Trans.). London, England: Oxford University Press.

A BOOK BY MORE THAN ONE AUTHOR

Belenky, M. F., Clinchy, B. M., Goldberger, N. R., & Torule, J. M. (1986). *Women's ways of knowing: The development of self, voice, and mind.* New York, NY: Basic Books.

A COLLECTION OF ESSAYS

Christ, C. P., & Plaskow, J. (Eds.). (1979). *Woman-spirit rising: A feminist reader in religion.* New York, NY: Harper & Row.

A WORK IN A COLLECTION OF ESSAYS

Fiorenza, E. (1979). Women in the early Christian movement. In C. P. Christ & J. Plaskow (Eds.), *Woman-spirit rising: A feminist reader in religion* (pp. 84-92). New York, NY: Harper & Row.

Articles in Periodicals

AN ARTICLE IN A JOURNAL

Tversky, A., & Kahneman, D. (1981). The framing of decisions and the psychology of choice. *Science, 211,* 453-458.

Foot, R. J. (1988-89). Nuclear coercion and the ending of the
    Korean conflict. *International Security, 13*(4), 92-112.

The reference informs us that the article appeared in issue number 4 of volume 13.

AN ARTICLE FROM A MAGAZINE

Bensman, D. (2015, December 4). Security for a precarious workforce.
    The American Prospect. Retrieved from http://prospect.org/

Greenwald, J. (1989, February 27). Gimme shelter. *Time, 133,* 50-51.

AN ARTICLE IN A NEWSPAPER

Connell, R. (1989, February 6). Career concerns at heart of 1980s
    campus protests. *Los Angeles Times,* pp. 1, 3.

Roberson, K. (2015, May 3). Innovation helps address nurse
    shortage. *Des Moines Register.* Retrieved from http://www
    .desmoinesregister.com/

(*Note:* If no author is given, simply begin with the title followed by the date in parentheses.)

AN ARTICLE FROM A DATABASE

Lyons, M. (2015). Writing upwards: How the weak wrote to the
    powerful. *Journal of Social History, 49*(2), 317-330. https://
    doi.org/10.1093/jsh/shv038

A BOOK REVIEW

Daniels, N. (1984). Understanding physician power [Review of the
    book *The social transformation of American medicine*]. *Philoso-
    phy and Public Affairs, 13,* 347-356.

Daniels is the reviewer, not the author of the book. The book under review is called *The Social Transformation of American Medicine,* but the review, published in volume 13 of *Philosophy and Public Affairs,* had its own title, "Understanding Physician Power."

If the review does not have a title, retain the square brackets and use the material within as the title. Proceed as in the example just given.

Government Publications

If the writer is not known, treat the government and the agency as the author. If a document number has been assigned, insert that number in parentheses between the title and the following period.

> U.S. Census Bureau, Bureau of Economic Analysis. (2015, December). *U.S. international trade in goods and services, October 2015* (Report No. CB15-197, BEA15-60, FT-900 [15-10]). Retrieved from http://www.census.gov/foreign-trade/Press-Release /current_press_release/ft900.pdf

Online Sources

WEBSITES AND PARTS OF WEBSITES

Do not include an entire website in the reference list; instead, give the URL in parentheses within your paper.

> Badrunnesha, M., & Kwauk, C. (2015, December). *Improving the quality of girls' education in madrasa in Bangladesh*. Retrieved from Brookings Institution website: http://www.brookings .edu/research/papers/2015/12/05-bangladesh-girls-education -madrasa-badrunnesha

BLOG POST

> Costandi, M. (2015, April 9). Why brain scans aren't always what they seem [Blog post]. Retrieved from http://www .theguardian.com/science/neurophilosophy/2015/apr/09 /bold-assumptions-fmri

COMMENT ON AN ONLINE ARTICLE

> MintDragon. (2015, December 9). Re: The very real pain of exclusion [Comment]. *The Atlantic*. Retrieved from http://www .theatlantic.com/

A SOCIAL MEDIA POST

> National Science Foundation. (2015, December 8). Simulation shows key to building powerful magnetic fields 1.usa.gov/1TZUiJ6 #supernovas #supercomputers [Tweet]. Retrieved from https:// twitter.com/NSF/status/674352440582545413

Multimedia Sources

WORK OF ART (INCLUDING PHOTOGRAPHS)

Sabogal, J. (2015). *Los hijos of the Revolution* [Outdoor mural]. San Francisco, CA.

Whitten, J. (2015). *Soul map* [Painting]. Retrieved from http://www.walkerart.org/

TELEVISION OR RADIO PROGRAM

Oliver, J. (Host), & Leddy, B. (Director). (2015, October 4). Mental health [Television series episode]. In *Last week tonight with John Oliver*. New York, NY: HBO.

PODCAST

Abumrad, J., & Krulwich, R. (2015, August 30). *Remembering Oliver Sacks* [Audio podcast]. Retrieved from https://www.wnycstudios.org/shows/radiolab/

DATA SET OR GRAPHIC REPRESENTATION OF DATA (GRAPH, CHART, TABLE)

Gallup. (2015). *Gallup worldwide research data collected from 2005-2018* [Data set]. Retrieved from http://www.gallup.com/services/177797/country-data-set-details.aspx

U.S. Department of Agriculture, Economic Research Service. (2015). *USDA expenditures for food and nutrition assistance, FY 1980-2014* [Chart]. Retrieved from http://www.ers.usda.gov/data-products/chart-gallery/detail.aspx?chartId=40105&ref=collection&embed=True

A VIDEO FROM AN ONLINE SOURCE (SUCH AS YOUTUBE)

Renaud, B., & Renaud, C. (2015, October 8). *Between borders: America's migrant crisis* [Video file]. Retrieved from https://www.youtube.com/watch?v=rxF0t-SMEXA

> **✓ A CHECKLIST FOR CRITICAL PAPERS USING SOURCES**
>
> ☐ Are all borrowed words and ideas credited, including those from internet sources?
>
> ☐ Are all summaries and paraphrases acknowledged as such?
>
> ☐ Are quotations and summaries not too long?
>
> ☐ Are quotations accurate? Are omissions of words indicated by three spaced periods? Are additions of words enclosed within square brackets?
>
> ☐ Are quotations provided with helpful lead-ins?
>
> ☐ Is documentation in proper form?
>
> Of course, you will also ask yourself the questions that you would ask of a paper that did not use sources, such as:
>
> ☐ Is the topic sufficiently narrowed?
>
> ☐ Is the thesis stated early and clearly, perhaps even in the title?
>
> ☐ Is the audience kept in mind? Are opposing views stated fairly and as sympathetically as possible? Are controversial terms defined?
>
> ☐ Is the purpose and focus clear (evaluation, recommendation of policy)?
>
> ☐ Is evidence (examples, testimony, statistics) adequate and sound?
>
> ☐ Is the organization clear (effective opening, coherent sequence of arguments, unpretentious ending)?
>
> ☐ Is the tone appropriate?
>
> ☐ Is the title effective?

AN ANNOTATED STUDENT RESEARCH PAPER IN MLA FORMAT

The following argument makes good use of sources. Early in the semester, students were asked to choose one topic from a list of ten and to write a documented argument of 750 to 1,250 words (three to five pages of double-spaced typing) as a prelude to working on a research paper of 2,500 to 3,000 words. Citations are given in the MLA form.

Lesley Timmerman

Professor Jennifer Wilson

English 102

15 August 2016

Title is
focused and
announces the
thesis.

An Argument for Corporate Responsibility

Opponents of corporate social responsibility (CSR) argue

that a company's sole duty is to generate profits. According

to them, by acting for the public good, corporations are

neglecting their primary obligation to make money. However,

Double-space
between the
title and first
paragraph—
and **all lines**
throughout
the essay.

as people are becoming more and more conscious of corporate

impacts on society and the environment, separating profits

from company practices and ethics does not make sense.

Employees want to work for institutions that share their values,

and consumers want to buy products from companies that are

making an impact and improving people's lives. Furthermore,

businesses exist in an interdependent world where the health of

the environment and the well-being of society really do matter.

Brief
statement of
one side of the
issue.

For these reasons, corporations have to take responsibility for

their actions, beyond making money for shareholders. For their

own benefit as well as the public's, companies must strive to be

socially responsible.

Summary of
the opposing
view.

In his article "The Case against Corporate Social Respon-

sibility," *Wall Street Journal* writer Aneel Karnani argues that

CSR will never be able to solve the world's problems. Thinking

it can, Karnani says, is a dangerous illusion. He recommends

1" margin on
each side and
at bottom.

that instead of expecting corporate managers to act in the

public interest, we should rely on philanthropy and government

Timmerman 2

regulation. Karnani maintains that "Managers who sacrifice profit for the common good [. . .] are in effect imposing a tax on their shareholders and arbitrarily deciding how that money should be spent." In other words, according to Karnani, corporations should not be determining what constitutes socially responsible behavior; individual donors and the government should. Certainly, individuals should continue to make charitable gifts, and governments should maintain laws and regulations to protect the public interest. However, Karnani's reasoning for why corporations should be exempt from social responsibility is flawed. With very few exceptions, corporations' socially responsible actions are not arbitrary and do not sacrifice long-term profits.

In fact, corporations have already proven that they can contribute profitably and meaningfully to solving significant global problems by integrating CSR into their standard practices and long-term visions. Rather than focusing on shareholders' short-term profits, many companies have begun measuring their success by "profit, planet and people" — what is known as the "triple bottom line." Businesses operating under this principle consider their environmental and social impacts, as well as their financial impacts, and make responsible and compassionate decisions. For example, such businesses use resources efficiently, create healthy products, choose suppliers who share their ethics, and improve economic opportunities for people in the communities they serve. By doing so, companies often save money. They also contribute to the sustainability of life on

Lead-in to quotation.

Essayist's response to the quotation.

Author concisely states her position.

Transitions ("For example," "also") alert readers to where the writer is taking them.

earth and ensure the sustainability of their own businesses. In their book *The Triple Bottom Line: How Today's Best-Run Companies Are Achieving Economic, Social, and Environmental Success,* coauthors Savitz and Weber demonstrate that corporations need to become sustainable, in all ways. They argue that "the only way to succeed in today's interdependent world is to embrace sustainability" (xi). The authors go on to show that, for the vast majority of companies, a broad commitment to sustainability enhances profitability (Savitz and Weber 39).

For example, PepsiCo has been able to meet the financial expectations of its shareholders while demonstrating its commitment to the triple bottom line. In addition to donating over $16 million to help victims of natural disasters, Pepsi has woven concerns for people and for the planet into its company practices and culture (Bejou 4). For instance, because of a recent water shortage in an area of India where Pepsi runs a plant, the company began a project to build community wells (Savitz and Weber 160). Though Pepsi did not cause the water shortage nor was its manufacturing threatened by it, "Pepsi realizes that the well-being of the community is part of the company's responsibility" (Savitz and Weber 161). Ultimately, Pepsi chose to look beyond the goal of maximizing short-term profits. By doing so, the company improved its relationship with this Indian community, improved people's daily lives and opportunities, and improved its own reputation. In other words, Pepsi embraced CSR and ensured a more sustainable future for everyone involved.

Another example of a wide-reaching company that is working toward greater sustainability on all fronts is Walmart. The corporation has issued a CSR policy that includes three ambitious goals: "to be fully supplied by renewable energy, to create zero waste and to sell products that sustain people and the environment" ("From Fringe to Mainstream"). As Dr. Doug Guthrie, dean of George Washington University's School of Business, noted in a recent lecture, if a company as powerful as Walmart were to succeed in these goals, the impact would be huge. To illustrate Walmart's potential influence, Dr. Guthrie pointed out that the corporation's exports from China to the United States are equal to Mexico's total exports to the United States. In committing to CSR, the company's leaders are acknowledging how much their power depends on the earth's natural resources, as well as the communities who produce, distribute, sell, and purchase Walmart's products. The company is also well aware that achieving its goals will "ultimately save the company a great deal of money" ("From Fringe to Mainstream"). For good reason, Walmart, like other companies around the world, is choosing to act in *everyone*'s best interest.

Recent research on employees' and consumers' social consciousness offers companies further reason to take corporate responsibility seriously. For example, studies show that workers care about making a difference (Meister). In many cases, workers would even take a pay cut to work for a more responsible, sustainable company. In fact, 45% of workers said they would take a 15% reduction in pay "for a job that makes

Author provides two examples of forward-thinking moves by major companies.

Author now introduces statistical evidence that, if introduced earlier, might have turned the reader off.

a social or environmental impact" (Meister). Even more said they would take a 15% cut in pay to work for a company with values that match their own (Meister). The numbers are most significant among Millennials (those born between, approximately, 1980 and the early 2000s). Fully 80% of Millennials said they "wanted to work for a company that cares about how it impacts and contributes to society," and over half said they would not work for an "irresponsible company" (Meister). Given this more socially conscious generation, companies are going to find it harder and harder to ignore CSR. To recruit and retain employees, employers will need to earn the admiration, respect, and loyalty of their workers by becoming "good corporate citizen[s]" (qtd. in "From Fringe to Mainstream").

Similarly, studies clearly show that CSR matters to today's consumers. According to an independent report, 80% of Americans say they would switch brands to support a social cause (Cone Communications 6). Fully 88% say they approve of companies' using social or environmental issues in their marketing (Cone Communications 5). And 83% say they "wish more of the products, services and retailers would support causes" (Cone Communications 5). Other independent surveys corroborate these results, confirming that today's customers, especially Millennials, care about more than just price ("From Fringe to Mainstream"). Furthermore, plenty of companies have seen what happens when they assume that consumers do not care about CSR. For example, in 1997, when Nike customers discovered that their shoes were manufactured by child laborers

Timmerman 6

in Indonesia, the company took a huge financial hit (Guthrie).
Today, Information Age customers are even more likely to
educate themselves about companies' labor practices and environmental records. Smart corporations will listen to consumer
preferences, provide transparency, and commit to integrating
CSR into their long-term business plans.

Author argues
that it is in
the *companies'*
interest to
be socially
responsible.

In this increasingly interdependent world, the case
against CSR is becoming more and more difficult to defend.
Exempting corporations and relying on government to be the
world's conscience does not make good social, environmental,
or economic sense. Contributors to a recent article in the online
journal *Knowledge@Wharton*, published by the Wharton School
of Business, agree. Professor Eric Orts maintains that "it is an
outmoded view to say that one must rely only on the government
and regulation to police business responsibilities. What we need
is re-conception of what the purpose of business is" (qtd. in
"From Fringe to Mainstream"). The question is, what should the
purpose of a business be in today's world? Professor of Business
Administration David Bejou of Elizabeth City State University has
a thoughtful and sensible answer to that question. He writes,

Author's
lead-in to the
quotation
guides the
reader's
response to
the quotation.

> . . . it is clear that the sole purpose of a business is
> not merely that of generating profits for its owners.
> Instead, because compassion provides the necessary
> equilibrium between a company's purpose and the
> needs of its communities, it should be the new phi-
> losophy of business. (Bejou 1)

Author
uses a block
quotation for
quotation
longer than
three lines in
text.

As Bejou implies, the days of allowing corporations to act in their own financial self-interest with little or no regard for their effects on others are over. None of us can afford such a narrow view of business. The world is far too interconnected. A seemingly small corporate decision — to buy coffee beans directly from local growers or to install solar panels — can affect the lives and livelihoods of many people and determine the environmental health of whole regions. A business, just like a government or an individual, therefore has an ethical responsibility to act with compassion for the public good.

Fortunately, corporations have many incentives to act responsibly. Customer loyalty, employee satisfaction, overall cost-saving, and long-term viability are just some of the advantages businesses can expect to gain by embracing comprehensive CSR policies. Meanwhile, companies have very little to lose by embracing a socially conscious view. These days, compassion is profitable. Corporations would be wise to recognize the enormous power, opportunity, and responsibility they have to effect positive change.

Timmerman 8

Works Cited

Bejou, David. "Compassion as the New Philosophy of Business."
    Journal of Relationship Marketing, vol. 10, no. 1, Apr.
    2011, pp. 1-6. *Taylor and Francis*, doi:10.1080/15332667
    .2011.550098.

Cone Communications. 2010 *Cone Cause Evolution Study*. Cone,
    2010, www.conecomm.com/research-blog/2010-cause
    -evolution-study.

"From Fringe to Mainstream: Companies Integrate CSR
    Initiatives into Everyday Business." *Knowledge@Wharton*,
    23 May 2012, knowledge.wharton.upenn.edu/article
    /from-fringe-to-mainstream-companies-integrate
    -csr-initiatives-into-everyday-business/.

Guthrie, Doug. "Corporate Social Responsibility: A State
    Department Approach." *Promoting a Comprehensive
    Approach to Corporate Social Responsibility (CSR)*, George
    P. Shultz National Foreign Affairs Training Center, 22 May
    2012. *YouTube*, 23 Aug. 2013, www.youtube.com
    /watch?v=99cJMe6wERc.

Karnani, Aneel. "The Case against Corporate Social
    Responsibility." *Wall Street Journal*, 14 June 2012, www
    .wsj.com/articles/SB10001424052748703338004575230
    112664504890.

Meister, Jeanne. "Corporate Social Responsibility: A Lever for
    Employee Attraction & Engagement." *Forbes*, 7 June
    2012, www.forbes.com/sites/jeannemeister/2012/06/07
    /corporate-social-responsibility-a-lever-for-employee
    -attraction-engagement/#6125425a7511.

Savitz, Andrew W., with Karl Weber. *The Triple Bottom Line:
    How Today's Best-Run Companies Are Achieving Economic,
    Social, and Environmental Success*, Jossey-Bass, 2006.

Works Cited
list begins on a
new page.

Alphabetical
by author's last
name.

Hanging
indent ½".

An article on a
blog without a
known author.

A clip from
YouTube.

AN ANNOTATED STUDENT RESEARCH PAPER IN APA FORMAT

The following paper is an example of a student paper that uses APA format.

Running head should be the title, or a shortened form of the title, no more than 50 characters (including spaces)

Running Head: DOES ABILITY DETERMINE EXPERTISE   1

The APA-style cover page gives title, author, and institution.

Does Ability Determine Expertise?

Hannah Smith Brooks

The University of Texas at Austin

Optional: You may choose to include an author note stating acknowledgments or course information.

Author Note

This paper was prepared for STM 385: Knowing and Learning in STEM Education, taught by Professor Flavio Azevedo.

Does Ability Determine Expertise?

To become an expert requires long-term commitment to the field of study, whether it be calculus or classroom instruction provided by a teacher. Thus, expertise is dependent upon the context of the required task or the domain specific information presented. Classifying individuals as novices means only that they have limited experience with a particular topic. If provided with an appropriate context, a novice may think deeply and demonstrate effective problem-solving strategies. An individual may be adept at managing student behavior, but he or she may have very little understanding of the biological brain development of adolescents. His or her expertise is defined by the required task of managing a classroom. Importantly, domain experts have extensive experience interacting with the content or skill throughout varied scenarios.

The Development of Expertise

Picture a classroom teacher who interacts with groups of students each day. That teacher develops a deep understanding of student behavior, instructional strategies, and building relationships with young people. During a year in the classroom, the teacher is presented with hundreds of students, each providing new information about how adolescence influences learning. Over time, the teacher becomes an expert in understanding how to effectively instruct student groups and manage student interactions, reinforcing the idea that expertise develops out of many different experiences within a domain.

Saxe (1992) suggests that cognitive development often follows along a pathway driven by goal-directed activities.

Short form of title and page number as running head.

Thesis explicitly introduced.

Headings aligned center and set in boldface to help readers navigate the essay.

DOES ABILITY DETERMINE EXPERTISE   3

These goals can shift based on the activity requirements and
accumulation of new knowledge. Our classroom teacher might
use goals embedded in lesson plan design and the building of
diverse student groups. As the teacher completes each goal, he
or she builds more understanding of the art of teaching. This
goal-directed model illustrates how novices can move through
the learning process to become experts if provided with
adequate supports and scaffolds. Constructivism theorizes that
all new learning is built on prior knowledge and conceptions.
Smith, diSessa, and Roschelle (1993/1994) discuss the role
of student conceptions in the development of expertise. They
argue that more complex cognitive structures must build on
existing structures, illustrating how expertise can be developed
exclusive of any innate ability. There must be a basic understanding of the foundational concepts in order for knowledge
and information to build towards expertise, but these foundational concepts are learned, not inherent.

    Many argue that an individual's natural interests may
dictate success across domains. However, interest and expertise
may not be directly related. Some would argue that all understanding occurs when new information is fully integrated into
one's existing cognitive structure (Carey, 1985). Using this
definition, interest could be seen as driving an individual to
understand and learn more about a particular topic or concept,
but does not guarantee integration of information into the
cognitive structure. Similarly, while an individual may move
through the learning process at a unique speed, the rate of
learning does not correlate to an underlying ability to become

*Author and
date cited for
summary or
paraphrase.*

a "better expert." Individuals are not born with an inherent ability or pre-existing cognitive structure that allows immediate and deep understanding of domain specific concepts, whether interested or not. In order to become recognized as an expert, the individual must actively build the domain-specific cognitive structure. Expertise is based on area specificity, where novices are only novices based on the contextual environment.

Author raises and refutes well-researched counter-arguments.

An important factor in the development of expertise is the learning environment in which the individual interacts. Cultural practices, social experiences, and the physical world influence how an individual sees and understands the world. The goal directed activities mentioned previously are determined by the specific cultural norms and expectations acting in the environment of the individual. In addition, the early interactions of childhood can greatly impact the belief system of a developing student. These influences can shape academic outcomes, but are not based on the inherent ability an individual may or may not be born with.

How Do Experts Differ From Novices?

There are some notable differences between experts and novices, and I would argue that each of the following skills or strategies is based on a repeated set of experiences and interactions with the domain specific content, not an inherent ability. Goldman and Petrosino (1999) conclude that experts are able to use acquired knowledge of their domain to improve the ability to notice subtle differences and characteristics of presented problems. They continue to suggest that expertise allows an individual to better develop problem-solving strategies and process information using complex creative mental

When author's name appears in text, only the date is cited parenthetically.

representations. Each of these strategies is based on the continued experience and exposure to content-specific concepts and ideas, not an individual's inherent problem-solving ability.

Bracketed word not in quotation in the original source. Author, date, and page number are cited for a direct quotation.

An expert is "not simply [a] 'general problem solver' who [has] learned a set of strategies that operate across all domains" (Bransford, Brown, & Cocking, 1999, p. 48). I consider myself a very creative problem solver inside the walls of a science classroom. If I was asked to solve for a derivative, I would be hopelessly lost and unable to draw upon my extensive problem-solving experience. As Goldman and Petrosino (1999) state, a deep domain-specific knowledge does not equate to an individual's general intelligence. Bransford, Brown and Cocking (1999) take this one step further and suggest that specialization within a specific domain actually reduces the amount of general knowledge an individual can hold at any given time.

Conclusion

Conclusion restates and strengthens thesis.

If provided with the supports and scaffolds to learn the required mathematical processes and calculations, I could grow into an expert within that domain. Successful acquisition of skills or knowledge in either area is based on my desire to improve and learn, not an inherent ability. Expertise arises with extended and extensive study and exposure to a specific area of study or content. While a student may be more interested in science, they are not born with an inherent ability that precedes the learning process. Everyone must learn how to incorporate new ideas, strategies, and skills into a unique cognitive structure that promotes increased understanding of the world around us to become an expert.

References

Bransford, J., Brown A. L., & Cocking, R. R. (1999). How experts differ from novices. In *How people learn: Brain, mind, experience, and school.* Retrieved from https://www.nap.edu/read/9853/chapter/1

Carey, S. (1985). *Conceptual change in childhood.* Cambridge, MA: MIT Press.

Goldman, S., & Petrosino, A. (1999). Design principles for instruction in content domains: Lessons from research on expertise and learning. In F. T. Durso & R. S. Nickerson (Eds.), *Handbook of applied cognition* (pp. 595-627). Chichester, NY: Wiley.

Saxe, G. B. (1992). Studying children's learning in context: Problems and prospects. *Journal of the Learning Sciences, 2,* 215-234.

Smith, J. P., diSessa, A., & Roschelle, J. (1993/1994). Misconceptions reconceived: A constructivist analysis of knowledge in transition. *Journal of the Learning Sciences, 3,* 115-163. Retrieved from http://www.jstor.org/stable/1466679

References begin on new page.

A book.

An article or a chapter in a book.

An article in a journal, retrieved from a database.

PART TWO

FURTHER VIEWS ON ARGUMENT

8

A Philosopher's View: The Toulmin Model

All my ideas hold together, but I cannot elaborate them all at once.
— JEAN-JACQUES ROUSSEAU

[Philosophy is] a peculiarly stubborn effort to think clearly.
— WILLIAM JAMES

Fight for the things you care about, but do it in a way that will lead others to join you.
— RUTH BADER GINSBURG

In Chapter 3, we explained the contrast between making *deductive* and *inductive* arguments, the two main methods people use to reason. Either

- we make explicit something concealed in what we already accept (**deduction**), or
- we use what we have observed as a basis for asserting something new (**induction**).

These two types of reasoning share some structural features, as we also noticed. Both deductive and inductive reasoning seek to establish a thesis (or reach a conclusion) by offering *reasons*. Thus, every argument contains both a thesis and one or more supportive reasons.

After a little scrutiny, we can in fact point to several features shared by all arguments, whether deductive or inductive, good or bad. We use the vocabulary popularized by Stephen Toulmin, Richard Rieke, and Allan Janik in their book *An Introduction to*

Reasoning (1979; second edition 1984) to explore the various elements of argument. Once these elements are understood, it is possible to analyze an argument using their approach and their vocabulary in what has come to be known as the Toulmin method.

The major components of arguments using this model are laid out in the Visual Guide to the Toulmin Method (below), and we go into more detail about each of them throughout this chapter.

Visual Guide: The Toulmin Method

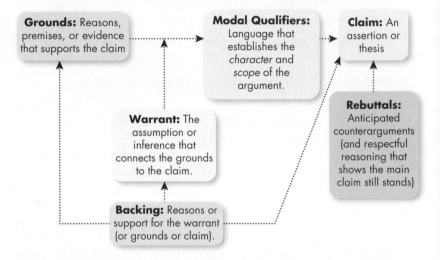

Grounds: Reasons, premises, or evidence that supports the claim

Modal Qualifiers: Language that establishes the *character* and *scope* of the argument.

Claim: An assertion or thesis

Warrant: The assumption or inference that connects the grounds to the claim.

Rebuttals: Anticipated counterarguments (and respectful reasoning that shows the main claim still stands)

Backing: Reasons or support for the warrant (or grounds or claim).

COMPONENTS OF THE TOULMIN MODEL

The Claim

Every argument has a purpose, goal, or aim—namely, to establish a **claim** (*conclusion* or *thesis*). Claims may be general or specific. As we have noted in earlier chapters, arguments may attempt to persuade readers simply to change an opinion or adopt a belief, or they may advocate for some action or seek to convince people to take some action. In other words, the *claim* being made in an argument is the whole point of making the argument in the first place. Consequently, when you read or analyze an argument, the first questions you should ask are these:

1. What is the argument intending to prove or establish?
2. What claim is it making?

Different types of claims will lead to different types of grounds, warrants, and backing and to different types of qualifiers and rebuttals.

Suppose you are arguing in a very general sense that men and women should receive equal pay for equal work. You might state your thesis or claim as follows:

> Men and women ought to be paid equally for the same kinds of jobs.

A more specific and precise claim might be the following:

> The Equal Pay Act of 1963 should be strengthened in order to guarantee that men and women are paid equally for the same kinds of jobs.

Both formulations are arguments with strong claims. They make similar but still distinguishable arguments. One is general, and the other is solution-based. Thus, the components of each argument—their grounds, warrants, backing, and so on—will also be slightly different.

Grounds

If a claim is clearly formulated and unambiguously asserts what it advocates, it does not matter how general or specific it is. As long as the argument's chief purpose or point is present, we can look for the reasons—in short, the **grounds**—for that claim. You may think of the word *groundwork* to understand better the meaning of an argument's *grounds*. You may ask, On what *groundwork*—what *ground*, what firmament of fact—does the claim rest? In *deductive* arguments, the grounds are the premises; in *inductive* arguments, the grounds are the samples, observations, or experimental results that make the claim possible and plausible.

Consider the differences in the grounds for the two claims about equal pay.

> *Claim 1:* Men and women ought to be paid equally for the same kinds of jobs.
> *Grounds:* According to the US Census Bureau in 2018, women on average make 19.5 percent lower incomes than men for the same kinds of work.

> *Claim 2:* The Equal Pay Act of 1963 should be strengthened in order to guarantee that men and women are paid equally for the same kinds of jobs.
> *Grounds:* The Equal Pay Act was passed in 1963 to eliminate the gender pay gap. Because women still earn on average 19.5 percent

lower incomes for the same kinds of work as men, the Equal Pay Act has not been effective.

But something is missing. We have provided the grounds and claim, but neither explains the reasoning or justifications that connects them. That women earn less money for similar work doesn't in and of itself justify the claim that pay should be equal among the sexes. One might simply counter that, no, women *should* make less money than men (and with only grounds and a claim you could not effectively argue back). Your opponent's argument might look like this:

> **Claim:** Women and men get paid exactly what they deserve.
> **Grounds:** According to the US Census Bureau in 2018, women on average currently make 19.5 percent lower incomes than men for the same kinds of work.

In this case, the grounds are the same as in the argument *against* pay inequity. Thus, good arguments exhibit — and require — another feature: the *warrant*.

Warrants

Once we have determined the claim of an argument and have isolated the grounds for its existence, the next question to ask is, What **warrants** it? That is, exactly what reasoning helps connect the claim and grounds, or why does the claim arise from the grounds?

The word *warrant* is related to the Old French word *gurant*, the root of our word *guarantee*. A warrant in this context is like the *warranty* you get when you buy something. It guarantees it. With an argument, you might ask, What *guarantees* that a rational claim may arise given these grounds? What reasons could be proffered to justify the claim?

Warrants help establish the *connections* between the claim and the grounds. Imagine you establish your grounds (the existence of the pay gap). You claim women and men should be paid equally for similar work. Someone might ask you, What *warrants* your claim? *Why* should women and men get equivalent pay for the same kinds of jobs? You might offer something such as:

> Well, we live in a society where people are not to be discriminated against based on sex, and unequal pay based on sex is discriminatory.

In this case, your warrant is the legal (and perhaps moral) proposition about equality that connects the claim and grounds. (Part of your warrant, too, is that the US Census Bureau numbers are reliable.) Warrants are, in a sense, *interpretations* of how the data and the arguments stemming from them are inherently related.

In ordinary and straightforward *deductive* arguments, warrants may be quite simple. If John is six feet tall and Mary is five feet tall, you have the grounds to argue that John is taller than Mary. The warrant here is just a matter of language: "Taller than" means exceeding something in a measurement of height, so the warrant is "People are said to be taller than other people when they exceed them in measurements of height." The *warrant* here is the common understanding of what the phrase "taller than" means.

In ordinary *inductive* arguments, we are likely to point to the way in which observations or sets of data constitute a *representative sample*. When Anne McKee, a neuropathologist, examined the brains of 110 deceased professional football players and found that 99 percent of them showed signs of chronic traumatic encephalopathy (CTE), she claimed that playing professional football increases the likelihood of brain damage. Her warrant was the reasoning about such a high percentage of her sample showing signs of CTE — that one (football) caused the other (CTE); the warrant is the logic that connected her grounds and her claim.

Establishing the warrants for our reasoning can be a highly technical and exacting procedure when we are making more complex, ambiguous, or values-based claims — that is, when we are explaining why our grounds really do support our claims about why something is right or wrong, moral or immoral, just or unjust. Developing a "feel" for why grounds are or are not relevant to what they are alleged to support is important. "That's just my view" is *not* a convincing warrant for any argument.

Even without formal training, however, one can sense that something is wrong with many bad arguments. Here is one example. British professor C. E. M. Joad found himself standing on a station platform, annoyed because he had just missed his train. Then another train, making an unscheduled stop, pulled up to the platform in front of him. Joad decided to jump aboard, only to hear the conductor say, "I'm afraid you'll have to get off, Sir. This train doesn't stop here." "In that case," replied the professor, "don't worry. I'm not on it."

Backing

Warrants, remember, explain why our *grounds* support our *claims*. The next task is to be able to show that we can back up what we have claimed by showing the reasons our warrants are good, reasonable, or rational. To establish that kind of further support for an argument is to provide **backing**.

What is appropriate backing for one kind of argument might be quite inappropriate for another kind of argument. For example, the kinds of reasons relevant to support the warrant that men and women should be paid equally may be completely different from the reason used to justify the claim that the Equal Pay Act should be amended. For the first argument, you might draw upon political documents, speeches, and other evidence showing that gender equality is a value and priority that necessitates action. In the second argument, you are claiming that the Equal Pay Act has been ineffective and needs strengthening, so your backing might consist of arguments about that piece of legislation specifically—theories and illustrations about what makes good, effective, and practical policy, for example. (Notice you are *not* arguing that women and men should be paid equally, per se; you are taking that for granted, making an assumption about shared beliefs.)

Another way of stating this point is to recognize that once you have given reasons for a claim, you are then likely to be challenged to explain why your reasons are good reasons—why, that is, anyone should believe your reasons rather than regard them skeptically. They have to be the right *kinds* of reasons given the field you are arguing about. A claim about the constitutionality of corporate personhood (in which corporations are regarded legally as sharing rights and responsibilities of natural persons) would have to be rationalized using backing quite different from the backing required to settle the question of what motivated Chinese people to immigrate to the United States in the nineteenth century. The *canons* (the established conventions, rules, laws, principles, and important texts) in two such dramatically different arguments have to do with the scholarly communities in law and history, respectively, that have developed over the years to justify, support, defend, challenge, and undermine ideas in those two areas of discourse.

Why (to give a simple example) should we accept the testimony of Dr. *X* when Dr. *Y*, equally renowned, supports the opposite side? What more do we need to know about "expert testimony" before it can be believably invoked? Consider a different kind of case: When and why is it safe to rest a prediction on a small—although admittedly carefully selected—sample? (McKee has been criticized for examining only the *donated* brains of professional football players, suggesting that those players or their families suspected CTE in the first place.) Why is it legitimate to argue that building a border wall, spanking children, or smoking cigarettes indoors is (or is not) appropriate? What evidence explains your thinking?

To answer questions of these sorts is to support one's reasons, to give them legitimate *backing*. No argument is any better than its backing.

Modal Qualifiers

As we have seen, all arguments are made up of assertions or propositions that can be sorted into four categories:

- *claims* (theses to be established)
- *grounds* (explicit reasons advanced)
- *warrants* (guarantees, evidence, or principles that connect grounds and claims)
- *backing* (relevant support)

All the kinds of propositions that emerge when we assert something in an argument have what philosophers call a **modality**. In other words, propositions generally indicate—explicitly or tacitly—the *character* and *scope* of what is believed to be their likely truth.

Character   **Character** has to do with the nature of the claim being made, the extent of an argument's presumed reach. Both making and evaluating arguments require being clear about whether they are

- *necessary,*
- *probable,*
- *plausible*, or
- *possible.*

Consider, for example, a claim that it is to the advantage of a college to have a racially diverse student body. Is that *necessarily* true or only *probably* true? What about an argument that a runner who easily wins a 100-meter race should also be able to win a 200-meter race? Is that *plausible*, or is it only *possible*? Indicating the *character* with which an assertion is advanced is crucial to any argument for or against it. Furthermore, if there is more than one reason for making a claim and all those reasons are *good*, it is still possible that one of those good reasons may be *better* than the others. If so, the better reason should be stressed.

Scope   Indicating the **scope** of an assertion is equally crucial to how an argument plays out. *Scope* entails such considerations as whether the proposition is thought to be true *always* or just *sometimes*. Further, is the claim being made supposed to apply in *all* instances or just in *some*? Assertions are usually clearer, as well as more likely to be true, if they are explicitly *quantified* and *qualified*. Suppose, for example, you are arguing against smoking, and the ground for your claim is this:

> Heavy smokers cut short their life span.

In this case, there are three obvious alternative quantifications to choose among: *All* smokers cut short their life span, *most* do, or only *some* do. Until the assertion is quantified in one of these ways, we really don't know what is being asserted, and so we don't know what degree and kind of evidence or counterevidence is relevant. Other quantifiers include *few, rarely, often, sometimes, perhaps, usually, more or less, regularly*, and *occasionally*.

Scope also reflects that empirical generalizations are typically *contingent* on various factors. Indicating such contingencies clearly is an important way to protect a generalization against obvious counterexamples. Thus, consider this empirical generalization:

> Students do best on final examinations if they study hard for them.

Are we really to believe that students who cram ("study hard" in that concentrated sense) for an exam will do better than those who do the work diligently throughout the whole course ("study hard" in that broader sense) and therefore do not need to cram for the final? Probably not; what is really meant is that, *all other things being equal* (in Latin, *ceteris paribus*), concentrated study just before an exam will yield good results. Alluding in this way to the contingencies—the things that might derail the argument—shows that the writer is aware of possible exceptions and is conceding them from the start.

In sum, sensitivity to both character and (especially) scope—paying attention to the role played by quantifiers, qualifiers, and contingencies and making sure you use appropriate ones for each of your assertions—will strengthen your arguments enormously. Not least of the benefits is that you will reduce the peculiar vulnerabilities of an argument that is undermined by exaggeration and other misguided generalizations.

Rebuttals

Very few arguments of any interest are beyond dispute, conclusively knockdown affairs. Only very rarely is the claim of an argument so rigidly tied to its grounds, warrants, and backing—and with its quantifiers and qualifiers argued in so precise a manner—that it proves its conclusion beyond any possibility of doubt. On the contrary, most arguments have many counterarguments, and sometimes one of these counterarguments is more convincing than the original argument. When writers raise counterarguments, they build their *ethos* and assure readers that other views are taken seriously; however, those counterarguments should not be raised simply to challenge your own position. If you indeed believe in your position, you can offer a **rebuttal** to the counterargument—telling your readers where it succeeds, perhaps, but also where it fails (thus implying or stating that *your* position is more convincing).

Suppose someone has taken a sample that appears to be random: An interviewer on your campus approaches the first ten students she encounters, and seven of them are fraternity or sorority members. She is now ready to argue that seven-tenths of enrolled students belong to Greek organizations.

You believe, however, that the Greeks are in the minority; you point out that she happens to have conducted her interview around the corner from the Panhellenic Society's office just off Sorority Row. Her random sample is anything but random. The ball is now back in her court as you await her response to your rebuttal.

As this example illustrates, it is safe to say that we do not understand our own arguments very well until we have tried to get a grip on the places in which they are vulnerable to criticism, counterattack, or refutation. As Edmund Burke astutely observed, "He that wrestles with us strengthens our nerves, and sharpens our skill. Our antagonist is our helper."

THINKING CRITICALLY CONSTRUCTING A TOULMIN ARGUMENT

Choose a topic or issue that interests you. In the spaces provided, supply a sentence or two for each step of a Toulmin argument about your topic.

Step of Toulmin Argument	Question This Step Addresses	Your Sentence(s)
Claim	What is your argument?	
Grounds	What is your evidence?	
Warrant	What reasoning connects your evidence to your argument?	
Backing	What can you provide as support to convince the reader to agree with your grounds, claims, and warrants?	
Qualifier	What are the limits of your argument?	
Rebuttal	What are the objections to your argument — and can you reason that your argument still holds?	

PUTTING THE TOULMIN METHOD TO WORK: RESPONDING TO AN ARGUMENT

Let's take a look at another argument — on why buying directly from farmers near you won't save the planet — and see how the Toulmin method can be applied. The checklist on page 350 can help you focus your thoughts as you read.

James E. McWilliams

James E. McWilliams (b. 1968), the author of Just Food: Where Locavores Get It Wrong and How We Can Truly Eat Responsibly *(2009), is a professor of history at Texas State University. This piece first appeared in* Forbes Magazine *on August 3, 2009.*

The Locavore Myth: Why Buying from Nearby Farmers Won't Save the Planet

Buy local, shrink the distance food travels, save the planet. The locavore movement has captured a lot of fans. To their credit, they are highlighting the problems with industrialized food. But a lot of them are making a big mistake. By focusing on transportation, they overlook other energy-hogging factors in food production.

Take lamb. A 2006 academic study (funded by the New Zealand government) discovered that it made more environmental sense for a Londoner to buy lamb shipped from New Zealand than to buy lamb raised in the U.K. This finding is counterintuitive—if you're only counting food miles. But New Zealand lamb is raised on pastures with a small carbon footprint, whereas most English lamb is produced under intensive factory-like conditions with a big carbon footprint. This disparity overwhelms domestic lamb's advantage in transportation energy.

New Zealand lamb is not exceptional. Take a close look at water usage, fertilizer types, processing methods, and packaging techniques and you discover that factors other than shipping far outweigh the energy it takes to transport food. One analysis, by Rich Pirog of the Leopold Center for Sustainable Agriculture, showed that transportation accounts for only 11 percent of food's carbon footprint. A fourth of the energy required to produce food is expended in the consumer's kitchen. Still more energy is consumed per meal in a restaurant, since restaurants throw away most of their leftovers.

Locavores argue that buying local food supports an area's farmers and, in turn, strengthens the community. Fair enough. Left unacknowledged, however, is the fact that it also hurts farmers in other parts of the world. The U.K. buys most of its green beans from Kenya. While it's true that the beans almost always arrive in airplanes—the form of transportation that consumes the most energy—it's also true that a campaign to shame English consumers with small airplane stickers affixed to flown-in produce threatens the livelihood of 1.5 million sub-Saharan farmers.

Another chink in the locavores' armor involves the way food 5 miles are calculated. To choose a locally grown apple over an apple trucked in from across the country might seem easy. But this decision ignores economies of scale. To take an extreme example, a shipper sending a truck with 2,000 apples over 2,000 miles would consume the same amount of fuel per apple as a local farmer who takes a pickup 50 miles to sell 50 apples at his stall at the green market. The critical measure here is not food miles but apples per gallon.

The one big problem with thinking beyond food miles is that it's hard to get the information you need. Ethically concerned consumers know very little about processing practices, water availability, packaging waste, and fertilizer application. This is an opportunity for watchdog groups. They should make life-cycle carbon counts available to shoppers.

Until our food system becomes more transparent, there is one thing you can do to shrink the carbon footprint of your dinner: Take the meat off your plate. No matter how you slice it, it takes more energy to bring meat, as opposed to plants, to the table. It takes 6 pounds of grain to make a pound of chicken and 10 to 16 pounds to make a pound of beef. That difference translates into big differences in inputs. It requires 2,400 liters of water to make a burger and only 13 liters to grow a tomato. A majority of the water in the American West goes toward the production of pigs, chickens, and cattle.

The average American eats 273 pounds of meat a year. Give up red meat once a week and you'll save as much energy as if the only food miles in your diet were the distance to the nearest truck farmer.

If you want to make a statement, ride your bike to the farmer's market. If you want to reduce greenhouse gases, become a vegetarian.

THINKING WITH THE TOULMIN METHOD

Remember to make use of the Visual Guide on page 338 as you work to find the claim(s), grounds, and warrant(s) that McWilliams puts forward in this short essay.

1. What **claim** is the author making? Is it in the title? Is it in the opening sentence? Or is it buried in the first paragraph?

McWilliams really gives away his game in the title, even though he opens the essay itself in a way that might make the reader think he is about to launch into a defense of the locavore movement. He even goes out of his way to praise its members ("To their credit . . .").

The signal that his claim really appears already in the title and that he is *not* going to defend the locavore movement is the way he begins the fourth sentence. Notice that although you may have been told that starting a sentence with *But* isn't the best way to write, McWilliams here does so to good effect. Not only does he dramatically counter what he said just prior to that, but he also sets up the final sentence of the paragraph, which turns out to be crucial. In this way, he draws sharp attention to his *claim*. How would you state his claim?

2. What are the **grounds**, the evidence or reasons, that the author advances in support of his claim?

As it turns out, McWilliams spells out only one example as evidence for his claim. What is it? Is it convincing? Should he have provided more evidence or reasons at this point? It turns out that he does have other grounds to offer, but he mentions them only later. What are those other pieces of evidence?

3. What **warrants** does McWilliams offer to show why we should accept his grounds? What authority does he cite? How effective and convincing is this way of trying to get us to accept the grounds he offered in support of his claim?

The essence of the Toulmin method lies in these three elements: the claim(s), the grounds, and the warrant(s). If you have extracted these from McWilliams's essay, you are well on the way to being able to identify the argument he is putting forward. So far, so good. Further probing, however—looking for the other three elements of the Toulmin method (the backing, the modal qualifiers and quantifiers, and the rebuttal)—is essential before you are in a position to actually evaluate the argument. So let's go on.

4. What **backing** does McWilliams provide? What reasons does he give that might persuade us to accept his argument? Look for what he claimed came out of the analysis that was his basic warrant. He certainly seems to be using factual information—but what if you challenged him? Has he provided adequate reasons for us to believe him? What could he (or would he have to) be able to tell us if we challenged him with questions like "How do you know . . . ?" or "Why do you believe . . . ?" In other words, has he provided adequate backing? Or does he want us to just accept his statement of the facts?

5. Does McWilliams use **modal qualifiers**? Can you find phrases like "in most cases" or "generally it is true that . . ."? Or does he write so boldly—with little in the way of qualifiers or quantifiers—that readers are left uncertain about whether to accept his position? Where might he have effectively used qualifiers?

6. Does McWilliams prepare **rebuttals**, the reasons given in anticipation of someone rejecting the author's claim or conceding the claim but rejecting the grounds? Does he offer anything to forestall criticisms? If so, what is it that he does? If not, what could or should he have done?

Just how good an argument has McWilliams made? Is he convincing? If you identified weak points in his argument, what are they? Can you help strengthen the argument? If so, how?

✓   A CHECKLIST FOR USING THE TOULMIN METHOD

☐ What claim does the argument make?

☐ What grounds are offered for the claim?

☐ What warrants connect the grounds to the claim?

☐ What backing supports the claim?

☐ With what modalities are the claim and grounds asserted?

☐ To what rebuttals are the claim, grounds, and backing vulnerable?

A Logician's View: Deduction, Induction, and Fallacies

Logic is the anatomy of thought.

— JOHN LOCKE

Logic takes care of itself; all we have to do is to look and see how it does it.

— LUDWIG WITTGENSTEIN

In Chapter 3, we introduced the terms *deduction*, *induction*, and *fallacy*. In this chapter, we discuss them in more detail and present some principles of *formal logic* to help you develop your ability to understand arguments.

USING FORMAL LOGIC FOR CRITICAL THINKING

Formal logic is a discipline of philosophy that studies the *nature* and *structure* of arguments abstracted from their content. Formal logic emerged in the ancient world and was developed further during the Enlightenment (ca. 1685–1815), a time of great scientific ferment, as an attempt to understand truth according to *a priori* rules—that is, rules that exist before, or *prior* to, any specific content. Formal logic is closely related to mathematics. Each expresses reality using symbols and variables. In math, the phrase *two plus two equals four* is true no matter if apples or oranges are being counted. Consider the structure of an equation:

If $A + B = C$, then $C + D = (A + B) + D$.

This formula expresses logical truth no matter what numbers you plug into the letters. The variables can change, but not the truth of the matter: If the first proposition is true, the second must be, too.

Perhaps for obvious reasons, formal logic is quite important in computer science, which is based on binaries of 0 and 1. But even in our everyday lives, we still use methods of formal logic to demonstrate truth ("If I take a lower-paying job, there will be less household income overall; if there is lower household income, there will be less money to pay for X, Y, and Z; therefore, some cuts to one or more of X, Y, or Z are inevitable if I take the lower-paying job").

But as soon as we enter the world of values, language, principles, and morals—where we encounter questions of what words mean and what we *should* or *ought* to do, or have a *right* to do—we must recognize the limits of formal logic's ability to demonstrate absolute truth. For arguments to work, the components must have meaning. Therefore, arguments that make assertions of human value involve applied reasoning, empirical observation, speculation, and other ways of thinking. Nevertheless, formal logic can assist us in seeing the ways even these types of arguments are structured and ultimately help us judge such arguments and think more carefully about our own.

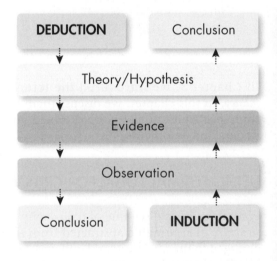

Visual Guide: Deduction and Induction

DEDUCTION

The basic aim of deductive reasoning is to start with some given premise and extract from it a conclusion—a logical consequence—that is concealed but implicit in it. When we introduced the idea of deduction in Chapter 3, we gave as our primary example the *syllogism*, and we provided a classical syllogism to represent how one aspect of formal logic, deduction, can lead to true conclusions:

Premise: All human beings are mortal.

Premise: Socrates is a human being.

Conclusion: Socrates is mortal.

If the premises are absolutely true, and the conclusion necessarily follows from them, the syllogism is *valid* and the argument is *sound*.
Here is another example:

Texas is larger than California.

California is larger than Arizona.

Therefore, Texas is larger than Arizona.

The conclusion in this syllogism can be derived from the two premises; that is, anyone who asserts the two premises is committed to accepting the conclusion as well, whatever one thinks of it. It is not a matter of perspective, opinion, or dispute.

Using formal logic, we can derive an equation of sorts to represent the argument graphically using nested circles:

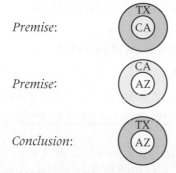

Premise:

Premise:

Conclusion:

We can see that this conclusion follows from the premises because it amounts to nothing more than what one gets by superimposing the two premises on each other. Thus, the whole argument can be represented like this:

$$\text{TX} \left(\text{CA}\right) \; + \; \text{CA} \left(\text{AZ}\right) \; = \; \text{TX} \left(\text{AZ}\right)$$

The so-called middle term in the argument — California — disappears from the conclusion; its role is confined to being the link between the other two terms, Texas and Arizona, in the premises.

In a graphic depiction, as with an equation, one can literally *see* that the conclusion follows from the premises. (This technique is an adaptation of one used in elementary formal logic known as Venn diagrams.)

In formal logic, the validity of a deductive inference depends on being able to show how the concepts in the premises are related to the concepts in the conclusion. In this case, the validity of the inference depends on the meaning of a key concept, *being larger than*. This concept has the property of *transitivity*, a property that many concepts share (e.g., *is equal to*, *is to the right of*, *is smarter than*). Transitive concepts can be represented symbolically in equations. Consequently, regardless of what is represented by A, B, and C, we can say:

If $A > B$, and $B > C$, then $A > C$.

This is all intended to show that the validity of deductive inference is a purely *formal* property of argument. You can substitute any state for Texas, California, and Arizona—or anything at all for the variables A, B, and C—as long as they adhere to the meaning of the transitive concept *larger than*.

Understanding this technique can help you see how some arguments can appear to be valid, but may also be challenged. For example:

If A is to the right of B and B is to the right of C, then A is to the right of C.

or

If A is smarter than B and B is smarter than C, then A is smarter than C.

Let's dig into these examples. First, on the earth, if A is to the right of B and B is to the right of C, it is purely logical that A is to the right of C, too—until we circle the globe and place A directly to the left of C, in which case the syllogism may be refuted on the grounds that it assumes an infinite plane surface. The very meaning of the phrase *to the right of* has been challenged. In the second example, *smarter than* is a category that needs definition. To challenge this argument, you can contest the comparative meaning of the term *smarter than*: Does "smart" refer to IQ level, grades earned in school, street smarts, or something else? Here you have two examples of valid syllogism, neither of which is necessarily true.

Now let's look at an example of another syllogism that is **valid** but not true.

Rhode Island is larger than Texas.

Texas is larger than Canada.

Therefore, Rhode Island is larger than Canada.

How, you might ask, can this syllogism be valid? Again, remember this about the formal properties of arguments: If you grant that the premises are true and the conclusion is inherently related to the premises, it is valid *even if it not true*.

Why is all this important to your learning about arguments? Well, if all one can say about an argument is that it is valid—that is, its conclusion follows from the premises—one has not given a sufficient reason for accepting the argument's conclusion. It has been said that the devil can quote scripture; similarly, an argument can be deductively valid and of no value whatsoever because valid (but false) conclusions can be drawn from false, misleading, or meaningless premises.

In short, a valid deductive argument doesn't prove anything unless the premises and the conclusion are *true*, but they can't be true unless they *mean* something in the first place. Consider this nonsense syllogism:

If the slithy toves, then the gyres gimble. The slithy toves. Therefore, the gyres gimble.

This argument has the following form:

If *A*, then *B*; *A*; therefore *B*.

As a piece of deductive inference, it is every bit as good (valid) as the other arguments above. Unlike them, however, it is of no interest at all because its assertions make no sense (unless you're a reader of Lewis Carroll's "Jabberwocky," and even then it is doubtful).

This example shows that the form of an argument can be good but the argument itself bad. We work through these problems because understanding the structures of arguments helps us better think about, analyze, and construct arguments ourselves. Think about this one:

If President Truman knew the Japanese were about to surrender, then it was immoral of him to order that atom bombs be dropped on Hiroshima and Nagasaki. Truman knew the Japanese were going to surrender. Therefore, it was immoral of him to order dropping those bombs.

Once again, anyone who assents to the *if . . . then* proposition in the premise and accepts that Truman knew the Japanese were about to surrender must assent to the conclusion. But do the premises *prove* the conclusion? That depends on whether both premises are true. Well, are they? The answer turns on a number of considerations, and it is worth pausing to examine how we might think critically about this argument.

Let's begin by examining the second premise, which proposes a fact: Did Truman really know the Japanese were about to surrender? This question is controversial even today. Autobiography, memoranda, other documentary evidence — all are needed to assemble the evidence to back up the grounds for the thesis or claim made in the conclusion of this argument. Evaluating this material effectively may involve further deductions (and perhaps inductive reasoning as well).

As to the first premise, its truth doesn't depend on facts about the past but, rather, on moral principles. The first premise contains a hypothetical ("if") and asserts a connection between two very different kinds of things (prior knowledge and morality). This premise as a whole can thus be seen as expressing *a principle of moral responsibility.* The principle is this: If we have knowledge that makes violence unnecessary, it is immoral to act violently anyway. Someone could compare Truman's decision to an argument that shares its form: If someone is surrendering, it is immoral to do violence to him. Such principles can, of course, be supported or contested.

Examples of Deduction

When we engage with and construct arguments, it is useful to keep in mind some of the basic structures (including but not limited to *syllogism*) because they help us see what is going on under the surface of an argument.

Disjunction   One common form of argument occurs through **disjunctive syllogism**, so called because its major premise is a **disjunction**, or a relationship between distinct alternatives. For example:

> Either censorship of fake news is overdue or our society is indifferent to hostile forces meddling in elections.

Our society is not indifferent to propaganda on social media affecting our elections.

Therefore, censorship of fake news is overdue.

Notice, by the way, that the validity of an argument, as in this case, does not turn on pedantic repetition of every word or phrase: Nonessential elements can be dropped or equivalent expressions substituted without adverse effect on the reasoning as long as those relationships are established. Thus, in conversation or in writing, this argument might actually be presented like this:

> Either censorship of fake news is overdue or our society is indifferent to the role fake news propaganda has in our elections. Of course, our political elections are susceptible to the effects of fake news, which is why some kind of censorship is overdue.

The key feature of disjunctive syllogism is that the conclusion is whichever of the alternatives remains after the others have been negated. We could easily have a very complex disjunctive syllogism with a dozen alternatives in the first premise and seven of them denied in the second, leaving a conclusion of the remaining five. Usually, however, a disjunctive argument is formulated in this manner: Assert a disjunction with two or more alternatives in the major premise, *deny all but one* in the minor premise, and then infer validly the remaining alternative(s) as the conclusion.

Dilemma   Another type of argument, especially favored by orators and rhetoricians, is the **dilemma**. Ordinarily, we use the term *dilemma* in the sense of an awkward predicament, as when we say, "His dilemma was that he didn't have enough money to pay the waiter." But when logicians refer to a dilemma, they mean a forced choice between two or more equally unattractive alternatives. For example, the predicament faced by the US government in fighting the Islamic State in Syria (ISIS) can be posed as a dilemma. The United States could ally itself with the Syrian government, a dictatorship under Bashar al-Assad, who is also trying to destroy ISIS influence in Syria. But al-Assad's government is hostile to the United States, has attempted to crush political reform movements in Syria, and actively supports groups the United States deems terrorist organizations. On the other hand, the United States could extend support to the Syrian Democratic Forces (SDF), a large militia inside Syria comprised mostly of Kurdish majority people who are fighting against ISIS and opposing al-Assad; however, in doing so, the United States risks expanding conflict in Syria, a Russian ally, and alienates its own ally, Turkey, which sees the SDF as a force of instability in its own country. The dilemma might be phrased as such:

> If the United States supports the Syrian government's fight against ISIS, it would be supporting a dictatorship linked to terrorism and crimes against humanity. If the United States supports the SDF, it risks further conflict with the Bashar al-Assad regime (and perhaps Russia) and also compromises its own relationship with Turkey. Thus, in fighting the Islamic State in Syria, either the United States supports a dictatorship or it supports a resistance group opposed to our own ally. In either case, unattractive consequences follow.

Notice first the structure of the argument: two conditional propositions asserted as premises followed by another premise that states a **necessary truth**. The premise, "Either we support the dictatorship or we support the SDF," is a disjunction; because the two alternatives are presented as exhaustive (the only options), one of the two alternatives must be true. (Such a statement is often called analytically true, or a *tautology*.) No doubt the conclusion of this dilemma ("unattractive consequences") follows from its premises.

But does the argument *prove*, as it purports to do, that whatever the US government does, it will suffer "unattractive consequences"? It is customary to speak of "the horns of the dilemma," as though the challenge posed by the dilemma were like a bull ready to gore us no matter which direction we turn. But if the two conditional premises failed to exhaust the possibilities, we can escape from the dilemma by going "between the horns" — by finding a third alternative (or a fourth or fifth).

If alternatives are not possible, we can still ask whether both of the main premises are true. Neither of the main premises spells out all or even most of the consequences that could be foreseen, and perhaps backing the SDF would not result in compromising our relationship with Turkey. In cases where both of the conditional premises are true, then, it may be that the consequences of one alternative are not as bad as those of the other. If that is true, but our reasoning stops before evaluating that fact, we may be guilty of failing to distinguish between the greater and the lesser of two evils. The logic of the dilemma itself cannot decide this choice for us. Instead, we must bring to bear empirical inquiry and imagination to the evaluation of the grounds of the dilemma.

Reductio Ad Absurdum

Finally, one of the most powerful and dramatic forms of argument is **reductio ad absurdum** (from the Latin, meaning "reduction to absurdity"). The idea of a reductio argument is to disprove a proposition by showing the absurdity of its inevitable conclusion. It is used, of course, to refute your opponent's position and prove your own. For example, in Plato's *Republic*, Socrates asks an old gentleman, Cephalus, to define *right conduct*. Cephalus says it consists of paying your debts and keeping your word. Socrates rejects

Socrates Looking in a Mirror by Bernard Vaillant, c. 17th century.

A. Hyatt Mayor Purchase Fund, Marjorie Phelps Starr Bequest, 1982

this answer by showing that it leads to a contradiction. He argues that Cephalus cannot have given the correct answer because if we believe that he did, we will quickly encounter contradictions; in some cases, when you keep your word, you will nonetheless be doing the wrong thing. Suppose, says Socrates, you borrowed a weapon from a man, promising to return it when he asks for it. One day he comes to your door, demanding his weapon and swearing angrily that he intends to murder a neighbor. Keeping your word under those circumstances would be absurd, Socrates implies, and the reader of the dialogue is left to infer that Cephalus's definition, which led to this result, has been refuted.

Let's look at another example. Suppose you are opposed to any form of gun control, whereas we are in favor of gun control. We might try to refute your position by attacking it with a reductio argument. We start out by assuming the very opposite of what we believe or favor and try to establish a contradiction that results from following out the consequences of your initial assumption:

> Your position is that there ought to be no legal restrictions of any kind on the sale and ownership of guns. That means that you'd permit having every neighborhood hardware store sell pistols and rifles to whoever walks in the door. But that's not all.

You apparently also would permit selling machine guns to children, antitank weapons to lunatics, and small-bore cannons to the nearsighted, as well as guns and ammunition to anyone with a criminal record. But that is utterly preposterous; no one could favor such a dangerous policy. So the only question worth debating is what kind of gun control is necessary.

Now in this example, our reductio of your position on gun control is not based on claiming to show that you have strictly contradicted yourself, for there is no purely logical contradiction in opposing all forms of gun control. Instead, what we have tried to do is to show that there is a contradiction between what you profess — no gun controls at all — and what you probably really believe, if only you'll stop to think about it — which is that no lunatic should be allowed to buy a loaded machine gun. Our refutation of your position rests on whether we succeed in establishing an inconsistency among your own beliefs. If it turns out that you really believe lunatics should be free to purchase guns and ammunition, our attempted refutation fails.

Contradiction, Consistency, and Conjunction   In explaining reductio ad absurdum, we have had to rely on another idea fundamental to logic, that of **contradiction**, or inconsistency. The opposite of contradiction is **consistency**, a notion important to good reasoning. These concepts deserve a few words of further explanation and illustration. Consider this pair of assertions:

A. Abortion is homicide.

B. Racism is unfair.

No one would plausibly claim that we can infer or deduce B from A or, for that matter, A from B. There is no evident connection between these two assertions. They are unrelated assertions; logically speaking, they are *independent* of each other. The two assertions are potentially *consistent*; that is, both could be true — or both could be false. But now consider another proposition:

C. Euthanasia is not murder.

Could a person assert A (*Abortion is homicide*) and also assert C (*Euthanasia is not murder*) and be consistent? Could you assert these two propositions as a **conjunction**? Now consider:

D. Abortion is homicide, and euthanasia is not murder.

It's not so easy to say whether these are consistent or inconsistent. One person could assert one of these propositions and reject the other, leading to a conclusion of general inconsistency. Another could be convinced that there is no inconsistency in asserting that *Abortion is homicide* and that *Euthanasia is not murder.* (For instance, suppose you believe both that the unborn are persons who deserve a chance to live and that putting terminally ill persons to death in a painless manner and with their consent confers a benefit on them.)

Let us generalize: We can say of any set of propositions that they are consistent *if and only if* all could be true together. Remember that, once again, the truth of the assertions in question doesn't matter. Two propositions can be consistent or not, quite apart from whether they are true. That's not so with falsehood: It follows from our definition of consistency that an *inconsistent* proposition must be *false.* (We have relied on this idea in explaining how a reductio ad absurdum argument works.)

Assertions or claims that are not consistent can take either of two forms. Suppose you assert that abortion is homicide, early in an essay you are writing, but later you assert that abortion is harmless. You have now asserted a position on abortion that is strictly contrary to the one with which you began—both cannot be true. It is simply not true that if an abortion involves killing a human being (which is what *homicide* strictly means), it causes no one any harm (killing a person always causes harm—even if it is excusable, justifiable, not wrong, the best thing to do in the circumstances, and so on). Notice that while both cannot be true, they *can* both be false. In fact, many people who are perplexed about the morality of abortion believe precisely this. They concede that abortion does harm the fetus, but they also believe that abortion doesn't kill a person.

Let's consider another, simpler case. If you describe the glass as half empty and I describe it as half full, both of us can be right; the two assertions are consistent, even though they sound vaguely incompatible. (This is the reason that disputing over whether the glass is half full or half empty has become the popular paradigm of a futile, purely *verbal disagreement.*) But if I describe the glass as half empty whereas you insist that it is two-thirds empty, we have a real disagreement; your description and mine are strictly contrary, in that both cannot be true—although both *can* be false. (Both are false if the glass is only one-fourth full.)

This, by the way, enables us to define the difference between a pair of **contradictory** propositions and a pair of **contrary** propositions. Two propositions are contrary if and only if both cannot be true (though both can be false); two propositions are contradictory if and only if they are such that if one is true the other must be false, and vice versa. Thus, if Jack says that Alice Walker's *The Color Purple* is a better novel than Mark Twain's *Huckleberry Finn*, and Jill says, "No, *Huckleberry Finn* is better than *The Color Purple*," she is contradicting Jack. If what either one of them says is true, then what the other says must be false.

A more subtle case of contradiction arises when two or more of one's own beliefs implicitly contradict each other. We may find ourselves saying "Travel is broadening" and saying an hour later "People don't really change." Just beneath the surface of these two beliefs lies a self-contradiction: How can travel broaden us unless it influences—and changes—our beliefs, values, and outlook? But if we can't really change ourselves, traveling to new places won't change us, either. (Indeed, there is a Roman saying to the effect that travelers change the skies above them, not their hearts.) "Travel is broadening" and "People don't change" collide with each other; something has to give.

Our point, of course, is not that you must never say today something that contradicts something you said yesterday. Far from it; if you think you were mistaken yesterday, of course you will take a different position today. But what you want to avoid is what George Orwell called *doublethink* in his novel *1984*: "*Doublethink* means the power of holding two contradictory beliefs in one's mind simultaneously, and accepting them both."

Paradox   While we're speaking of inconsistency, let's spend a moment on **paradox**. The word refers to two different things:

- an assertion that is essentially self-contradictory and therefore cannot be true
- a seemingly contradictory assertion that nevertheless may be true

An example of the first might be "Evaluations concerning quality in literature are all a matter of personal judgment, but Shakespeare is the world's greatest writer." It is hard to make any sense out of this assertion. Contrast it with a paradox of the second sort, a *seeming* contradiction that may make sense, such as "The longest way around is the shortest way home," or "Work is more fun than fun," or "The best way to find happiness is not to look for it." Here we have assertions that are striking because as soon as we hear them we realize that although they seem inconsistent and self-defeating, they contain (or may contain) profound truths. If you use the word *paradox* in your own writing—for instance, to characterize an argument you're reading—be sure the reader will understand in which sense you're using the word. (And, of course, you won't want to write paradoxes of the first, self-contradictory sort.)

INDUCTION

Deduction involves logical thinking that applies to absolutely any assertion or claim—because every possible statement, true or false, has deductive logical consequences. Induction, remember, is the type of thinking that begins with specific **empirical** or *factual* observations and leads to general conclusions. Induction is relevant to one kind of assertion only. Other kinds of assertions (such as definitions, mathematical equations, and moral or legal norms) simply are not the product of inductive reasoning and cannot serve as a basis for further inductive thinking.

So, in studying the methods of induction, we are exploring tactics and strategies useful in gathering and then using **evidence**—empirical, observational, experimental—in support of a belief as its ground. Modern scientific knowledge is the product of these methods, and they differ somewhat from one science to another because they depend on the theories and technology appropriate to each of the sciences. Here all we can do is discuss generally the more abstract features common to inductive inquiry. For fuller details, you must eventually consult a physicist, chemist, geologist, or their colleagues and counterparts in other scientific fields.

Observation and Inference

Let's begin with a simple example. Suppose we have evidence (actually we don't, but that won't matter for our purposes) in support of this claim:

> In a sample of 500 smokers, 230 persons observed have cardiovascular disease.

The basis—the evidence or grounds—for asserting this claim would be, presumably, straightforward physical examination of the 500 persons in the sample, one by one.

With this claim in hand, we can think of the purpose and methods of induction as pointing in two opposite directions: toward establishing the basis or ground of the very empirical proposition with which we start (in this example, the observation stated above) or toward understanding what that observation indicates or suggests as a more general, inclusive, or fundamental fact of nature.

In each case, we start from something we *do* know (or take for granted and treat as a sound starting point)—some fact of nature, perhaps a striking or commonplace event that we have observed and recorded—and then go on to something we do *not* fully know and perhaps cannot directly observe. In the smoking example above, only the second of these two orientations (the 230 persons with cardiovascular disease) is of any interest, so let's concentrate exclusively on it.

Generalization   Anyone truly interested in the observed fact that *230 of 500 smokers have cardiovascular disease* is likely to start speculating about, and thus be interested in finding out, whether any or all of several other propositions are also true. For example, one might wonder whether the following claim is true:

> *All* smokers have cardiovascular disease or will develop it during their lifetimes.

This claim is a straightforward generalization of the original observation as reported in the first claim. When we think inductively, we are reasoning from an observed sample (some smokers—i.e., 230 of the 500 *observed*) to the entire membership of a more inclusive class (*all* smokers, whether observed or not). The fundamental question raised by reasoning from the narrower claim to the broader claim is whether we have any ground for believing that what is true of *some* members of a class is true of them *all*. So the difference between these claims is that of *quantity* or scope.

Relation   We can also think inductively about the *relation* between the factors mentioned in the original claim, *In a sample of 500 smokers, 230 persons observed have cardiovascular disease*. Having observed data, we may be tempted to assert a different and more profound kind of claim:

> Smoking *causes* cardiovascular disease.

Here our interest is not merely in generalizing from a sample to a whole class; it is the far more important one of *explaining* the observation with which we began. Certainly, the preferred, even if not the only, mode of explanation for a natural phenomenon is a *causal* explanation. In this claim, we propose to explain the presence of one phenomenon (cardiovascular disease) by the prior occurrence of an independent phenomenon (smoking). The original observation about the number of diseased smokers is now serving as evidence or support for this new conjecture.

But there is a third way to think inductively beyond our original claim. Instead of a straightforward generalization or a pronouncement on the cause of a phenomenon, we might have a more complex and cautious further claim in mind, such as this:

> Smoking is a factor in the causation of cardiovascular disease in some persons.

This proposition also advances a claim about causation, although it is obviously weaker than the claim *Smoking causes cardiovascular disease*. That is, other observations, theories, or evidence that would support the "factor" claim could easily fail to be enough to support the claim that smoking is the sole or main cause. Claiming that smoking is only one factor allows for other (unmentioned) factors in the causation of cardiovascular disease (e.g., genetic or dietary factors) that may not be found in all smokers.

Inductive Inference (or Hypothesis)   We began by assuming that our first proposition states an empirical fact based on direct observation but that the propositions that follow do not. Instead, they state empirical *hypotheses* or conjectures—tentative generalizations not fully confirmed—each of which goes beyond the observed facts. As such, they can be regarded as an *inductive inference* from the first proposition or observation.

Probability

Another way of thinking about inferences and hypotheses is to say that whereas a statement of observed fact (*230 out of 500 smokers have cardiovascular disease*) has a **probability** of 1.0 — that is, it is absolutely certain — the probability of each of

Al Ross/The New Yorker Collection/The Cartoon Bank

the hypotheses that followed, *relative* to 1.0, is smaller than 1.0. (We need not worry here about how much smaller than 1.0 the probabilities are, nor about how to calculate these probabilities precisely.) But it takes only a moment's reflection to realize that no matter what the probability actually is, those probabilities in each case will be quite different relative to different information, such as this:

> Ten persons observed in a sample of 500 smokers have cardiovascular disease.

The idea that *a given proposition can have different probabilities* relative to different bases is fundamental to all inductive reasoning. The following example makes a convincing illustration. Suppose we want to consider the probability of this proposition being true:

> Susanne Smith will live to be eighty.

Taken as an abstract question of fact, we cannot even guess what the probability is with any assurance. But we can do better than guess; we can, in fact, even calculate the answer—if we get some further information. Thus, suppose we are told that Susanne Smith is seventy-nine. Our original question then becomes one of determining the probability that the proposition is true given this fact—that is, relative to the evidence. There's no doubt that if Susanne Smith really is seventy-nine, the probability that she will live to be eighty is greater than if we know only that Suzanne Smith is more than nine years old. Obviously, a lot can happen to Susanne in the seventy years between nine and seventy-nine that isn't very likely to happen in the one year between seventy-nine and eighty. So our proposition is more probable relative to the evidence of Susanne's age of seventy-nine than of "more than nine years old."

Let's suppose for the sake of the argument that the following is true:

> Ninety percent of women alive at age seventy-nine live to be eighty.

Given this additional information and the information that Susanne is seventy-nine, we now have a basis for answering our original question about our proposition about Susanne's longevity with some precision. But suppose, in addition, we are also told that

> Susanne Smith is suffering from inoperable cancer.

and also that

> The survival rate for women suffering from inoperable cancer is 0.6 years (i.e., the average life span for women after a diagnosis of inoperable cancer is about seven months).

With this new information, the probability that Susanne will live to eighty drops significantly, all because we can now estimate the probability in relation to a new body of evidence.

The probability of an event, thus, is not a fixed number but one that varies because it is always relative to some evidence—and given different evidence, one and the same event can have different probabilities. In other words, the probability of any event is always relative to how much is known (assumed, believed), and because different persons may know different things about a given event or the same person may know different things at different times, one and the same event can have two or more probabilities. This conclusion is not a paradox but, rather, a logical consequence of the concept of what it is for an event to have (i.e., to be assigned) a probability.

Mill's Methods

Now let's return to our earlier discussion of smoking and cardiovascular disease and consider in greater detail the question of a causal connection between the two phenomena. We began thus:

> In a sample of 500 smokers, 230 persons observed have cardiovascular disease.

We regarded this claim as an observed fact, although in truth, of course, it is mere supposition. Our question now is how we might augment this information so as to strengthen our confidence of our causal hypotheses that

> Smoking *causes* cardiovascular disease.

or at least that

> Smoking is a factor in the causation of cardiovascular disease in some persons.

Suppose further examination showed that

> In the sample of 230 smokers with cardiovascular disease, no other suspected factor (such as genetic predisposition, lack of physical exercise, age over fifty) was also observed.

Such an observation would encourage us to believe that our hypotheses are true. Why? Because we're inclined to believe also that no matter what the cause of a phenomenon is, it must *always* be present when its effect is present. Thus, the inference from observed fact to our hypotheses is supported by this new evidence, using **Mill's Method of Agreement**, named after the British philosopher John Stuart Mill (1806–1873), who first formulated it. It's called a method of agreement because of the way in which the inference relies on *agreement* among the observed phenomena where a presumed cause is thought to be *present.*

Let's now suppose that in our search for evidence to support our hypotheses we conduct additional research and discover that

> In a sample of 500 nonsmokers, selected to be representative of both sexes, different ages, dietary habits, exercise patterns, and so on, none is observed to have cardiovascular disease.

This observation would further encourage us to believe that we had obtained significant additional confirmation of our hypotheses.

Why? Because we now know that factors present (such as male sex, lack of exercise, family history of cardiovascular disease) in cases where the effect is absent (no cardiovascular disease observed) cannot be the cause. This is an example of **Mill's Method of Difference**, so called because the cause or causal factor of an effect must be *different* from whatever factors are present when the effect is *absent*.

Suppose now that, increasingly confident we've found the cause of cardiovascular disease, we study our first sample of 230 smokers ill with the disease, and we discover this:

> Those who smoke two or more packs of cigarettes daily for ten or more years have cardiovascular disease either much younger or much more severely than those who smoke less.

This is an application of **Mill's Method of Concomitant Variation**, perhaps the most convincing of the three methods. Here we deal not merely with the presence of the conjectured cause (smoking) or the absence of the effect we are studying (cardiovascular disease), as we were previously, but with the more interesting and subtler matter of the *degree and regularity of the correlation* of the supposed cause and effect. According to the observations reported here, it strongly appears that the more we have of the "cause" (smoking), the sooner or the more intense the onset of the "effect" (cardiovascular disease).

Notice, however, what happens to our confirmation if, instead, we had discovered this:

> In a representative sample of 500 nonsmokers, cardiovascular disease was observed in 34 cases.

(We won't pause here to explain what makes a sample more or less representative of a population, although the representativeness of samples is vital to all statistical reasoning.) Such an observation would lead us almost immediately to suspect some other or additional causal factor: Smoking might indeed be *a* factor in causing cardiovascular disease, but it can hardly be *the* cause because (using Mill's Method of Difference) we cannot have the effect, as we do in the observed sample of 34 cases reported above, unless we also have the cause.

An observation such as this is likely to lead us to think our hypothesis that *smoking causes cardiovascular disease* has been disconfirmed. But we have a fallback position ready—we can still defend our weaker hypothesis: *Smoking is a factor in the causation of cardiovascular disease in some persons.* It is still quite possible that smoking is a factor in causing this disease, even if it isn't the *only* factor.

FALLACIES

The straight road on which sound reasoning proceeds gives little latitude for cruising about. Irrationality, carelessness, passionate attachment to one's unexamined beliefs, and the sheer complexity of some issues occasionally spoil the reasoning of even the best of us. An inventory of some common fallacies proves an instructive and potentially amusing exercise—instructive because the diagnosis and repair of error help us understand more principles of sound reasoning and amusing because we are so constituted that our perception of the nonsense of others can stimulate our minds, warm our hearts, and give us comforting feelings of superiority.

The discussion that follows, then, is a quick tour through the twisting paths, mudflats, and quicksands one sometimes encounters in reading arguments that stray from the way of clear thinking.

Common Fallacies

	Fallacy	Definition	Example
Fallacies of Ambiguity	Ambiguity (p. 373)	Using a word, phrase, or claim that gives rise to more than one possible interpretation.	People have equal rights, and so everyone has a right to property.
	Division (p. 374)	Assuming all members of a set share characteristics of the set as a whole.	PETA is a radical organization; therefore, anyone who is a member of PETA is radical.
	Composition (p. 374)	Assuming that a set shares characteristics with a given member of a set (the reverse of division fallacy).	Kimberly is a freelance writer and makes a lot of money; freelance writers must make a lot of money.
	Equivocation (p. 374)	Making two words or phrases equivalent in meaning while ignoring contextual differences.	Evolution is a natural process, so this company's growth is natural and good.
	Non sequitur (p. 375)	Literally, "it does not follow." Drawing conclusions that are unrelated or do not follow logically from the premises.	Because Sammy is good at math, we should let him draw up our annual budget.

	Fallacy	Definition	Example
Fallacies of Presumption	Distorting the Facts (p. 376)	Misrepresenting information, data, or facts in an argument.	Video games have been shown to cause violence in one out of five kids; 20 percent of the next generation will be violent citizens.
	Post Hoc, Ergo Propter Hoc (p. 376)	Literally, "after this, therefore because of this." Assuming that sequence equals consequence.	After the invention of the birth control pill, the divorce rate increased; therefore, the "pill" contributed to the rising divorce rate.
	Many Questions (p. 377)	Presupposing facts that are assumed in the question itself.	Can selfish and self-interested politicians be trusted to do anything to bring about banking reform?
	Hasty Generalization (p. 377)	Jumping to conclusions based on insufficient evidence or biases.	I'm not moving to that neighborhood. When I visited it, there were two people fighting in the street.
	Slippery Slope (p. 377)	Arguing that an idea or action will lead inevitably to unrealistically steeper and steeper consequences.	If we allow legal recreational marijuana, other drugs will soon follow, and soon there will be addicts everywhere.
	False Analogy (p. 378)	Comparing two things that may be similar in some ways but remain different in other ways.	Building a border wall is just like fencing in our backyards; it is simply a safe and reasonable precaution.
	Straw Man (p. 378)	Misrepresenting an argument so that you can attack the misrepresentation rather than the actual argument.	If you want prison reform, you are basically saying you want to treat criminals like they're at a resort. We should not be rewarding criminals!
	Special Pleading (p. 379)	Making an unwarranted claim by misapplying or misusing rules and standards.	I should get an A because I worked really hard.
	Begging the Question (p. 379)	Making an argument in which the premises are based on the truth of the conclusion.	We have a free press because the Constitution guarantees it.

(Continued)

Common Fallacies (*Continued*)

	Fallacy	Definition	Example
Fallacies of Presumption	False Dichotomy (p. 379)	Establishing only two opposing positions or points when more might be available or when the opposing positions are not mutually exclusive.	Either we drill for natural gas, or we keep using carbon fuel.
	Oversimplification (p. 380)	Reducing a complex thing to a simple cause or consequence.	With all the bullying on the internet, it is no wonder school shootings are happening.
	Red Herring (p. 380)	Presenting a question or issue intended to divert and distract from the central or most relevant question or issue.	I recognize that the issue of race and police violence needs to be addressed, but the real question is whether or not athletes should kneel during the national anthem.
Fallacies of Irrelevance	Tu Quoque (p. 381)	Literally, "you also." Discrediting an argument by attacking the speaker's failure to adhere to his or her conclusion.	How can my professor say that electric vehicles are the future when he stil drives a fuel-cell car?
	Genetic Fallacy (p. 381)	Arguing a position based on the real or imagined origin, history, or source of the idea.	In ancient times, men were hunters and women were gatherers — that's why women tend to be more domestic than men.
	Appeal to Ignorance (p. 381)	Saying that something is true because there is no evidence against it.	No one has complained about our new chili recipe, so it must be good.
	Poisoning the Well (p. 382)	Creating negative associations preemptively to discredit another person or position.	Now that I have highlighted the importance of keeping the controversial monument on campus, watch out because all the liberal snowflakes are going to argue that it "injures" them.
	Ad Hominem (p. 382)	Literally, "against the man [person]." Attacking the character of a person by providing irrelevant negative information.	How can this woman be the mayor when she can't even hold her own family together?

	Fallacy	Definition	Example
Fallacies of Irrelevance	Appeal to Authority (p. 382)	Asserting that a claim is true by citing someone thought to be an authority, regardless of the merits of the position or the relevance of the authority's expertise.	If the coach says throwing balls at the players makes them tougher, it must be true.
	Appeal to Fear (p. 383)	Supporting a position by instilling irrational fear of the alternatives.	If we don't strengthen our drug laws, drug dealers will see our community as a place to buy and sell openly on the streets.
Other	Death by a Thousand Qualifications (p. 384)	Justifying a weak idea or position by changing (or qualifying) it each time it is challenged.	Television is so bad for kids. (Well, not all television, and not all kids, and not in moderation, etc.)
	Protecting the Hypothesis (p. 384)	Distorting evidence to support a preexisting belief or idea.	According to the prophecy, the world was supposed to end. It didn't end. Therefore, the prophecy was not wrong, but we must have misinterpreted it.

Fallacies of Ambiguity

Ambiguity   Near the center of the town of Concord, Massachusetts, is an empty field with a sign reading "Old Calf Pasture." Hmm. A pasture in which calves grazed in former times? Or a pasture now in use for elderly calves? Or something that used to be a calf pasture but is now something else? These alternative readings arise because of **ambiguity**; brevity in the sign has produced a group of words that give rise to more than one possible interpretation, confusing the reader and (presumably) frustrating the sign writer's intentions.

Consider a more complex example. Suppose someone asserts *People have equal rights* and also *Everyone has a right to property.* Many people believe both these claims, but their combination involves an ambiguity. According to one interpretation, the two claims entail that everyone has an *equal right* to property. (That is, you and I each have an equal right to whatever property we have.) But the two claims can also be interpreted to mean that everyone has a *right to equal property.* (That is, whatever property you have a right to,

I have a right to the same, or at least equivalent, property.) The latter interpretation is revolutionary, whereas the former is not. Arguments over equal rights often involve this ambiguity.

Division   In the Bible, we read that the apostles of Jesus were twelve and that Matthew was an apostle. Does it follow that Matthew was twelve years old? No. To argue in this way from a property of a group to a property of a member of that group is to commit the **fallacy of division**. The example of the apostles may not be a very tempting instance of this error. A classic version may be a bit more interesting: If it is true that the average American family has 1.8 children, does it follow that your brother and sister-in-law are likely to have 1.8 children? If you think it does, you have committed the fallacy of division.

Composition   Could an all-star team of professional basketball players beat the Boston Celtics in their heyday — say, the team of 1985–1986? Perhaps it could in one game or two, but probably not in seven out of a dozen games in a row. As students of the game know, teamwork is an indispensable part of outstanding performance, and the 1985–1986 Celtics were famous for their self-sacrificing style of play.

The **fallacy of composition** can therefore be convincingly illustrated in this argument: *A team of five NBA all-stars is the best team in basketball if each of the five players is the best at his position.* The fallacy is called composition because the reasoning commits the error of arguing from the true premise that each member of a group has a certain property to the not necessarily true conclusion that the group (the composition) itself has the property (i.e., because *A* is the best player at forward, *B* is the best center, and so on; therefore, the team of *A*, *B*, . . . is the best team).

Equivocation   In a delightful passage in Lewis Carroll's *Through the Looking-Glass*, the king asks his messenger, "Who did you pass on the road?" and the messenger replies, "Nobody." This prompts the king to observe, "Of course, Nobody walks slower than you," provoking the messenger's sullen response: "I do my best. I'm sure nobody walks much faster than I do." At this the king remarks with surprise, "He can't do that or else he'd have been here first!" (This, by the way, is the classic predecessor of the famous comic dialogue "Who's on First?" between the comedians Bud Abbott and Lou Costello.) The king and the messenger are equivocating on the term *nobody*. The messenger uses it in the normal way as an indefinite pronoun equivalent to "not anyone." But the king uses the word as though it were a proper noun, *Nobody*, the rather odd name of some person. It's no wonder the king and the messenger talk right past each other.

Equivocation (from the Latin for "equal voice" — i.e., giving utterance to two meanings at the same time in one word or phrase) can ruin otherwise good reasoning, as in this example: *Euthanasia is a good death; one dies a good death when one dies peacefully in old age; therefore, euthanasia is dying peacefully in old age.* The etymology of *euthanasia* is literally "a good death," so the first premise is true. And the second premise is certainly plausible. But the conclusion of this syllogism is false. Euthanasia cannot be defined as a peaceful death in one's old age for two reasons. First, euthanasia requires the intervention of another person who kills someone (or lets the person die); second, even a very young person can be euthanized. The problem arises because "a good death" works in the second premise in a manner that does not apply to euthanasia. Both meanings of "a good death" are legitimate, but when used together, they constitute an equivocation that spoils the argument.

Non Sequitur   The fallacy of equivocation takes us from the discussion of confusions in individual claims or grounds to the more troublesome fallacies that infect the linkages between the claims we make and the grounds (or reasons) for them. These fallacies occur in statements that, following the vocabulary of the Toulmin method, are called the *warrant* of reasoning. Each fallacy is an example of reasoning that involves a **non sequitur** (Latin for "it does not follow"). That is, the *claim* (the conclusion) does not follow from the *grounds* (the premises).

For a start, here is an obvious non sequitur: "He went to the movies on three consecutive nights, so he must love movies." Why doesn't the claim ("He must love movies") follow from the grounds ("He went to the movies on three consecutive nights")? Perhaps the person was just fulfilling an assignment in a film course (maybe he even hated movies so much that he had postponed three assignments to see films and now had to see them all in quick succession), or maybe he went with a girlfriend who was a movie buff, or maybe . . . — there are any number of other possible reasons.

Fallacies of Presumption

Distorting the Facts   Facts can be distorted either intentionally (to deceive or mislead) or unintentionally, and in either case usually (but not invariably) to the benefit of whoever is doing the distortion. Consider this case. In 1964, the US surgeon general reported that smoking cigarettes increased the likelihood that smokers would eventually suffer from lung cancer. The cigarette manufacturers vigorously protested that the surgeon general relied on inconclusive research and was badly misleading the public about the health risks of smoking. It later turned out that the tobacco companies knew that smoking increased the risk of lung cancer—a fact established by the company's own laboratories but concealed from the public. Today, thanks to public access to all the facts, it is commonplace knowledge that inhaled smoke—including secondhand smoke—is a risk factor for many illnesses.

Post Hoc, Ergo Propter Hoc   One of the most tempting errors in reasoning is to ground a claim about causation on an observed temporal sequence—that is, to argue "after this, therefore because of this" (which is what *post hoc, ergo propter hoc* means in Latin). When the medical community first announced that smoking tobacco caused lung cancer, advocates for the tobacco industry replied that doctors were guilty of this fallacy.

These industry advocates argued that medical researchers had merely noticed that in some people, lung cancer developed *after* considerable smoking—indeed, years after—but (they insisted) that this correlation was not at all the same as a causal relation between smoking and lung cancer. True enough. The claim that *A causes B* is not the same as the claim that *B comes after A*. After all, it was possible that smokers as a group had some other common trait and that this factor was the true cause of their cancer.

As the long controversy over the truth about the causation of lung cancer shows, to avoid the appearance of fallacious post hoc reasoning one needs to find some way to link the observed phenomena (the correlation between smoking and the onset of lung cancer). This step requires some further theory and preferably some experimental evidence for the exact sequence or physical mechanism, in full detail, of how ingestion of tobacco smoke is a crucial factor—and is not merely an accidental or happenstance prior event—in the subsequent development of the cancer.

Many Questions   Some questions contain presuppositions that are presented as true and are built into the question itself. Loaded questions, leading questions, and trick questions are all part of the many questions fallacy. The old saw, "When did you stop beating your wife?" is sometimes used to illustrate the **fallacy of many questions**. This question, as one can readily see, is unanswerable unless all three of its implicit presuppositions are true. The questioner presupposes that (1) the addressee has or had a wife, (2) he or she has beaten her, and (3) he or she has stopped beating her. If any of these presuppositions is false, the question is pointless; it cannot be answered strictly and simply with a date or time.

Hasty Generalization   From a logical point of view, **hasty generalization** is the precipitous move from true assertions about *one* or a *few* instances to dubious or even false assertions about *all*. For example, although it may be true that the only native Hungarians you personally know do not speak English very well, that is no basis for asserting that all Hungarians do not speak English very well. Likewise, if the clothes you recently ordered online turn out not to fit very well, it doesn't follow that *all* online clothes turn out to be too large or too small. A hasty generalization usually lies behind a **stereotype**—that is, a person or event treated as typical of a whole class.

Slippery Slope   One of the most familiar arguments against any type of government regulation is that if it is allowed, it will be just the first step down the path that leads to ruinous interference, overregulation, and totalitarian control. Fairly often we encounter this mode of argument in the public debates over handgun control, the censorship of pornography, and physician-assisted suicide. The argument is called the **slippery slope** (or the wedge argument, from the way people use the thin end of a wedge to split solid things apart; it is also called, rather colorfully, "letting the camel's nose under the tent"). The fallacy here is in implying that the first step necessarily leads to the second and so on down the slope to disaster, when in fact there is no necessary slide from the first step to the second. (Would handgun registration lead to a police state? Well, it hasn't in Switzerland.)

Closely related to the slippery slope is what lawyers call a **parade of horrors**, an array of examples of terrible consequences that will or might follow if we travel down a certain path. A good example appears in Justice William Brennan's opinion for the US Supreme

Court in *Texas v. Johnson* (1989) regarding a Texas law against burning the American flag in political protest. If this law is allowed to
stand, Brennan suggests, we may next find laws against burning
the presidential seal, state flags, and the Constitution.

False Analogy   Argument by analogy, as we point out in Chapter 3
and as many of the selections in this book show, is a familiar and
even indispensable mode of argument. But it can be treacherous
because it runs the risk of the **fallacy of false analogy**. Unfortunately, we have no simple or foolproof way of distinguishing
between the useful, legitimate analogies and the others. The key
question to ask yourself is, Do the two things put into analogy differ
in any essential and relevant respect, or are they different only in
unimportant and irrelevant aspects?

   In a famous example from his discussion in support of suicide,
philosopher David Hume rhetorically asked: "It would be no crime
in me to divert the Nile or Danube from its course, were I able to
effect such purposes. Where then is the crime of turning a few
ounces of blood from their natural channel?" This is a striking
analogy—except that it rests on a false assumption. No one has the
right to divert the Nile or the Danube or any other major international watercourse; it would be a catastrophic crime to do so without the full consent of people living in the region, their government,
and so forth. Therefore, arguing by analogy, one might well say that
no one has the right to take his or her own life either. Thus, Hume's
own analogy can be used to argue against his thesis that suicide
is no crime. But let's ignore the way in which his example can be
turned against him. The analogy is a terrible one in any case. Isn't it
obvious that the Nile, regardless of its exact course, would continue
to nourish Egypt and the Sudan, whereas the blood flowing out of
someone's veins will soon leave that person dead? The fact that the
blood is the same blood, whether in a person's body or in a pool on
the floor (just as the water of the Nile is the same body of water no
matter what path it follows to the sea) is, of course, irrelevant to the
question of whether one has the right to commit suicide.

Straw Man   It is often tempting to reframe or report your opponent's thesis to make it easier to attack and perhaps refute it. If you
do so in the course of an argument, you are creating a straw man,
a thing of no substance that's easily blown away. The straw man
you've constructed is usually a radically conservative or extremely
liberal thesis, which few if any would want to defend. That is why

it is easier to refute the straw man than refute the view your opponent actually holds: "So you defend the death penalty—and all the horrible things done in its name." It's highly unlikely that your opponent supports *everything* that has been done in the name of capital punishment—crucifixion and beheading, for example, or execution of the children of the guilty offender.

Special Pleading   We all have our favorites—relatives, friends, and neighbors—and we're all too likely to show that favoritism in unacceptable ways. Here is an example: "I know my son punched another boy but he is not a bully, so there must have been a good reason."

Begging the Question   The fallacy called "begging the question," *petitio principii* in Latin, is so named because the conclusion of the argument is hidden among its assumptions—and so the conclusion, not surprisingly, follows from the premises. The argument over whether the death penalty is a deterrent to crime illustrates this fallacy. From the facts that you live in a death-penalty state and were not murdered yesterday, we cannot infer that the death penalty was a deterrent. Yet it is tempting to make this inference, perhaps because—all unaware—we are relying on the **fallacy of begging the question**. If someone tacitly assumes from the start that the death penalty is an effective deterrent, the fact that you weren't murdered yesterday certainly looks like evidence for the truth of that assumption. But it isn't, as long as there are competing but unexamined alternative explanations, as in this case.

Of course, that you weren't murdered is *consistent* with the claim that the death penalty is an effective deterrent, just as someone else being murdered is also consistent with that claim (because an effective deterrent need not be a *perfect* deterrent). In general, from the fact that two propositions are consistent with each other, we cannot infer that either is evidence for the other.

Note: "Begging the question" is often wrongly used to mean "raises the question," as in "His action of burning the flag begs the question, What drove him to do such a thing?"

False Dichotomy   Sometimes, oversimplification takes a more complex form in which contrary possibilities are wrongly presented as though they were exhaustive and exclusive. "Either we get tough with drug users, or we must surrender and legalize all drugs."

Really? What about doing neither and instead offering education and counseling, detoxification programs, and incentives to "Say no"? A favorite of debaters, **either/or reasoning** always runs the risk of ignoring a third (or fourth) possibility. Some disjunctions are indeed exhaustive: "Either we get tough with drug users, or we do not." This proposition, although vague (what does "get tough" really mean?), is a tautology; it cannot be false, and there is no third alternative. But most disjunctions do not express a pair of *contradictory* alternatives: They offer only a pair of *contrary* alternatives, and mere contraries do not exhaust the possibilities (recall our discussion of contraries versus contradictories on pp. 360–62).

Oversimplification   "Poverty causes crime," "Taxation is unfair," "Truth is stranger than fiction"—these are examples of generalizations that exaggerate and therefore oversimplify the truth. Poverty as such can't be the sole cause of crime because many poor people do not break the law. Some taxes may be unfairly high, others unfairly low—but there is no reason to believe that *every* tax is unfair to all those who have to pay it. Some true stories do amaze us as much or more than some fictional stories, but the reverse is true, too. (In the language of the Toulmin method, **oversimplification** is the result of a failure to use suitable modal qualifiers in formulating one's claims or grounds or backing.)

Red Herring   The fallacy of **red herring**, less colorfully named "irrelevant thesis," occurs when one tries to distract one's audience by invoking a consideration that is irrelevant to the topic under discussion. (This fallacy probably gets its name from the fact that a rotten herring, or a cured herring, which is reddish, will throw pursuing hounds off the right track.) Consider this case: Some critics, seeking to defend the US government's refusal to sign the Kyoto accords to reduce climate change, argue that signing is supported mainly by left-leaning scientists. This argument supposedly shows that climate change is not a serious, urgent issue. But claiming that the supporters of these accords are left-inclined is a red herring, an irrelevant thesis. By raising doubts about the political views of the advocates of signing, critics distract attention from the scientific question (Is there climate change?) and also from the separate political question (Ought the US government to sign the accords?). The refusal of a government to sign the accords doesn't show there is no such thing as climate change. And even if all the advocates of signing were left-leaning (they aren't), this fact (if it were a fact, but it isn't) would not show that worries about climate change are exaggerated.

Fallacies of Irrelevance

Tu Quoque   The Romans called one particular type of fallacy *tu quoque*, for "you also." Consider this: "You're a fine one, trying to persuade me to give up smoking when you indulge yourself with a pipe and a cigar from time to time. Maybe I should quit, but then so should you. It's hypocritical of you to complain about my smoking when you persist in the same habit." The fallacy is this: The merit of a person's argument has nothing to do with the person's character or behavior. Here the assertion that smoking is bad for one's health is *not* weakened by the fact that a smoker offers the argument.

Genetic Fallacy   A member of the family of fallacies that includes poisoning the well and ad hominem (see below) is the **genetic fallacy**. Here the error takes the form of arguing against a claim by pointing out that its origin (genesis) is tainted or that it was invented by someone deserving our contempt. For example, an opponent of the death penalty might argue this:

> Capital punishment arose in barbarous times, but we claim to be civilized; therefore, we should discard this relic of the past.

Such reasoning shouldn't be persuasive because the question of the death penalty for our society must be decided by the degree to which it serves our purposes—justice and defense against crime, presumably—to which its historic origins are irrelevant. The practices of beer- and wine-making are as old as human civilization, but their origin in antiquity is no reason to outlaw them in our time. The curious circumstances in which something originates usually play no role in its validity. Anyone who would argue that nothing good could possibly come from molds and fungi is refuted by Sir Alexander Fleming's discovery of penicillin in 1928.

Appeal to Ignorance   In the controversy over the death penalty, the issues of deterrence and executing the innocent are bound to be raised. Because no one knows how many innocent persons have been convicted for murder and wrongfully executed, it is tempting for abolitionists to argue that the death penalty is too risky. It is equally tempting for proponents of the death penalty to argue that since no one knows how many people have been deterred from murder by the threat of execution, we abolish it at society's peril.

Each of these arguments suffers from the same flaw: the **fallacy of appeal to ignorance**. Each argument invites the audience to draw an inference from a premise that is unquestionably true, but what is that premise? It asserts that there is something "we don't know." But what we *don't* know cannot be *evidence* for (or against) anything. Our ignorance is no reason for believing anything, except perhaps that we ought to undertake an appropriate investigation so as to replace our ignorance with reliable information.

Poisoning the Well   During the 1970s, some critics of the Equal Rights Amendment (ERA) argued against it by pointing out that Marx and Engels, in their *Communist Manifesto*, favored equality of women and men — and therefore the ERA was immoral, undesirable, and perhaps even a Communist plot. This kind of reasoning is an attempt to **poison the well**; that is, it is an attempt to shift attention from the merits of the argument — the validity of the reasoning, the truth of the claims — to the source or origin of the argument. Such criticism deflects attention from the real issue — namely, whether the view in question is true and what the quality of evidence is in its support. The mere fact that Marx (or Hitler, for that matter) believed something does not show that the belief is false or immoral; just because some scoundrel believes the world is round is no reason for you to believe it is flat.

Ad Hominem   Closely allied to poisoning the well is another fallacy, **ad hominem** argument (from the Latin for "against the person"). A critic can easily yield to the temptation to attack an argument or theory by trying to impeach or undercut the credentials of its advocates.

Consider this example: Jones is arguing that prayer should not be permitted in public schools, and Smith responds by pointing out that Jones has twice been convicted of assaulting members of the clergy. Jones's behavior doubtless is reprehensible, but the issue is not Jones, it is prayer in school, and what must be scrutinized is Jones's argument, not his police record or his character.

Appeal to Authority   One might easily imagine someone from the South in 1860 defending the slave-owning society of that day by appealing to the fact that no less a person than Thomas Jefferson — a brilliant public figure, thinker, and leader by any measure—owned slaves. Or today one might defend capital punishment on the ground that Abraham Lincoln, surely one of the nation's greatest presidents, signed many death warrants during the Civil War, authorizing the execution of Union soldiers. No doubt the esteem in which such figures as Jefferson and Lincoln are deservedly held amounts to impressive endorsement for whatever acts and practices, policies, and institutions, they supported. But the **authority** of these figures in itself is not evidence for the truth of their views, so their authority cannot be a reason for anyone to agree with them.

Sometimes, the appeal to authority is fallacious because the authoritative person is not an expert on the issue in dispute. The fact that a high-energy physicist has won the Nobel Prize is no reason for attaching any special weight to her views on the causes of cancer, the reduction of traffic accidents, or the legalization of marijuana. We all depend heavily on the knowledge of various experts and authorities, so we tend to respect their views. Conversely, we should resist the temptation to accord their views on diverse subjects the same respect that we grant them in the area of their expertise.

Appeal to Fear   The Romans called the **appeal to fear** fallacy *ad baculum*, for "resorting to violence" (*baculum* means "stick" or "club"). Trying to persuade people to agree with you by threatening them with painful consequences is obviously an appeal that no rational person would contemplate. The violence need not be physical; if you threaten someone with the loss of a job, for instance, you are still using a stick. Violence or the threat of harmful consequences in the course of an argument is beyond reason and always shows the haste or impatience of those who appeal to it. It is also an indication that the argument on its merits would be unpersuasive, inconclusive, or worse. President Theodore Roosevelt's epigrammatic doctrine for the kind of foreign policy he favored—"Speak softly but carry a big stick"—illustrates an attempt to have it both ways; an appeal to reason for starters, but a recourse to coercion, or the threat of coercion, as a backup if needed.

Additional Fallacies

Finally, we add two fallacies, not easily embraced by the three categories that have served us well thus far (ambiguity, erroneous presumption, and irrelevance): death by a thousand qualifications and protecting the hypothesis.

Death by a Thousand Qualifications   **Death by a thousand qualifications** gets its name from the ancient torture of death by a thousand small cuts. Thus, a bold assertion can be virtually killed and its true content reduced to nothing, bit by bit, as all the appropriate or necessary qualifications are added to it. Consider an example. Suppose you hear a politician describing another country (let's call it Ruritania so as not to offend anyone) as a "democracy"—except it turns out that Ruritania doesn't have regular elections, lacks a written constitution, has no independent judiciary, prohibits religious worship except of the state-designated deity, and so forth. So what remains of the original claim that Ruritania is a democracy is little or nothing. The qualifications have taken all the content out of the original description.

Protecting the Hypothesis   In Chapter 3, we contrasted *reasoning* and *rationalization* (or the finding of bad reasons for what one intends to believe anyway). Rationalization can take subtle forms, as the following example indicates. Suppose you're standing with a friend on the shore or on a pier and you watch as a ship heads out to sea. As it reaches the horizon, it slowly disappears—first the hull, then the upper decks, and finally the tip of the mast. Because the ship (you both assume) isn't sinking, it occurs to you that this sequence of observations provides evidence that the earth's surface is curved. Nonsense, says your companion. Light waves sag, or bend down, over distances of a few miles, and so a flat surface (such as the ocean) can intercept them. Therefore, the ship, which appears to be going "over" the horizon, really isn't: It's just moving steadily farther and farther away in a straight line. Your friend, you discover to your amazement, is a card-carrying member of the Flat Earth Society, a group who insists the earth is a plane surface. Now most of us would regard the idea that light rays bend down in the manner required by the Flat Earther's argument as a rationalization whose sole purpose is to protect the flat-earth doctrine against counterevidence. We would be convinced it was a rationalization, and not a very good one at that, if the Flat Earther held to it despite a patient and thorough explanation from a physicist that showed modern optical theory to be quite incompatible with the view that light waves sag.

     This example illustrates two important points about the *backing* of arguments. First, it is always possible to **protect a hypothesis** by abandoning adjacent or connected hypotheses; this is the tactic our Flat Earth friend has used. This maneuver is possible, however, only because—and this is the second point—whenever we test a hypothesis, we do so by taking for granted (usually, quite unconsciously) many other hypotheses as well. So the evidence for the hypothesis we think we are confirming is impossible to separate entirely from the adequacy of the connected hypotheses. As long as we have no reason to doubt that light rays travel in straight lines (at least over distances of a few miles), our Flat Earth friend's argument is unconvincing. But once that hypothesis is itself put in doubt, the idea that seemed at first to be a pathetic rationalization takes on an even more troublesome character.

There are, then, not one but two fallacies exposed by this example. The first and perhaps graver one is in rigging your hypothesis so that *no matter what* observations are brought against it, you will count nothing as falsifying it. The second and subtler one is in thinking that as you test one hypothesis, all your other background beliefs are left safely to one side, immaculate and uninvolved. On the contrary, our beliefs form a corporate structure, intertwined and connected to one another with great complexity, and no one of them can ever be singled out for unique and isolated application, confirmation, or disconfirmation to the world around us.

✔ A CHECKLIST FOR EVALUATING AN ARGUMENT WITH LOGIC

- ☐ Can I identify the premises and the conclusion of the argument?
- ☐ Given the premises, is the argument valid?
- ☐ If it is valid, are all its premises true?
- ☐ If all the premises are true, does the conclusion necessarily follow from them?
- ☐ Are there any claims that are inconsistent in the argument?
- ☐ Does the argument contain one or more fallacies?
- ☐ If the argument is inductive, on what observations is it based?
- ☐ Do the observations or data make the conclusion probable?
- ☐ Is there enough evidence to disconfirm the conclusion?

THINKING CRITICALLY IDENTIFYING FALLACIES

Here are some fallacies in action. Using the explanations in this section, identify what type of fallacy the argument example commits and then explain your reasoning.

Example	Type of Fallacy	Explanation
Senator Case was friends with a disgraced racketeer; he shouldn't be your selection in the upcoming election.		
These activists say they want justice, but is it really justice to clog up the streets with the protests?		
East Coast urban liberals are going to say that hunting is inhumane. They do not realize how narrow-minded they are.		
There have been few terrorist attacks since September 11, 2001; therefore, our national security efforts must be working.		
If you start out with a bottle of beer a day and then go on to a glass or two of wine on the weekends, you're well on your way to becoming a hopeless drunk.		
My marriage was a failure, which just proves my point: Don't ever get married in the first place.		
Not until astronauts sailed through space around the moon did we have adequate reason to believe that the moon even had a back side.		
Going to church on a regular basis is bad for your health. Instead of sitting in a pew for an hour each Sunday, you'd be better off taking an hour's brisk walk.		
A professional baseball player has a good-luck charm. When he wears it, the team wins.		
How come herbivores don't eat herbs?		

Max Shulman

Max Shulman (1919–1988) began his career as a writer when he was a journalism student at the University of Minnesota. Later he wrote humorous novels, stories, and plays. One of his novels, Barefoot Boy with Cheek *(1943), was made into a musical, and another,* Rally Round the Flag, Boys! *(1957), was made into a film starring Paul Newman and Joanne Woodward. The* Tender Trap *(1954), a play he wrote with Robert Paul Smith, still retains its popularity with theater groups.*

"Love Is a Fallacy" was first published in 1951, when demeaning stereotypes about women and minorities were widely accepted in the marketplace, as well as the home. Thus, jokes about domineering mothers-in-law or about dumb blondes routinely met with no objection.

Love Is a Fallacy

Cool was I and logical. Keen, calculating, perspicacious, acute, and astute — I was all of these. My brain was as powerful as a dynamo, as precise as a chemist's scales, as penetrating as a scalpel. And — think of it! — I was only eighteen.

It is not often that one so young has such a giant intellect. Take, for example, Petey Bellows, my roommate at the university. Same age, same background, but dumb as an ox. A nice enough fellow, you understand, but nothing upstairs. Emotional type. Unstable. Impressionable. Worst of all, a faddist. Fads, I submit, are the very negation of reason. To be swept up in every new craze that comes along, to surrender yourself to idiocy just because everybody else is doing it — this, to me, is the acme of mindlessness. Not, however, to Petey.

One afternoon I found Petey lying on his bed with an expression of such distress on his face that I immediately diagnosed appendicitis. "Don't move," I said. "Don't take a laxative. I'll call a doctor."

"Raccoon," he mumbled thickly.

"Raccoon?" I said, pausing in my flight.   5

"I want a raccoon coat," he wailed.

I perceived that his trouble was not physical, but mental. "Why do you want a raccoon coat?"

"I should have known it," he cried, pounding his temples. "I should have known they'd come back when the Charleston came back. Like a fool I spent all my money for textbooks, and now I can't get a raccoon coat."

"Can you mean," I said incredulously, "that people are actually wearing raccoon coats again?"

"All the Big Men on Campus are wearing them. Where've you been?"   10

"In the library," I said, naming a place not frequented by Big Men on Campus.

He leaped from the bed and paced the room. "I've got to have a raccoon coat," he said passionately. "I've got to!"

"Petey, why? Look at it rationally. Raccoon coats are unsanitary. They shed. They smell bad. They weigh too much. They're unsightly. They ——"

"You don't understand," he interrupted impatiently. "It's the thing to do. Don't you want to be in the swim?"

"No," I said truthfully.   15

"Well, I do," he declared. "I'd give anything for a raccoon coat. Anything!"

My brain, that precision instrument, slipped into high gear. "Anything?" I asked, looking at him narrowly.

"Anything," he affirmed in ringing tones.

I stroked my chin thoughtfully. It so happened that I knew where to get my hands on a raccoon coat. My father had had one in his undergraduate days; it lay now in a trunk in the attic back home. It also happened that Petey had something I wanted. He didn't *have* it exactly, but at least he had first rights on it. I refer to his girl, Polly Espy.

I had long coveted Polly Espy. Let me emphasize that my desire   20 for this young woman was not emotional in nature. She was, to be sure, a girl who excited the emotions, but I was not one to let my heart rule my head. I wanted Polly for a shrewdly calculated, entirely cerebral reason.

I was a freshman in law school. In a few years I would be out in practice. I was well aware of the importance of the right kind of wife in furthering a lawyer's career. The successful lawyers I had observed were, almost without exception, married to beautiful, gracious, intelligent women. With one omission, Polly fitted these specifications perfectly.

Beautiful she was. She was not yet of pin-up proportions, but I felt sure that time would supply the lack. She already had the makings.

Gracious she was. By gracious I mean full of graces. She had an erectness of carriage, an ease of bearing, a poise that clearly indicated the best of breeding. At table her manners were exquisite. I had seen her at the Kozy Kampus Korner eating the specialty of the house — a sandwich that contained scraps of pot roast, gravy, chopped nuts, and a dipper of sauerkraut — without even getting her fingers moist.

Intelligent she was not. In fact, she veered in the opposite direction. But I believed that under my guidance she would smarten up. At any rate, it was worth a try. It is, after all, easier to make a beautiful dumb girl smart than to make an ugly smart girl beautiful.

"Petey," I said, "are you in love with Polly Espy?"   25

"I think she's a keen kid," he replied, "but I don't know if you'd call it love. Why?"

"Do you," I asked, "have any kind of formal arrangement with her? I mean are you going steady or anything like that?"

"No. We see each other quite a bit, but we both have other dates. Why?"

"Is there," I asked, "any other man for whom she has a particular fondness?"

"Not that I know of. Why?"   30

I nodded with satisfaction. "In other words, if you were out of the picture, the field would be open. Is that right?"

"I guess so. What are you getting at?"

"Nothing, nothing," I said innocently, and took my suitcase out of the closet.

"Where you going?" asked Petey.

"Home for the weekend." I threw a few things into the bag.   35

"Listen," he said, clutching my arm eagerly, "while you're home, you couldn't get some money from your old man, could you, and lend it to me so I can buy a raccoon coat?"

"I may do better than that," I said with a mysterious wink and closed my bag and left.

"Look," I said to Petey when I got back Monday morning. I threw open the suitcase and revealed the huge, hairy, gamy object that my father had worn in his Stutz Bearcat in 1925.

"Holy Toledo!" said Petey reverently. He plunged his hands into the raccoon coat and then his face. "Holy Toledo!" he repeated fifteen or twenty times.

"Would you like it?" I asked.   40

"Oh yes!" he cried, clutching the greasy pelt to him. Then a canny look came into his eyes. "What do you want for it?"

"Your girl," I said, mincing no words.

"Polly?" he said in a horrified whisper. "You want Polly?"

"That's right."

He flung the coat from him. "Never," he said stoutly.   45

I shrugged. "Okay. If you don't want to be in the swim, I guess it's your business."

I sat down in a chair and pretended to read a book, but out of the corner of my eye I kept watching Petey. He was a torn man. First he looked at the coat with the expression of a waif at a bakery window. Then he turned away and set his jaw resolutely. Then he looked back at the coat, with even more longing in his face. Then he turned away, but with not so much resolution this time. Back and forth his head swiveled, desire waxing, resolution waning. Finally he didn't turn away at all; he just stood and stared with mad lust at the coat.

"It isn't as though I was in love with Polly," he said thickly. "Or going steady or anything like that."

"That's right," I murmured.

"What's Polly to me, or me to Polly?"   50

"Not a thing," said I.

"It's just been a casual kick—just a few laughs, that's all."

"Try on the coat," said I.

He complied. The coat bunched high over his ears and dropped all the way down to his shoe tops. He looked like a mound of dead raccoons. "Fits fine," he said happily.

I rose from my chair. "Is it a deal?" I asked, extending my hand.   55

He swallowed. "It's a deal," he said and shook my hand.

I had my first date with Polly the following evening. This was in the nature of a survey; I wanted to find out just how much work I had to do to get her mind up to the standard I required. I took her first to dinner. "Gee, that was a delish dinner," she said as we left the restaurant. Then I took her to a movie. "Gee, that was a marvy movie," she said as we left the theater. And then I took her home. "Gee, I had a sensaysh time," she said as she bade me good night.

I went back to my room with a heavy heart. I had gravely underestimated the size of my task. This girl's lack of information was terrifying. Nor would it be enough merely to supply her with information. First she had to be taught to *think*. This loomed as a project of no small dimensions, and at first I was tempted to give her back to Petey. But then I got to thinking about her abundant physical charms and about the way she entered a room and the way she handled a knife and fork, and I decided to make an effort.

I went about it, as in all things, systematically. I gave her a course in logic. It happened that I, as a law student, was taking a course in logic myself, so I had all the facts at my fingertips. "Polly," I said to her when I picked her up on our next date, "tonight we are going over to the Knoll and talk."

"Oo, terrif," she replied. One thing I will say for this girl: You   60
would go far to find another so agreeable.

We went to the Knoll, the campus trysting place, and we sat down under an old oak, and she looked at me expectantly: "What are we going to talk about?" she asked.

"Logic."

She thought this over for a minute and decided she liked it. "Magnif," she said.

"Logic," I said, clearing my throat, "is the science of thinking. Before we can think correctly, we must first learn to recognize the common fallacies of logic. These we will take up tonight."

"Wow-dow!" she cried, clapping her hands delightedly.   65

I winced, but went bravely on. "First let us examine the fallacy called Dicto Simpliciter."

"By all means," she urged, batting her lashes eagerly.

"Dicto Simpliciter means an argument based on an unqualified generalization. For example: Exercise is good. Therefore everybody should exercise."

"I agree," said Polly earnestly. "I mean exercise is wonderful. I mean it builds the body and everything."

"Polly," I said gently, "the argument is a fallacy. *Exercise is good*   70 is an unqualified generalization. For instance, if you have heart disease, exercise is bad, not good. Many people are ordered by their doctors *not* to exercise. You must *qualify* the generalization. You must say exercise is *usually* good, or exercise is good *for most people*. Otherwise you have committed a Dicto Simpliciter. Do you see?"

"No," she confessed. "But this is marvy. Do more! Do more!"

"It will be better if you stop tugging at my sleeve," I told her, and when she desisted, I continued. "Next we take up a fallacy called Hasty Generalization. Listen carefully: You can't speak French. I can't speak French. Petey Bellows can't speak French. I must therefore conclude that nobody at the University of Minnesota can speak French."

"Really?" said Polly, amazed. "*Nobody?*"

I hid my exasperation. "Polly, it's a fallacy. The generalization is reached too hastily. There are too few instances to support such a conclusion."

"Know any more fallacies?" she asked breathlessly. "This is   75 more fun than dancing even."

I fought off a wave of despair. I was getting nowhere with this girl, absolutely nowhere. Still, I am nothing if not persistent. I continued. "Next comes Post Hoc. Listen to this: Let's not take Bill on our picnic. Every time we take him out with us, it rains."

"I know somebody just like that," she exclaimed. "A girl back home — Eula Becker, her name is. It never fails. Every single time we take her on a picnic ——"

"Polly," I said sharply, "it's a fallacy. Eula Becker doesn't *cause* the rain. She has no connection with the rain. You are guilty of Post Hoc if you blame Eula Becker."

"I'll never do it again," she promised contritely. "Are you mad at me?"

I sighed. "No, Polly, I'm not mad."   80

"Then tell me some more fallacies."

"All right. Let's try Contradictory Premises."

"Yes, let's," she chirped, blinking her eyes happily.

I frowned, but plunged ahead. "Here's an example of Contradictory Premises: If God can do anything, can He make a stone so heavy that He won't be able to lift it?"

"Of course," she replied promptly.   85

"But if He can do anything, He can lift the stone," I pointed out.

"Yeah," she said thoughtfully. "Well, then I guess He can't make the stone."

"But He can do anything," I reminded her.

She scratched her pretty, empty head. "I'm all confused," she admitted.

"Of course you are. Because when the premises of an argu-   90
ment contradict each other, there can be no argument. If there is an irresistible force, there can be no immovable object. If there is an immovable object, there can be no irresistible force. Get it?"

"Tell me some more of this keen stuff," she said eagerly.

I consulted my watch. "I think we'd better call it a night. I'll take you home now, and you go over all the things you've learned. We'll have another session tomorrow night."

I deposited her at the girls' dormitory, where she assured me that she had had a perfectly terrif evening, and I went glumly home to my room. Petey lay snoring in his bed, the raccoon coat huddled like a great hairy beast at his feet. For a moment I considered waking him and telling him that he could have his girl back. It seemed clear that my project was doomed to failure. The girl simply had a logic-proof head.

But then I reconsidered. I had wasted one evening; I might as well waste another. Who knew? Maybe somewhere in the extinct crater of her mind a few embers still smoldered. Maybe somehow I could fan them into flame. Admittedly it was not a prospect fraught with hope, but I decided to give it one more try.

Seated under the oak the next evening I said, "Our first fallacy   95
tonight is called Ad Misericordiam."

She quivered with delight.

"Listen closely," I said. "A man applies for a job. When the boss asks him what his qualifications are, he replies that he has a wife and six children at home, the wife is a helpless cripple, the children have nothing to eat, no clothes to wear, no shoes on their feet, there are no beds in the house, no coal in the cellar, and winter is coming."

A tear rolled down each of Polly's pink cheeks. "Oh, this is awful, awful," she sobbed.

"Yes, it's awful," I agreed, "but it's no argument. The man never answered the boss's question about his qualifications. Instead he appealed to the boss's sympathy. He committed the fallacy of Ad Misericordiam. Do you understand?"

"Have you got a handkerchief?" she blubbered.   100

I handed her a handkerchief and tried to keep from screaming while she wiped her eyes. "Next," I said in a carefully controlled tone, "we will discuss False Analogy. Here is an example: Students should be allowed to look at their textbooks during examinations. After all, surgeons have X rays to guide them during an operation, lawyers have briefs to guide them during a trial, carpenters have blueprints to guide them when they are building a house. Why, then, shouldn't students be allowed to look at their textbooks during an examination?"

"There now," she said enthusiastically, "is the most marvy idea I've heard in years."

"Polly," I said testily, "the argument is all wrong. Doctors, lawyers, and carpenters aren't taking a test to see how much they have learned, but students are. The situations are altogether different, and you can't make an analogy between them."

"I still think it's a good idea," said Polly.

"Nuts," I muttered. Doggedly I pressed on. "Next we'll try   105 Hypothesis Contrary to Fact."

"Sounds yummy," was Polly's reaction.

"Listen: If Madame Curie had not happened to leave a photographic plate in a drawer with a chunk of pitchblende, the world today would not know about radium."

"True, true," said Polly, nodding her head. "Did you see the movie? Oh, it just knocked me out. That Walter Pidgeon is so dreamy. I mean he fractures me."

"If you can forget Mr. Pidgeon for a moment," I said coldly, "I would like to point out that the statement is a fallacy. Maybe Madame Curie would have discovered radium at some later date. Maybe somebody else would have discovered it. Maybe any number of things would have happened. You can't start with a hypothesis that is not true and then draw any supportable conclusions from it."

"They ought to put Walter Pidgeon in more pictures," said Polly.   110 "I hardly ever see him anymore."

One more chance, I decided. But just one more. There is a limit to what flesh and blood can bear. "The next fallacy is called Poisoning the Well."

"How cute!" she gurgled.

"Two men are having a debate. The first one gets up and says, 'My opponent is a notorious liar. You can't believe a word that he is going to say.' . . . Now, Polly, think. Think hard. What's wrong?"

I watched her closely as she knit her creamy brow in concentration. Suddenly a glimmer of intelligence — the first I had seen — came into her eyes. "It's not fair," she said with indignation. "It's not a bit fair. What chance has the second man got if the first man calls him a liar before he even begins talking?"

"Right!" I cried exultantly. "One hundred percent right. It's 115 not fair. The first man has *poisoned the well* before anybody could drink from it. He has hamstrung his opponent before he could even start. . . . Polly, I'm proud of you."

"Pshaw," she murmured, blushing with pleasure.

"You see, my dear, these things aren't so hard. All you have to do is concentrate. Think — examine — evaluate. Come now, let's review everything we have learned."

"Fire away," she said with an airy wave of her hand.

Heartened by the knowledge that Polly was not altogether a cretin, I began a long, patient review of all I had told her. Over and over and over again I cited instances, pointed out flaws, kept hammering away without letup. It was like digging a tunnel. At first everything was work, sweat, and darkness. I had no idea when I would reach the light, or even *if* I would. But I persisted. I pounded and clawed and scraped, and finally I was rewarded. I saw a chink of light. And then the chink got bigger and the sun came pouring in and all was bright.

Five grueling nights this took, but it was worth it. I had made 120 a logician out of Polly; I had taught her to think. My job was done. She was worthy of me at last. She was a fit wife for me, a proper hostess for my many mansions, a suitable mother for my well-heeled children.

It must not be thought that I was without love for this girl. Quite the contrary. Just as Pygmalion loved the perfect woman he had fashioned, so I loved mine. I decided to acquaint her with my feelings at our very next meeting. The time had come to change our relationship from academic to romantic.

"Polly," I said when next we sat beneath our oak, "tonight we will not discuss fallacies."

"Aw, gee," she said, disappointed.

"My dear," I said, favoring her with a smile, "we have now spent five evenings together. We have gotten along splendidly. It is clear that we are well matched."

"Hasty Generalization," said Polly brightly.   125

"I beg your pardon," said I.

"Hasty Generalization," she repeated. "How can you say that we are well matched on the basis of only five dates?"

I chuckled with amusement. The dear child had learned her lessons well. "My dear," I said, patting her hand in a tolerant manner, "five dates is plenty. After all, you don't have to eat a whole cake to know that it's good."

"False Analogy," said Polly promptly. "I'm not a cake. I'm a girl."

I chuckled with somewhat less amusement. The dear child had   130 learned her lesson perhaps too well. I decided to change tactics. Obviously the best approach was a simple, strong, direct declaration of love. I paused for a moment while my massive brain chose the proper words. Then I began:

"Polly, I love you. You are the whole world to me, and the moon and the stars and the constellations of outer space. Please, my darling, say that you will go steady with me, for if you will not, life will be meaningless. I will languish. I will refuse my meals. I will wander the face of the earth, a shambling, hollow-eyed hulk."

There, I thought, folding my arms, that ought to do it.

"Ad Misericordiam," said Polly.

I ground my teeth. I was not Pygmalion; I was Frankenstein, and my monster had me by the throat. Frantically I fought back the tide of panic surging through me. At all costs I had to keep cool.

"Well, Polly," I said, forcing a smile, "you certainly have learned   135 your fallacies."

"You're darn right," she said with a vigorous nod.

"And who taught them to you, Polly?"

"You did."

"That's right. So you do owe me something, don't you, my dear? If I hadn't come along you never would have learned about fallacies."

"Hypothesis Contrary to Fact," she said instantly.   140

I dashed perspiration from my brow. "Polly," I croaked, "you mustn't take all these things so literally. I mean this is just classroom stuff. You know that the things you learn in school don't have anything to do with life."

"Dicto Simpliciter," she said, wagging her finger at me playfully.

That did it. I leaped to my feet, bellowing like a bull. "Will you or will you not go steady with me?"

"I will not," she replied.

"Why not?" I demanded.   145

"Because this afternoon I promised Petey Bellows that I would go steady with him."

I reeled back, overcome with the infamy of it. After he promised, after he made a deal, after he shook my hand! "That rat!" I shrieked, kicking up great chunks of turf. "You can't go with him, Polly. He's a liar. He's a cheat. He's a rat."

"Poisoning the Well," said Polly, "and stop shouting. I think shouting must be a fallacy too."

With an immense effort of will, I modulated my voice. "All right," I said. "You're a logician. Let's look at this thing logically. How could you choose Petey Bellows over me? Look at me — a brilliant student, a tremendous intellectual, a man with an assured future. Look at Petey — a knothead, a jitterbug, a guy who'll never know where his next meal is coming from. Can you give me one logical reason why you should go steady with Petey Bellows?"

"I certainly can," declared Polly. "He's got a raccoon coat."   150

Topic for Critical Thinking and Writing

After you have finished reading "Love Is a Fallacy," consider the following hypothetical conversation and then join the conversation: Write your own, final response that points out to these three peers how their arguments succeed or fail, using the elements of logic from this chapter (premises, conclusions, assumptions, fallacies, etc.). Finally, make your own argument about the nature of this story and how it bears on the question of sexism and publication.

CAITLYN: The story is condescending and even insulting to women. You could even call it sexist. Sexist stories should not be in college textbooks, and therefore this story should not have been published in this college textbook.

JOSHUA: This story may be sexist, but that is acceptable in the context of learning. Now if any story were racist, you would have a point about not including it in a textbook. But this story was written in 1951, and it wasn't considered sexist in its own time.

SAM: Max Shulman was a great humorist who worked in old-time television and invented the iconic character Dobie Gillis. The story is intended to be funny; therefore, it is not sexist. If anything, it should not be included in this textbook because it is not funny.

A Psychologist's View: Rogerian Argument

Real communication occurs . . . when we listen with understanding.

— CARL ROGERS

The first duty of a wise advocate is to convince his opponents that he understands their arguments, and sympathizes with their just feelings.

— SAMUEL TAYLOR COLERIDGE

ROGERIAN ARGUMENT: AN INTRODUCTION

Carl R. Rogers (1902–1987), perhaps best known for his book entitled *On Becoming a Person* (1961), was a psychotherapist, not a teacher of writing. Nonetheless, Rogers's approach to argument (put forth in the short essay by Rogers beginning on p. 401) has exerted much influence on instructors who teach argument.

On the surface, many arguments seem to show *A* arguing with *B*, presumably seeking to change *B*'s mind, but *A*'s argument is really directed not to *B* but to *C*. This attempt to persuade a nonparticipant is evident in the courtroom, where neither the prosecutor (*A*) nor the defense lawyer (*B*) is really trying to convince the opponent. Rather, both are trying to convince a third party, the jury (*C*). Prosecutors don't care whether they convince defense lawyers; they don't even mind infuriating defense lawyers because their only real goal is to convince the jury. Similarly, the writer of a letter to a newspaper, taking issue with an editorial, doesn't expect

Michael Rougier/Getty Images

Carl R. Rogers (second from the right) leading a panel discussion in 1966.

to change the paper's policy. Rather, the writer hopes to convince a third party, the reader of the newspaper.

But suppose *A* really does want to bring *B* around to *A*'s point of view and suppose *B* is also arguing with *A*, too, trying to persuade *A* that his or her way is best. Politicians often argue with one another in just such ways. In such instances, both parties may be reluctant to listen to the other. Rogers points out that when we engage in an argument, if we feel our integrity or our identity is threatened, we will stiffen our position. The sense of threat may be so great that we are unable to consider the alternative views being offered, and we therefore remain unpersuaded. Threatened, we may defend ourselves rather than our argument, and little communication will take place. Of course, a third party might say that we or our opponent presented the more convincing case, but we, and perhaps the opponent, have scarcely listened to each other, and so the two of us remain apart.

Rogers therefore suggests that a writer who wishes to communicate with someone (as opposed to convincing a third party) needs to reduce the threat. In a sense, the participants in the argument need to become partners rather than adversaries. Rogers, a therapist, was keen to highlight **empathy**, the understanding of someone else's perspective or experiences, as a fundamental part of effective communication. But writers, like therapists, also must work toward understanding their partners in communication. That is achieved partially through an honest attempt to inhabit the psyche of the other, to see and feel the issues through the other's perspectives, in light of their perceptions and feelings. Instead of point–counterpoint argument, the goal is to foster emotional and intellectual reciprocity. Listeners are more willing to be persuaded when they see their partner in communication as an honest collaborator instead of an opponent. Rogers wrote, "Mutual communication tends to be pointed toward solving a problem rather than toward attacking a person or group."

Visual Guide: Rogerian Argument

1 State the problem.

2 Give the opponent's position.

3 Grant whatever validity the writer finds in that position.

4 (If possible) Attempt to show how the opposing position will be improved if the writer's own position is accepted.

Thus, in an essay on standardized testing, for instance, the writer need not—and probably should not—see the issue as black or white, as *either/or.* Such an essay might indicate that testing is undesirable because it has negative effects on students or teaching, *but in some circumstances* it may be seen as reasonable and acceptable. This qualification does not mean that one must compromise. Thus, the essayist might argue that high-stakes testing increases student anxiety, constrains teachers, and devalues the arts, but may also recognize the value of the tests in ensuring educational consistency across public school systems.

A writer who wishes to reduce the psychological threat to the opposition and thus facilitate partnership in the study of some issue can do several things:

- Show sympathetic understanding of the opposing argument.
- Recognize what is valid in it.
- Recognize and demonstrate that those who take the other side are nonetheless persons of goodwill.

Advocates of Rogerian argument are likely to contrast it with Aristotelian argument, saying that the style of argument associated with Aristotle (384–322 BCE, Greek philosopher and rhetorician) has these two characteristics:

- It is adversarial, seeking to refute other views.
- It sees the listener as wrong, as someone who now must be overwhelmed by evidence.

In contrast to the confrontational Aristotelian style, which allegedly seeks to present an airtight case that compels belief, Rogerian argument (it is said) has the following characteristics:

- It is nonconfrontational, collegial, and friendly.
- It respects other views and allows for multiple truths.
- It seeks to achieve some degree of assent and empathy rather than convince utterly.

Sometimes, of course, the differing positions may be so far apart that no reconciliation can be proposed, in which case the writer will probably seek to show how the problem can best be solved by adopting the writer's own position. These matters are discussed in Chapter 6, but not from the point of view of a psychotherapist, and so we reprint Rogers's essay here.

✓ A CHECKLIST FOR ANALYZING ROGERIAN ARGUMENT

☐ Have I stated the problem and indicated that a dialogue is possible?

☐ Have I stated at least one other point of view in a way that would satisfy its proponents?

☐ Have I been courteous to those who hold views other than mine?

☐ Have I enlarged my own understanding to the extent that I can grant validity, at least in some circumstances, to at least some aspects of other positions?

☐ Have I stated my position and indicated the contexts in which I believe it is valid?

☐ Have I pointed out the ground that we share?

☐ Have I shown how other positions will be strengthened by accepting some aspects of my position?

Carl R. Rogers

Carl R. Rogers (1902–1987), perhaps best known for his book On Becoming a Person *(1961), was a psychotherapist. The following essay was originally presented on October 11, 1951, at Northwestern University's Centennial Conference on Communications. In it, Rogers reflects the political climate of the cold war between the United States and the Soviet Union, which dominated headlines for more than forty years (1947–1989). Several of Rogers's examples of bias and frustrated communication allude to the tensions of that era.*

Communication: Its Blocking and Its Facilitation

It may seem curious that a person whose whole professional effort is devoted to psychotherapy should be interested in problems of communication. What relationship is there between providing therapeutic help to individuals with emotional maladjustments and the concern of this conference with obstacles to communication? Actually the relationship is very close indeed. The whole task of psychotherapy is the task of dealing with a failure in communication. The emotionally maladjusted person, the "neurotic," is in difficulty first because communication within himself has broken down, and second because as a result of this his communication with others has been damaged. If this sounds somewhat strange, then let me put it in other terms. In the "neurotic" individual, parts of himself which have been termed unconscious, or repressed, or denied to awareness, become blocked off so that they no longer communicate themselves to the conscious or managing part of himself. As long as this is true, there are distortions in the way he communicates himself to others, and so he suffers both within himself, and in his interpersonal relations. The task of psychotherapy is to help the person achieve, through a special relationship with a therapist, good communication within himself. Once this is achieved he can communicate more freely and more effectively with others. We may say then that psychotherapy is good communication, within and between men. We may also turn that statement around and it will still be true. Good communication, free communication, within or between men, is always therapeutic.

It is, then, from a background of experience with communication in counseling and psychotherapy that I want to present here two ideas. I wish to state what I believe is one of the major factors in blocking or impeding communication, and then I wish to present what in our experience has proven to be a very important way to improving or facilitating communication.

I would like to propose, as an hypothesis for consideration, that the major barrier to mutual interpersonal communication is our very natural tendency to judge, to evaluate, to approve or disapprove, the statement of the person, or the other group. Let me illustrate my meaning with some very simple examples. As you leave the meeting tonight, one of the statements you are likely to hear is, "I didn't like that man's talk." Now what do you respond? Almost invariably your reply will be either approval or disapproval of the attitude expressed. Either you respond, "I didn't either. I thought it was terrible," or else you tend to reply, "Oh, I thought it was really good." In other words, your primary reaction is to evaluate what has just been said to you, to evaluate it from *your* point of view, your own frame of reference.

Or take another example. Suppose I say with some feeling, "I think the Republicans are behaving in ways that show a lot of good sound sense these days," what is the response that arises in your mind as you listen? The overwhelming likelihood is that it will be evaluative. You will find yourself agreeing, or disagreeing, or making some judgment about me such as "He must be a conservative," or "He seems solid in his thinking." Or let us take an illustration from the international scene. Russia says vehemently, "The treaty with Japan is a war plot on the part of the United States." We rise as one person to say "That's a lie!"

This last illustration brings in another element connected with   5 my hypothesis. Although the tendency to make evaluations is common in almost all interchange of language, it is very much heightened in those situations where feelings and emotions are deeply involved. So the stronger our feelings, the more likely it is that there will be no mutual element in the communication. There will be just two ideas, two feelings, two judgments, missing each other in psychological space. I'm sure you recognize this from your own experience. When you have not been emotionally involved yourself, and have listened to a heated discussion, you often go away thinking, "Well, they actually weren't talking about the same thing." And they were not. Each was making a judgment, an evaluation, from his own frame of reference. There was really nothing which could be called communication in any genuine sense. This tendency to react to any emotionally meaningful statement by forming an evaluation of it from our own point of view, is, I repeat, the major barrier to interpersonal communication.

But is there any way of solving this problem, of avoiding this barrier? I feel that we are making exciting progress toward this goal and I would like to present it as simply as I can. Real communication occurs, and this evaluative tendency is avoided, when we listen with understanding. What does that mean? It means *to see the expressed idea and attitude from the other person's point of view, to sense how it feels to him, to achieve his frame of reference in regard to the thing he is talking about.*

Stated so briefly, this may sound absurdly simple, but it is not. It is an approach which we have found extremely potent in the field of psychotherapy. It is the most effective agent we know for altering the basic personality structure of an individual, and improving his relationships and his communications with others. If I can listen to what he can tell me, if I can understand how it seems to him, if I can see its personal meaning for him, if I can sense the emotional flavor which it has for him, then I will be releasing potent forces of change in him. If I can really understand how he hates his father, or hates the university, or hates communists—if I can catch the flavor of his fear of insanity, or his fear of atom bombs, or of Russia—it will be of the greatest help to him in altering those very hatreds and fears, and in establishing realistic and harmonious relationships with the very people and situations toward which he has felt hatred and fear. We know from our research that such empathic understanding—understanding *with* a person, not *about* him—is such an effective approach that it can bring about major changes in personality.

Some of you may be feeling that you listen well to people, and that you have never seen such results. The chances are very great indeed that your listening has not been of the type I have described. Fortunately I can suggest a little laboratory experiment which you can try to test the quality of your understanding. The next time you get into an argument with your wife, or your friend, or with a small group of friends, just stop the discussion for a moment and for an experiment, institute this rule. "Each person can speak up for himself only *after* he has first restated the ideas and feelings of the previous speaker accurately, and to that speaker's satisfaction." You see what this would mean. It would simply mean that before presenting your own point of view, it would be necessary for you to really achieve the other speaker's frame of reference—to understand his thoughts and feelings so well that you could summarize them for him. Sounds simple, doesn't it? But if you try it you will discover it one of the most difficult things you have ever tried to do.

However, once you have been able to see the other's point of view, your own comments will have to be drastically revised. You will also find the emotion going out of the discussion, the differences being reduced, and those differences which remain being of a rational and understandable sort.

Can you imagine what this kind of an approach would mean if it were projected into larger areas? What would happen to a labor-management dispute if it was conducted in such a way that labor, without necessarily agreeing, could accurately state management's point of view in a way that management could accept; and management, without approving labor's stand, could state labor's case in a way that labor agreed was accurate? It would mean that real communication was established, and one could practically guarantee that some reasonable solution would be reached.

If then this way of approach is an effective avenue to good 10 communication and good relationships, as I am quite sure you will agree if you try the experiment I have mentioned, why is it not more widely tried and used? I will try to list the difficulties which keep it from being utilized.

In the first place it takes courage, a quality which is not too widespread. I am indebted to Dr. S. I. Hayakawa, the semanticist, for pointing out that to carry on psychotherapy in this fashion is to take a very real risk, and that courage is required. If you really understand another person in this way, if you are willing to enter his private world and see the way life appears to him, without any attempt to make evaluative judgments, you run the risk of being changed yourself. You might see it his way, you might find yourself influenced in your attitudes or your personality. This risk of being changed is one of the most frightening prospects most of us can face. If I enter, as fully as I am able, into the private world of a neurotic or psychotic individual, isn't there a risk that I might become lost in that world? Most of us are afraid to take that risk. Or if we had a Russian communist speaker here tonight, or Senator Joe McCarthy, how many of us would dare to try to see the world from each of these points of view? The great majority of us could not *listen*; we would find ourselves compelled to *evaluate*, because listening would seem too dangerous. So the first requirement is courage, and we do not always have it.

But there is a second obstacle. It is just when emotions are strongest that it is most difficult to achieve the frame of reference of the other person or group. Yet it is the time the attitude is most needed, if communication is to be established. We have not found this to be an insuperable obstacle in our experience in psychotherapy.

A third party, who is able to lay aside his own feelings and evaluations, can assist greatly by listening with understanding to each person or group and clarifying the views and attitudes each holds. We have found this very effective in small groups in which contradictory or antagonistic attitudes exist. When the parties to a dispute realize that they are being understood, that someone sees how the situation seems to them, the statements grow less exaggerated and less defensive, and it is no longer necessary to maintain the attitude, "I am 100 percent right and you are 100 percent wrong." The influence of such an understanding catalyst in the group permits the members to come closer and closer to the objective truth involved in the relationship. In this way mutual communication is established and some type of agreement becomes much more possible. So we may say that though heightened emotions make it much more difficult to understand *with* an opponent, our experience makes it clear that a neutral, understanding, catalyst type of leader or therapist can overcome this obstacle in a small group.

This last phrase, however, suggests another obstacle to utilizing the approach I have described. Thus far all our experience has been with small face-to-face groups — groups exhibiting industrial tensions, religious tensions, racial tensions, and therapy groups in which many personal tensions are present. In these small groups our experience, confirmed by a limited amount of research, shows that this basic approach leads to improved communication, to greater acceptance of others and by others, and to attitudes which are more positive and more problem-solving in nature. There is a decrease in defensiveness, in exaggerated statements, in evaluative and critical behavior. But these findings are from small groups. What about trying to achieve understanding between larger groups that are geographically remote? Or between face-to-face groups who are not speaking for themselves, but simply as representatives of others, like the delegates at Kaesong?[1] Frankly we do not know the answers to these questions. I believe the situation might be put this way. As social scientists we have a tentative test-tube solution of the problem of breakdown in communication. But to confirm the validity of this test-tube solution, and to adapt it to the enormous problems of communication breakdown between classes, groups, and nations, would involve additional funds, much more research, and creative thinking of a high order.

[1] **the delegates at Kaesong** Representatives of North Korea and South Korea met at the border town of Kaesong to arrange terms for an armistice to hostilities during the Korean War (1950–1953). [Editors' note]

Even with our present limited knowledge we can see some steps which might be taken, even in large groups, to increase the amount of listening *with*, and to decrease the amount of evaluation *about*. To be imaginative for a moment, let us suppose that a therapeutically oriented international group went to the Russian leaders and said, "We want to achieve a genuine understanding of your views and even more important, of your attitudes and feelings, toward the United States. We will summarize and resummarize the views and feelings if necessary, until you agree that our description represents the situation as it seems to you." Then suppose they did the same thing with the leaders in our own country. If they then gave the widest possible distribution to these two views, with the feelings clearly described but not expressed in name-calling, might not the effect be very great? It would not guarantee the type of understanding I have been describing, but it would make it much more possible. We can understand the feelings of a person who hates us much more readily when his attitudes are accurately described to us by a neutral third party, than we can when he is shaking his fist at us.

But even to describe such a first step is to suggest another obsta-   15
cle to this approach of understanding. Our civilization does not yet have enough faith in the social sciences to utilize their findings. The opposite is true of the physical sciences. During the war[2] when a test-tube solution was found to the problem of synthetic rubber, millions of dollars and an army of talent was turned loose on the problem of using that finding. If synthetic rubber could be made in milligrams, it could and would be made in the thousands of tons. And it was. But in the social science realm, if a way is found of facilitating communication and mutual understanding in small groups, there is no guarantee that the finding will be utilized. It may be a generation or more before the money and the brains will be turned loose to exploit that finding.

In closing, I would like to summarize this small-scale solution to the problem of barriers in communication, and to point out certain of its characteristics.

I have said that our research and experience to date would make it appear that breakdowns in communication, and the evaluative tendency which is the major barrier to communication, can be avoided. The solution is provided by creating a situation in which each of the different parties come to understand the other from the *other's* point of view. This has been achieved, in practice, even when

---

[2]**the war** World War II. [Editors' note]

feelings run high, by the influence of a person who is willing to understand each point of view empathically, and who thus acts as a catalyst to precipitate further understanding.

This procedure has important characteristics. It can be initiated by one party, without waiting for the other to be ready. It can even be initiated by a neutral third person, providing he can gain a minimum of cooperation from one of the parties.

This procedure can deal with the insincerities, the defensive exaggerations, the lies, the "false fronts" which characterize almost every failure in communication. These defensive distortions drop away with astonishing speed as people find that the only intent is to understand, not judge.

This approach leads steadily and rapidly toward the discovery   20 of the truth, toward a realistic appraisal of the objective barriers to communication. The dropping of some defensiveness by one party leads to further dropping of defensiveness by the other party, and truth is thus approached.

This procedure gradually achieves mutual communication. Mutual communication tends to be pointed toward solving a problem rather than toward attacking a person or group. It leads to a situation in which I see how the problem appears to you, as well as to me, and you see how it appears to me, as well as to you. Thus accurately and realistically defined, the problem is almost certain to yield to intelligent attack, or if it is in part insoluble, it will be comfortably accepted as such.

This then appears to be a test-tube solution to the breakdown of communication as it occurs in small groups. Can we take this small-scale answer, investigate it further, refine it; develop it and apply it to the tragic and well-nigh fatal failures of communication which threaten the very existence of our modern world? It seems to me that this is a possibility and a challenge which we should explore.

Topics for Critical Thinking and Writing

1. What obstacles to effective argument does Carl R. Rogers outline in his essay? Consider that it was written in the 1950s. Are there any additional obstacles we face today? How might they be overcome through critical thinking and effective argument?

2. Rogers writes in paragraph 12 that it is "when emotions are strongest that it is most difficult to achieve the frame of reference of the other person or group." Select a current debate in the news

and explain how strong emotions — about issues or in relation to particular factors — inhibit effective communication in that debate. Is each side equally emotional, or do emotions inhibit one side more than the other? How can one or the other side argue more effectively not by discounting the emotions of the other but expressing understanding?

3. List three additional debate topics with two generally opposing positions. Then identify potentially shared goals or outcomes among the two positions. (Use the Visual Guide on p. 399 as a model.) Reflect on the exercise: What challenges did you face following the Rogerian framework for argument? What do you think may help and hinder empathy between the two positions?

Edward O. Wilson

Edward O. Wilson, born in Birmingham, Alabama, in 1929, is an emeritus professor of evolutionary biology at Harvard University. A distinguished writer as well as a researcher and teacher, Wilson has twice won the Pulitzer Prize for General Non-Fiction. We reprint a piece first published in 2006 in Wilson's book The Creation: An Appeal to Save Life on Earth.

Letter to a Southern Baptist Minister

Dear Pastor:

We have not met, yet I feel I know you well enough to call you friend. First of all, we grew up in the same faith. As a boy I too answered the altar call; I went under the water. Although I no longer belong to that faith, I am confident that if we met and spoke privately of our deepest beliefs, it would be in a spirit of mutual respect and good will. I know we share many precepts of moral behavior. Perhaps it also matters that we are both Americans and, insofar as it might still affect civility and good manners, we are both Southerners.

I write to you now for your counsel and help. Of course, in doing so, I see no way to avoid the fundamental differences in our respective worldviews. You are a literalist interpreter of Christian Holy Scripture. You reject the conclusion of science that mankind evolved from lower forms. You believe that each person's soul is immortal, making this planet a way station to a second, eternal life. Salvation is assured those who are redeemed in Christ.

I am a secular humanist. I think existence is what we make of it as individuals. There is no guarantee of life after death, and heaven and hell are what we create for ourselves, on this planet. There is no other home. Humanity originated here by evolution from lower forms over millions of years. And yes, I will speak plain, our ancestors were apelike animals. The human species has adapted physically and mentally to life on Earth and no place else. Ethics is the code of behavior we share on the basis of reason, law, honor, and an inborn sense of decency, even as some ascribe it to God's will.

For you, the glory of an unseen divinity; for me, the glory of the universe revealed at last. For you, the belief in God made flesh to save mankind; for me, the belief in Promethean[1] fire seized to set men free. You have found your final truth; I am still searching. I may be wrong, you may be wrong. We may both be partly right.

Does this difference in worldview separate us in all things? It 5 does not. You and I and every other human being strive for the same imperatives of security, freedom of choice, personal dignity, and a cause to believe in that is larger than ourselves.

Let us see, then, if we can, and you are willing, to meet on the near side of metaphysics in order to deal with the real world we share. I put it this way because you have the power to help solve a great problem about which I care deeply. I hope you have the same concern. I suggest that we set aside our differences in order to save the Creation. The defense of living Nature is a universal value. It doesn't rise from, nor does it promote, any religious or ideological dogma. Rather, it serves without discrimination the interests of all humanity.

Pastor, we need your help. The Creation—living Nature—is in deep trouble. Scientists estimate that if habitat conversion and other destructive human activities continue at their present rates, half the species of plants and animals on Earth could be either gone or at least fated for early extinction by the end of the century. A full quarter will drop to this level during the next half century as a result of climate change alone. The ongoing extinction rate is calculated in the most conservative estimates to be about a hundred times above that prevailing before humans appeared on Earth, and it is expected to rise to at least a thousand times greater or more in the next few decades. If this rise continues unabated, the cost

---

[1]**Promethean** In Greek mythology, Prometheus was a Titan who looked after mankind, going so far as to steal fire from Mount Olympus to give it to humans. [Editors' note]

to humanity, in wealth, environmental security, and quality of life, will be catastrophic.

Surely we can agree that each species, however inconspicuous and humble it may seem to us at this moment, is a masterpiece of biology, and well worth saving. Each species possesses a unique combination of genetic traits that fits it more or less precisely to a particular part of the environment. Prudence alone dictates that we act quickly to prevent the extinction of species and, with it, the pauperization of Earth's ecosystems—hence of the Creation.

You may well ask at this point, Why me? Because religion and science are the two most powerful forces in the world today, including especially the United States. If religion and science could be united on the common ground of biological conservation, the problem would soon be solved. If there is any moral precept shared by people of all beliefs, it is that we owe ourselves and future generations a beautiful, rich, and healthful environment.

I am puzzled that so many religious leaders, who spiritually represent a large majority of people around the world, have hesitated to make protection of the Creation an important part of their magisterium.[2] Do they believe that human-centered ethics and preparation for the afterlife are the only things that matter? Even more perplexing is the widespread conviction among Christians that the Second Coming is imminent, and that therefore the condition of the planet is of little consequence. Sixty percent of Americans, according to a 2004 poll, believe that the prophecies of the book of Revelation are accurate. Many of these, numbering in the millions, think the End of Time will occur within the life span of those now living. Jesus will return to Earth, and those redeemed by Christian faith will be transported bodily to heaven, while those left behind will struggle through severe hard times and, when they die, suffer eternal damnation. The condemned will remain in hell, like those already consigned in the generations before them, for a trillion trillion years, enough for the universe to expand to its own, entropic death, time enough for countless universes like it afterward to be born, expand, and likewise die away. And that is just the beginning of how long condemned souls will suffer in hell—all for a mistake they made in choice of religion during the infinitesimally small time they inhabited Earth.

For those who believe this form of Christianity, the fate of 10 million other life forms indeed does not matter. This and other

[2]**magisterium**   The official teaching of the Roman Catholic Church. [Editors' note]

similar doctrines are not gospels of hope and compassion. They are gospels of cruelty and despair. They were not born of the heart of Christianity. Pastor, tell me I am wrong!

However you will respond, let me here venture an alternative ethic. The great challenge of the twenty-first century is to raise people everywhere to a decent standard of living while preserving as much of the rest of life as possible. Science has provided this part of the argument for the ethic: the more we learn about the biosphere, the more complex and beautiful it turns out to be. Knowledge of it is a magic well: the more you draw from it, the more there is to draw. Earth, and especially the razor-thin film of life enveloping it, is our home, our wellspring, our physical and much of our spiritual sustenance.

I know that science and environmentalism are linked in the minds of many with evolution, Darwin, and secularism. Let me postpone disentangling all this (I will come back to it later) and stress again: to protect the beauty of Earth and of its prodigious variety of life forms should be a common goal, regardless of differences in our metaphysical beliefs.

To make the point in good Gospel manner, let me tell the story of a young man, newly trained for the ministry, and so fixed in his Christian faith that he referred all questions of morality to readings from the Bible. When he visited the cathedral-like Atlantic rainforest of Brazil, he saw the manifest hand of God and in his notebook wrote, "It is not possible to give an adequate idea of the higher feelings of wonder, admiration, and devotion which fill and elevate the mind."

That was Charles Darwin in 1832, early into the voyage of HMS 15 *Beagle*, before he had given any thought to evolution.

And here is Darwin, concluding *On the Origin of Species* in 1859, having first abandoned Christian dogma and then, with his newfound intellectual freedom, formulated the theory of evolution by natural selection: "There is grandeur in this view of life, with its several powers, having been originally breathed into a few forms or into one; and that, whilst this planet has gone cycling on according to the fixed law of gravity, from so simple a beginning endless forms most beautiful and most wonderful have been, and are being, evolved."

Darwin's reverence for life remained the same as he crossed the seismic divide that divided his spiritual life. And so it can be for the divide that today separates scientific humanism from mainstream religion. And separates you and me.

You are well prepared to present the theological and moral arguments for saving the Creation. I am heartened by the movement growing within Christian denominations to support global conservation. The stream of thought has arisen from many sources, from evangelical to unitarian. Today it is but a rivulet. Tomorrow it will be a flood.

I already know much of the religious argument on behalf of the Creation, and would like to learn more. I will now lay before you and others who may wish to hear it the scientific argument. You will not agree with all that I say about the origins of life—science and religion do not easily mix in such matters—but I like to think that in this one life-and-death issue we have a common purpose.

TOPICS FOR CRITICAL THINKING AND WRITING

1. Edward O. Wilson claims to be a "secular humanist" (para. 3). How would you define that term? Are you a secular humanist? Why, or why not?

2. What does Wilson mean by "metaphysics" (para. 6)? Which if any of his views qualify as metaphysical?

3. Wilson obviously seeks to present his views in a fashion that makes them as palatable as possible to his reader. Do you think he succeeds in this endeavor? Write an essay of about 500 words arguing for or against his achievement in this regard, pointing to instances in the text where he succeeds or fails.

APPENDIX

SENTENCE GUIDES for ACADEMIC WRITERS

Being a college student means being a college writer. No matter what field you are studying, your instructors will ask you to make sense of what you are learning through writing. When you work on writing assignments in college, you are, in most cases, being asked to write for an academic audience.

Writing academically means thinking academically—asking a lot of questions, digging into the ideas of others, and entering into scholarly debates and academic conversations. As a college writer, you will be asked to read different kinds of texts; understand and evaluate authors' ideas, arguments, and methods; and contribute your own ideas. In this way, you present yourself as a participant in an academic conversation.

What does it mean to be part of an *academic conversation*? Well, think of it this way: You and your friends may have an ongoing debate about the best film trilogy of all time. During your conversations with one another, you analyze the details of the films, introduce points you want your friends to consider, listen to their ideas, and perhaps cite what the critics have said about a particular trilogy. This kind of conversation is not unlike what happens among scholars in academic writing—except they could be debating the best public policy for a social problem or the most promising new theory in treating disease.

If you are uncertain about what academic writing *sounds like* or if you're not sure you're any good at it, this appendix offers guidance for you at the sentence level. It helps answer questions such as these:

How can I present the ideas of others in a way that demonstrates my understanding of the debate?

How can I agree with someone, but add a new idea?

How can I disagree with a scholar without seeming, well, rude?

How can I make clear in my writing which ideas are mine and which ideas are someone else's?

The following sections offer sentence guides for you to use and adapt to your own writing situations. As in all writing that you do, you will have to think about your purpose (reason for writing) and your audience (readers) before knowing which guides will be most appropriate for a particular piece of writing or for a certain part of your essay.

The guides are organized to help you present background information, the views and claims of others, and your own views and claims—all in the context of your purpose and audience.

ACADEMIC WRITERS PRESENT INFORMATION AND OTHERS' VIEWS

When you write in academic situations, you may be asked to spend some time giving background information for or setting a context for your main idea or argument. This often requires you to present or summarize what is known or what has already been said in relation to the question you are asking in your writing.

SG1   Presenting What Is Known or Assumed

When you write, you will find that you occasionally need to present something that is known, such as a specific fact or a statistic. The following structures are useful when you are providing background information.

As we know from history, _____.

X has shown that _____.

Research by X and Y suggests that _____.

According to X, _____ percent of _____ are/favor _____.

In other situations, you may have the need to present information that is assumed or that is conventional wisdom.

People often believe that _____.

Conventional wisdom leads us to believe _____.

Many Americans share the idea that _____.

_____ is a widely held belief.

In order to challenge an assumption or a widely held belief, you have to acknowledge it first. Doing so lets your readers believe that you are placing your ideas in an appropriate context.

> Although many people are led to believe X, there is significant benefit to considering the merits of Y.

> College students tend to believe that _____ when, in fact, the opposite is much more likely the case.

SG2   Presenting Others' Views

As a writer, you build your own *ethos*, or credibility, by being able to represent the views of others fairly and accurately. As an academic writer, you will be expected to demonstrate your understanding of a text by summarizing the views or arguments of its author(s). To do so, you will use language such as the following.

> X argues that _____.

> X emphasizes the need for _____.

> In this important article, X and Y claim _____.

> X endorses _____ because _____.

> X and Y have recently criticized the idea that _____.

> _____, according to X, is the most critical cause of _____.

Although you will create your own variations of these sentences as you draft and revise, the guides can be useful tools for thinking through how best to present another writer's claim or finding clearly and concisely.

SG3   Presenting Direct Quotations

When the exact words of a source are important for accuracy, authority, emphasis, or flavor, you will want to use a direct quotation. Ordinarily, you will present direct quotations with language of your own that suggests how you are using the source.

> X characterizes the problem this way: ". . ."

> According to X, _____ is defined as ". . ."

"...," explains *X*.

X argues strongly in favor of the policy, pointing out that "..."

Note: You will generally cite direct quotations according to the documentation style your readers expect. MLA style, often used in English and in other humanities courses, recommends using the author name paired with a page number, if there is one. APA style, used in most social sciences, requires the year of publication generally after the mention of the source, with page numbers after the quoted material. In *Chicago* style, used in history and in some humanities courses, writers use superscript numbers (like this[6]) to refer readers to footnotes or endnotes. In-text citations, like the ones shown below, refer readers to entries in the works cited or reference list.

MLA   Lazarín argues that our overreliance on testing in
           K-12 schools "does not put students first" (20).

APA   Lazarín (2014) argues that our overreliance on testing
           in K-12 schools "does not put students first" (p. 20).

Chicago   Lazarín argues that our overreliance on testing in
           K-12 schools "does not put students first."[6]

Many writers use direct quotations to advance an argument of their own:

> Standardized testing makes it easier for administrators   *Student*
> to measure student performance, but it may not be the   *writer's*
> best way to measure it. Too much testing wears students   *idea*
> out and communicates the idea that recall is the most
> important skill we want them to develop. Even educa-   *Source's*
> tion policy advisor Melissa Lazarín argues that our over- *idea*
> reliance on testing in K-12 schools "does not put students
> first" (20).

SG4   Presenting Alternative Views

Most debates, whether they are scholarly or popular, are complex — often with more than two sides to an issue. Sometimes you will have to synthesize the views of multiple participants in the debate before you introduce your own ideas.

On the one hand, *X* reports that _____, but on the other hand, *Y* insists that _____.

Even though *X* endorses the policy, *Y* refers to it as ". . ."

X, however, isn't convinced and instead argues _____.

X and *Y* have supported the theory in the past, but new research by *Z* suggests that _____.

ACADEMIC WRITERS PRESENT THEIR OWN VIEWS

When you write for an academic audience, you will indeed have to demonstrate that you are familiar with the views of others who are asking the same kinds of questions as you are. Much writing that is done for academic purposes asks you to put your arguments in the context of existing arguments—in a way asking you to connect the known to the new.

When you are asked to write a summary or an informative text, your own views and arguments are generally not called for. However, much of the writing you will be assigned to do in college asks you to take a persuasive stance and present a reasoned argument—at times in response to a single text and at other times in response to multiple texts.

SG5 Presenting Your Own Views: Agreement and Extension

Sometimes you agree with the author of a source.

X's argument is convincing because _____.

Because *X*'s approach is so _____, it is the best way to _____.

X makes an important point when she says _____.

Other times you find you agree with the author of a source, but you want to extend the point or go a bit deeper in your own investigation. In a way, you acknowledge the source for getting you so far in the conversation, but then you move the conversation along with a related comment or finding.

X's proposal for _____ is indeed worth considering. Going one step further, _____.

X makes the claim that _____. By extension, isn't it also true, then, that _____?

_____ has been adequately explained by *X*. Now, let's move beyond that idea and ask whether _____.

SG6   Presenting Your Own Views: Queries and Skepticism

You may be intimidated when you're asked to talk back to a source, especially if the source is a well-known scholar or expert or even just a frequent voice in a particular debate. College-level writing asks you to be skeptical, however, and approach academic questions with the mind of an investigator. It is OK to doubt, to question, to challenge—because the end result is often new knowledge or new understanding about a subject.

Couldn't it also be argued that _____?

But is everyone willing to agree that this is the case?

While *X* insists that _____ is so, he is perhaps asking the wrong question to begin with.

The claims that *X* and *Y* have made, while intelligent and well-meaning, leave many unconvinced because they have failed to consider _____.

SG7   Presenting Your Own Views: Disagreement or Correction

You may find at times that the only response you have to a text or to an author is complete disagreement.

X's claims about _____ are completely misguided.

X presents a long metaphor comparing _____ to _____; in the end, the comparison is unconvincing because _____.

A NOTE ABOUT USING FIRST PERSON "I"

Some disciplines look favorably upon the use of the first person "I" in academic writing. Others do not and instead stick to using third person. If you are given a writing assignment for a class, you are better off asking your instructor what he or she prefers or reading through any samples given than *guessing* what might be expected.

First person (*I, me, my, we, us, our*)

I question Heddinger's methods and small sample size.

Harnessing children's technology obsession in the classroom is, I believe, the key to improving learning.

Lanza's interpretation focuses on circle imagery as symbolic of the family; my analysis leads me in a different direction entirely.

We would, in fact, benefit from looser laws about farming on our personal property.

Third person (names and other nouns)

Heddinger's methods and small sample size are questionable.

Harnessing children's technology obsession in the classroom is the key to improving learning.

Lanza's interpretation focuses on circle imagery as symbolic of the family; other readers' analyses may point in a different direction entirely.

Many Americans would, in fact, benefit from looser laws about farming on personal property.

You may think that not being able to use "I" in an essay in which you present your ideas about a topic is unfair or will lead to weaker statements, but know that you can make a strong argument even if you write in the third person. Third-person writing allows you to sound more assertive, credible, and academic.

It can be tempting to disregard a source completely if you detect a piece of information that strikes you as false or that you know to be untrue.

> Although *X* reports that _____, recent studies indicate that this is not the case.

> While *X* and *Y* insist that _____ is so, an examination of their figures shows that they have made an important miscalculation.

SG8 Presenting and Countering Objections to Your Argument

Effective college writers know that their arguments are stronger when they can anticipate objections that others might make.

> Some will object to this proposal on the grounds that _____.

> Not everyone will embrace _____; they may argue instead that _____.

Countering, or responding to, opposing voices fairly and respectfully strengthens your writing and your *ethos*, or credibility.

> *X* and *Y* might contend that this interpretation is faulty; however, _____.

> Most _____ believe that there is too much risk in this approach. But what they have failed to take into consideration is _____.

ACADEMIC WRITERS PERSUADE BY PUTTING IT ALL TOGETHER

Readers of academic writing often want to know what's at stake in a particular debate or text. Aside from crafting individual sentences, you must, of course, keep the bigger picture in mind as you attempt to persuade, inform, evaluate, or review.

SG9 Presenting Stakeholders

When you write, you may be doing so as a member of a group affected by the research conversation you have entered. For example, you may be among the thousands of students in your state whose level of debt may change as a result of new laws about financing a college education. In this case, you are a *stakeholder* in the matter. In other words, you have an interest in the matter as a person who could be impacted by the outcome of a decision. On the other hand, you may be writing as an investigator of a topic that interests you but that you aren't directly connected with. You may be persuading your audience on behalf of a group of interested stakeholders—a group of which you yourself are not a member.

You can give your writing some teeth if you make it clear who is being affected by the discussion of the issue and the decisions that have been or will be made about the issue. The groups of stakeholders are highlighted in the following sentences.

Viewers of Kurosawa's films may not agree with X that _____.

The research will come as a surprise to parents of children with type 1 diabetes.

X's claims have the power to offend potentially every low-wage earner in the state.

Marathoners might want to reconsider their training regimen if stories such as those told by X and Y are validated by the medical community.

SG10 Presenting the "So What"

For readers to be motivated to read your writing, they have to feel as if you're either addressing something that matters to them or addressing something that matters very much to you or that should matter to us all. Good academic writing often hooks readers with a sense of urgency—a serious response to a reader's "So what?"

Having a frank discussion about _____ now will put us in a far better position to deal with _____ in the future. If we are unwilling or unable to do so, we risk _____.

Such a breakthrough will affect _____ in three significant ways.

It is easy to believe that the stakes aren't high enough to be alarming; in fact, _____ will be affected by _____.

Widespread disapproval of and censorship of such fiction/films/art will mean _____ for us in the future. Culture should represent _____.

_____ could bring about unprecedented opportunities for _____ to participate in _____, something never seen before.

New experimentation in _____ could allow scientists to investigate _____ in ways they couldn't have imagined _____ years ago.

SG11 Presenting the Players and Positions in a Debate

Some disciplines ask writers to compose a review of the literature as a part of a larger project—or sometimes as a freestanding assignment. In a review of the literature, the writer sets forth a research question, summarizes the key sources that have addressed the question, puts the current research in the context of other voices in the research conversation, and identifies any gaps in the research.

Writing that presents a debate, its players, and their positions can often be lengthy. What follows, however, can give you the sense of the flow of ideas and turns in such a piece of writing.

_____ affects more than 30% of children in America, and signs point to a worsening situation in years to come because of *A*, *B*, and *C*. Solutions to the problem have eluded even the sharpest policy minds and brightest researchers. In an important 2003 study, *W* found that _____, which pointed to more problems than solutions. [. . .] Research by *X* and *Y* made strides in our understanding of _____ but still didn't offer specific strategies for children and families struggling to _____. [. . .] When *Z* rejected both the methods and the findings of *X* and *Y*, arguing that _____, policymakers and health-care experts were optimistic. [. . .] Too much discussion of _____, however, and too little discussion of _____ may lead us to solutions that are ultimately too expensive to sustain.

Student writer states the problem.

Student writer summarizes the views of others on the topic.

Student writer presents her view in the context of current research.

VERBS MATTER

Using a variety of verbs in your sentences can add strength and clarity as you present others' views and your own views.

When you want to present a view fairly neutrally

acknowledges	observes
adds	points out
admits	reports
comments	suggests
contends	writes
notes	

X **points out** that the plan had unintended outcomes.

When you want to present a stronger view

argues   emphasizes
asserts   insists
declares

Y argues in favor of a ban on _____, but Z insists that the plan is misguided.

When you want to show agreement

agrees
confirms
endorses

An endorsement of X's position is smart for a number of reasons.

When you want to show contrast or disagreement

compares   refutes
denies   rejects
disputes

The town must come together and reject X's claims that _____ is in the best interest of the citizens.

When you want to anticipate an objection

admits
acknowledges
concedes

Y admits that closer study of _____, with a much larger sample, is necessary for _____.

Text Credits

Index